Francis Ernest Gigot

**Outlines of Jewish History from Abraham to Our Lord**

Francis Ernest Gigot

**Outlines of Jewish History from Abraham to Our Lord**

ISBN/EAN: 9783743310971

Manufactured in Europe, USA, Canada, Australia, Japa

Cover: Foto ©Thomas Meinert / pixelio.de

Manufactured and distributed by brebook publishing software
(www.brebook.com)

Francis Ernest Gigot

**Outlines of Jewish History from Abraham to Our Lord**

# PREFACE.

THE present volume has been prepared for the special use of theological students, who, being already acquainted with the leading facts of the Biblical narrative as found in most Bible Histories, need to be introduced to the scientific study of Holy Writ upon which they enter, by a more accurate and thorough knowledge of the History of the Jews. Not, indeed, that the present work is intended to supply students with a detailed and continuous narrative of all the historical facts recorded in the Bible such as would enable them to dispense with a careful perusal of the Sacred Books themselves. The writer is fully persuaded, on the contrary, that the Inspired Text should ever remain pre-eminently the text-book of Biblical students, and that whatever else may be placed at their disposal should be only helps calculated to promote their closer acquaintance with the Sacred records. Whilst therefore describing the events of Jewish history in such a way as to recall them sufficiently to the minds of the careful readers of the inspired books of the Old Testament, whilst also constantly referring to the Bible for further details, the writer has aimed at supplying theological students with much of what is needed for a scientific study of the History of the Jews.

It is with this distinct purpose in view that he has embodied concisely in this work the best ascertained results of modern criticism and recent exploration through Bible Lands, and has availed himself of every source of information to make Jewish history at once more intelligible and more attractive. It is for the same purpose that he has taken notice of the principal difficulties which are daily being made on historical grounds to the facts narrated in the Biblical records, and has suggested briefly the best answers which have been offered. It is believed that the Biblical student will also be greatly benefited by the references to sources, which he will constantly find in the text-book now placed at his disposal.

Whilst aiming principally at meeting the requirements of clerical students, the writer is not without hopes of doing service to a much larger number of readers. For example, teachers of Sacred History in Sunday-schools, colleges, academies, and the like, who constantly feel the need of something more consecutive and methodic than is supplied by the Sacred Text itself or by the popular manuals, will rejoice to meet it in the present volume. Perhaps even the deeper student of Biblical history will occasionally find in its pages views and suggestions new and helpful.

Finally, if the writer of the present work has not dealt with the great facts of the Creation of the World, or the Fall of Man, etc., which are narrated in the opening chapters of Genesis, it is chiefly because their study is not directly connected with the history of the Jewish people as a nation, for this history begins strictly with Abraham, the first distinct ancestor of the chosen people, and also because this study may be more profitably postponed to a later period in the Biblical training of theological students.

OCTOBER 19, 1897.

# CONTENTS.

| | PAGE |
|---|---|
| INTRODUCTION | 1 |

## FIRST PERIOD.

*The Patriarchal Age: From the Call of Abraham to Moses.*

### ABRAHAM.

#### CHAPTER I.

| | |
|---|---|
| *Section I.* A SUMMARY ACCOUNT OF HIS LIFE | 6 |

#### CHAPTER II.

| | |
|---|---|
| *Section II.* SOCIAL AND RELIGIOUS ASPECTS OF HIS LIFE, | 17 |

#### CHAPTER III.

| | |
|---|---|
| JACOB | 27 |

#### CHAPTER IV.

| | |
|---|---|
| JOSEPH | 37 |

#### CHAPTER V.

| | |
|---|---|
| THE ISRAELITES IN EGYPT | 46 |

## SECOND OR TRIBAL PERIOD.

*From Moses to the Institution of the Monarchy.*

### CHAPTER VI.
THE DELIVERANCE FROM EGYPT . . . . . 58

### CHAPTER VII.
SINAI AND THE LAW . . . . . . . . 70

#### THE MOSAIC LAW.

### CHAPTER VIII.
*Section I.* GENERAL REMARKS. THE TABERNACLE AND ITS MINISTERS . . . . . . . 78

### CHAPTER IX.
*Section II.* SACRIFICIAL AND FESTIVAL RITES . . 89

### CHAPTER X.
FROM SINAI TO THE SOUTHERN BORDER OF PALESTINE . . 100

### CHAPTER XI.
GEOGRAPHY OF PALESTINE . . . . . . . 109

### CHAPTER XII.
CONQUEST OF EASTERN PALESTINE . . . 117

### CHAPTER XIII.
CONQUEST OF WESTERN PALESTINE . . . 130

### CHAPTER XIV.
THE TIME OF THE JUDGES . . . 145

### CHAPTER XV.
HISTORY OF THE JUDGES . . . . . . 156

## THIRD OR ROYAL PERIOD.

*From the Institution of the Monarchy to the Babylonian Captivity.*

### CHAPTER XVI.
The Beginning of the Monarchy . . . . . 171

### CHAPTER XVII.
The Reign of Saul and Youth of David . . 183

### CHAPTER XVIII.
The Reign of David . . . . . . . 196

#### The Kingdom of Solomon.

### CHAPTER XIX.
*Section I.* Its Beginning and Prosperous Period . 211

### CHAPTER XX.
*Section II.* Its Decline and Disruption . . . 228

### CHAPTER XXI.
The Kingdom of Israel . . . . . . 240

### CHAPTER XXII.
The Kingdom of Juda . . . . . . . 255

#### The Prophetical Office in the Old Testament.

### CHAPTER XXIII.
*Section I.* Nature and History . . . 272

### CHAPTER XXIV.
*Section II.* Predictions and Influence . . . 284

## FOURTH PERIOD.

*The Restoration: From the Babylonian Captivity to Our Lord.*

### CHAPTER XXV.
THE BABYLONIAN CAPTIVITY. . . 296

### CHAPTER XXVI.
RETURN FROM THE EXILE . 310

### CHAPTER XXVII.
RULE OF THE HIGH PRIESTS . . . 323

### CHAPTER XXVIII.
THE NATIONAL INDEPENDENCE RECONQUERED . . 335

### CHAPTER XXIX.
THE LAST JEWISH DYNASTY . . 347

### CHAPTER XXX.
THE JEWS OF THE DISPERSION . 360

GENERAL INDEX . . . 373

# OUTLINES OF JEWISH HISTORY.

### INTRODUCTION.

**1. Object of Jewish History.** The history of the Jews, like that of all nations, is the narrative of the past events connected with a particular people. Its object is to represent to the modern eye, in a vivid and accurate manner, the several phases of the actual existence of the Jewish nation. For this purpose, it narrates the facts supplied by every available source of information, illustrates the manners and customs of the Jews, describes the countries which they have successively occupied, and taking notice of every development in their literary, commercial, political and religious life, it sets forth a faithful picture of the origin, growth and decline of Jewish civilization.

Jewish history is not, however, simply the picture of the civilization which the Jews attained in the various periods of their national existence, it is also the history of the true Religion from Abraham to the coming of our Lord. From beginning to end, Israel's history is most intimately bound up with Divine Revelation. A Divine covenant with Abraham, "the Father" of the Jews, marks the very beginning of the chosen people, and the various stages of this Divine covenant are intimately connected with the social and political changes of the Jewish nation. Israel is ever God's "peculiar people," and its judges and kings, its priests and prophets, are but the visible representatives of Jehovah, the Almighty King of the Jews. National prosperity or public calamities are meted out to the theocratic nation according to its faithfulness or unfaithfulness in keeping alive the pure worship of the true God. In fine, under God's special guidance, the principal personages and leading events of Jewish history foreshadow the corresponding personages and events of the Christian dispensation. From all this it follows that Jewish history is essentially identical with *Sacred* history.

2. **Importance of Jewish History.** The *religious* importance of the history of the Jews has ever been felt in the Church of God. The Fathers of the early centuries, and the ecclesiastical writers of all ages, ever considered the facts which it records and the predictions which it contains as the real preparation and the sure basis of Christianity. They read the history of Israel with the religious respect which man owes to the Word of God, and they delighted in drawing from the inspired records of the Jews the instructions, encouragements, warnings, promises, etc., which they needed for their own spiritual welfare or for the good of those intrusted to their care. In point of fact, to the Christian mind, the main importance of Jewish history will ever consist in that religious character which makes of it the authentic record of God's dealings with the children of men.

Viewed from another, viz., from a *historical*, standpoint, Jewish history has also a special importance. "It is the most complete history of the Oriental world in our possession, and is not confined to one people, but is full of references to many and great Eastern nations. It is the beaten track through Oriental times, to which and from which numerous pathways lead. Taking it as a starting-point, and making it our own, we shall have little difficulty in increasing our knowledge of the contemporaneous history of the surrounding peoples" (IRA M. PRICE, Syllabus of Old Testament History, third edition, p. 2).

A thorough acquaintance with Jewish history presents another precious advantage: it enables us to grasp the exact meaning of the Sacred Scriptures, particularly of the Old Testament. It makes us conversant, for instance, with those Eastern manners and customs which are so constantly referred to, but so seldom explained in the Sacred Scriptures, and it thereby furnishes us with a key for the right interpretation of countless passages of the Inspired volume. For the prophetical writings in particular, Jewish history has a special *exegetical* importance. The exhortations, threats and predictions of the prophets are usually suggested by, and natually connected with, the events and conditions of the time when they were uttered, and, in consequence, only a man really conversant with Jewish history has the true data by which these important portions of Holy Writ can be rightly interpreted.

Finally, the study of Jewish history has acquired during this century a great *apologetical* importance. On the one hand, there is hardly a book of Holy Writ whose authority has not been assailed on historical grounds by some of the ablest scholars of the Rationalistic school, and their objections naturally demand to be met with genuine historical knowledge. On the other hand, as a careful study of Jewish history shows that many of these objections, once apparently so formidable, have lost their force, chiefly in face of the recent discoveries in Bible lands, the apologist of the present day may justly feel that the objections which have not yet been fully disposed of, will sooner or later meet with a similar fate.

3. **Sources of Jewish History.** The Sacred Books of the Old Testament are the first source of Jewish History.

They all, in their several degrees, supply materials for the narrative of the events connected with the chosen people. Those among them which are called **Historical** because they detail directly and almost exclusively the events of one or several periods of Israel's existence, stand naturally the first as sacred sources of Jewish history. Next come the **Prophetical** writings with their numerous references to past or present events, and with their vivid descriptions of the moral, social, political and religious condition of the time. Lastly, the **Didactic** works of the Old Testament contain also precious indications about the customs and civilization of the Jews, and at times they furnish detailed information about some great personages or leading events of the Jewish nation.

Outside these authentic sources of Jewish history, useful materials may be gathered from secondary sources of information, such as ancient History and Geography, Archæology and Ethnography. By means of the **ancient history** of the greatest countries of antiquity, such as Egypt, Assyria, Babylonia, Phenicia, Syria, Medo-Persia, and especially of their condition when Israel comes in contact with them, many facts of Jewish history are better realized, because viewed in the light of the actual circumstances which influenced their production. In like manner a fair acquaintance with the **Geography** and scenery of these great countries is very desirable to render more living and more interesting the events of Jewish history which occurred in these ancient regions. **Archæology**, or the science of the domestic, social, political, and religious antiquities of the nations which surrounded or conquered Israel, may furnish at times the best illustrations of the antiquities of the Jews, either by way of resemblance or by way of contrast. Finally, ancient and modern **Ethnography**, or description of the customs and manners of the various nations, especially in the form of books of Eastern travel, can be of the greatest use, because of the unchanging character of Oriental life, even in its minutest details.

**4. Division of Jewish History.** The history of the Jews from Abraham to Our Lord may be divided into four great periods of about equal duration, and corresponding to the most important political changes undergone by the Jewish nation:

(1) The **Patriarchal** age, from the call of Abraham to Moses.

(2) The **Tribal** period, from Moses to the institution of the monarchy.

(3) The **Royal** period, from the institution of the monarchy to the Babylonian captivity.

(4) The period of the **Restoration**, from the Babylonian captivity to Our Lord.

## SYNOPSIS OF CHAPTER I.

ABRAHAM (Gen. xi, 27–xxv, 10).

*Section I. A Summary Account of His Life.*

HISTORY OF ABRAHAM.
- 1. *Birthplace.* Ur of the Chaldees.
  - General aspect of Chaldæa.
  - Site of *Ur*, description of its *ruins*.
- 2. *Wanderings.*
  - 1. Ur, Haran, Sichem, Bethel, Egypt.
  - 2. Bethel again, Mambre near Hebron.
  - 3. Gerara, Bersabee, Hebron finally.
- 3. *Relations* with
  - 1. The Chanaanites.
  - 2. Egypt.
  - 3. Melchisedech.
  - 4. Abimelech.
- 4. *Domestic Life.*
  - Agar and Ismael.
  - Sara and Isaac.
  - Eliezer and Rebecca.
  - Lot (separation, rescue).
  - Cetura.
- 5. *Burial-Place.* Machpelah (double cave)
  - purchase.
  - description.

# FIRST PERIOD.

## THE PATRIARCHAL AGE: FROM THE CALL OF ABRAHAM TO MOSES.

### CHAPTER I.

ABRAHAM (Gen. xi, 27–xxv, 10).

SECTION I. A SUMMARY ACCOUNT OF HIS LIFE.

1. **Birthplace.** The man selected by God to be the ancestor of the chosen people was **Abraham,** or as he was first called, **Abram.** He was the youngest son of Thare, the ninth descendant from Sem, and was born in "the land the Chaldeans" (Acts vii, 4), whereby is meant the southern part of the country fertilized by the Tigris and the Euphrates. As Chaldæa is strictly an alluvial region, its aspect is that of a level plain whose monotony is unrelieved by mountain or hill. But its natural fertility is wonderful, and with its former large and industrious population (Gen. x, 10), it must have presented in Abraham's time a great contrast with its present barren and depopulated condition. Among its many cities was "Ur of the Chaldees" the birthplace of Abraham, and whose long disputed site has been recently identified with **Mugheir,** some six miles distant from the right bank of the Euphrates, and about 125 miles northwest of the Persian Gulf. In the time of Abraham, Ur was most likely a thriving seaport, for recently discovered inscriptions, whilst proving that Mugheir was formerly called Ur, "constantly speak

of the ships of Ur and of the brisk commerce of its inhabitants " (BLAIKIE, Heroes of Israel, p. 9). The ruins of Ur are extensive, consisting mostly of low mounds, near the northern end of which are the remains of a Chaldean temple built in brick, partly sunburnt and partly baked, and dedicated to Hurki, the moon-god, from whom the town derived its name. As Ur was for long centuries used as a cemetery-city, because of the notions entertained about its great sanctity, its ruins present mainly the aspect of a city of tombs.

2. **Wanderings.** The wanderings of Abraham began during the lifetime of his father. For some unknown reason — perhaps simply because of the restlessness natural to nomads — the family of Thare left their settlement at Ur, and under his leadership started towards the land of Chanaan (Gen. xi, 31). Proceeding northward, the emigrants naturally followed the road which is along or near the banks of the Euphrates, because it presented no special difficulty for the conveyance of either man or cattle. For upwards of 170 miles they moved along the rich plain of Sennaar and passed by the great cities of Arach, Chalanne and Babylon; next they entered a highland region, and about 200 miles northwest of Babylon crossed the river Khabur, whence they easily reached **Haran**, the frontier town of Babylonia. There the family of Thare settled, captivated by the great fertility of the plain in the centre of which Haran is built. There, also, after his father's death, Abraham received the Divine call recorded in Genesis (chap. xii, 1, sq.) bidding him leave his own country and the idolatrous house of his father (Josue xxiv, 2, 3) and repair to another land (cfr. CRELIER, Genèse, p. 153).

Accordingly, Abraham, now seventy-five years old, leaving his brother Nachor in Haran (Gen. xxiv, 10), proceeded on his journey with his wife Sarai, and his nephew Lot. Both Abraham and Lot had prospered in Haran, and their large possessions and retinue formed a long caravan which moved slowly towards the Euphrates (Gen. xii, 4, 5). Having crossed this river — probably at the ford still in use near Zeugma — they naturally took the old track or road to Damascus across the great Syrian desert. They stopped but a little time in Damascus (Gen. xv, 2, 3) and then resumed their southwesterly road by one of the ordinary caravan routes which passed, as they still pass, through Palestine to Egypt. Thus did Abraham reach the land of Chanaan, but not knowing yet whether this was the land of promise, "he passed through the country into the place of **Sichem**" as far as the turpentine tree of Moreh (cfr. Gen. xii, 6; xxxiv, 4). Here it was that Jehovah appeared to Abraham and promised to his seed this very land; here it was also that the grateful patriarch erected his first altar to Jehovah (Gen. xii, 7).

But the plain was small, and not without proprietors. This led Abraham to pass southward to a mountain east of **Bethel**, a fine district for pasturage, which, however, soon proved insufficient for his numerous flocks. He therefore went southward to *"the Negeb," "the dry"* region which forms the southern limit of the Holy Land, till the pressure of famine compelled him to go down into Egypt, the fertile granary to which the Bedouins of the present day repair willingly under similar circumstances (Gen. xii, 8, sq.).

Compelled to withdraw from Egypt under Pharao's orders, Abraham went back to his former camping-ground near **Bethel,** where he soon separated from Lot, his nephew, who hitherto had accompanied him in all his wanderings, and where he was greatly encouraged by a more explicit promise of Jehovah that his seed should possess the Holy Land. Thence he removed and took up his abode under the terebinths of Mambre, an Amorrhite prince (Gen. xiv, 13), near Hebron (Gen. xii, 20–xiii).

After a long residence at Mambre, Abraham resumed his

wanderings, and proceeding towards the south he "dwelt between Cades and Sur, and sojourned in **Gerara**," a place now known as **Umm el Jerar**. Here, or not far from it, at **Bersabee** — about 25 miles south of Hebron — he sojourned for a long time, highly respected by the Philistine authorities, who considered him as a powerful chieftain not to be interfered with. But although Bersabee afforded plenty of roaming space for his flocks and several wells for their watering, Abraham finally removed to **Hebron**: the death of Sara could not be very distant, and in preparation for her demise he wished to secure for himself and his descendants a burial-place in the locality whose possession had been several times promised him for his posterity (Gen. xx, 1; xxi, 22-34).

3. **Outward Relations.** The first class of people with whom Abraham came in contact during his long wanderings after reaching the holy land, are those tribes which, under the general name of **Chanaanites**, were "at that time in the land" (Gen. xii, 6). His general relations with them present a twofold aspect: (1) he ever remains separated from the surrounding tribes, professing to be a stranger among them (Gen. xxiii, 4), not accepting any gift from their hands (Gen. xiv, 23), not willing to have any intermarriage between his race and theirs (Gen. xxiv, 3), etc.; (2) there is no trace in his actual dealings with them of the unrelenting enmity of later ages. This, however, should not be accounted for by community of creed and identity of religious worship, but rather by the fact that Palestine was then but thinly peopled and offered many tracts of unappropriated grounds fit for pasturage. Dwelling in their towns and satisfied with their immediate neighborhood, the Chanaanites did not interfere with a chieftain no less really powerful than ostensibly peaceful and disinterested.

Abraham's relations with the **Egyptians** were naturally of shorter duration than with the Chanaanites, and their brief description in Genesis (chap. xii, 11-20) is quite in harmony with recent Egyptian discoveries. Thus the fears of Abraham for his own life, if Sarai was known to be his wife, are illustrated in the Egyptian "Tale of Two Brothers," where we are told that a King of Egypt sent two armies to bring a beautiful woman to him and to murder her husband. The notification to the king of Abraham's arrival with his beautiful sister, is in perfect accordance with the extant reports made under similar circumstances by officers posted on the Egyptian frontier. In like manner, the well-known customs of the country required that Sarai's supposed brother should be offered presents calculated to secure his ready consent to her future marriage with Pharao. Finally, it is generally admitted that all the animals mentioned in the Bible as presented to Abraham by Pharao, were then known in Egypt (See VIGOUROUX, Bible et Découvertes Modernes; GEIKIE, Hours with the Bible, vol. i, pp. 320-322).

Few things found in the Biblical records have appeared more strange and incredible than Abraham's relations with **Melchisedech**. In this connection, Genesis (chap. xiv, 18-20) tells us that on his return from a victorious battle against eastern kings who had invaded Palestine, Abraham was met by Melchisedech, the King of Salem and priest of the most high God, received his blessing and gave him the tithes of all the spoil. This sudden introduction of a Chanaanite personage bearing a Semitic name, at once king and priest, without any mention of his parentage, place of birth, successor in office, etc., has ever appeared most mysterious and supplied matter for more or less improbable conjectures. Quite lately, however, an unexpected light has been thrown upon several points connected with Melchisedech, which enables us to realize the historical character of this illustrious type of our Lord (Heb. v, 6, 10). Among the cuneiform tablets discovered in 1887 at Tell el-Amarna on the Nile, were found despatches going back to a time long before the

Exodus and addressed to the kings of Egypt by the governor of Jerusalem. From some of them we learn that Semitic words were then current in Palestine, that the town over which this official ruled as an ally to Egypt was **Uru' Salim**, and that his office was not hereditary, nor dependent on the appointment of the Egyptian monarch, but filled by the direct oracle of a God whom he calls the Mighty King and who had his shrine in Uru' Salim. As appointed by a direct divine oracle, the ruler over Jerusalem was naturally at the same time the priest of the God to whom he would offer a sacrifice of thanksgiving for the glorious victory of Abraham, and in whose name he would bless this illustrious patriarch. Abraham, recognizing Jehovah in the God worshipped by Melchisedech, willingly gave to this king and priest the tithes of all the spoil.[1]

The last class of Abraham's outward relations which we intend briefly to mention here are those which this patriarch had for long years with the Philistines, who, apparently at that time, were a pastoral tribe under the leadership of a king bearing the official title of Abimelech. In reaching their country, Abraham — according to his general agreement with Sara — gave out that she was his sister, and in consequence she was taken to become the wife of Abimelech. The narrative of this second seizure, whilst bearing much general resemblance with the preceding narrative of Sara's capture in Egypt, differs from it in several important particulars, such as the explanation now given of his conduct by Abraham (Gen. xx, 11–13), and the kind manner with which Abimelech deals with him (Gen. xx, 14–18). The sojourn of Abraham in the land of the Philistines is also marked by the first act of appropriation on the part of his

[1] As the God at whose altar Melchisedech ministered was the God of the territory of Jerusalem which then extended to Carmel in the south, and to Geth and Ceila in the west, it is not unlikely that He was identified by Abraham with Jehovah whom he knew to be the God of the promised Land and who had appeared to him in that region. (See Records of the Past, new series, vol. v, pp. 54–101.)

servants — the digging of the wells of Bersabee — which was indeed resented by the pastoral population of the tribe, but which simply led to a firmer alliance between him and the Philistine authorities (Gen. xxi, 22-34).

4. **Domestic Life.** In connection with the members of Abraham's household we notice first of all that **Agar**, one of his female slaves — probably one of the gifts of Pharao (cfr. Gen. xii, 16; xvi, 1) — appears as a secondary wife of the patriarch. She became such at the instigation of Sarai, according to a custom still known in the East, and in virtue of which children born in this manner are considered as legitimate offspring and treated as the children of the mistress of the establishment. Agar having conceived, forgot her condition to the extent of despising her barren mistress, but she had to "run away" from Sarai's resentment. The angel of Jehovah found her in the wilderness of Sur — which separated Palestine from Egypt her native land — assured her that Jehovah had heard her affliction, and that Ismael her son, would be a free, indomitable son of the desert. Whereupon Agar returned to her mistress, and in due time bore a son to Abraham (Gen. xvi). Evidently Ismael became dear to the old patriarch and was treated by him as the heir of the Divine promise, up to the birth of Isaac from Sarai. This explains how Abraham was so reluctant to expel him as requested by Sarai, who could not bear the idea that the son of a bond-woman should share the paternal inheritance, but it makes it difficult to realize how despite his paternal love he consented to dismiss Ismael and his mother with a scanty supply of bread and a bottle of water, unless we admit that under the name of bread other provisions are included. However this may be, the picture of the sufferings of the youth in the desert of Bersabee is true to life (GEIKIE, p. 343), and had not the angel of Jehovah intervened in his behalf, Ismael would have perished from

thirst. Saved from a cruel death, the lad grew up in the wilderness of Pharan which forms the northeastern division of the peninsula of Sinai, was married to an Egyptian woman and became the ancestor of numerous nomadic tribes spread over the deserts of Northern Arabia between the Red Sea and the Euphrates (Gen. xvi ; xxxvii, 25, 28).

But however dear to Abraham were Ismael and his mother, two other members of his family lay closer to the heart of the patriarch, viz., **Sara** his half-sister and wife (Gen. xx, 11, 12) and **Isaac** the son of promise and the heir of all things (Gen. xxv, 5). Of course, the history of Sara is that of Abraham, whom she accompanied in all his wanderings, yet her independent action appears in connection with family affairs, such as Abraham's connection with Agar and the difficulties between her and Agar, between Isaac and Ismael. Her ironical laughter at the promise of a child (Gen. xviii, 10), her trembling denial of that laughter (Gen. xviii, 15), her laughter of thankful joy for the birth of Isaac (Gen. xxi, 6), are traits of her character to be noticed. It was probably at Bersabee that she brought forth Isaac, and on the eighth day the child was circumcised according to the Divine command. When two or three years old Isaac was weaned, and it was soon after the festival celebration which marked this event, that God declared that through Isaac alone Abraham would be the ancestor of the chosen people (Gen. xxi). And yet the time came when Jehovah asked from the patriarch the sacrifice of this beloved son, but was satisfied with Abraham's firm faith and ready obedience (Gen. xxii, 1-19).

The time came also when a suitable partner was to be provided for Isaac, and in consequence, Abraham ever anxious to keep his seed separate from the idolatrous Chanaanites, sent his chief servant the Damascene, **Eliezer**, to Mesopotamia, where Nachor had remained. In this connection, the sacred narrative pictures Eliezer's departure, meeting with

Rebecca, petition for her hand in behalf of his young master, etc., with a faithfulness to Oriental life which has never been surpassed (Gen. xxiv).

The mutual attachment of Abraham and his nephew **Lot** deserves also a mention here. On the one hand, Lot follo s willingly his uncle whithersoever he goes (to Damascus, Sichem, Egypt, etc.), and consents to depart from him only when their common interest requires it manifestly (Gen. xiii, 5, sq.). On the other hand, Abraham willingly gives Lot his choice of the best land before him (Gen. xiii, 9, sq.), and after the actual departure of his nephew, shows himself ever ready to come to his help as is exemplified in the promptitude with which Abraham "the Hebrew" (*i. e.*, the one who came from beyond the Euphrates) started to rescue him when made captive by the eastern kings who had invaded Chanaan (Gen. xiv, 1–16).[1]

Finally, it is in connection with another wife of Abraham, named **Cetura**, by whom he had several children, that we learn the prudent measures to which he resorted to preclude all discussion about his inheritance between his lawful heir and his other children. To the latter "he gave gifts, and separated them from Isaac his son, while he yet lived, to the east country" (Gen. xxv, 1–6).

5. **Death and Burial-Place.** Abraham was 175 years old when "he was gathered to his people." Isaac and Ismael, his sons, buried him by the side of his beloved wife, Sara, in the cave of **Machpelah** (Gen. xxv, 7–10).

As we already noticed, this burial-place was bought by the holy patriarch on the occasion of the death of Sara, and

---

[1] Later on Lot was miraculously saved from the destruction of Sodom, the details of which are recorded in Genesis (chap. xix). The statements of the Bible in connection with this catastrophe are in perfect harmony with the accounts of such writers as Philo, Tacitus and Strabo; they are also made by the sacred writer in such a manner as to clearly imply the supernatural character of the destruction of the guilty cities (cfr. V, GUERIN, Terre Sainte, vol. ii, p. 287, sq.; DEANE, Abraham, p. 110, sq.; BLAIKIE, Heroes of Israel, p. 132, sq).

its purchase is recorded in Genesis (chap. xxiii) with great minuteness, and also with perfect faithfulness to Eastern customs. Then, as now, the order of the transactions was ceremony, compliment, and then business; then, as now, the sellers offered anything, everything, as a gift, but all are politely declined; then, as now, every article must be specified in the deed (the field, the cave, the trees), *all* rights must be paid in current money, and then the deed "is made sure" (HENRY A. HARPER, From Abraham to David; see also DEANE, Abraham, p. 150, sq.).

The mosque at Hebron is built over the cave of Machpelah, and even the mosque is guarded with the most jealous care by the Mussulmans, a few great personages being the only ones who were allowed to visit it for several centuries. The only visitor of the cave itself who has left a credible account of his inspection is the rabbi Benjamin, of Tudela, who in 1163 was allowed to examine it. He says: "The Gentiles have erected six sepulchres in this place, which they pretend to be those of Abraham and Sarah, of Isaac and Rebecca, and of Jacob and Lia . . . if any Jew come, who gives an additional fee to the keeper of the caves, an iron door is opened and with a burning candle in his hand, the visitor descends into a first cave which is empty, traverses a second in the same state, and at last reaches a third, which contains the six sepulchres, one opposite the other. All these sepulchres bear inscriptions. . . . A lamp burns in the cave and upon the sepulchres, continually both night and day." Whatever may be thought of this description by one who visited the cave during the occupation of Palestine by the Christians, it may be said with great probability that the cave "resembles the rock-cut sepulchres of Palestine, with a square antechamber carefully quarried, and two interior sepulchral chambers, to which access has been made at a later period through the roofs" (C. R. CONDER, Survey Memoirs, vol. iii, p. 346).

# SYNOPSIS OF CHAPTER II.

## ABRAHAM.

*Section II. Social and Religious Aspects of His Life.*

**I. SOCIAL ASPECT: A Nomad Life.**
- **A.** *In general:* The Nomad Life
  - still exists is Western Asia.
  - is now better known than ever before.
  - singularly illustrative of the Patriarchal life.
- **B.** *In particular:* Some of its particulars described:
  1. The Tent.
  2. The Wandering Life:
     - Its motives.
     - Its principal features.
  3. Dealings with others: hospitality.
  4. Domestic Life: children, women, slaves.
  5. Burial-place and funeral rites.

**II. RELIGIOUS ASPECT: A Life of Faith.**
- **A.** "The Friend of God." A life little known *before* the Call, but *afterwards* a life of Faith
  - Shown by
    - a constant sense of the Divine Presence.
    - a trustful love and deep veneration for Jehovah.
    - an unlimited devotion to His service.
  - Rewarded by
    - earthly blessings.
    - familiar intercourse with God.
- **B.** "The Father of the Faithful."
  1. Of the *Jews*:
     - Repeated promises.
     - Covenant.
  2. Of the *Christians* (spiritually): universality of the promises.
  3. Claimed even by *Mussulmans*.

# CHAPTER II.

## ABRAHAM.

SECTION II.  SOCIAL AND RELIGIOUS ASPECTS OF HIS LIFE.

### § *1. Social Aspect: A Nomad Life.*

1. **The Nomad Life in General.** The inhabitants of Palestine and neighboring countries have, from the earliest ages, been divided into two great classes, according as they dwell in permanent or in movable habitations (Gen. iv, 17, 20), and this division holds good down to the present day. In all parts of Western Asia, beside the people settled in villages and cities, tribes are now met with dwelling in tents, and "moving about with their flocks according to the demands of the season, the state of the herbage and the supply of water" (KITTO, art. Pasturage). They are *nomad* tribes leading the same wandering life as their ancestors long centuries before Christ, wearing the same garb, and speaking almost the same language. Their roaming habits, their apparent lack of all civilization, together with the difficulty in past centuries to reach the East, and the great insecurity of travel through the vast deserts of Western Asia, have long prevented Biblical scholars from acquiring a close acquaintance with customs and manners so different from those of Western Europe. But of late most of those obstacles have disappeared: as the means of transportation have become more rapid and less expensive, travels through Eastern lands have been multiplied, the manners and customs of nomad tribes have been studied in their own country, and interesting narratives have placed the result of patient and

careful investigation within the reach of Biblical students. In point of fact the nomad life is better known now than ever before, and our greater knowledge of it enables us to realize with peculiar vividness the various features of the patriarchal age, inasmuch as the life and habits of modern nomads are almost in every particular identical with those of the nomads of ancient times (J. L. PORTER, Five Years in Damascus, p. 178, sq.; GEIKIE, The Holy Land and the Bible, chap. xiii).

**Some Particulars of the Nomad Life described.** The first feature common to the nomads of to-day and to the wandering patriarchs of old consists in the use of the tent as a dwelling (Gen. xii, 8 ; xiii, 3 ; xviii, 1, etc.). The tents of Arabs are usually oblong and higher in front than behind. They are formed by setting poles — nine in all — in the ground, and spreading over them a covering made of goat's-hair cloth and along the border of which ropes are fastened. To keep the whole structure in position, the ropes are stretched to their utmost and fixed by their loops to pegs driven fast into the ground. The interior is divided into two parts by a curtain hanging upon the three central poles: the part on the left, in entering, is reserved for the women and contains the provisions of the household, the cooking utensils, the skin water-bottles, etc.; the part on the right, forms the men's apartment and is the place where passing guests and visitors are usually received (cfr. Gen. xviii, 6, 9, sq.; xxvii, 5, sq., etc.).

Dwellings of this description are easily transported, and as such are very convenient for that *wandering life* which perseveres down to the present day for the same motives as in the times of the patriarchs of old. Among these motives may be reckoned (1) the amount of personal adventure and tribal independence it allows ; (2) the means it affords for raising flocks and cattle by moving according to seasons, conditions of pastures, etc.; (3) the harmony it presents with olden traditions and ancestral habits; (4) the natural charms it offers under a blue Eastern sky, etc.

Of course, now, as during the patriarchal age, it is rare to meet solitary tents, for households united by kindred naturally dwell in the same region or move together in their migrations. "In the desert, the tents are often arranged in a circle or quadrangle, so that the cattle can be gathered together into the central space, and thus be more effectually defended against marauders" (VAN LENNEP, Bible Lands, p. 403). When migrating to new pastures the appearance of a large tribe — not unlike the large caravans of Abraham (cfr. Gen. xii, 4, sq.; xiii, 1, sq., etc.); and of Jacob (xxxii, 1-8, 13-21; xxxiii, 4-14),— is most picturesque, and is thus graphically described by Layard: "We soon found ourselves in the midst of wide-spreading flocks of sheep and camels. As far as the eye could reach, to the right, to the left, and in front, still the same moving crowd. Long lines of asses and bullocks laden with black tents, huge caldrons and variegated carpets; aged women and men, no longer able to walk, tied on the heap of domestic furniture; infants crammed into saddle-bags, their tiny heads thrust out through the narrow opening, balanced on the animal's back by kids or lambs tied on the opposite side; young girls clothed only in the close-fitting Arab shirt, which displayed rather than concealed their graceful forms; mothers with their children on their shoulders; boys driving flocks of lambs; horsemen armed with their long, tufted spears, scouring the plain on their fleet mares; riders urging their dromedaries with their short, hooked sticks, and leading their high-bred steeds by the halter; colts galloping amongst the throng" (Nineveh and its Remains, vol. i, p. 90).

On the arrival of a tribe at their camping-ground, the pitching of tents occasions a great deal of confusion, every one appearing desirous to outdo his neighbor in vehemence of shouting and of action. This is, however, but a friendly debate on the site of the respective tents, and after it has been settled by no more violent measure than mere yelling, each family begins to raise its temporary dwelling. The camels are made to kneel down, the donkeys to stop in the places fixed upon, and the loads are rolled off their backs. The women next spread the black tent covering, the men rush about with wooden mallets to drive in the stakes and pegs, and in a few minutes the temporary abodes are complete. The women and girls are then sent forth to fetch water, or to collect brushwood and dry twigs for fire, whilst the men, assembling in the tent of the sheikh and crouching in a circle round the entire trunk of an old tree, which is soon enveloped in flames, prepare to pass the rest of the day in that desultory talk relating to stolen sheep, stray donkeys, or successful robberies, which fills up the leisure of an Arab (cfr. LAYARD, Nineveh, vol. ii, pp. 49, 50).

In all encampments the sheikh's tent can easily be known by a long spear stuck upright in the ground in front of it, and distinguished travellers naturally make for it. As oftentimes, like the patriarchs of old, the sheikh sits under the awning of his tent or the shade of a tree watching for wayfarers, he soon notices that they are approaching, and at once the scene described in Genesis (chap. xviii) is renewed in their behalf. With the same formulas as those used by Abraham, they are invited to remain until they have partaken of refreshments; with the same speed, a lamb or a calf is brought in, stretched upon the ground and slaughtered, and with almost the same inconceivable expedition it is dressed and served up with butter and milk, together with the bread baked on the hearth. Finally, if his guests are persons of high rank, the sheikh *stands by* them while they eat, as Abraham did in the circumstance recorded in Genesis (cfr. L. J. PORTER, Five Years in Damascus, pp. 61, 178).

Of course, only sheikhs can afford to undergo such expenses in welcoming their guests, but all modern nomads feel bound to do all in their power to exercise the duty of hospitality, the sacredness of which is scarcely ever broken in the East notwithstanding the well-known dishonesty, treachery and cruelty of the inhabitants of the desert.

In the family circle, the head of the household is absolute lord and master of the lives and property of every member, so that had Abraham sacrificed his son Isaac, he would not have exceeded the authority granted to every father by the nomad tribes (Gen. xxii, 10). Now, as during the patriarchal age, the chief wife rules indeed over the other women, dispenses the provisions of the household and enjoys the privilege of preparing the meals destined for her husband and his guests, but this does not prevent frequent jealousies and intrigues, and in consequence one of the secondary wives is sometimes dismissed in order to restore peace to the disturbed household (See LAYARD, Babylon and Nineveh, p. 316). The sending of Eliezer to the country of Abraham's kindred to seek a wife for Isaac is exactly what an Arab chief would do to-day, "and it is very common among the Arabs of Egypt and other countries for a man to marry his first cousin . . . a union of this kind being generally lasting because of this tie of blood" (LANE, Modern Egyptians, p. 215). The fondness of Orientals for children, and especially for sons, is well known, and now, as in the time of the ancient patriarchs, the birth of a son is considered by the father as most welcome news (Gen. xxi, 7).

Of course, slavery has existed in the East from time immemorial, and the power of the master over his slaves is unbounded. It should be borne in mind, however, that the husband has no power over his wife's slaves — whom she may have received as a part of her dowry — unless there be an express agreement on her part to that effect (VAN LENNEP, Bible Lands, pp. 567, 568).

As a natural consequence of their wandering life, the nomads do not collect the remains of their dead in a cemetery;

if, however, some of their kindred have already been buried in a particular spot, they regard it as a preferable burial-place for themselves and for the members of their household. Public demonstrations of intense grief over their dead are a very ancient custom with Orientals (cfr. Gen. xxiii, 2, with W. THOMPSON, The Land and the Book, vol. i, p. 243), and the noise of their lamentations is naturally proportionate to the dignity and power of the deceased   It is not unlikely that the funeral rites of a sheikh, witnessed by Wm. Thompson at Hebron and so graphically described by him, bear a close resemblance to the public marks of honor and mourning which surrounded the burial of Abraham, one of the most powerful chieftains of his time (cfr. The Land and the Book, vol. i, p. 245, sq.; and also DEANE, Abraham, pp. 173, 174).

### § 2. *Religious Aspect: A Life of Faith.*

The religious aspect of Abraham's life is distinctly set forth by the sacred writers when they call him (1) "THE FRIEND OF GOD" (ii Paralip. xx, 7; Isaias xli, 8; James ii, 23), (2) "THE FATHER OF THE FAITHFUL" (Rom. iv, 11).

The first of these titles suggests a real, living, personal intercourse of the great patriarch with the Almighty, and it was well deserved by his strong, practical, persevering life of faith as the chosen servant of Jehovah. Various reasons have been alleged to account for the *beginning* of his belief in the true God whilst surrounded on all sides, even in the house of his father, by Assyrian idolatry, as, for instance, that he was born before Thare became an idolater, that he was himself converted from idolatry by a special revelation from God, etc.; these, however, are but suppositions more or less in harmony with the Biblical data respecting the life of Abraham, and it must be confessed that the origin of his faith in Jehovah is still a matter of conjecture. No less uncertainty prevails as regards the circumstances in the midst of which Abraham's faith, once begun, acquired the wonderful strength which characterizes it at the very first moment we see it tried by a Divine command (Gen. xii, 1, sq.), for it is far from being proved that Abraham's faith grew stronger and stronger in Ur of the Chaldees under the influence of religions persecutions started by the Assyrian King, Sargon I, and of which we would still hear in legends and traditions (cfr. HANNEBERG, Histoire de la Révélation Biblique, vol. i, p. 52, sq. ; DEANE, Abraham, chaps. i, ii).

Be all this as it may, there can be no doubt that, after the Divine call, Abraham ever evinced the most implicit, practical and generous faith. Indeed his life is less admirable for the *moral virtues* he practised, such as unselfishness (Gen. xiii, 8, 9; xiv, 23, etc.); nobility of disposition (xiv, 20); uprightness and courtesy in his dealings with others (Gen. xxiii), etc.; than for (1) a constant sense of the presence of an unseen God, raising Him altars whithersoever he goes (Gen. xii, 7, 8; xiii, 4, 18, etc.); (2) his trustful love and deep veneration for Jehovah (Gen. xvii, 3 ; xviii, 27 ; xxiv, 7); (3) an unlimited devotion to God's service, leaving at once and repeatedly everything (Epistle to the Hebrews xi, 8, sq. ); believing God's word notwithstanding all the suggestions of reason to the contrary (Gen. xv, 5, 6 ; Rom. iv, 19) ; willing to sacrifice his dearly beloved son (Gen. xxii) and teaching his family and posterity to be faithful to Jehovah (Gen. xviii, 19).

It is not therefore to be wondered at, if such a life was rewarded by the most splendid blessings (Gen. xxi, 22 *b*); and first of all by *earthly* blessings, such as worldly possessions (Gen. xiii, 6 ; xxiv, 35), the miraculous gift of an heir (Gen. xxiv, 37); a large posterity (Gen. xxv, 1, sq., etc.) ; high consideration from men (Gen. xxi, 23) and, finally, a robust and long life (Gen. xxv, 8); and next, by wonderful blessings of the *spiritual* order, God guiding and protecting him on every occasion (Gen. xiii, 17 ; xii, 17 ; xxi, 22), appearing to him (Gen. xv, 1, etc.), conversing familiarly with him and revealing to him His secrets (Gen. xviii, 17), granting readily his petitions (Gen. xvii, 18, 20; xviii, 23, sq.; xx, 7, 17), etc.

In virtue of the second title — that of "THE FATHER OF THE FAITHFUL" — given to Abraham in Holy Writ, the great patriarch stands before us as the glorious ancestor of the chosen people of God under the old and the new dispensation. He is, first of all, the *natural* ancestor of the Jewish nation, through Isaac his son and the heir of all his possessions. Such was from the first the design of God, who in bidding Abraham leave his country, his kindred and his father's house promised " to make of him a great nation " (Gen. xii, 1, 2), to which He would give the Land of Chanaan (Gen. xii, 7; xiii, 15; xv, 13). As time went on, the Divine promises multiplied and became more distinct. Abraham was made sure that he would have a son from Sara, that Isaac would be his only heir, and that from him a great and powerful nation should arise (Gen. xviii, 10; xxi, 10; xxii, 17). These various promises were also confirmed, first, by a solemn although transient covenant, as we read in Genesis, xv, 18, and next by the permanent covenant, of the circumcision (Gen. xvii). There is, therefore, no doubt that Abraham is the glorious ancestor "according to the flesh" of that people chosen of old by Jehovah to preserve here below the true faith (Gen. xvii, 7, 8) together with the expectation of the future redeemer of the world, but now long rejected to give place to another nation as numerous as the stars of the heavens and walking in the footsteps of the "faithful Abraham" (Gal. iii, 9). "According to the spirit," Abraham is the father of all Christians, God's chosen people under the new covenant, and in a special manner of those who earnestly strive to live up to their belief after his example (Gal. iii, 7, 29; Rom. iv, 12). In the Divine plan, Abraham was ever destined to be the father of all those who would through ages share in the blessing immediately granted through him to the Jewish people, for it must be noticed that the promises made by God to Abraham are always *universal* (Gen. xii, 2; xviii, 17, 18; xxii, 18), and the covenant of the circumcision has been transformed from the circumcision of the flesh into that of the heart (Rom. ii, 29; Galat. vi, 15).

But God destined Abraham to become "the father of *many* nations" even physically, and as a fact, he is not the natural ancestor of the Jews alone, he is also the father of a branch of the Arabs through Ismael (Gen. xvi, 15; xxv, 13), of the descendants of Cetura enumerated in Genesis (xxv, 1, sq.), and of the Edomites through his grandson Esau (Gen. xxv, 23). In Arabia proper, Mussulmans do not hesitate to claim him as their ancestor, the more so because Mohammed, having recognized that all that the Arabs had of good in his time was due to this great patriarch, bethought himself of restoring among them the religion of Abraham (see HANNEBERG, Histoire de la Révélation Biblique, vol. i, pp. 60, 61).

# SYNOPSIS OF CHAPTER III.

## JACOB.

HISTORY OF JACOB.
1. *Importance of Jacob in Jewish History.*

2. *Birth and First Period of Life:*
   - A. Birth of Esau and Jacob.
   - B. Purchase of Birthright.
   - C. Acquisition of Paternal Blessing.

3. *Journey to and Sojourn in Haran:*
   - A. Reasons and Incidents of the Journey.
   - B. Jacob and Laban's Household.
   - C. His Shepherd Life.

4. *Return from Haran and Subsequent Life:*
   - A. Motives of Departure.
   - B. Principal Incidents
     - *East* of the Jordan (Mt. Galaad, Mahanain, Phanuel, Socoth).
     - *West* of the Jordan (Sichem, Bethel, Ephrata, Mambre).
   - C. Life in Hebron; removal to and Death in Egypt.

5. *Character:* Contrast with
   - Abraham,
   - Isaac,
   - Esau.

## CHAPTER III.

### JACOB.

**1. Importance of Jacob in Jewish History.** As might naturally be expected, Isaac was treated by God, after his father's death, as the lawful and sole heir of the Divine promises, and, in fact, his history resembles in many ways that of Abraham. Like him, he moves under Jehovah's guidance and protection (Gen. xxvi, 1-3, 11) and receives glorious promises of a large posterity "in which shall all the nations of the earth be blessed" (Gen. xxvi, 3, 4, 24); like Abraham, he exhibits genuine devotion to Jehovah (Gen. xxvi, 25), and God makes him very prosperous, victorious over his enemies, grants him children and length of years (Gen. xxvi, 12-14; 27-31; xxv, 21-26; xxxv, 29). And yet the patriarch next to Abraham in importance in Jewish history is not his son Isaac, whose deeds are only summarized in the Book of Genesis, but his grandson Jacob, whose history is recorded with so many details in the Sacred narrative. If we possess so many particulars about Jacob's life, it is not simply because his was a very eventful life. It is also because (1) even before his birth, he was chosen by God, in preference to his twin-brother Esau, to become the actual father of the twelve heads of the tribes of Israel (Gen. xxv, 22, 23); because (2) during the first period of his life he succeeded in purchasing Esau's birthright (Gen. xxv, 28-34) and in obtaining the last blessing of Isaac (Gen. xxvii); and, finally, because (3) the tribes which eventually united into a powerful (the Jewish) nation, trace back their respective origin to his immediate posterity.

2. **Birth and First Period of Life.** Great, indeed, must have been the love of Isaac for Rebecca and his faith in the Divine promises, since he remained twenty long years without the blessing of children, and yet neither thought of taking another wife — as allowed by Oriental customs — nor gave up all hope of obtaining children through her. At length, his trustful and earnest entreaty with God in Rebecca's behalf secured the long-desired offspring. Rebecca conceived twins who seemed to struggle in her womb, and filled with apprehension she appealed to Jehovah who returned this prophetic answer:

> Two nations are in thy womb,
> And two peoples shall be separated from thy bowels;
> And a people shall overcome a people,
> And the elder shall serve the younger.

In due time the twins were born, and were called respectively **Esau** and **Jacob**, from the well-known circumstances which accompanied their coming forth.

Esau was the elder, and as such was beloved by Isaac, who naturally considered him as his lawful heir, and who, later on, enjoyed — as Orientals do down to the present day — the game which Esau's love of the chase often secured in the surrounding country of Bersabee. On the other hand, Jacob was the favorite of Rebecca who ever considered him as the lawful heir of Jehovah's promises to Abraham, soon acquainted him with the Divine oracle in his behalf, taught him how invaluable was the birthright therein promised to his exertions, and urged him to avail himself of every opportunity that might make sure the attainment of so desirable an object. To this maternal influence of Rebecca over Jacob's mind and feelings we may naturally ascribe the eagerness with which Jacob proposed to Esau the selling of his birthright for a savory dish, a transaction to which the latter readily agreed, through a lack of proper appreciation of the Divine blessings then connected with primogeniture (Genesis xxv, 21-34).

The Sacred narrative does not tell us whether this transfer of Esau's birthright to his brother was made known to Isaac; but we can easily gather from it that Esau, relying on his father's special affection, continued to feel sure of the paternal inheritance, and that Isaac really intended to transmit it to him with his last blessing. This would have indeed occurred if Rebecca had not, in her part of the tent, overheard the words of Isaac, when, in his old age, he directed Esau to "go abroad," bring him of his hunting and "make him savory meat thereof," and if, under her influence, Jacob had not taken advantage of his father's dimness of sight to obtain the last paternal blessing intended for Esau. Jacob's blessing was irreversible and gave him henceforth the most unquestionable outward claim to all the privileges of birthright, and this is why now, sadly frustrated in his expectations, Esau begins to cherish murderous designs against his brother (Gen. xxvii, 1-41).

3. **Journey to and Sojourn in Haran.** Two reasons demanded that leaving Bersabee, the actual residence of his father, Jacob should start for Mesopotamia. He would thereby (1) secure himself against the wrath of Esau, who only waited for the decease of Isaac to recover the advantages of birthright by the death of Jacob (Gen. xxvii, 41-45); and (2) avoid all connection with the surrounding tribes by obtaining a wife from among the descendants of his forefathers (Gen. xxvii, 46; xxviii, 1-6). On his way northwards Jacob soon reached the spot "where Abraham had already erected an altar, and at which he may have determined to make a halt on that account" (RAWLINSON, Isaac and Jacob, p. 91). This was then, as it is now, a stony district; and at night, the fatigued traveller used for a pillow one of the many smooth stones scattered around him. Comforted by a

mysterious dream, wherein God renewed to him the glorious promises already made to Abraham and Isaac, Jacob dedicated this spot the next morning to God, and called it **Bethel** (that is, the House of God) and vowed exclusive worship to Jehovah should He accompany him during his wanderings and bring him back safely home. Then he went on his way, following probably the same road as Eliezer, and reached **Haran** after a journey of upwards of four hundred miles (Gen. xxviii, 10–22).

The relations of Jacob with Laban's household in Haran form an interesting episode, the details of which are perfectly true to Eastern life. "The well (by which Jacob met Rachel) is *in the field*, that is in the open pasture-land. Water being scarce, all the flocks, for miles round, meet at it to be watered. The heavy stone rolled over its mouth may be seen by any traveller in many parts of Palestine. The daughters of the flock-masters still go, in many places, to tend and water the flocks. . . . That Laban kissed Jacob effusively is only what one sees Orientals doing every day, on meeting a neighbor or a friend. The wily Syrian, in admitting that it is better to give Rachel to the son of Isaac than to another man, acted simply on the Bedouin law that a suitor has the exclusive right to the hand of his first cousin. . . . To give a female slave to a daughter as a part of her dowry is usual now, where means permit, so that **Zelpha's** being given to **Lia** at her marriage is another proof of the unchanging sameness of Eastern life in all ages. Excuses for sending home an elder daughter, instead of a younger, to the bridegroom, need still to be made in not a few cases, and are exactly the same as those with which Laban palliated the substitution of Lia for Rachel" (GEIKIE, The Holy Land and the Bible, chap. xx). Even the agreement of Jacob with Laban to serve long years to obtain Rachel in marriage is not without parallel in modern Eastern life (cfr. MILMAN, History of the Jews). He indeed succeeded in marrying **Rachel**, to whom Laban gave **Bala** as a part of her dowry, but this, instead of securing his domestic happiness, brought only in its train the many evils naturally entailed by the practice of polygamy, and to which allusion has already been made in connection with Abraham (Genesis xxix, 30–xxx, 26).

It was through Lia and her sister Rachel and their two handmaids that Jacob obtained a large family, all destined by God to share in the paternal inheritance, and to become in their turn the fathers of numerous descendants who later on developed into the twelve tribes of Israel.

Jacob's manner of life during his entire sojourn in Haran was that of an Eastern shepherd. Soon after his arrival in Mesopotamia, Laban had realized how valuable his services could prove in this line and entrusted to him the care of his flocks, and the book of Genesis tells us not only how these prospered under Jacob's skilful management, but also how Laban succeeded in keeping him twenty long years in his service. It is easy to picture to ourselves the mode of life followed by Jacob during this period, for the life of an Eastern shepherd has varied little from what it was in the patriarchal age; even in its minutest details, it is the same hard and responsible life. Now as then, the shepherd must defend his flock against robbers and wild beasts and "make good all the damage"; now as then, he has to suffer from the heat of the day and from the frost of the night, especially in those places where the flocks are kept out of the sheep-fold at night all the year round, and as of old, his share in the flock for the reward of his hard labors is but small, although years of persevering efforts may increase it so that finally he may possess a flock of his own (Gen. xxxi, 39, sq.); etc. (For a full description of this arduous life, see GEIKIE, The Holy Land and the Bible, chap. x; and VAN-LENNEP, Bible Lands, p. 182, sq.)

**4. Return from Haran and Subsequent Life.** It was for two principal reasons that after his long sojourn in Haran, Jacob started for his father's house. He justly feared the ill-will of Laban if he remained longer in Mesopotamia (Gen. xxxi, 1, 2) and Jehovah had bidden him return to the Promised Land (Gen. xxxi, 3). As he fled with all that he had (Gen. xxxi, 18), with wives and children, maid-servants and men-servants, flocks and herds, camels and asses (Gen. xxxii, 5, 15) his retinue formed a large Oriental caravan which moved but slowly in a south-western direction. The Euphrates once passed (Gen. xxxi, 21), he hastened with all speed to cross the mountainous region of Galaad, but was overtaken in its northern part by Laban, who bitterly accused him of a breach of courtesy and even of theft. Jacob vindicated himself with truly Eastern vehemence, but finally agreed to a covenant between him and his father-in-law. Neither party was to trespass the limits now agreed upon to injure the other, and by a common repast — as is customary down to the present day — the covenant of peace was solemnly ratified (Gen. xxxi, 22-55. See H. A. Harper, Bible and Modern Discoveries, fifth edition, p. 31).

Delivered from all anxiety on that side, Jacob continued his journey, deeply concerned as to the best means of appeasing his brother Esau whose rancor he still feared. Whilst in this painful frame of mind, he was favored with two visions calculated to encourage him greatly. The first occurred before he crossed the Jaboc river, at a place which he called **Mahanain**, the second after he had passed this river, at a place which he surnamed **Phanuel** and where his own name was changed into that of **Israel** (Gen. xxxii). It was also at Phanuel that the much dreaded meeting of Jacob and Esau took place. It was a friendly one, and Jacob could have continued his journey homewards, had he not preferred to interrupt it so as to give a much needed rest to his household; in consequence, he sojourned in a place East of the

Jordan which he called **Socoth** from the more permanent kind of dwellings (viz.: *booths* instead of *tents*) which he erected there (Gen. xxxiii, 1-17).

Leaving Socoth, Jacob crossed the Jordan, passed on in peace to **Sichem** and pitched his tents by the town. To be independent of the Chanaanite inhabitants, he bought from them a parcel of ground wherein he dug a well — which still bears his name — and erected an altar to Jehovah, the God of Israel, probably on the very spot where Abraham had set up his first altar to God in the land of Chanaan. Soon followed the sad story of Dina's outrage by Sichem and the perfidious and awful revenge of Jacob's children upon the Sichemites, after which the prudent patriarch withdrew from the neighborhood and according to Divine direction, repaired to **Bethel** where he probably fulfilled the vow which he had made when on his way to Haran. Resuming his journey southward, he halted first at **Ephrata** (the ancient name of Bethlehem) where Rachel died in giving birth to Benjamin, and next a little beyond the **Tower of Eder**, and finally reached **Mambre** beside **Hebron**, the actual residence of his father (Gen. xxxiii, sq.).

It was probably but a short time after the return of Jacob, that both he and his brother Esau joined in paying the last tribute of respect to the mortal remains of Isaac (Gen. xxxv, 29). After their father's burial, Esau withdrew to his possessions in Mount Seir and Jacob dwelt in Chanaan, leading probably the same manner of life as his father. Like him, he had near Hebron a permanent abode, and was considered by the neighboring Chanaanite tribes as a prosperous and powerful head of a pastoral family. Like him also, he evinced partiality towards one of his children, the young Joseph, and this gave rise to family dissensions which prepared the way for the most important changes in the history of the children of Israel. We shall soon see how Jacob was induced to repair to Egypt to rejoin the object of his special affection, and how he died there after a settlement of his descendants in the land of Gessen "which seemed to break forever the connection between the sons of Abraham and the Promised Land, but ended in establishing them as the sole possessors of the whole territory" (MILMAN, History of the Jews).

5. **Character of Jacob.** "Abraham was a hero, Jacob was a 'plain man dwelling in tents.' Abraham we feel to be above ourselves, Jacob to be like ourselves." Such is the contrast drawn between the two patriarchs by Cardinal Newman (Sermons, vol. v, p. 91) and amply justified by an examination of the main features of their character. In Abraham we easily notice a nobility of soul, a firmness of faith, a perfect devotion to God's service seldom met with in men's nature, and because of which he became "the Friend of God" and "the Father of the Faithful," but which we would look for in vain in the character of his grandson. Jacob is above all a shrewd man of the world, not indeed deprived of religion, yet relying much more on his exertions to attain the object of his ambition than on God's power and providence, and even at times using means whose lawfulness was at least questionable. Again, whilst Abraham was ever kind and considerate towards every member of his household, Jacob formed passionate attachments to some, like Rachel and Joseph, and was barely just to others, such as Lia and the majority of his sons (BLAIKIE, Manual of Bible History, p. 75).

Jacob's character appears also inferior in many respects to that of Isaac his father. Of course they were two very different men, each one having both strong and weak points of character. Jacob had more strength of will, and, all things considered, seemed better fitted to push his way through opposition and difficulty, and to govern a numerous household, but Isaac had more gentleness of disposition, greater submission to God's holy will, and in the end succeeded as well as Jacob in getting the better of those who thwarted him; and one instinctively feels that although Isaac's nature seems at times too passive and his life too retired, yet his character is on the whole much nobler and better than that of his son.

But it is beyond question that Jacob has the advantage in a comparison with his brother Esau. The latter is the very type of ardent and rough natures, frank but impulsive, regardless of lawful social customs, and animated by such low feelings as to make him sell his birthright for a passing pleasure and contemplate with satisfaction both the near death of his father and the possible murder of his brother. The former is a living model of self-command combined with shrewdness and perseverance, of faithful compliance with social duties, and especially of that frame of mind which whilst it pursues the increase of earthly possessions, never loses altogether sight of higher blessings promised to its untiring exertions. Esau is indeed "the likeness of the fickle, uncertain Edomite, now allied, now hostile to the seed of promise," whilst Jacob is no less truly the likeness of the crafty persecuted Jew, with "his unbroken endurance and undying resolution which keep the nation alive in its present outcast condition, and which, in its brighter days, were the basis of the heroic zeal, long-suffering and hope of Moses, of David, of Jeremias and of the Maccabees" (STANLEY, Lectures on the History of the Jewish Church, vol. i, p. 61).

# SYNOPSIS OF CHAPTER IV.

## JOSEPH.

HISTORY OF JOSEPH.

- A. *In Chanaan:* (Gen. xxxvii).
  1. Hated of his brothers.
  2. Sold by them.
  3. Abiding grief of Jacob.

  Illustrations from Eastern and Egyptian manners.

- B. *In Egypt:*
  1. Joseph in the House of Putiphar ((Gen. xxxix, 1–19).
  2. Joseph in Prison (Gen, xxxix, 20–xli, 37):
     - The prison described.
     - The dreams of the two co-prisoners.
     - The dreams of Pharao.
  3. Joseph in the House of Pharao (Gen. xli, 38–xlv, 28):
     - Power and Marriage.
     - Treatment of his brothers.
     - Sending for his father.

*Character of Joseph:* A Type of our Lord.

## CHAPTER IV.

### JOSEPH.

### § *1. History of Joseph in Chanaan.*

**1. Joseph Hated by his Brethren.** The sacred narrative points out the reasons for which Joseph gradually became an object of hatred to his brothers. First of all, he had witnessed some very wicked deed of several among them, and they knew that he had revealed it to his father. Their next grievance consisted in the manifest partiality of Jacob for this elder son of Rachel born to him in his old age. They contemplated with a jealousy which soon grew into intense hatred, the fine garment which the patriarch had given to his beloved child. Whilst they had to be satisfied with the shepherd's sleeveless tunic reaching only to the knees, Joseph wore an ample garment covering nearly the whole frame, and probably made of fine linen, in stripes of many colors, such as it is usual still in the East to give to favorite children. Finally, with the imprudence of youth, Joseph narrated to them dreams which clearly portended his future elevation above them all, but which, for the present, simply caused them to envy and hate him all the more (Gen. xxxvii, 1-11. See VIGOUROUX, Bible et Découvertes Modernes, vol. ii, p. 7).

**2. Joseph Sold by his Brethren.** The cruel revenge soon taken upon Joseph by his brothers as related in the book of Genesis (xxxvii, 12-28) is perfectly true both to Biblical topography and to Oriental customs. The wide expanse of the valley of Sichem where Jacob's children had fed their flocks for some time and to which Joseph was sent by his father, contrasts indeed favorably with the barren hills of the country farther south, but it cannot compare with the pasture-ground of Dothain, and this is why the children of Jacob, who had first moved from Hebron to Sichem, had left it for Dothain, now identified with a spot bearing this ancient name and about 20 miles north of Sichem. In repairing to Dothain to find out his brothers, Joseph, after climbing the high hill north of Samaria, had to descend the steep northern slope of the ridge, and at Dothain in the plain below, he would easily be seen "afar off" and even recognized by his brothers "sharp-sighted, as all Arab shepherds are to-day." (HARPER, p. 41). At first they intended to put him to death, but they next agreed to cast him into one of the many dry pits or underground cisterns still visible in the district. Finally, they acceded to Juda's proposal to sell their brother to Ismaelite merchants whom they noticed coming by the great caravan road from Galaad to Egypt which still passes by Dothain. "The brown-skinned children of Ismael, who brought camels richly laden from the East to the Nile, are drawn to the life on the Egyptian monuments"[1]; and of the three kinds of spices they were carrying into Egypt — and are even now the principal articles of commerce of their descendants between the East and that country — two are named in recently discovered papyri, whilst the odor of the third may still be detected among those of other materials used in the embalming of mummies. That they should willingly purchase Joseph on their way down to Egypt is all the more natural because Syrian slaves had a special value on Egyptian markets, and it seems beyond doubt that "their descendants would not now hesitate to make such a purchase, and actually do so in certain parts of the country" (THOMPSON, quoted by RAWLINSON, Isaac and Jacob, p. 142).

[1] Ebers, Ægypten und die Bücher Moses, quoted in Vigouroux, vol. ii, p. 12, and in Geikie, vol. i, p. 422, footnote 6.

3. **Abiding Grief of Jacob.** Before casting Joseph into the pit, his brothers had stripped him of his fine garment, and it is this garment which, dipped in the blood of a kid, they sent to their father to make him believe that a wild beast had devoured his beloved son. They succeeded but too well in deceiving Jacob, who gave at once all the customary signs of intense grief, "tearing his garments and putting on sackcloth, and mourning for his son a long time." In vain did his children gather around him to comfort him, he refused every proffered consolation, saying "I will go down to my son into the grave, mourning" (Gen. xxxvii, 31-35). For long years afterwards, Jacob centred indeed his affection in Benjamin, the younger son of Rachel, yet all the while, even this other child of his most tenderly loved wife filled but partly the vacant place in the patriarch's heart (cfr. Gen. xlii, 4, 36-38; xlv, 26-28).

### § 2. *History of Joseph in Egypt.*

1. **Joseph in the House of Putiphar** (Gen. xxxix, 1-19). Whilst thus bewailed by his father, Joseph was carried to Egypt and sold to **Putiphar** (a word which signifies dedicated to *Ra* or the Sun," the chief divinity of On, or Heliopolis), an officer of Pharao and apparently a captain of the State police in charge "of prisoners and prisons, of bodily punishments and executions" (GEIKIE, Hours with the Bible, vol. i, p. 425). Egyptian monuments make us acquainted with the various duties of the position of "overseer" soon held by Joseph in his master's house. He is a slave placed over all the rest, "now directing the laborers in the field, now taking account of the crops, writing down on tablets the goodly store of goods; introducing what strangers might come to the master, or meting out punishment to offenders" (HARPER, p. 43); he has the special title of "governor of the house," as we read of Joseph in Genesis xxxix, 4,

and to him is entrusted the care of all things "both at home and in the fields."

Whilst Joseph was discharging with perfect success his manifold duties in his master's house, he was often brought in contact with the wife of Putiphar, for at that time, as implied in the Bible and clearly shown on Egyptian monuments, there was as much free intercourse between men and women in Egypt, as among us in the present day. Oftentimes she noticed the youthful and handsome Hebrew overseer, and with a passion too much in harmony with the profligacy for which Egyptian women have ever been notorious, she repeatedly tempted him to commit adultery with her, till at length, resenting his virtuous conduct, she charged him to her husband with the very criminal solicitations wherewith she had herself pursued him. The credulous Putiphar believed the report of his wife, and in consequence "cast Joseph into the prison where the King's prisoners were kept." Several details of the Biblical narrative of Joseph's temptation are strikingly similar to those found on a papyrus which goes back to the time before the Exodus, and is known as the "Tale of the Two Brothers." In it, the younger was tempted to adultery by the wife of his elder brother, and as he refused she "made herself like one who had suffered violence," falsely accused the younger brother, and her husband in a rage threatened his life, which was saved by the protection of the *Sun-God* (cfr. BUDGE, the Dwellers on the Nile, p. 115 sq.; VIGOUROUX, tome ii, chap. iii).

2. **Joseph in Prison.** (Gen. xxxix, 20-xli, 37). The fact that Putiphar in his anger did not at once put Joseph to death is in harmony with the old Egyptian law which denied to the master power over the life of his slave. The prison to which Joseph was now confined was not a single building, but something like a walled fortress including the barracks of the garrison, some temples and the prisons, a special part

of which was reserved for prisoners of state, and where later on two great officers of Pharao (the chief butler and the chief baker) rejoined Joseph because, for some reason unknown to us, they had displeased the Egyptian monarch.

After a little while, Joseph's co-prisoners had each a dream which caused them all the more sadness because in their prison, they had no access to professional interpreters of dreams. Their dreams were naturally in harmony with each one's occupation, and the details with which they are described in the Bible correspond most exactly to what Egyptian pictures represent were the occupations of bakers and butlers in that period, wine being freely served at Egyptian banquets, and bread and other articles of food, when carried by men, being carried in baskets on their *heads*, not on their *shoulders* as was wont for women. Joseph's interpretation of each dream came indeed to pass, but, despite the promise of the chief butler to remember him when restored to his office, he had to remain in prison, till his interpretation of two dreams of Pharao secured to him the royal favor.

It would indeed be difficult to imagine something more in harmony with the Egyptian country and civilization than the details connected with Pharao's dreams, such as the cows feeding on the reeds and sedge of the marshy banks of the Nile, the ears of corn for which Egypt was ever so famous and in which at times, however, it was completely wanting, the number *seven* common to both dreams and so sacred to Egyptian minds, etc. So is it likewise with the recourse which Pharao had at once to interpreters of dreams, for whilst dreams were in Egypt the object of superstitious fear, several kinds of interpreters — two of which are mentioned with their official *Egyptian* title in the Hebrew Text — were ever in attendance at Court. Finally, in the care with which Joseph, when taken out of prison, must be shaved and change his garments, it is easy to discover an allusion to that perfect ceremonial cleanness required before any one could be brought in to Pharao (see GEIKIE, vol. i, p. 432 sq.; VIG-OUROUX, vol. ii, chap. iv).

3. **Joseph in the House of Pharao** (Gen. xli, 38–xlv, 25). The clear and plausible interpretation of Pharao's dreams by Joseph struck the King with such admiration that, in virtue of his supreme will, he raised him at once from the lowest to the highest rank in the State. The raising of Joseph to a dignity inferior to none but that of Pharao consisted in three distinct things. (1) He received the insignia of his office — the signet-ring to seal, in the royal name, all public documents; robes of the finest linen, as befitting Pharao's prime minister; and the golden neck chain, the official badge of his authority. (2) He was carried through the streets of the capital on the second royal chariot, that all might do homage to him as the second ruler over Egypt. (3) He assumed an Egyptian name, and became a member of the highest class of Egypt through marriage with the daughter of a priest of Heliopolis, named **Putiphare.**

Soon the seven years of plenty predicted by Joseph set in, during which he stored up corn in each of the cities from the lands of which it was gathered. They were followed by seven years of dearth, during which by his skilful management he saved Egypt from the worst features of want and hunger,[1] and not only Egypt, but also the various countries around, which had to suffer from the same protracted famine. At an early period during the seven years of famine Jacob sent his sons to Egypt to buy corn, keeping back, however, Benjamin "lest perhaps he take any harm in the journey." What occurred on the occasion of this their first journey, as well as in connection with a second one they were compelled to make a little later — this second time in company with Benjamin — is too well known to require a detailed description here. The narrative of the manner in which Joseph

---

[1] For illustration of these facts, see HARPER, p. 49.

discovered himself finally to them is peculiarly beautiful and touching, and shows how little in all his dealings with them, he intended to take revenge on them for their past unworthy conduct. He even went so far as to excuse in some manner, their greatest crime "Let it not seem to you a hard case that you sold me into these countries. . . . Not by your counsel was I sent hither, but by the will of God" (Gen. xlv, 5, 8).

The rumor of the arrival of the brothers of Joseph soon spread and reached the ears of Pharao, who gladly entered into the designs of his prime minister that he should send for his aged father, and cause him to settle with all his family in the land of Egypt. Accordingly, the sons of Jacob, supplied with Egyptian chariots, large provisions for the journey and magnificent gifts in money and raiment for their father, went out of Egypt, and brought to the old Jacob the almost incredible, and yet the most certain as well as most welcome news that Joseph "was living, and was ruler in all the land of Egypt." Convinced at length that this wonderful news was but the expression of a glorious reality, Jacob revived and said, "It is enough for me, if Joseph my son be yet living, I will go and see him before I die."

**4. Character of Joseph.** Old Testament history presents few, if any characters more beautiful than that of Joseph. As a boy he has the most vivid horror for the evil done by his brothers, and as a youth he resists with heroic constancy the repeated and pressing solicitations of his master's wife. Cast into prison, he exhibits great power of endurance, and when raised to the highest rank in the State, he shows himself worthy of that exalted dignity by his modesty no less than by his energetic efforts to promote in the most effective manner the welfare of his adoptive countrymen. His wonderful flexibility enables him to adapt himself to each new position in life and his great amiability endears him to almost all who come in contact with him. His tenderness of heart is revealed in a variety of ways, such as the tears he sheds at the first visit of his brothers after they had sold him, his loving feelings towards Benjamin, his filial respect and devotion for his aged father after years of separation and in the midst of the greatest honors of Pharao's court.

It would indeed be difficult to point out a character more worthy than that of Joseph to be one of the types of our Lord. In point of fact, there is a manifold resemblance between Jacob's beloved son and the dearly beloved Son of God. Like Jesus, Joseph was hated and cast out by his brethren, and yet wrought out their salvation through the sufferings they had brought upon him; like Jesus, Joseph obtained his exaltation only after passing through the deepest humiliations, and in the kingdom over which he ruled, he invited his brethren to join those whom heretofore they had looked upon as strangers, in order that they also might enjoy the blessings he had stored up for them; like the Saviour of the world, Joseph had but words of forgiveness and blessing for all who, recognizing their misery, had recourse to his supreme power; finally, it was to Joseph of old, as to Jesus, that all had to appeal for relief, offer homages of the deepest respect and yield ready obedience in all things.

# SYNOPSIS OF CHAPTER V.

## The Israelites in Egypt.

**I. The Land of Egypt:**
- 1. *Physical Description:* Situation; two great divisions; the Nile.
- 2. *History:*
  - Little known up to a very recent period.
  - Now opened by study of hieroglyphic inscriptions.
  - Principal dynasties before the Israelites went down into Egypt.
- 3. *Civilisation:*
  - Social Organization.
  - Domestic Life and Manners.
  - Religion (Esoteric and Exoteric Aspects).

**II. Sojourn of the Israelites in Egypt.**

- A. *The last years of Jacob and Joseph:*
  - 1. Entrance into Egypt.
    - In what manner effected?
    - Under what dynasty?
  - 2. The Land of Gessen: Situation and description.
  - 3. Death and Funeral honors of Jacob and Joseph.
- B. *After the Death of Joseph:*
  - 1. Period of Prosperity:
    - From a Nomad Tribe, Israel becomes a settled people.
    - Families remain distinct; no common head.
  - 2. Period of Oppression:
    - At what time began the oppression?
    - How exercised?
    - How illustrated
      - A. by Egyptian monuments?
      - B. in modern Fellahin?

[46]

## CHAPTER V.

#### THE ISRAELITES IN EGYPT.

§ *1. The Land of Egypt.*

1. **Physical Description.** Egypt, the country in which the descendants of Jacob dwelt for several centuries, occupies the north-east angle of Africa. It lies on both sides of the Nile and is bounded on the north by the Mediterranean Sea, on the east by Arabia and the Red Sea, on the south by Nubia (which country the Nile traverses before it enters Egypt at the first cataract), and on the west by Lybia. In ancient times, however, the territory of Egypt was much less extensive, because its width included then little more than the fertile strip of land on both sides of the Nile, the deserts beyond on either side being considered as parts of Arabia and Lybia respectively.

Ancient Egypt had two great natural divisions, (1) the **Delta**, so called from its resemblance with the Greek letter $\Delta$; (2) the **Valley of the Nile.** The Delta is a vast triangular plain watered by the branches of the Nile and extending along the Mediterranean coast for about 200 miles, and up the Nile for 100 miles. The Valley of the Nile extends from this point — about the site of the present city of Cairo — to the First Cataract, a distance of about 500 miles, and its width varies from 10 to 30 miles. The Delta and the Valley of the Nile have together an area of about 9,600 square miles, or about equal to the two States of Massachusetts and Rhode Island together.

Nothing is more exact than the saying of the old Greek

historian Herodotus (fifth century B. C.), who affirms that Egypt "is the gift of the Nile" (History, Book ii, chap. v), for owing to the periodical rainy season which inundates Upper Abyssinia, where the Nile takes its rise, this river is periodically swollen and by its overflow secures to the country of Egypt its wonderful fertility. The rising of the Nile usually begins towards the end of June, and as the waters rise they turn from greenish to dark red, which latter color does not interfere in the least with their wholesome and palatable properties. During the following months, the lowlands of Egypt are inundated and thereby supplied with the moisture and alluvial deposit required for farming purposes. If the annual inundation reaches a sufficient height — in ancient times, the most favorable height was 16 cubits or about 28 feet — all is well with Egypt and its inhabitants, but if the reverse occurs — if it is only 12 cubits, for instance — a famine is the result. As the fertility of Egypt has ever depended on the water of the Nile, canals were dug from a remote antiquity, to distribute it in various directions.

2. History. Up to a very recent period, little could be known with certainty about the history of ancient Egypt, for every writer on Egypt depended almost entirely on Greek historians whose statements were too often at variance, and whose comparative authority could not be defined. Moreover as these historians were unacquainted with the Egyptian language, they did not utilize the original documents of the banks of the Nile, but simply recorded obsolete traditions with which they mingled their own views, and as a necessary consequence, the history of ancient Egypt was for centuries little more than a collection of groundless statements.

A more accurate and certain knowledge of Egyptian history began only with the deciphering of the Egyptian **hieroglyphics** by François Champollion in the first quarter of the present century. By years of hard and persevering efforts he succeeded not only in making out the value of a large number of Egyptian characters, but also in understanding the meaning of the words through his acquaintance with the Coptic language, a legitimate descendant from the old Egyptian and bearing with it a very close resemblance. Since that time, pyramid and obelisk, sarcophagus and coffin, stele and papyrus have spoken and their inscriptions, ranging from 4000 B. C. to the time of our Lord, have yielded an outline of Egypt's dynasties and political vicissitudes, and better still a vivid picture of its beliefs, manners and customs (cfr. BUDGE, Dwellers on the Nile, chaps. i, ii).

Despite all these discoveries, the earliest history of Egypt is still very obscure; it cannot be doubted, however, that about 4000 B. C., Egypt was already a well-organized State. Its first dynasty is supposed to have had for its founder **Mena** or **Menes**, about whose laws and institutions little is known for certain. Of the following dynasties, twelve ruled in succession before the children of Jacob went down into Egypt; and the principal of these were two: (1) The **Fourth**, to whose kings Egypt is indebted for much of its ancient glory, and in particular for its greatest *pyramids* or royal tombs, viz.: those of Cheops, Chephren and Mycerinus at Gizeh, on the western bank of the Nile, near Cairo; (2) the **Twelfth**, famous for its warlike undertakings, and also for the formation of the enormous lake Moeris and the building of the wonderful palace of the Labyrinth. From the twelfth to the eighteenth dynasty, there is a gap of about 500 years during which both the rule of the Hyksos or "Shepherd Kings" and the settlement of the Israelites in Egypt are to be placed.

3. **Civilization.** Egypt is one of the most ancient civilized nations of the world, and in the present day we are allowed a clear insight into the manifold features of its antique civilization through the numberless paintings, sculptures, in-

scriptions, etc., brought to light by recent explorations. Among these features we may notice first of all, the political and social organization of the ancient Egyptians, at the basis of which lay their division into classes. Two of these classes, those of the *priests* and of the *warriors*, were deemed most honorable, and together with the King, owned the soil of Egypt. The priests constituted the learned class; they were exempt from taxation, received daily rations of the sacred food together with contributions of oxen, sheep and wine, were allowed to have only one wife, and were submitted to minute ritual observances, such as frequent ablutions, the exclusive use of linen robes, etc. Next to the priests in honor, came the soldiers, whose profession, like that of the priests, was hereditary. They possessed nearly a third of the soil and were exempt from all taxes, and of course, when on duty in the field or about the King's person, they were given special pay and rations. The rest of the free population of Egypt formed a sort of third order subdivided into the classes of *shepherds, husbandmen* and *artisans*, whose various occupations are represented with the minutest detail and accuracy in the pictures in the tombs and on the monuments of the ancient Egyptians.

At the head of the State, was the King, bearing the title of **Pharao**, at once priest and warrior, and the actual god of all his subjects both during his lifetime and after his death. For him the Egyptians were trembling slaves, compelled even from religious motives to carry out his orders blindly, and to set at the same time the highest value on his most trifling favors. "The first object of the King was supposed to be the welfare of his people both temporal and spiritual. Minor matters of administration would be disposed of by his subordinates, but things of importance would come before him and be discussed with his leading advisers and councillors" (BUDGE, Dwellers on the Nile, page 183).

The domestic life of the ancient Egyptians is perhaps better known than their social organization, for their paintings and inscriptions make us acquainted with the minute details of their daily life. Their houses were generally only two stories high, had small windows, lofty ceilings and terraced roofs surrounded by a balustrade or battlement. The houses of the wealthy often covered a very large extent of ground, had an inner court planted with trees, and their walls were beautifully sculptured and decorated, whilst the rooms were supplied with the most elegant furniture. At an entertainment, the dinner was served up at noon, men and women sat side by side at tables covered with numerous dishes and supplied with wine of various sorts, each guest being placed according to his rank. "After dinner, games, music, dancing and other amusements were provided for the guests" (BLAIKIE, Manual of Bible History, p. 98).

Polygamy was certainly practised by some of the nobles and Kings of Egypt, but even where several wives were taken one of them enjoyed a real superiority over all the others. Children were educated according to their future position in life, those of the priests being carefully taught the various kinds of Egyptian writing together with astronomy, mathematics, etc., in a word, "all the wisdom of the Egyptians." (For fuller information see WILKINSON, The Ancient Egyptians, vol. ii.)

The religion of Egypt deserves also a special notice here. It presented, as in all pagan countries, a twofold aspect, the one *esoteric*, exhibiting whatever was most elevated, most philosophical, but kept hidden in the sanctuary for the honor and profit of the priests and of a small number of initiated, — the other *exoteric*, the sole known to the people at large, consisting only of the outer form of the esoteric doctrine and made up of the grossest superstitions.

The esoteric doctrine of the Egyptian priests had for its basis the great idea of the unity of a God who is described in the sacred texts of Ancient Egypt as eternal, infinite, loving and just (cfr. extract from an Egyptian hymn in BUDGE, p. 130 sq.); that the primitive Egyptian worship was thus monotheistic is rendered the more probable from the fact that religious edifices of the primitive ages were without sculptured images and without idols. Unfortunately, this sublime idea was very early obscured and disfigured by the conceptions of the priests, as well as by the ignorance of the multitude. The attributes and qualities of the one sole, absolute and eternal God were by degrees invested with a concrete and personal existence, and transformed in the eyes of the people into absolutely distinct gods. For the purposes of external and public worship these almost countless gods were grouped into triads — after the image of a human family having a father, mother and son — and each triad was worshipped in the sanctuary of one of the capitals of the Egyptian districts or *nomes*. Again, through a further abuse of symbolic representations so entirely in harmony with Egypt's genius, the attributes, qualities and nature of the various gods were symbolized by means of animals, each god being represented under the figure of a particular animal, or as was more usually the case, by the conjunction of the head of that animal with a human body, and this finally led the Egyptian multitudes to the worship of the animals themselves, not simply as representations but as incarnations of the deity (see FRANÇOIS LENORMANT, Manual of the Ancient History of the East, vol. i, p. 317-327).

One of the principal religious beliefs common to both people and priests was the doctrine of a future life with its eternal rewards for the just, and its punishments for the wicked.

§ 2. *Sojourn of the Israelites in Egypt.*

1. **The Last Years of Jacob and Joseph** (Gen. xlvi-l). The first impulse of Jacob on learning of Joseph's

preservation and exalted dignity in Egypt was to go down to that country and spend his last years with his beloved son. He soon, however, hesitated in carrying out a plan which seemed to run counter to God's designs by settling down far from the Promised Land, but a vision from Jehovah near Bersabee, put an end to every hesitation on his part, and he started without delay with all his family and possessions, sending Juda ahead to apprise Joseph of his coming. The meeting of the patriarch with his beloved son was most affectionate, and was soon followed by the presentation, first of five brothers of Joseph, and next of the old man himself to the Egyptian monarch. The Pharao of the time belonged most likely to a dynasty established by nomad hordes of Arabia, Chanaan and Syria after their conquest of Northern Egypt, and known under the name of the Hyksos or " Shepherd Kings." Once settled in Egypt, the Hyksos soon adopted Egyptian manners and customs, and their court resembled in every respect that of the ancient Pharaòs, and yet all the time they had to fight against the native Kings who maintained themselves in Southern Egypt, and who ultimately succeeded in expelling those whom the Egyptian population ever regarded as intruders. These historical data concerning the Hyksos agree perfectly with the Biblical statements regarding the dynasty which ruled in Egypt at the time when the Israelites entered that country. On the one hand, although this dynasty had a foreign origin, it had already adopted the customs of Egypt, and in consequence it is justly described in the Bible as holding a thoroughly Egyptian court; and on the other hand, because of its foreign origin and also because of the hatred wherewith it was pursued by the native princes and population, it would not only welcome, but even readily grant a portion of territory to a pastoral tribe coming also from Asia and in which they hoped to secure allies, when necessary, against the conquered Egyptians.

The portion of Egyptian territory ascribed to Jacob and

his family as their residence was the "Land of Gessen" whose boundaries gradually "extended with the increase of the people over the territory they inhabited" (NAVILLE, quoted by HARPER, Bible and Modern Discoveries, p. 55). In the time of Joseph it probably comprised little more than the present **Wady Et Tumilat,** a district east of the Delta and not far from Tanis or Zoan, the actual capital of the Hyksos. The land of Gessen counted but few Egyptian inhabitants, because its former settlers had fled before the invading Asiatic hordes, and although it was capable of yielding excellent crops, it was yet — as we learn from a recently discovered Egyptian document — "not cultivated, but left as a pasture for cattle." All this enables us to understand why Joseph was desirous that this region should be assigned to his brothers who had come with flocks and herds, were "shepherds from their infancy," and as such would be an object of hatred for the native population "because the Egyptians had all shepherds in abomination."

After his migration into Egypt, Jacob lived seventeen years, towards the end of which he requested that his mortal remains should be transported into the land of Chanaan and deposited in "the burying-place of his ancestors." In his last sickness, the dying patriarch blessed all his children, uttering at the same time prophetic words concerning the future of their respective descendants. His blessing of Juda is particularly remarkable not only because it promised the temporal supremacy to the tribe of Juda, but also because it distinctly foretold that from Juda's posterity should arise "He to whom nations shall yield obedience," that is, the Messias in whom "shall all the nations of the earth be blessed" (Gen. xii, 3; xxvi, 4. For a careful study of Jacob's blessing of Juda, see VIGOUROUX, Manuel Biblique; CORLUY, Spicilegium Dogmatico-biblicum, vol. i; PELT, Histoire de l'Ancien Testament, vol. i, chap. xv).

Joseph honored his father (1) by a costly embalming, of

which the Bible speaks in a manner which agrees perfectly with the process as depicted on Egyptian monuments, (2) by a long time of mourning in the Land of Egypt, (3) by a large and distinguished funeral cortege which accompanied the embalmed body to the Promised Land, finally (4) by "full seven days of great and vehement lamentation" when arrived at Machpelah, where Jacob's remains were laid by the side of his great ancestors (cfr. GEIKIE, vol. i, p. 471).

Very little is told us about Joseph in the Biblical narrative after the burial of his father. We read simply that he ever bore himself kindly to his brothers, saw the grandchildren of his sons Ephraim and Manasses, and required from his brothers a solemn oath that they should carry his remains out of Egypt, when God would bring them back to Chanaan. His body was carefully embalmed and "laid in a coffin in Egypt."

2. **After the Death of Joseph.** The prosperity which the Israelites enjoyed in Egypt during the lifetime of Joseph long continued after his death. During this period of peace and plenty, which the opening chapter of the book of Exodus rather hints at than describes, they multiplied very rapidly and soon covered much more territory than the district originally ascribed to them. Many of the new districts presented much better opportunities for agricultural or industrial purposes than for pastoral pursuits, and in consequence many families gave up gradually their despised primitive shepherd life, and learned to till the fertile soil of northeastern Egypt, or became acquainted with the various arts of the Egyptians, such as weaving, dyeing, etc. Their social importance naturally grew apace with their wealth, and intermarriage gave them access to the highest circles in the State (cfr. i Paralip. iv, 18). Thus, from a nomad tribe, Israel was by degrees transformed into a numerous and powerful settled people conversant with the arts and civilization of Egypt, and also,

it must be added, deeply influenced by the splendor of its temples and worship. Finally, they were allowed a fair amount of political independence, for they governed themselves in pretty much the same manner as the nations kindred to them (the Edomites and the Ismaelites) having like them elders who presided over the interests of distinct districts, but no common head.

Had this wonderful prosperity of the Israelites lasted much longer, it seems not improbable that they would have gradually forgotten Chanaan, and even lost their faith in the God of their ancestors; but these two great evils were averted by a providential course of events, which brought about a long period of severe oppression followed by their departure from Egypt. The precise time at which this oppression began cannot be determined; but it is now universally granted that the "*new King who arose over Egypt and did not know Joseph*" (Exod. i, 8) belonged to the old native dynasty which had finally succeeded in expelling the Hyksos from the country. There is also little doubt that the particular King who persecuted so severely the Israelites was **Ramesses II**, whom Egyptian inscriptions concur with the Bible in representing as having had a very long reign, as a passionate builder, and as the founder of Ramesses and Phithom. His aim was so to weaken the Israelites as to render them of no account in case of a foreign invasion from the east, and for this purpose he had recourse to three devices: (1) he imposed upon them an excessive amount of work of the most exhausting kind; (2) he gave order to the Egyptian midwives to kill every Israelite man-child at its birth; (3) he charged all his people to cast into the Nile any male child who might have escaped (Exod. i, 9-22).

Egyptian monuments make us acquainted with brickmaking as it was then imposed upon the Israelites, when they represent to us some men digging clay, others mixing it, others laden with the prepared clay, others again carrying bricks or stacking them, whilst just by is the task master, his stick ever lifted up to enforce labor. By "all the other manners of service" exacted from the Israelites (Exod. i, 14, cfr. also verse 11) we are doubtless to understand the hewing out of enormous blocks of granite and limestone, and the drawing of them for the building of Ramesses's temples and cities, the digging of canals, etc. (Cfr. inscriptions of Ramesses in GEIKIE, Hours with the Bible, vol. ii, p. 98, sq.)

The frightful hardships and enormous expenditure of life naturally entailed by such work carried on with no machinery and with but little mechanical help, are most vividly illustrated in the Fellahin or Egyptian husbandmen who, during this very century, were taken by force from their villages and compelled to work for the Egyptian authorities. Thus, for instance, out of 250,000 fellahin torn away from their homes and employed at making the canal which connects Alexandria with the Nile, 30,000 actually died, falling worn out with the toil exacted from them by the blows of their pitiless taskmasters. Similar barbarities with similar results were also noticed in connection with the beginning of the Suez canal, and all travellers relate like tales of woe concerning the forced labor imposed upon the poor fellahin in the sugar factories of the late Khedive (that is, the viceroy of Egypt). (Cfr. HARPER, Bible and Modern Discoveries, p. 69; VIGOUROUX, vol. ii, p. 249, sq.)

# SYNOPSIS OF CHAPTER VI.

## The Deliverance from Egypt.

**I. Moses the Deliverer:**
- Birth and Education (Exodus ii, 1–10; Acts vii, 20–22).
- Flight and Sojourn in Madian (Exodus ii, 11–22; Acts, vii, 23–29).
- Return into Egypt (Exodus ii, 23–iv; Acts vii, 30–35).

**II. Departure of the Israelites:**

A. *Opposition to Departure:*
  1. Why and how raised by Pharao (Exodus v–vii, 9)?
  2. How met by Moses? (Exodus vii, 10–x).
     - The Nine First Plagues.
       - Analogy with natural scourges.
       - Miraculous character.
       - Opposition to Egyptian idolatry.

B. *The Departure:*
  1. Preparatory events.
     - The First Pasch.
     - The Tenth Plague (No Egyptian record).
  2. Execution.
     - The gathering and simultaneous departure of the Israelites.
     - Their number; the spoils of Egypt.

C. *The length of stay in Egypt* (Exodus xii, 40, 41; Galatians iii, 17).

**III. The Passage of the Red Sea.**
1. The road followed from Ramesses to the Red Sea.
2. *The passage of the Sea:*
   - A. Northern limit of the western arm of the Red Sea in the time of Moses.
   - B. The pursuit of the Israelites by Pharao.
   - C. The passage described: its miraculous character.
   - D. Egyptian account of this escape, and other traditions.
3. *The Canticle of Moses* (Exodus xv, 1–21).

# SECOND OR TRIBAL PERIOD.

## FROM MOSES TO THE INSTITUTION OF THE MONARCHY.

### CHAPTER VI.

#### THE DELIVERANCE FROM EGYPT.

§ *1. Moses the Deliverer.*

**1. Birth and Education** (Exod. ii, 1-10). Whilst the King of Egypt was bent on crushing Israel out of existence, a child was born of the tribe of Levi destined to free forever God's people from Egypt's bondage, and to introduce a new era into the history of the Jewish religion and nation. His parents Amram and Jochabed (Exod. vi, 20) who lived apparently near the habitual residence of Ramesses II, had had already two children, one daughter called Mary and a son named Aaron. Struck with the infantine beauty of her second son, Jochabed resolved to save him by concealing his birth from the Egyptians who, according to Pharao's recent order, cast into the Nile any newly-born Israelite male child they could lay their hands on. The story of the manner in which after three months of concealment the child was exposed on the waters of the Nile, and then rescued, adopted and trusted by the daughter of Pharao to the fostering care of Jochabed herself, is known to all, and needs no further mention here.

During his youth and early manhood, Moses — for thus was the child called henceforth because he had been "saved from the waters" of the Nile — underwent a twofold influence. On the one hand, as the son of Jochabed, he learned from his real mother who and what he was, and what great designs God ever had respecting His chosen people; on the other hand, as the adopted son of Pharao's daughter "he was instructed in all the wisdom of the Egyptians" (Acts vii, 22), that is, in all the learning, literary, scientific and religious, of the priests.

2. **Flight and Sojourn in Madian** (Exod. ii, 11-22). The deep influence of Jochabed on the mind of Moses is evidenced by the fact that though brought up in the midst of the refinement and luxury of Pharao's court, he did not hesitate, when the time came, to cast his lot with the oppressed children of Israel (cfr. Heb. xi, 24 sq.). One day, in his indignation against an Egyptian taskmaster whom he saw striking an Israelite, he slew him, buried him hastily in the sand and relied on the discretion of those whose defence he had thus boldly taken. Moses, however, was deceived in his expectation, his bold deed was soon known, and he took to flight from the vengeance of Pharao.

The place of his retreat was the "Land of Madian," a pastoral district beyond the Egyptian possessions in the peninsula of Sinai, and somewhat to the north and to the east of them. There he remained long years during which he led the humble shepherd life of the patriarchs of old, and became the son-in-law of Jethro the prince and priest of Madian.

3. **Return into Egypt** (Exod. ii, 23-iv). Meantime Ramesses II died, and was succeeded by Meneptah I, to whom the Israelites appealed in vain for relief. But Jehovah "heard their groaning" and took actual steps to rescue them from their misery. For this purpose He first appeared to

Moses in the vicinity of Mount Horeb, in the southern part of the peninsula of Sinai, revealed to him the name under which He was to be made known to the Israelites and directed him to return to Egypt. He also bade Moses gather together the ancients of Israel, announce to them the good news of Divine deliverance, and together with them deliver to Pharao God's message, that he should allow Israel to go a three days' journey to offer a sacrifice to Jehovah, their God. This mission appeared to Moses fraught with difficulties, but he finally accepted it because God supplied him with miraculous powers and promised that he would find in his brother Aaron a faithful and eloquent spokesman. With Jethro's consent, Moses left Madian and soon met Aaron, whom he made acquainted both with the mission and with the power of performing miracles Jehovah had entrusted to him.

Upon their arrival at the Israelite settlements, the two brothers gathered together the ancients of the people, and, agreeably to the Divine promise, Aaron proved a most successful spokesman near them; finally, Aaron's words backed up by miracles convinced the people at large that Jehovah had indeed "visited the children of Israel and that He had looked upon their affliction."

§ *2. Departure of the Israelites.*

1. **Opposition to Departure** (Exod. v–x). As might naturally be expected, Pharao was not to be so easily persuaded of the Divine mission of Moses as the children of Israel, and, in point of fact, when Moses and Aaron together with the ancients of the people requested him in the name of Jehovah, "the God of Israel," that he should let His people go and offer Him a sacrifice in the desert, the King of Egypt answered that Jehovah was a god unknown to him and that he would not let Israel go. What was asked of him was in

entire opposition with his twofold policy of using every available man for his public works and of preventing the increase of the Israelites by excessive labor, and in consequence, the very same day he gave to the Egyptian taskmasters orders of an almost incredible severity against the children of Israel. Henceforth these bondmen of Pharao must find for themselves the chopped straw they needed to make brick, and yet furnish each day exactly the same number of bricks as when straw was supplied to them. They indeed appealed to the King against such oppression, but Pharao maintained his orders that they must keep on supplying bricks, sun-baked, and made with whatever straw, or even sedges, rushes and water-plants, they could find, with such binding materials, in a word, as we know were employed in the construction of the brick walls of Phithom discovered by M. de Naville in 1884.

It is not, therefore, to be wondered at, that, groaning under their increased misery, the children of Israel complained against Moses and Aaron, who had brought it upon them, and positively refused to give credence to the message which a little later Moses delivered to them in the name of Jehovah.

At this juncture, God bade Moses and Aaron appear again before Pharao, requesting him that he should allow the departure of the Israelites, and instructed the two brothers to change into a serpent the rod Aaron was supplied with, as a sign of their Divine mission. This they did, to the amazement of Pharao, who, however, having called upon his wise men and magicians and having witnessed what seemed to be the performance of a prodigy similar to that of Moses and Aaron, refused to grant what was requested of him. After this refusal of Pharao, God inflicted on the country, by the ministry of Moses and Aaron, the various scourges so well known under the name of the **Plagues of Egypt.** The first of these plagues — the turning of the water of the Nile into blood — is clearly analogous with the annual phenomenon of the **Red** Nile, already referred to in the preceding chapter, and whereby this river appears in the eyes of all as a river of blood. The same close resemblance of the next eight plagues with corresponding natural scourges which occur from time to time in Egypt, is also borne witness to by very reliable recent travellers, and this has led many Rationalists to look upon the first nine plagues described in the Bible as mere natural phenomena. But if this analogy of the plagues with natural scourges is undoubted and in so far proves the historical character of the Biblical narrative, it is no less unquestionable that several things connected with the production of the plagues of Egypt prove their miraculous character. Take for instance the first of these plagues: the turning of the water of the Nile into blood cannot be identified absolutely with the annual and natural phenomenon of the Red Nile, since the ordinary redness at the time of the Nile's overflow does not render the water unfit for use or injurious to the fish in the river, whilst the reverse is positively affirmed by the Bible in connection with the first plague (Exod. vii, 20, 21). Again, it should be noticed that the effect of the stretching of Aaron's rod was immediate, that it had been predicted, that it extended at once to all the canals, trenches and pools connected with the Nile, and even to the water which had previously been taken from the river (Exod. vii, 19-21), which circumstances, of course, are not realized in connection with the annual phenomenon of the Red Nile. It is plain therefore that several features of the first plague clearly distinguish it from the natural phenomenon of the Red Nile and mark it as a miraculous event, and a similar conclusion is forced upon us about the eight following plagues when we compare them with the corresponding natural scourges which occur from time to time in the valley of the Nile. (For details respecting the plagues of Egypt, see VIGOUROUX, vol. ii; GEIKIE, vol. ii.)

These various miracles had not however for their sole object to wrest from Pharao his consent to the departure of the Israelites (Exod. vi, 1), they were also intended to teach the children of Israel the utter powerlessness of the Egyptian gods when confronted with Jehovah (Numb. xxxiii, 4; Exod. x, 2; Wisdom xii, 27). Thus the beneficent power of the Nile, worshipped as the representation of Osiris, felt the stroke of Jehovah's power in the first plague; in the second plague, that of the frogs, Heki, "the driver away of the frogs," proved powerless in behalf of his worshippers; in the third plague, the soil of Egypt, adored as "the father of the gods," under the name of Seb, was defiled, and its dust seemed turned into sciniphs to torment its worshippers; in the next plagues, the several animal-deities of the land were in like manner derided, whilst in the ninth, even the Sun, the supreme Egyptian god, had to veil its face before Jehovah.

2. **The Departure of the Israelites** (Exod. xi–xii, 36). It was to complete the Divine judgment upon the gods of Egypt (Exod. xiii, 12), and also finally to compel Pharao and his subjects to send away His chosen people, that Jehovah, setting aside the agency of the elements of nature He had heretofore used against the Egyptians, declared that He would Himself smite "every first-born in the land of Egypt, from the first-born of man to the first-born of beasts." The time fixed for this tenth and last plague was the hour of midnight on the fourteenth of the month which was already begun, and which was henceforth to be considered by the Israelites as the first month of their sacred year. Meantime, each Israelite household was (1) to select, on the tenth of the month, a lamb or kid, one year old and without blemish; (2) to slay it on the fourteenth, just before the evening twilight, and to sprinkle some of its blood upon the door-posts of each house, and (3) on the very same evening, before midnight, to eat it with unleavened bread and bitter herbs, and in haste, with their loins girded, their shoes on

their feet, and their staves in hand, like persons in a hurry to depart. All the Divine orders relating to this first Pasch, were, of course, carried out with the utmost exactitude by the children of Israel, and at midnight on the fourteenth of the month of Abib, Jehovah *passing over* the houses which He saw marked with blood, smote all the first-born in the land of Egypt.

Such was the tenth plague, a most unquestionable exercise of Divine power in behalf of Israel, and also of Divine judgment upon Pharao and his subjects. No wonder therefore, that whilst according to Jehovah's orders, the Israelites kept most gladly year by year the remembrance of it in the celebration of the Passover, the Egyptians, on the contrary, did not preserve any record of such an awful and humbling event. It must be said, however, that the inscription recently discovered on the gigantic statue of Meneptah I, which states that his eldest son had been associated with the empire and died before him, although it is not an explicit record of the death of the son of the Pharao spoken of in Exodus, seems singularly illustrative of the Biblical statement, that Jehovah "smote the *first-born* of Pharao, who *sat on his throne*."

Struck with terror by the awful blow which the God of Israel had dealt to every Egyptian family, Pharao and his subjects pressed the Israelites to depart at once. As has been well said by Rawlinson, "Moses had no need to give any signal, or to send his orders by messengers, that all the Israelites should set out at early dawn on the fifteenth of the month. For by fixing the Passover feast for a definite day, and requiring that after eating it none should go forth "until the morning" (Exod. xii, 22), he had made all acquainted with the day and hour of departure; he had also caused all to be prepared for setting forth; and, if any had been inclined to linger, the Egyptians themselves would not have allowed it (Exod. xii, 33). So that an almost simultaneous departure was actually secured" (Moses, p. 118).

The sacred text informs us that when they left Egypt, the Israelites were "about 600,000 men besides children," which makes it probable that they formed a body of emigrants which exceeded two millions of souls. This great number renders it indeed difficult for us to imagine how the whole Hebrew nation could depart under the circumstances narrated; yet this actual migration of an entire people is not without parallel in profane history, for we read in the history of Russia that, in the last century, 400,000 Tartars, under the cover of a single night, departed from Russia and made their way over several thousand miles of steppes to the frontiers of China.

Together with their national freedom, the Israelites obtained most valuable gifts from the panic-stricken Egyptians. They had been instructed by Moses that on the night of the exodus, they should ask jewels of silver and gold, and raiment from their oppressors, and under the excitement which the tenth plague caused in each Egyptian household, they obtained at once whatever they asked for. These were, of course, very valuable things, but however precious, they were but a feeble compensation secured by Jehovah to His chosen people for their long years of unpaid labor.

Thus ended the sojourn of the Israelites in the land of Egypt. The length of their stay is variously given in the Hebrew text and in the Septuagint or oldest Greek translation of the Old Testament. According to the former it extended to 430 years, according to the latter (cfr. also Galat. iii, 17) it was much shorter, about 125 years; the longer duration is more probable (cfr. CRELIER, Exode, p. 103).

3. **The Passage of the Red Sea** (Exod. xii, 37-xv, 21). Of the road which the Israelites followed from Ramesses to the Red Sea, nothing is known except its general

direction. As the goal of their journey was the Land of Chanaan, they naturally made for the Arabian desert, and having reached its borders, they turned south toward the Red Sea, in order to avoid the armed opposition they would have met with from the Philistines had they continued their journey to the northeast. It is true that besides this general direction, the sacred narrative mentions the encampments of the children of Israel at Soccoth, Etham and Phihahiroth; but these stages of their road are now little more than names of places which cannot be identified, because of the scantiness of biblical and archæological data concerning them.

Great uncertainty prevails also among scholars as to the exact place where the Hebrews crossed the western arm of the Red Sea, for it is still a debated question whether the northern limit of this western arm is now practically the same as in the time of Moses. Various writers maintain that at the time of the exodus, this arm — now called the Gulf of Suez, from the town built near its northern extremity — extended some thirty or forty miles farther north, and they admit for the actual place of crossing some point of this former extension of the Red Sea. Others, on the contrary, and apparently with greater probability, think that in the time of Moses the northern limit of the Gulf of Suez did not vary much, if at all, from what it is in the present day, and they maintain that the crossing took place at some point of the present head of the Gulf, either a little above or a little below the town of Suez. (For an able discussion of this question, see BARTLETT, From Egypt to Palestine, chap. vii; VIGOUROUX, vol. ii.)

Whilst the Israelites moved slowly towards the nearest desert, and next towards the Red Sea, Pharao and his subjects recovering from their first terror, regretted that these numerous slaves should have been allowed to depart, and with a view to compel them to return, started hurriedly after them. Great indeed was the distress of the Hebrews when they noticed the Egyptian hosts approaching, and in point of fact the position of the chosen people was extremely perilous; eastward was the sea, and whilst the mountains barred their escape to the south and west, the well-trained and numerous army of Pharao approached Israel from the north. Thus hemmed in on all sides, the Israelites naturally expected their prompt and utter destruction; but it was not so with their leader, who, trustful in God's protection, foretold both the timely help of Jehovah and the complete overthrow of the Egyptians.

The sacred narrative makes known to us how perfectly this prediction of Moses was fulfilled. It tells us how, on the one hand, about nightfall and at the stretching forth of Moses' hand over the sea, there arose a violent wind which, by dividing the waters, secured a safe passage to the children of Israel and how, on the other hand, at break of day and at the same stretching of Moses' hand after the Hebrews had passed over, the waters returned to their former place and drowned the Egyptian army.

This wonderfu. passage of the Red Sea by the Hebrews was ever considered by them not only as a great event in their national history, but also as one of the most stupendous miracles wrought by the Almighty in behalf of His chosen people In point of fact, no unprejudiced reader of the book of the Exodus can help noticing that whilst the inspired writer clearly admits the actual play of natural forces — such as that of a violent northeastern wind — in the production of this event, he speaks of several particulars which point no less clearly to his conviction that the safe passage of Israel was no mere result of these natural forces, but was brought about by a timely intervention of Jehovah, who superadded to their energy all the power necessary to secure the deliverance He had so distinctively foretold by the mouth of Moses. (See VIGOUROUX, vol. ii, livre iv, chap. viii.)

But whilst the Jewish writers refer repeatedly to this miraculous deliverance of their ancestors (Ps. lxxvi, 17-21; cxiii; Wisdom x, 18, 19; etc.), the Egyptian monuments, as might naturally be expected, keep the strictest silence about the ignominious overthrow of Pharao's army on this occasion. It must be said, however, that Josephus, in his "Treatise against Apion," has quoted the accounts of this event as recorded by the three Egyptian writers, Manetho, Chæremon and Lysimachus, but as these accounts present numerous contradictions, they deserve but little credence. Perhaps more value is to be set upon the local traditions which have retained the remembrance of this great catastrophe. The Arabs of the Sinaitic peninsula still call fountains or wells by the names of Moses and Pharao, and look upon the whole coast with a superstitious awe. Nor should we reject at once these traditions of the modern Arabs, for Diodorus Siculus states that even in his time these tribes ascribed them to their very remote ancestors; yet, it will ever remain true that these local traditions may have originated in the Biblical account of the passage of the Red Sea, and that consequently they cannot be brought forth as an independent confirmation of this memorable event (cfr. EWALD, History of Israel, vol. ii, p. 76, sq.).

Immediately after their miraculous deliverance, the children of Israel sang unto Jehovah that joyous canticle of praise and thanksgiving which Moses, their great leader, composed for the occasion and which we find recorded in the book of Exodus (xv, 1-21).

# SYNOPSIS OF CHAPTER VII.

## SINAI AND THE GIVING OF THE LAW.

**I. THE JOURNEY TO SINAI:**
1. *The stations indicated* (Exodus xv, 22–xix, 2; Numbers xxxiii, 3–15).
2. *The chief incidents on the way:*
   - A. Difficulties arising from
     - the country.
     - Amalec.
   - B. Helps from Heaven (quails, manna, etc).
   - C. Moses and Jethro.

**II. SINAI:**
1. *Physical description.*
2. *The Giving of the Law:*
   - A. The traditional Mount Sinai: its fitness for the giving of the Law.
   - B. Accompanying incidents.
     - Various ways in which God communicates with his people.
     - The Golden Calf.

## CHAPTER VII.

#### SINAI AND THE LAW.

1. **The Journey to Sinai** (Exod. xv, 22–xix, 2; Numb. xxxiii, 3–15). Of the various stations of the Israelites on their way to Sinai, several have very probably been identified. Thus there is hardly a doubt that their first camping-place was at the modern **'Ayun Musa**, or "Wells of Moses," about half an hour distant from the eastern shore of the Gulf of Suez. Their next stage is no less certainly identified with the spring **Awarah**, because it corresponds exactly with the Mara spoken of in the Bible, both as to position — a three days' journey from 'Ayun Musa — and as to the *bitter* taste of its waters which gave it its name. From 'Ain Awarah or Mara a short march brought the Israelites to the oasis of **Elim**, probably the **Wady Gharandel**, whose palatable waters and delightful shade they so highly appreciated as to remain "encamped by the waters" no less than a month (cfr. HARPER, Bible and Modern Discoveries, pp. 95, 96).

The book of Numbers mentions next an encampment of Israel by the **Red Sea**. This statement, formerly a puzzle to interpreters who could not understand how the Israelites should come back upon the Red Sea on their way to Sinai, which lay in the heart of the peninsula, is now justly quoted by travellers as a proof of the wisdom of the Jewish leader. In conducting the chosen people by what was unquestionably the less direct road to Sinai, Moses, who was well acquainted with the country, simply caused them to avoid the mines worked by Egyptians in the heart of the peninsula and defended by strong garrisons, and prudently put between the Egyptian warriors and his own untrained hosts a barrier of mountains.

From the Red Sea, the Israelites struck inland and entered the **Wilderness of Sin**, probably identified with the great plain **El Markha**. The next two stations mentioned in the book of Numbers are those of **Daphca** and **Alus**, but of these there is no satisfactory identification. Not so however with the next encampment at **Raphidim**, which Biblical scholars justly identify with the long and fertile plain called **Wady Feiran**, overhung by the granite rocks of **Mount Serbal**, probably the **Horeb** of Holy Writ. Finally, leaving Raphidim, the Israelites came into "the **Desert of Sinai** and there encamped over against the mountain," after a journey of more than two months, during which they had to overcome serious difficulties both from the country itself and from its inhabitants.

For about 150 miles they had had to traverse a country spoken of in Deuteronomy (viii, 15) as "the great and terrible wilderness" and supplied with no better roads than the pebbly ground of its wâdies, or torrent-beds. Several times they had to suffer from the bitter taste and even from the want of water, and as the provisions they had brought from Egypt were soon exhausted, they naturally feared for the very preservation of their large multitude.

To these difficulties, arising from the character of the country, were also added the attacks of the Amalecites, a tribe of the wilderness, less numerous indeed than the Israelites, but better armed and thoroughly acquainted with the mountain-passes. Hence it is likely enough that Israel would never have succeeded in overcoming all the difficulties it had to contend with in its way to Sinai, had not Jehovah repeatedly intervened in behalf of His chosen people.

Bearing this in mind, it will be easy for us to recognize as positive helps from heaven granted to the children of Israel, not only the spring of water which issued for them from the rock of Horeb, and their victory over Amalec, but also other facts which, notwithstanding their close analogy with mere natural phenomena, are clearly described by the sacred writer as actual miracles. Such is the case, for instance, with the plentiful supply of quails spoken of in the sixteenth chapter of Exodus, for, whilst the various details recorded in this connection agree very well with what travellers tell us of the usual migration of quails from Africa, it is plain that the Biblical narrative implies a miraculous intervention, inasmuch as the exact time for the sending of the quails had been most distinctly foretold by Moses. Such is also the case with the supply of manna granted to the Hebrews during the forty long years of their wandering in the wilderness. It must be granted indeed, that this wonderful food resembles closely the resinous substance which the tamarisk-tree of the Sinaitic peninsula yields under the prick of an insect, and which is collected usually in June. But this mere natural product — called also "manna" by modern writers — cannot be identified with the manna described in the Bible; for, differently from the latter, it cannot be gathered all the year round, and its quantity is very far short of what would suffice to constitute the principal article of food for so great a multitude of men as the Hebrews of old. (For other no less striking differences, see VIGOUROUX, vol. ii; cfr. also GEIKIE, vol. ii, p. 245, sq.)

A last incident well worthy of mention here in connection with the journey of the Israelites to Sinai is the meeting of Moses and Jethro, narrated in Exodus, after the defeat of Amalec at Raphidim. This was a peaceful interview, in which Israel and Madian entered into a close and lasting alliance, and it was followed by an important change in the manner in which Moses had heretofore administered justice in Israel; henceforth subordinate judges were to decide minor matters, and only the more important cases were to be brought before the Jewish leader. It seems also that on his return to his own estates Jethro left behind him his son Hobab, who proved a most reliable guide for the chosen people from Sinai to the border of Chanaan (Numb. x, 29, sq.).

2. **Sinai.** The whole mountain-mass now designated under the name of Mount Sinai comprises three parallel mountains, separated by the valleys Wady el Leja and Wady ed Deir. One of these mountains — that to the northeast — is called Jebel ed Deir and looks upon the convent of St. Catharine, erected at its base; the mountain to the south of the group bears the name of Jebel el Hamr, or Jebel Catharine, whilst between these two mountains is Mount Sina proper, now called Jebel Musa. This last mountain is oblong in form and about two miles in length by one mile in width. Its summit presents many syenite peaks of considerable height and ends north and south in still higher peaks, the one to the south being over 7,000 feet above the level of the sea and bearing the name of Jebel Musa, like the mountain itself, whilst the other, to the north, is almost 7,000 feet in altitude and is known as Ras Sufsâfeh.

The old tradition which connects Mount Sinai proper with the giving of the Law has of late been powerfully confirmed by the labors of the Ordinance Survey Expedition to the peninsula of Mount Sinai. From these long labors, it clearly follows that neither Jebel Catharine, nor Mount Serbal, nor any other mountain which has been spoken of as identical with the Mount of the Law, "has a plain at its foot where a multitude could encamp, and vegetation in its front on which flocks and herds could feed, as the Bible tells us they did at Sinai" (HARPER, Bible and Modern Discoveries, p. 111). From these same labors, it follows also that the various conditions required by the Biblical narrative are fully realized in Mount Sinai. Its wellnigh perfect isolation from the surrounding mountains would easily allow Moses "to appoint certain limits to the people round about" (Exod. xix, 12, 23), and its abrupt rise from the plain agrees well with the statement that the Israelites might "stand at the bottom of the mount" (Exod. xix, 17). Directly in front of Ras Sufsâfeh is the immense plain Er Rahah, which offers more than sufficient standing ground for all the children of Israel, and from the summit of the same peak it is easy to be heard by a very large multitude. The southern summit of Mount Sinai (the particular peak called Jebel Musa) was most likely the secluded spot to which Moses went when Jehovah called him up to the top of the Mount (Exod. xix, 20), for, besides its being completely hidden from the plain Er Rahah, it was formerly called the Mount of **Moneijah** or of the **Conference.**

Again, near the base of Ras Sufsâfeh, an old tradition points justly to a hill at the opening of the Wady ed Deir and visible from every part of the valley Er Rahah as "the hill of the golden calf" (Exod. xxxii, 4, sq.), for, whilst the Hebrews could with equal facility share in this idolatrous worship and witness the Divine manifestations taking place on the summit of Ras Sufsâfeh, "Moses and Josue when descending from that mount through a ravine between two peaks might have first heard the shouts of the people (Exod. xxxii, 17) before they saw them dancing round the golden calf" (SCHAFF, Bible Dictionary, p. 809). Finally, "in the torrent which cometh down from the mountain" (Deuter. ix, 21), through the ravine into the plain Er Rahah, Moses could cast the dust of the destroyed idol (Exod. xxxii, 19).

In these and other such striking coincidences of the traditional Mount Sinai with the sacred narrative we find plainly a strong argument not only for its identity with the scene described in the book of Exodus "but also that the scene itself was described by an eye-witness" (STANLEY, Sinai and Palestine, p. 43).

It was then in the plain Er Rahah and at the foot of the cliffs of Ras Sufsâfeh that the children of Israel collected in a single encampment, prepared themselves carefully, according to the directions of Moses, for the glorious manifestation Jehovah was about to make of Himself to them, and which actually took place on the morning of the third day (Exod. xix, 3, sq.). Everything in this mysterious event was calculated to impress upon the people the greatest and most lasting idea of the power and majesty and holiness of Jehovah. From amid the thunders and lightnings and the darkness which had settled on the mount, they first heard the Almighty speaking to Moses and treating him openly as His ambassador to them, and next, with feelings of indescribable terror, they heard this same voice of God addressing Himself to them and giving forth the Law by which they were to live, that is the **Ten Commandments**, on which all other laws were to be founded (Exod. xx, 1–18; Deuter. v, 5–21).

With this revelation of the Ten Commandments ended the direct outward communication of Jehovah with His people (Deut. v, 22), for they were struck with such terror as to pray their leader that he would henceforth speak to them in the place of God, lest they should die, and Jehovah acceded to their request. Moses was accordingly invested with the office of **mediator** between God and His people, and during the forty days and forty nights he remained with Jehovah in the cloud he received from Him those various and detailed precepts the perfect fulfilment of which would make of Israel at once a holy and a happy nation.

In point of fact, the Israelites had solemnly pledged themselves to do all that Jehovah would require of them (cfr. Exod. xix, 8; Deut. v, 27), but as Moses delayed long to come down from the mount, they thought him lost, and their idolatrous instincts revived. To please them, Aaron, who governed them in the absence of his brother, made them a molten calf, the symbol of the Egyptian Apis, or Mnevis, and proclaimed for the morrow a festival, which the people celebrated with sacrifices followed by those licentious orgies which were so common among heathen nations (Exod. xxxii, 1-6; I Cor. x, 7, sq.). This awful breach of the Divine Covenant drew forth vengeance from both Jehovah and Moses, in a manner too well known to need more than a passing mention here; suffice it to say that, after Moses had repeatedly and earnestly pleaded for Israel, God at length forgave entirely His people, renewed His covenant with them, and in a second period of forty days and forty nights of communion with the Jewish leader on the holy mount, He imparted to Moses fresh instructions respecting the various laws of the Theocracy (Exod. xxxii, 7-xxxiv).

# SYNOPSIS OF CHAPTER VIII.

## THE MOSAIC LAW.

*Section I. General Remarks. — The Tabernacle and its Ministers.*

I. GENERAL REMARKS ABOUT THE MOSAIC LAW:

1. *Main purposes of the Mosaic Law.*
2. *Its principal features:*
   - A. Constitutional (the Jewish Theocracy).
   - B. Civil (no distinction of castes; high regard for individual rights).
   - C. Criminal (human and disciplinary character of punishments).
   - D. Judicial (judges the representatives of God; their principal qualities).
   - E. Religious (enforcement of Monotheistic belief and worship).

II. THE TABERNACLE AND ITS MINISTERS.

1. *The Tabernacle* (Exod. xxxvi–xl):
   - General idea of this centre of Jewish worship.
   - Its principal parts:
     - The Court and its contents.
     - The Sanctuary (size, divisions and contents).

2. *Its Ministers* (Exod. xxviii, xxix; Levit. viii, ix; Numb. iii, iv):
   - The Tribe of Levi (why selected? how divided)?
   - The simple Levites (dedication and functions).
   - The Jewish Priests (consecration; sacred vestments; duties and maintenance).
   - The High Priest (sacred character; special garments and functions).

# CHAPTER VIII.

### THE MOSAIC LAW.

SECTION 1. GENERAL REMARKS. THE TABERNACLE AND ITS MINISTERS.

§ *1. General Remarks about the Mosaic Law.*

1. **Main Purposes.** If we except the Christian law, no legislation was ever enacted for higher and better purposes than the Mosaic law, the record of which occupies a large portion of the books of **Exodus** and **Numbers** and almost the whole of the books of **Leviticus** and **Deuteronomy**. It aimed, first of all, at organizing into a civilized nation hordes of slaves but recently delivered from the most abject servitude, and, as such, very little fitted for the duties and privileges of personal freedom and national independence. It aimed, in the second place, at making Israel a monotheistic nation, and indeed succeeded in making it the sole monotheistic nation of antiquity, that is, the sole nation of the ancient world, which possessed the correct idea of the Divinity. But more particularly was the Mosaic law intended to fashion the Jewish people into "a priestly kingdom and a holy nation" (Exod. xix, 6), bound to be holy because Jehovah their God is holy, destined to offer to the true God the only sacrifices acceptable to the Divine Majesty, and to preserve and spread among all the nations of the earth, together with the belief in Jehovah, the expectation of the promised Redeemer of the world. Of course some of these purposes could be obtained but slowly and gradually, and this is why the student of the Mosaic law should never consider it was

its purpose to bring all things at once to perfection, but rather to correct old abuses as far as allowed by the present religious and moral condition of the Jewish nation, and usually to suggest, and even at times simply foreshadow, the perfection which was to be introduced into the world by Christianity.

2. **General Features.** At the basis of the Hebrew commonwealth, the Mosaic law placed a theocratic constitution in virtue of which Jehovah was to be not only the God but also the *King* of Israel, as He was indeed the founder of the state and the proprietor of the land which He would bestow upon His people. In accepting freely this order of things, the Jews acknowledged themselves as Jehovah's tenants, holding their lands on well-defined terms of vassalage, foremost among which was their faithfulness to the exclusive worship of the one great and invisible Creator. The social compact in Israel was not therefore primarily between the people at large and one or several members of the community, but between the entire nation and its God, and as long as this fundamental relation of Jehovah to His people was fully secured, it mattered but little in the eyes of Moses what manner of political organization was in vigor among the Hebrews. Hence while retaining the time-honored organization of the people into tribes, families and houses, under their respective heads (cfr. Josue vii, 14), he did not consider as incompatible with the Jewish theocracy the monarchical form of government which he foresaw would one day exist in Israel (Deuter. xvii, 14, sq.).

As a natural consequence of this same theocratic character of the Jewish polity, Moses looked upon all the members of God's people as being equally His subjects, and, in consequence, he granted to all equal civil rights. Differently from the Egyptians, they were to constitute but one great caste, that of husbandmen cultivating their own inalienable property; and although the Levites formed in the Jewish state a distinct class analogous in several ways to the priestly caste of Egypt, yet, differently from the Egyptian priests, they were forbidden to own lands and prevented from accumulating riches and exercising any influence which might endanger the liberties of the people. With the same high regard for civil freedom, the Jewish lawgiver made but few changes in all that concerned the organization and government of the natural basis of society, — the family. He deprived, however, the father of the right of life and death upon his household, and restricted the practice of divorce. The regulations of the Mosaic law respecting the poor, the slaves, the strangers, the travellers, the working-classes, etc., bespeak also the greatest regard for man's life, individual rights and personal freedom. Its deep concern for the religious education of children, and the strict practice not only of justice but also of equity in business transactions, is no less remarkable.

When we pass from the civil to the criminal code of the Jews we find that it also is permeated with the theocratic spirit. "Each breach of the law was an act of disobedience to God's holy will, and not merely an offence against society; the rewards of obedience and the punishment of sin had reference to the covenant under which the people lived" (SMITH, Old Testament History, p. 220). In virtue of this same theocratic character of the Mosaic law, crimes directly against God, such as idolatry, blasphemy, etc., were naturally considered as most heinous, and many others, usually beyond the cognizance of ordinary codes, were really amenable to the tribunal of Jehovah, the great King of Israel and the all-knowing Judge of men's deeds. Many offences were indeed punishable with death — which was inflicted by stoning, by fire, or by the sword — but no torture could be resorted to in order to force the confession of crimes, no cruelty was allowed after the guilt of a man had been proven, and in opposition to the political custom of Asia, the punishment of a father did not entail that of his children. The other forms of punishment were (1) scourging, which was not to exceed forty stripes of the lash at a time; (2) mutilation, and (3) various fines. But whatever the punishments threatened or the rewards promised, the chief object of the criminal code in Israel was "*disciplinary*, and to this its retributive element was subordinate" (SMITH, ibid, p. 221). It should also be noticed that some customs — such as that of retaliation applied to malicious or accidental wounding — which appear to us extremely severe, not to say barbarous, were indeed allowed to exist, but only as minor evils destined to be mitigated as soon as the conditions of a more settled life would permit.

As Jehovah was the real King of Israel, so was He also its Supreme Judge, who intervened at times to mete out to the transgressors of His Law the chastisements which they deserved. But however numerous and striking these instances of direct Divine judgment in Jewish history, it remains true that the ordinary application of laws was among the Hebrews, as among all other nations, intrusted to a judiciary whose members acted as ministers of the Head of the State. The Law required that they should be "able, godly, truthful and incorrupt" (SMITH, ibid, p. 275), and this is why they were selected from among the elders of Israel, and also later on, from among the Levites, that is, from the best instructed and most independent members of the community. As the representatives of God's power and majesty they are oftentimes called "gods" in Holy Writ, and their persons and characters were held sacred by all the Jews. After the settlement in Chanaan, they rendered justice in the gates of the cities, so that trials were actually held in public.

The last general feature to be mentioned here in connection with the Mosaic law is its religious character. Viewed from this standpoint, the Mosaic legislation will ever appear the greatest effort of antiquity to promulgate and maintain the belief in, and worship of, one only God, for such was unquestionably the object of its dogmatic teaching, and of many of its moral precepts and ceremonial enactments. The chief dogma of Israel is absolute Monotheism, which — as might naturally be expected — is inculcated in such a manner as to imply a formal opposition to Egyptian idolatry (cfr. Exod. xxii, 2, sq., the wording of which points back to the custom long witnessed by the Hebrews in Egypt of worshipping countless images of the Divinity and of its various attributes).[1] Many moral precepts of the Mosaic law — however closely this law may resemble Egyptian legislation in other respects — tend no less manifestly to enforce among the chosen people the exclusive worship of Jehovah (cfr. for instance, Exod. xxiii, 13, 24; Deuter. vii, 2, sq.; xvii, 2-7); and it is not unlikely that the entire omission of the rewards and punishments in the next life from the Pentateuch, as a sanction of the moral law, must be explained by the desire of the Jewish lawgiver not to recall, even indirectly, to the Israelites the idolatrous practices with which the Egyptians had surrounded the burials and tombs of their dead. But it is more particularly in connection with the ceremonial enactments of the Mosaic law that the desire of the great lawgiver of Israel to guard his people against Egyptian idolatry appears evident, for, whilst he borrowed from Egypt many of the externals of Jewish worship, he is very careful to divest them of their polytheistic character (cfr. W. Smith, The Pentateuch, Authorship, etc., p. 289, sq.). As this ceremonial law plays a very important part in the history of the Jewish nation, and is described with many details in the sacred narrative, we now proceed to give, though briefly, its principal features.

[1] Perhaps the familiarity of the Israelites with the worship of the Egyptian gods in *triads*, together with their tendency to retain the idolatrous beliefs and practices of Egypt (Exod. xxxii, 4, sq.), may account for the fact that the mysterious existence of one God in *three* persons was not included in the revelation of Mount Sinai.

## § 2. *The Tabernacle and its Ministers.*

1. **The Tabernacle** (Exod. xxxvi–xl). The centre of public worship in Israel was the **Tabernacle**, or Tent, which Jehovah, as God and King of His people, wished to have among them. Erected by means of the free-will offerings of the Israelites it ever reminded them that they were a theocratic nation, since their God, like the chieftain of a tribe, resided in their midst, and in a portable building, whose form exhibited at the same time several features of the more solid and more majestic temples of Egypt. This portable temple was surrounded by an oblong court wherein were found the Altar of Holocausts, and between it and the Sacred Tent itself the laver of brass at which God's ministers washed their hands and feet on entering the Tabernacle. The Tabernacle itself, called also the Sanctuary, was placed toward the western end of the court, and was an oblong rectangular tent, 52 feet long by 17 feet in height and width. It was divided by a magnificently embroidered veil, into two parts: the Holy Place and the Holy of Holies. The Holy Place contained, beside the sacred utensils, (1) the table whereon the twelve loaves of proposition were placed every Sabbath day, (2) the golden candlestick with its seven branches, and (3) the small portable altar of wood covered with gold, called the Altar of Incense. Whilst the simple priests were allowed to enter the Holy Place for the exercise of their sacred functions, only Moses and the high priest had the privilege of penetrating into the mysterious darkness of the Holy of Holies, which contained nothing but the Ark of the Covenant. This ark was a wooden chest three feet nine inches in length by two feet three inches in width and height, and, as the symbol of the covenant between Jehovah and His people, it contained the two stone tables of the Law. Its lid, made of the purest gold, was called the Mercy Seat, or propitiatory, because it was considered as the throne whence Jehovah exercised mercy and

forgiveness towards His people; it was also overshadowed by the outstretched wings of two symbolical figures which the Bible calls Cherubim. This Biblical description of the Ark shows that it resembled in a striking manner the Naos, or portable wooden chapel which was found in the sanctuary of every Egyptian temple and which contained the image of a deity over whom two symbolical figures extended their wings. But however close this resemblance, it should never make us forget that a most important difference existed between the Jewish ark and the Egyptian naos; whilst the latter contained an image of the deity to whom it was dedicated, the former offered to the eyes of the Hebrews no visible representation of Jehovah (Exod. xxv, sq.).

2. **The Ministers of the Tabernacle** (Exod. xxviii, xxix; Levit. viii, ix; Numb. iii, iv). For the service of His Tabernacle, God selected the whole tribe of Levi, apparently as a reward for the zeal in favor of religious unity which they had exhibited on the occasion of the idolatrous worship of the golden calf (Exod. xxxii, 25, 29). Moreover, as Moses belonged to this tribe, he might naturally depend more on them than on any other tribe in Israel to establish and forward His religious institutions among the chosen people.

Although the special mission of the whole tribe seems to be described as that of mediating between Jehovah and His people (Numb. xviii, 22, 23), it is probable that, from the beginning, a distinction was established between the sons of Aaron and the rest of the tribe; the former and their descendants alone were the *priests* of Jehovah, the latter and their descendants were simply the *assistants* of the priests and retained the distinctive name of **Levites.**

The **simple Levites** were dedicated to the service of Jehovah in the person of His priests, by solemn ceremonies which are detailed in the book of Numbers (viii, 5-22), and which were not repeated at the induction of each Levite into his office. Besides their general function of assisting the sons of Aaron in the discharge of their priestly duties, the Levites were charged to carry the Tabernacle and its vessels, to keep watch about the sanctuary, etc., and other like duties which required a man's full strength, and hence they did not enter upon their functions before the age of thirty.

The sons of Aaron, together with their male descendants, were the only lawful priests of Jehovah. If properly qualified for the exercise of the priestly ministry, they had to be individually consecrated by special ceremonies, which lasted seven days and which consisted in sacrifices, purifications, the putting on of the holy garments, the sprinkling of blood, and anointing with oil. During their ministrations, they wore vestments in several respects similar to those of the Egyptian priests, and the principal of which were: fine linen drawers, a close-fitting tunic, also of white linen, and reaching to the feet, a long linen girdle confining the tunic round the waist; upon their heads they wore a kind of a tiara, formed by the foldings of a linen cloth, and of a round turban-like shape. Their manifold duties were briefly as follows: In the court of the Tabernacle they kept ever burning the fire on the Altar of Holocausts and offered various sacrifices to God; in the Holy Place they were charged to offer the morning and evening sacrifice of the incense, to take care of the golden candlestick and its lights, and to place, every week, on the table the loaves of proposition; independently of these functions connected with the Tabernacle, they also acted as judges, and as teachers and interpreters of the law. Finally, for their maintenance, they had a considerable share in the victims offered to Jehovah, and received dues of various kinds, such as first-fruits, one-tenth of the tithes of the produce of the country paid to the Levites, the redemption-money for the first-born of man and beast, etc.

At the head of the whole Jewish priesthood was Aaron with the title and dignity of **High Priest**, which were to pass to his son Eleazar and his male descendants. The high priest was to be a person especially sacred, as was clearly set forth by the gold plate which was attached to his tiara and on which was engraved "*Holy to the Lord,*" and hence any bodily imperfection or blemish excluded him from the office. He was consecrated in the same manner as the simple priests, with this difference, however, that the sacred oil was poured upon his head. His *special* garments were: (1) the **Robe of the Ephod**, which the high priest wore in place of the close-fitting tunic of the simple priests. It was a robe of woven work, without sleeves, drawn over the head through an opening, and its skirt was set with a remarkable trimming of pomegranates alternating with golden bells; (2) the **Ephod**, a short cloak made of two parts, one covering the back and the other the breast and upper part of the body; they were clasped together on the shoulder with two onyx stones, on each of which were engraved the names of six of the tribes; (3) just above the very fine girdle of the high priest which gathered around the waist both the Robe of the Ephod and the Ephod itself was the **Breastplate.** This was an ornament of embroidered cloth, set with four rows of precious stones, three in each row, and on each stone was engraved the name of one of the tribes of Israel. It was about ten inches square in size and had its two upper corners fastened to the two onyx stones on the shoulders, whilst the two lower ones were fixed to the ephod. Within the Breastplate, or "**Breastplate of Judgment,**" were the **Urim and Thummim**, whose meaning, now so mysterious to us, was so well known to the Hebrews as not to require any explanation from the sacred writer. They were most likely analogous to the small figure of sapphire which the Egyptian supreme judge (who was ordinarily the high priest) wore suspended from his neck when delivering judgment, and which was a representation of the goddess worshipped under the character of Truth and Justice (W. SMITH, The Pentateuch, authorship, credibility, etc., p. 298, sq.). When using them, the Jewish high priest appealed not to a pagan deity but to Jehovah, who by their means was pleased to make known to Israel His true and just judgment (cfr. I Kings, xxviii, 6; xiv, 3, 18; etc.).

Besides the right of presiding over the court of judgment (Deuter. xvii, 9) and of consulting the Divine Oracle (Numb. xxvii, 21), the high priest enjoyed the exclusive privilege of officiating on the great Day of Atonement, and of entering on that same day into the Holy of Holies. He held his office for life, and was naturally recognized as the supreme administrator of sacred things and the final arbiter of all religious controversies.

# SYNOPSIS OF CHAPTER IX.

### THE MOSAIC LAW.

*Section II.  Sacrificial and Festival Rites.*

**I. MOSAIC SACRIFICES:**
(Exod. xxix, xxx,
Levit. i–vii.
Numb. xv.)

1. *Sacrifice, an Expression of Religious Worship.*
2. *Bloody Sacrifices:*
   - Principal kinds (Holocausts; Expiatory and Pacific sacrifices).
   - Features common to them all.
   - Animals selected: why offered to the true God?
3. *Unbloody Sacrifices:*
   - Principal kinds.
   - Chief objects of unbloody sacrifices.
4. *Place where the Sacrifices were to be Offered.*
5. *Laws of Purity.*

**II. MOSAIC HOLIDAYS:**

1. *The Sabbath and Holidays connected therewith:*
   - A. The Weekly Sabbath (why and how sanctified?)
   - B. The Feast of the New Moon.
   - C. The Feast of Trumpets (why called so? how celebrated?)
   - D. The Sabbatical Year (meaning and special regulations).
   - E. The Year of Jubilee (special enactments; their importance).
2. *The Three Great Joyous Festivals:*
   - A. The Paschal Festival (Levit. xxiii, 5–8; Numb. xxviii, 16–25; Deut. xvi, 1–8).
   - B. The Feast of Pentecost (Levit. xxiii, 15–22; Numb. xxviii, 26–31; Deut. xvi, 9–12).
   - C. The Feast of Tabernacles (Levit. xxiii, 34–43; Numb. xxix, 12–39; Deut. xvi, 13–15).
3. *The Day of Atonement* (Levit. xvi; xxiii, 26–32).

# CHAPTER IX.

### THE MOSAIC LAW.

## Section II. Sacrificial and Festival Rites.

### § 1. *The Mosaic Sacrifices.*

1. **Sacrifice, an Expression of Religious Worship.** The rite of sacrifice, as a public expression of religious worship, goes back to the most remote antiquity, and will ever remain not only the most fitting acknowledgment of God's supreme Majesty, infinite holiness, justice and liberality, but also the means best calculated to impress upon, and develop in, the minds and hearts of men, the feelings which they should bear towards their almighty Maker and Preserver. In the time of the exodus, numerous sacrifices were offered to their gods by the Egyptians, as well as by the other nations of the ancient world, and it behooved Moses, who was so anxious to preserve in its purity the religious belief in Israel, to determine, in detail, which sacrificial rites the Hebrews should retain from the Egyptian ceremonial, and which they should discard. This, therefore, he did with a completeness and precision all the more necessary, because he knew he was legislating in a most important matter and for all future ages. The numerous sacrifices which he prescribed to the Jewish people can be divided into two great classes: (1) the **bloody** sacrifices, in which the Israelites testified, by the slaying of animals, the supreme power of God over the life and death of His creatures; (2) the **unbloody** sacrifices, by which they acknowledged Jehovah as the bestower of the land and of its produce.

2. **The Bloody Sacrifices.** Three principal kinds of bloody sacrifices can be distinguished in the Mosaic ceremonial, namely, the **Holocausts**, the **Expiatory** and the **Pacific** sacrifices. The distinguishing feature of the holocausts consisted in the burning of all the parts of the victim upon the altar, whereby it was signified that the offerer belonged wholly to Jehovah, dedicated himself entirely to His honor and glory, and placed his life at His disposal. In the Expiatory sacrifices, which were to be offered for sins of ignorance or for sins committed knowingly, only the fat of the victim was burned on the altar, and in some cases the flesh of the animal was burned without the camp, whilst in others it belonged to the priests. The leading characteristic of the Pacific sacrifices was the sacrificial meal by which they were followed. After the fat of the victim had been burned on the altar, its right shoulder and breast were "waved before Jehovah," and then became the portion of the priest, whilst the remaining parts were restored to the offerer, who, the same day, feasted thereon, in a meal which was both the symbol and the pledge of God's friendship to His worshippers.

But however different in many particulars they might appear, these various kinds of bloody sacrifices exhibited important features common to them all. Thus in all cases the *offerer* was required to bring the victim into the court of the Tabernacle, there to lay his hand on its head and then to slay it himself. In all cases also the *priest* received the blood of the animal in a basin, and then sprinkled it in different ways upon the Altar of the Holocausts. In all these sacrifices, finally, the selection of the victims was limited to animals of the herd, of the flock and to all clean birds, and the victim offered was required to be perfect of its kind and without blemish.

Thus, then, the animals to be selected as victims were those "most nearly connected with man, and of these again, such as were most meek, innocent, pure and valuable" (MACLEAR, Old Testament History, p. 136,), such, in a word, as would entail a real sacrifice upon the man who willingly parted with them, and would suggest the purity and innocence with which Jehovah was to be worshipped. Moreover, in prescribing animal sacrifices, God not only affirmed His supreme dominion over living things — even over animals which were regarded as gods by the Egyptians — but He also helped to prevent His people from falling back into idolatry, as might indeed be apprehended had He not required from them bloody sacrifices similar to those which were then offered by all the nations of the earth and which the Israelites had offered themselves in the land of Egypt. Finally, these animal sacrifices — however imperfect — suggested to the Hebrews inward sentiments of piety, such as thanksgiving for benefits received, sorrow for sins committed, etc., and foreshadowed the great and perfect sacrifice which Jesus, the High Priest of the New Law and the true Lamb of God, was to offer in fulfilment of all the bloody sacrifices of the old Covenant.

3. **Unbloody Sacrifices.** The second class of Mosaic sacrifices included all those which were to be offered to God, either in conjunction with, or independently of, the bloody sacrifices. These unbloody offerings were of three principal kinds, namely: (1) **First-fruits and Tithes** of the produce of the land, which were presented either in their natural state, as grain, fruit, wool, etc., or prepared for man's use, such as flour, oil, wine; (2) **Meat-offerings and Drink-offerings**, the latter consisting in wine poured out at the foot of the altar, the former consisting in corn either in the form of fine flour seasoned with salt and mingled with frankincense and oil, but without leaven, or made into cakes offered with oil and salt, but without leaven or honey; (3) offering of **Incense**, which, besides accompanying every meat-offering,

was also made separately every day on the golden altar in the Holy Place, and in the Holy of Holies on the great Day of Atonement.

As the Holocaust " signified the consecration of *life* to God, both that of the offerer himself and of his living property, so in the meat-offering the produce of the land was presented before Jehovah as being His gift" (SMITH, Old Testament History, p. 247). Another object of the first-fruits, and especially of the tithes, was, as we already noticed, to provide for the maintenance of the priests and Levites who were not allowed territorial possessions in Israel. Finally, even admitting, as supposed by many, that the incense which was burned with the various sacrifices was intended to make a sweet odor in the court of the Tabernacle, it can hardly be denied that the sacrifice of the incense when made separately was meant, even perhaps from the first, to have the symbolical signification of the prayer of the worshipper rising before the throne of God (cfr. Psalm cxl, 2).

4. **Place where the Sacrifices were to be Offered.** As might naturally be expected from a legislation framed for a nation which was encamped around the tent of its God, the court of the Tabernacle was the only place where the Hebrews were allowed to offer sacrifices to Jehovah (Levit. xvii, 3-9). The enactment of this rule was also in perfect harmony with the great wish of the Mosaic lawgiver, namely: to secure the monotheism of Israel, inasmuch as it prescribed that all sacrifices should be offered under the very eyes of priests whose plain duty it was to exclude all idolatry from the sacrificial rites of the people. Notwithstanding these and other such reasons in favor of the view that the *Unity of Sanctuary* was prescribed to the Hebrews at the time of the exodus, many scholars think that this point of Jewish worship was defined only centuries after the death of Moses, and that meanwhile the Israelites were at liberty to

offer sacrifices in different places. To substantiate their position these scholars appeal (1) to Exodus xx, 22–26, which seems clearly to allow the use of several altars whereon to offer sacrifices to Jehovah; (2) to the constant and apparently lawful practice in Israel of offering sacrifices in many places besides the court of the Tabernacle, such as Mount Ebal (Josue viii, 30, 31), Bochim (Judges ii, 5), Bethsames, (I Kings vi, 15), Hebron, (II Kings xv, 7–9), etc.

5. **Laws of Purity.** Under the name of "Laws of Purity" may be designated many Mosaic regulations which are intimately connected with the offering of sacrifices, inasmuch as any one who was not legally clean was forbidden the approach of God's sanctuary until he had first undergone a purification which often entailed various kinds of offerings according to the character of the legal impurity he had contracted. It cannot be doubted that many of these regulations were laws of hygiene regulating diet, enforcing cleanliness, and preventing the spread of contagious diseases. Yet it must be admitted that they had all a higher object, namely: that of reminding the Jews of their separation from the other nations and from all that is impure, because they had been chosen as the special people of the thrice holy God (Levit. xx, 24–26).

The principal laws of purity regarded (1) **Things unclean to touch**, such as the dead body of any animal, the body, bones or grave of a dead man; (2) **Things unclean to eat**, wherein were included all quadrupeds which did *not both divide the hoof and chew the cud*, all birds of prey and nearly all the water-fowl, all fishes that have not both fins and scales, all the reptiles and insects except the locusts; (3) **Unclean conditions**, such as those which resulted from the use of marriage, from childbirth, and particularly the uncleanness entailed by leprosy (Levit. xi–xv).

It should also be noticed that partaking of the blood of all animals, whether clean or unclean, was most strictly prohibited by the Mosaic law (Levit. iii, 17; xvii, 10, 12), and that the rites prescribed for purification varied very considerably according to the character of the legal uncleanness which had been contracted.

### § 2. *Mosaic Holidays.*

1. **The Sabbath and Holidays connected therewith.** Of all the holidays prescribed by the Mosaic law, none was to be observed more strictly than the **Sabbath** or seventh day of the week. Absolute rest from worldly toil was enjoined on this weekly holiday in remembrance of God's rest after the six days of Creation, and for this reason it was called "Sabbath" or "Rest" (Exod. xx, 8–11; xxxi, 13–17). Bodily labor was prohibited under penalty of death, and work apparently most necessary, such as kindling the fire, cooking food, etc., was to be done on the preceding day. This strict prohibition of bodily labor extended also to slaves and strangers, even to beasts of burden. Besides this prescribed rest, a few religious services were enjoined on the Sabbath day; they consisted in the doubling of the morning and evening sacrifice which was offered on ordinary days (Numb. xxviii, 3–10), the renewal of the loaves of proposition (Levit. xxiv, 8), and finally some kind of religious meeting for the people.

Just as every week was marked by a day especially consecrated to Jehovah, so was also every month of the Jewish year. The feast of the **New Moon**—a kind of monthly Sabbath—was celebrated on the first day of the month by the sounding of the two sacred silver trumpets and by the sacrifice of eleven victims over and above the daily offerings (Numb. x, 10; xxviii, 11–15).

The seventh month of the ecclesiastical year among the Jews had a kind of Sabbatic character, and hence its new moon was observed with special solemnity. It was a holy convocation and was called the **Feast of Trumpets**, because it was "a day for the sounding of trumpets" (Numb. xxix, 1), and in addition to the daily sacrifices and the eleven victims offered on the first day of the other months, ten other victims were offered to Jehovah.

During the seventh or **Sabbatical Year**, the land was to enjoy its Sabbath. It was not to be sown, nor the vineyards and olive-trees dressed, nor the spontaneous produce of the year to be gathered, but left entirely for the poor, the slave, the stranger and even the cattle. By this rest, the land did homage to its Lord and Creator in the same way as man by the rest of the seventh day. The seventh year was also called the "year of remission," because in it creditors were bound to release poor debtors from their obligations, and its religious character was emphasized by the solemn reading of the Law to the people assembled at the feast of Tabernacles (Levit. xxv, 3–7 ; Deuter. xv; xxxi, 10–13).

At the end of seven times seven years was the **Year of Jubilee**. During this fiftieth year, the land was left uncultivated, as in the Sabbatical year; all the territorial possessions, which poor owners had alienated, were to return to the families to which they had been originally allotted, and all slaves of Hebrew blood were set free. By this semi-centennial restitution of land and liberation of Hebrew bondmen, it was clearly asserted that both land and people belonged to Jehovah alone, whilst the accumulation of riches and the formation of castes were effectively prevented.

2. **The Three Great Joyous Festivals.** Besides the Sabbath and Sabbatic holidays, the Mosaic law enjoined the celebration of three annual festivals of a joyous character, because intended to return thanks to God for benefits received. The first and greatest of them all was the **Pasch**, whose original institution was noticed in connection with

Israel's departure from Egypt. It commemorated this great national event, and at the same time marked the beginning of the harvest. It lasted seven days, from the evening of the 14th to the end of the 21st of the first month of the Jewish ecclesiastical year, and during its celebration no leavened bread was to be eaten. Each paschal lamb was slain on the evening of the 14th of the first month (Nisan), in the court of the Tabernacle, its blood, received by priests in basins, was sprinkled on the altar, and the fat was burned upon the Altar of Holocausts. Thence the lamb was carried into private houses, where it was roasted whole with fire, and eaten with unleavened bread and a salad of bitter herbs. On the 15th and the six following days an offering of eleven animals was made, in addition to the daily sacrifices, and the first and last days (the 15th and 21st) were holy convocations. Finally, on the 16th of Nisan, the first ripe sheaf of barley was offered to Jehovah, and this marked the beginning of the harvest, whose first-fruits had thus been dedicated to the God of Israel (Levit. xxiii, 5-8; Numb. xxviii, 16-25; Deuter. xvi, 1-8).

The second great joyous festival of the Jewish year was the **Feast of Pentecost**, called the **Feast of Weeks** in the Pentateuch, because celebrated **seven weeks** after the Pasch. It lasted but one day, which was kept as a holy convocation, and during which the whole people were especially exhorted to rejoice before Jehovah with free-will offerings. Eleven animals were also publicly offered in the court of the Tabernacle, in addition to the daily sacrifices. But the chief and distinguishing feature of this festival was the offering of *two leavened loaves*, made from the new corn of the now completed harvest, together with two lambs, which were sacrificed as peace-offerings. "The whole ceremony was the completion of that dedication of the harvest to God, as its Giver, which was begun by the offering of the wave-sheaf at the Passover" (SMITH, p. 265).

The last great, joyous, annual festival of the Jews was the **Feast of Tabernacles**, which was celebrated in the autumn, on the 15th of the seventh month, and was at once a thanksgiving for the completion of the harvest and a commemoration of the time when the Israelites dwelt in tents during their sojourn in the wilderness. Its duration was strictly only of seven days, the first and last of which were holy convocations; as, however, it was followed by a day of holy convocation, the festival is sometimes spoken of as lasting eight days. During it the Israelites were commanded to live in tents or booths of green boughs, and to make burnt-offerings far more numerous than at any other festival. When this feast fell on a Sabbatical year, portions of the Law were read each day in public. The Feast of Tabernacles completed the cycle of the annual festivals, and was one of the most joyous of them all, for it marked the crowning of Divine mercy, which had just allowed the chosen people to complete the ingathering of the vintage and of all the fruits of the year.

For the celebration of these three great festivals, all male Israelites were required to appear before Jehovah.

3. **The Day of Atonement.** To these great national holidays was added another, of a very different character. The tenth day of the seventh month — five days only before the Feast of Tabernacles — was the **Day of Atonement,** that is, the great day of expiation for the sins of both priests and people. From the evening of the 9th to the evening of the 10th of the seventh month no bodily labor could be done, no food taken under penalty of death. All the ritual of the day was carried out by the high priest himself. Having bathed himself and dressed in the white linen garments common to himself and the rest of the priesthood, he brought forward a young bullock as sin-offering and a ram as burnt-offering for himself and for the priests; and next, two he-

goats as a sin-offering and a ram as a burnt-offering for the people. The two goats were then led to the entrance of the Tabernacle, and lots cast upon them, one lot being-marked "*for Jehovah,*" the other "*for Azazael.*" This done, the high priest, making atonement for himself and for the priesthood, offered the bullock, carried live coals in a censer with two handfuls of incense into the Holy of Holies, where he threw the incense upon the coals, and soon after sprinkled the blood of the bullock seven times before the Mercy-Seat. He then killed the goat that was "for Jehovah," and sprinkled its blood in the same manner. Over the goat that was "for Azazael" he solemnly confessed the sins of the people and then sent it away into the desert. After this, the high priest bathed again, put on his special gorgeous robes and offered the two rams as a burnt-offering, one for himself and the other for the people.

The typical meaning of these victims and ceremonies is set forth in the Epistle to the Hebrews (chaps. viii-x).

# SYNOPSIS OF CHAPTER X.

## FROM SINAI TO THE SOUTHERN BORDER OF PALESTINE.

I. FROM SINAI TO CADES:
- 1. *Departure:* Time; Manner; Aim.
- 2. *Route followed:* (General direction. — Stations indicated.)
- 3. *Principal Incidents:*
  - Israel's murmurings.
  - Seventy elders appointed.
  - The land espied.

II. THE WILDERNESS AND THE FORTY YEARS' WANDERING:
- 1. *The Wilderness:*
  - Its boundaries and divisions.
  - Its general aspect and productions.
- 2. *The forty years' wandering:*
  - A. Why imposed by God.
  - B. The road followed by Israel: Almost unknown. Various opinions.
  - C. History: Facts unknown. Conditions conjectured. A few incidents related.

## CHAPTER X.

#### FROM SINAI TO THE SOUTHERN BORDER OF PALESTINE.

### § 1. *From Sinai to Cades.*

1. **Departure from Sinai.** The great events which occurred at Mount Sinai — the giving of the law, the consecration of the priests, the construction and erection of the Tabernacle — had detained Israel very nearly a year in that region (Exod. xix, 1; Numb. i, 1); after which time Jehovah commanded Moses to take a census of all who were fit for war. This first signal of their approaching departure from Sinai was followed by a due celebration of the anniversary of the Passover, soon after which the Israelites — numbering altogether between two and three millions — received the final signal for departure (Numb. x, 11).

Under the guidance of Hobab, the brother-in-law of Moses, who intimately knew the usual resting-places, the water-springs, etc., of the country which the Israelites were about to traverse, the twelve tribes, divided into four great bodies and preceded by the Ark, began their march. At this solemn moment, the Jewish lawgiver and leader of Israel broke the silence of the desert, and exclaimed :

> " Arise, Jehovah, and let Thy enemies be scattered,
> And let them that hate Thee, flee from before Thy face."

In these poetical words Moses clearly set forth the object of Israel's present departure; headed by Jehovah, the chosen people was starting to conquer the idolatrous tribes of Chanaan, which were the enemies of both God and His people, and to enter at once upon the possession of the land promised to the patriarchs of old (Numb. x, 35; Deuter. i, 6-8).

2. **Route followed by Israel.** The general direction of the road followed by the Israelites lay northward, between Sinai on the south and Cades on the north, the distance between these two points being an "eleven days' journey," or about one hundred and seventy miles, "by the way of Mount Seir" (Numb. xxxii, 8; Deuter. i, 2). They most likely took the ordinary route, which passes first along the eastern arm of the Red Sea — now called the **Gulf of Akabah** — and next through the wide plain of the **Arabah**, between Mount Seir on the east and the desert of *Et-Tih*, that is, of the Wandering, on the west.

Of the twenty stations indicated in the book of Numbers (xxxiii, 16-35), only the first two belong most likely to the present journey of the Israelites; these are (1) *Kibroth Hattaavah* (graves of lust), a three days' journey from Sinai, and probably to be identified with Erweis el Ebeirig; (2) *Hazeroth*, identical with the modern 'Ain Hudherah both in name and in position (one day's journey from Kibroth Hattaavah). The next encampment spoken of in the book of Numbers (xiii, 1) was in *the desert of Pharan*, that is in that part of the northeastern division of the Peninsula of Sinai in which Cades — called also **Cadesbarne** — was situated. The position of the city of Cades, so important in the topography of the exodus, has not yet been identified with certainty; it may be said, however, with great probability, that Cades is identical with '*Ain Gadis*, some fifty miles south of Bersabee (cfr. art. *Cades*, in VIGOUROUX, Dictionnaire de la Bible; see also *Revue Biblique*, July, 1896, p. 440, sq).

3. **Principal Incidents.** During their lengthened stay in the wadies of Mount Sinai, the Israelites had lost a great

deal of their power of endurance, and this is why shortly after setting out for Cades they openly "repined at their fatigue." This first murmuring, however natural under the circumstances, was not left unpunished; a fire broke out in the encampment, and ceased only at the prayer of Moses. It is likely that this fire was not looked upon by the children of Israel as a divine punishment, for we see them very soon afterwards rising in an almost general rebellion against Moses and against Jehovah Himself. Sitting and weeping, they longed for their fill of flesh, and speaking scornfully of the manna they were ever supplied with, regretted the fish and the vegetables of Egypt. It was springtime, and a plentiful supply of quails was granted to Israel — as it had been granted a year before — not however, without entailing the dreadful punishment of a plague, which gave the place its name, "the graves of lust."

Out of this second murmuring there also arose an important institution. In presence of such widespread discontent, Moses had complained to God of the great burden he had to bear alone in leading the Hebrew nation, and had asked for relief. Jehovah granted the request of His faithful servant, and appointed seventy elders, to whom He imparted something of Moses' spirit, and who were to help him in the government of the chosen people, and it is to this appointment of seventy elders that the tradition of the Jews traces back the origin of the Sanhedrim, the supreme tribunal of their nation, and made up also of seventy members (Numb. xi).

Another severe trial befell Moses, when, in Hazeroth, his very brother and sister (Aaron and Mary) claimed an authority equal to his own. The Jewish lawgiver bore this new insult with his wonted patience, but Jehovah not only vindicated in words His chosen servant, He also struck Mary with a leprosy, which would have been permanent had not Moses successfully intervened in her behalf (Numb. xii, 1–16).

The last incident to be mentioned here in connection with this period is the spying of the Promised Land after the Israelites had reached Cades. Before attacking the Chanaanites, the Hebrews wished to know what sort of country lay before them, and whether its conquest was not too difficult, and, accordingly, one man from each tribe was sent to make a thorough examination of the land of Chanaan. After an absence of forty days, the spies came back, carrying on a staff, borne by two men, one cluster of grapes, of enormous size, as a proof of the fertility of the land, and reported at the same time that giants of the race of Enac occupied the country. Only two of the Jewish messengers, Caleb and Josue, represented the conquest of Chanaan as possible if an immediate attack was made, and, in consequence, the multitude, giving themselves to despair, openly murmured against Moses and Aaron, and proposed to select a leader who would bring them back into Egypt. As the mutiny increased, Jehovah interfered, threatening to destroy utterly the rebels with pestilence, but, touched again by the entreaty of Moses, He announced that the chosen people, as a people, would indeed be preserved, but that not one of the rebellious generation — save Caleb and Josue — should enter the land of Chanaan. They were condemned to die during a forty years' wandering in the Wilderness, and after a mad effort to evade this awful sentence by rushing against their enemies — Amorites and Amalecites combined — routed and discomfited, they had to resign themselves to their well-deserved fate (Numb. xiii, xiv; Deuter. i, 19b-45).

§ *2. The Wilderness and the Forty Years' Wandering.*

1. **The Wilderness of the Wanderings.** The desert through which the Israelites were now condemned to wander — whence its modern name of **Badiet et Tih,** or "Wilderness of the Wanderings" — occupies about one-third of the Sinaitic Peninsula. Its precise limits cannot

be determined; it is commonly admitted, however, that it was bounded on the north by the land of Chanaan; on the west by the River of Egypt, which parted it from the wilderness of Sur; on the south by a great sand belt, extending from the Gulf of Suez to the Gulf of Akabah, and forming the line of demarcation between it and the Sinaitic range; on the east by the Gulf of Akabah and the deep valley of the Arabah.

The principal divisions of this immense region are designated in Holy Writ under the respective names of the **Negeb** or **South Country** of Chanaan, the desert of **Pharan** (under which name the whole Wilderness of the Wanderings is also known), and the desert of **Sin**, probably the southeastern part of the Badiet et Tih. The general aspect of the Wilderness is that of a series of limestone plateaus ascending in successive steps from the Sinaitic range to the hill country of Southern Palestine. "To European eyes it is a blanched and dreary waste, intersected by water-courses, almost always dry, except in the rainy season, and crossed by low ranges of horizontal hills, which relieve but little the general monotony of its appearance. It does not exhibit the savage and frightful desolation of the Arabah; but neither is it enlivened by the fertile valleys to be found amid the granite mountains of Sinai.

"Its soil is mostly strewn with pebbles, through which a slight coating of vegetation struggles; yet here and there level plains may be found in it of rich, red earth fit for culture, or valleys abounding in shrubs and trees, and offering coverts for hares. It has been remarked that vegetation is readily produced wherever the winter rains do not at once run to waste. But this vegetation has probably been long on the decrease, and is still decreasing, principally from the reckless destruction of trees for charcoal, and the aspect of the Wilderness has been proportionately deteriorated" (The Speaker's Bible, vol. i, part 2, p. 685).

2. **The Forty Years' Wandering.** It was not the original purpose of God that the Israelites should spend long years in the Wilderness before conquering the land of Chanaan (cfr. Deuter. 1, 21, 26, sq.), but their conduct at Cades had shown how little they were worthy of entering at once upon their inheritance. Their very sending of spies to explore the land of Chanaan implied a great distrust of God's goodness and power, and their despair, together with the acts of positive disobedience to Moses and to God, which followed the report of the spies, clearly proved that, although selected by Jehovah as His covenanted people, they were yet but hordes of slaves, so utterly unable to appreciate their dignity and privileges as to be ready to set at naught all the past mercies of God and all His glorious promises regarding the future, by entertaining the project of going back into the land of Egypt. Their unworthy conduct well deserved the awful punishment which awaited them in the Wilderness, and which was to be a solemn warning to their immediate descendants. Finally, whilst these descendants would thus learn to fear Jehovah, to desire the fulfilment of His promises to their forefathers, their very life in the Wilderness would fit them for undertaking, in due time, the conquest of the Holy Land.

For these, and other such reasons, the children of Israel were condemned to wander 40 years — this is, however, simply a round figure for their actual 38 years of wandering — in the Wilderness. The road they followed during this long period is almost entirely unknown, for nearly all the 18 stations which are enumerated in the book of Numbers (chap. xxxiii, 18-35) cannot be identified even with probability. Opinions vary also concerning the character, time and general locality of these encampments, and only the following points can be regarded as probable in reference to them. The stations named in the book of Numbers (xxxiii) are likely enough, only those headquarters where the Tabernacle was pitched, and where Moses and the priests encamped, while the main body of the Israelites was scattered in various directions. Again, these stations belong most likely, not to the journey of Israel from Sinai to Cades, already described, but to the period of wandering whose starting-point and terminus was Cades on the southern border of Chanaan. Finally, most of these stations were made by the children of Israel in the Badiet et Tih, rather than in the tract between this desert and the eastern shore of the gulf of Akabah.

The student of the Bible will easily notice that the sacred writer deals with this considerable period of Jewish history in pretty much the same reticent manner as he dealt with the much longer period of Israel's sojourn in Egypt, apparently because in both these periods nothing of great importance occurred either on the part of the Israelites or on the part of God. Besides, of course, the present sojourn of the Hebrews in the wilderness was an inglorious time spent in expiating national unfaithfulness to Jehovah, and consequently hardly deserving more than a passing mention, after God's dealings with His chosen people had been amply shown both just and merciful by the detailed account of Israel's most unworthy conduct in Cades.

It is not difficult, however, conjecturally to picture to ourselves the conditions in the midst of which the children of Israel spent the 40 years of their wanderings. The people naturally spread themselves widely in search of pasture for their flocks and herds from which they drew — as do the Arabs of the present day whom they undoubtedly resembled in their mode of life — ample means for their sustenance. They would also buy provisions from the neighboring tribes (cfr. Deuter. ii, 26-29) or from the caravans which crossed the desert on their way to Egypt. Perhaps the soil of the Et Tih was then in many places much more fertile than it is now, and they could easily tarry long enough in one place for sowing and reaping; finally, they certainly had during this long period the miraculous help of the manna. But, whilst they thus adapted themselves to what may be called a Bedouin life, by a reversion to the patriarchal, that is to the nomad, traditions of their race, it is most likely that they lost much of that knowledge of the industrial arts which they had acquired in the land of the Pharaohs.

Finally, from the few incidents which the sacred narrative has preserved to us regarding this nomadic life of the Hebrews, it may readily be inferred that they also persevered in their murmuring frame of mind, and that, at times, they were severely dealt with by Jehovah (cfr. Numb. xvi, xvii).

# SYNOPSIS OF CHAPTER XI.

## GEOGRAPHY OF PALESTINE.

I. VARIOUS NAMES:
- *Palestine:* The most common; origin.

II. SITE AND SIZE:
- A. *Site:* Latitude and longitude. — Boundaries. — Admirable situation.
- B. *Size:* Length. — Breadth. — Total area.

III. GENERAL ASPECT AND DIVISIONS.

IV. PHYSICAL DESCRIPTION OF
- 1. *Eastern Palestine:*
  - The high table-land beyond Jordan.
  - Rivers and mountains.
  - Pastoral character of the Transjordanic region.
- 2. *Western Palestine:*
  - Three long Parallel tracts:
    - Sea-coast.
    - The hilly country.
    - The Jordan valley.
  - Mountains: begin in the South and proceed Northward.
  - Lowlands: (three principal).
  - Rivers: Only one; streams or torrents.
  - Lakes.

# CHAPTER XI.

### GEOGRAPHY OF PALESTINE.

1. **Various Names.** Palestine, whose conquest the children of Israel were about to undertake, has in different ages been designated by the following names: (1) the land of **Chanaan**; (2) the land of **Promise**; (3) the land of **Israel**; (4) the land of **Juda** or **Judæa**; (5) the **Holy Land**; (6) **Palestine**. This last, by far the most common name, was originally applied by the Hebrews merely to the strip of maritime plain inhabited by their encroaching neighbors; but ultimately it became the usual appellation for the whole country of the Jews.

2. **Site and Size.** Although the extent of Palestine varied considerably in the different periods of Jewish history, it may be said that the region where the children of Israel settled was probably comprised between the 31° and 33° 20′ of north latitude, and between the 34° 20′ and 36° 20′ of east longitude. The country within these limits was bounded on the west by Phenicia and the Great or Mediterranean Sea; on the south by the Brook of Egypt, the Negeb, the south end of the Dead Sea and the Arnon River; on the east by Arabia; on the north by Anti-Lebanon, Lebanon and Phenicia. Its situation in the temperate zone, in the centre of the ancient world, has often been admired; it combined, with a sufficient isolation from heathen influences, a position well suited to the preservation and spread of the true religion among mankind.

As many countries which have played a great part in the world's history, Palestine is a very small country. Its average length is about 150 miles, and its average breadth west of the Jordan a little more than 40 miles, east of the Jordan a little less than 40 miles. The total area between the Jordan and the Great Sea is about 6,600 square miles; the portion east of the Jordan has an area of about 5,000 or perhaps 6,000 square miles, — making the whole area of Palestine 12,000 or 13,000 square miles, or about equal to the two States of Massachusetts and Connecticut together.

3. **General Aspects and Divisions.** A single glance at a physical map of the Holy Land is quite sufficient to make us realize that its general aspect is that of a mountainous country. It owes this hilly appearance to the great Lebanon range, whose eastern branch (the Anti-Lebanon) is prolonged through Palestine by two distinct chains of mountains, the one to the west, with the exception of one broad depression, extending as far as the Desert of Sinai, the other to the east, reaching as far as the mountains of Arabia Petræa (cfr. STANLEY, Sinai and Palestine, chap. ii). To the west of each one of its mountain-chains Palestine has one large plain, namely, the valley of the Jordan and the sea-coast, so that the Holy Land is naturally divided into four long parallel tracts extending north and south. Three of these parallel tracts are almost entirely situated to the west of the Jordan and are usually designated under the name of **Western** Palestine, whilst the tract altogether east of the Jordan, is known as **Eastern** Palestine or the **Transjordanic** region.

4. **Physical Description of Eastern and Western Palestine.** The region beyond Jordan consists in a table-land whose length is about 150 miles from the Anti-Lebanon on the north to the Arnon River on the south, and whose breadth varies from 30 to 80 miles from the edge of

the Jordan valley to the edge of the Arabian desert. Its surface, which is tolerably uniform, has an average elevation of about 2,000 feet above the level of the sea, and whilst its western edge is broken by deep ravines running into the valley of the Jordan, its eastern edge melts away into the desert.

Eastern Palestine has three natural divisions marked by the three large rivers which cut it at right angles to the Jordan — the **Arnon**, the **Jaboc** and the **Yarmuk**. Across the norhernmost of these divisions, which extends from Anti-Lebanon to the Yarmuk, "the limestone which forms the basis of the country is covered by volcanic deposits. The stone is basalt, the soil is rich, red loam, resting on beds of ash, and there are vast "harras" or eruptions of lava, suddenly cooled and split open into the most tortuous shapes. Down the edge of the Jordan valley and down the border of the desert run rows of extinct volcanoes. The centre of this northern province is a great plain, perhaps fifty miles long by twenty broad, scarcely broken by a hill, and almost absolutely without trees. This is Hauran proper. To the west of this, above the Jordan, is the hilly and once well-wooded district of Jaulan (Golan of Scripture); to the east the "harras" and extinct volcanoes already noticed; and in the southeast, the high range of Jebel Hauran. All beyond is desert draining to the Euphrates" (G. A. SMITH, The Historical Geography of the Holy Land, 1897, p. 534).

In the second division of Eastern Palestine, which extends from the Yarmuk to the Jaboc rivers, the volcanic elements almost entirely disappear and the limestone comes into view again. The surface of the oountry is generally made up of high ridges covered with forests and furnishing rich pasturage; eastward, however, there are plains covered with luxuriant herbage.

The third division of the Transjordanic region lies between the Jaboc and the Arnon rivers. In it "the ridges and forests alike diminish, till by the north of the Dead Sea the country assumes the form of an absolutely treeless plateau, in winter bleak, in summer breezy and fragrant. This plateau is broken only by deep, wide, warm valleys like the Arnon, across which it rolls southward; eastward it is separated from the desert by low rolling hills" (SMITH, Ibid, p. 535).

The principal ranges of mountains are those of Basan and those of Galaad, the latter of which include the following mountains named in Scripture: (1) the Abarim (Numb. xxvii, 12; xxxiii, 47, 48), (2) Mount Phasga (Numb. xxi, 20; xxiii, 14, etc.); (3) Mount Nebo (Deuter. xxxii, 4; xxxiv, 1); (4) Mount Phogor (Numb. xxiii, 28; xxv, 18, etc.).

Of the two great divisions of the Holy Land, Eastern Palestine was unquestionably the better fitted for pastoral pursuits, and this is why it became the share of the two main pastoral tribes of Israel even before the conquest of the country west of the Jordan was attempted; this is why also "so large a part of the annals of Eastern Palestine is taken up with the multiplying of cattle, tribute in sheep and wool, and the taking of spoil by tens of thousands of camels and hundreds of thousands of sheep" (SMITH, ibid, p. 524).

The region west of the Jordan, or Western Palestine, by far the most important in Jewish history, is naturally divided into three long parallel tracts extending north and south:

(1) **Sea-Coast.** This tract is a plain, the main portion of which extends without a break from the desert below Gaza to the ridge of Mount Carmel. A great part of this plain is flat and naturally fertile. It is intersected by deep gullies, which have high earthen banks, and through some of which flow perennial streams. The neighborhood of these streams is marshy, especially towards the north. This main portion of the maritime plain is some 80 miles long and from 100 to 200 feet above the sea, with low cliffs near the Mediterranean; towards the north it is 8 miles, and near Gaza 20 miles broad. North of the headland of the Carmel, which

comes within 200 yards of the sea, is the second and narrower portion of the maritime plain extending to Phenicia through the territory of Acre; very near this town the plain has an average width of about five miles and is remarkably fertile.

(2) **The Hilly Country.** Next to the coast-plain eastward comes the high table-land, which gives to Western Palestine the aspect of a hilly region. This tract is about 25 miles wide, and its eastern slopes are extremely steep and rugged. The fertility of this highland region improves gradually as one goes northward.

The southern district below Hebron is mostly made up of barren uplands. Passing a little farther north into what was called later **Judæa**, we find the central and northern parts of the hilly country scarcely more fertile, for the soil is poor and scanty, and springs are very rare; its western and northwestern parts being reached by sea-breezes offer a better vegetation, olives abound, and some thickets of pine and laurel are to be noticed; the eastern part is an unhabitable tract known as the Wilderness of Judæa.

Passing northward from Judæa to the central section of Western Palestine, the **Samaria** of later days, the country gradually opens and is more inviting. Its rich plains become gradually larger; the valleys are tillable and possess springs; there are orange-groves and orchards; the mountains are still bare of wood; northwest of Nablous, however, the slopes are dotted with fields of corn and tracts of wood.

Proceeding northward, we reach the northernmost division of Western Palestine, so well known under the name of **Galilee,** and where we find the plain of Esdrælon, 15 square miles in extent. The vegetation is more luxuriant here than elsewhere west of the Jordan, and springs are abundant. The hills are richly wooded with oaks, maples, poplars; covered with wild flowers, rich herbage, etc. East of these hills is the rounded mass of Mount Tabor, covered with oaks and contrasting with the bare slopes of the Little Hermon about four miles distant to the southwest. North of Tabor is the plain El Buttauf, of a similar nature to that of Esdrælon, but much more elevated.

(3) **The Jordan Valley.** This valley extends from the base of Mount Hermon to the southern shore of the Dead Sea. Its width varies from one-half a mile to five miles; at some points it is 12 miles broad. At the foot of Mount Hermon this valley is about 1,000 feet above the sea; 12 miles below, it is upon the sea-level; 10 miles farther south it is still lower by 692 feet; and 65 miles farther, at the Dead Sea, it is 1,292 feet below the level of the Mediterranean. The mountains on either side reach a great altitude, some points being 4,000 feet high. These heights combined with the deep depression of the valley, afford a great variety of temperature, and bring into close proximity productions usually found widely apart.

**Mountains, Lowlands, Rivers and Lakes, of Western Palestine.** Along the coast, the only mountain of importance is the ridge of Carmel, the highest point of which is about 1,750 feet. In the hilly region, the best-known points of elevation are: Hebron, 3,000 feet; Mount Olivet, 2,600 feet; Mounts Ebal and Garizim, 3,000 feet; Little Hermon and Tabor, 1,900 feet.

The three principal lowlands are: (1) the Maritime plain subdivided into Philistia, the plain of Saron and the plain of Acre; (2) the plain of Esdrælon; (3) the valley of the Jordan.

The most important river of Palestine is the **Jordan**. At the junction of its three principal sources it is 45 feet wide and flows in a channel from 10 to 20 feet below the level of the plain. It traverses successively the lakes of Merom and Genesareth, and empties itself into the Dead Sea after an actual course of 260 miles, although the distance between its source and the Dead Sea is not more than 136 miles in a straight line. Its width varies from 45 to 180 feet, and its depth from 3 to 12 feet.

Three things are chiefly noticeable in connection with this river, namely: (1) its enormous fall of nearly 3,000 feet; (2) its endless windings; (3) the absence of towns on its banks. The other streams of Western Palestine worthy of mention are, the **Leontes**, the **Belus**, the **Cison** and the **Zerka**.

The three principal lakes are the lake of **Merom**, the lake of **Genesareth**, and the **Dead Sea**.

# SYNOPSIS OF CHAPTER XII.

## Conquest of Eastern Palestine.

**I. The Advance to Chanaan:**
1. *Manifold difficulties in the way of reaching Palestine from the South.*
2. *Circuitous Route followed by the Israelites.*
3. *Accompanying events:*
   - The death of Aaron.
   - The victory over Arad.
   - The Brazen Serpent.

**II. Conquest of the Region East of the Jordan:**
1. *Political divisions* (The Kingdoms of Og and Sehon).
2. *Rapid Conquest by the Israelites:*
   - Kingdoms north of the Arnon River conquered.
   - Moab and Madian (History of Balaam).
3. *Settlement:*
   - By whom made?
   - Under what conditions?
   - With what subsequent results?

**III. The Last Days of Moses.** — His Character.

[117]

# CHAPTER XII.

#### CONQUEST OF EASTERN PALESTINE.

§ *1. The Advance to Chanaan.*

1. **Manifold Difficulties in the Way of Reaching Palestine from the South.** In the beginning of the fortieth year of their wanderings, the hosts of Israel were encamped again at Cades, on the southern border of Palestine. At this place Mary, the sister of Moses, died; here also the great Jewish leader, when causing water to flow from the rock, distrusted the Divine assistance, and because of this, received the sentence that he should not bring the nation into the land of Chanaan (Numb. xx, 1–13). But, although thus deprived of the hope he had so long cherished, namely, that of entering the Holy Land and that of leading into it the chosen people, Moses did not for a moment shrink from doing all in his power to bring the Israelites nearer and nearer their inheritance. He did not think it prudent, however, to attempt an invasion into Chanaan from the south, because many formidable difficulties forbade such an attempt at this time. Directly north of the Jewish camp lay the lofty mountains of Southern Palestine, inhabited by warlike tribes which could no longer be surprised by a sudden invasion, as was certainly possible when Israel reached the southern border of Chanaan for the first time. These various tribes would have the further advantage of defending defiles, with which they were perfectly acquainted, and of fighting on their own territory, the hills of which were protected by strong fortresses. To have attempted either of the narrow passes

which led into Southern Palestine, besides the difficulty of transporting baggage and driving the flocks and herds, would have exposed the Israelites to the danger of being cut off by piecemeal, and, finally, the Philistines, who occupied the coast, might have fallen on their rear (F. G. HIBBARD, Palestine, p. 230, sq.).

For these, and other such reasons, Moses gave up all project of reaching Palestine from the south, and determined to make a circuit, to pass round the Dead Sea and cross the Jordan into the richest and least defended part of the Holy Land.

2. **Circuitous Route Followed by the Israelites.** The Jewish leader had all the more willingly adopted this method of advancing towards Chanaan, because on their way eastward the children of Israel would have to traverse the territories of Edom, Moab and Ammon, who all three were connected by descent with the chosen people, and who, he had every reason to hope, would show themselves friendly to him and his hosts, since he only wished to pass quietly through their territory. But the permission he had asked to cross the mountainous tracts of Edom was refused with a great display of force, to be used if needed (Numb. xx, 14—21).

Thus denied the most direct route towards the country east of the Jordan, the Israelites were forced to journey southward down the Arabah towards the Gulf of Akabah, or eastern arm of the Red Sea, and then make a long circuit round the territory of Edom; the whole extra journey thus imposed on them was probably not less than one hundred and fifty miles. On their way they reached Mount Hor, where they delayed thirty days, and after encamping at the eastern end of the Red Sea, rounded the southern possessions of the Edomites. Thence they marched northwards, skirting the eastern frontier first of Edom and next of Moab, and, finally, encamped over against the Arnon River, which then, as ever, marked the southern limit of Eastern Palestine.

3. **Accompanying Events.** Of the many events which must have accompanied this long circuitous advance of the Hebrews towards Chanaan, only three, because of their especial importance in Jewish history, are recorded in the book of Numbers (chaps. xx, xxi). The first was the death of Aaron, the first Jewish high priest, at the age of one hundred and twenty-three years. He was buried on Mount Hor, a mountain which tradition identifies with the **Jebel Nebi Harun** (the mountain of the Prophet Aaron), which rises to the height of 4,350 feet above the level of the Mediterranean, and on the top of which Aaron's place of burial is still pointed out by the natives. As, however, the traditional Jebel Harûn is on the *east* side of Edom, it can hardly be the place where Aaron died and was buried, since Holy Writ clearly implies that the Israelites were still on the western border of the possessions of the Edomites, when this melancholy event occurred. It is, therefore, much more probable that the modern **Jebel Madurah,** on the western side of the Arabah, and at a comparatively short distance of Cades, is the actual Mount Hor, the more so because the actual place of Aaron's death and burial is called **Mosera** in Deuteronomy (x, 6). Upon the death of Aaron, his son Eleazar was solemnly invested with the insignia of the high priesthood, and regularly inducted into that most important office in Israel.

The second incident noted in the sacred narrative is the brilliant victory which the Israelites won over **Arad,** a Chanaanite king, who had attacked them on the borders of Edom. The importance of this event should be measured far less by the greatness of its actual consequences, than by the considerable change it denotes in the temper of Israel after the forty years' wandering. Differently from their conduct thirty.

eight years before, the Hebrews are now careful to call upon Jehovah before going to battle, and their actual success against Arad does not betray them either into a further advance into Chanaan, or into a conflict with Edom, when this nation so rudely refused them passage through its own territory, because they wished faithfully to comply with the Divine will, that they should pass by the borders of the Edomites without fighting against them (Deuter. ii, 4, sq.).

This does not mean, however, that the children of Israel had fully profited by their training in "The Wilderness of the Wanderings," for as we learn from the third event, which is recorded as accompanying their advance to Chanaan, their inveterate murmuring frame of mind awaited only peculiarly trying circumstances to show itself again. But their murmurs were severely punished; venomous serpents — which still abound, as travellers tell us, in the very neighborhood of the encampment of the Israelites — "bit them and killed many of them" (cfr. GEIKIE, Hours with the Bible, vol. ii, p. 396). As a remedy, Moses caused a serpent of brass to be made, "which when they that were bitten looked upon, they were healed." This brazen serpent, which became later an idolatrous object in Israel (IV Kings, xviii, 4), was the mysteuiors symbol of "the Son of Man lifted up like the serpent in the desert, that whosoever believeth in Him may not perish, but may have life everlasting" (John iii, 14, 15).

§ *2. Conquest of the Region East of the Jordan.*

1. **Political Divisions of Eastern Palestine.** At the time of Israel's encampment on the Arnon, the territory between this river and Mount Hermon was politically divided into two powerful kingdoms, whose common boundary was the Jaboc River. The kingdom to the north of that river extended northward to the foot of Mount Hermon, and was known as the Kingdom of Basan. This country, so famous

by its pastures, cattle and forests, was then crowded with cities and villages, and their ruins are not improbably those which, in the present day, attest to recent travellers present distress and former grandeur. The ruler over this vast and prosperous country was an Amorrhite king named Og, a man of gigantic stature, and whose huge iron bedstead was long preserved as a curiosity (Deuter. iii, 1-11). The second kingdom east of the Jordan included that territory between the Jaboc and the Arnon rivers, which an Amorrhite colony, come from across the Jordan, had recently wrested from the Moabites (Numb. xxi, 26, 29). Its ruler was King Sehon, and its capital the Fortress of Hesebon, whose ruins still exist about fifteen miles east of the northern end of the Dead Sea. (For details concerning recent discoveries east of the Jordan, see SELAH MERRILL; HERR SCHUMACHER, etc.)

The other political divisions east of the Jordan consisted of the distinct territories of Moab, Madian and Ammon, but as the Israelites were forbidden to conquer them, they lay beyond the territory promised to the chosen people, and consequently require here but a passing mention. The possessions of the Ammonites at this time lay to the east of the Kingdom of Sehon, being limited to the west by a branch of the river Jaboc, on which indeed their capital, Rabbath, or Rabbath Ammon, stood, whilst the territory of the Madianites extended far to the east and south of the Moabites.

2. **Rapid Conquest by the Israelites.** Whilst still camping outside the territory of King Sehon, the Israelites sent him a message, asking a peaceful passage through his territory, and promising the same regard for his possessions, which they had already promised to the Edomites. Sehon not only refused, but assembling his army, went forth to give battle against Israel. The battle was fought at Jasa (Jahaz, in the Hebrew Text), probably "in the southeast corner of Sehon's territory" (G. A. SMITH, p. 559). The

result was the total defeat of the Amorrhite king, and as a further consequence the capture of his capital and his walled towns, of his numerous flocks and herds, and even the possession of the entire country between the Arnon and the Jaboc rivers (Numb. xxi, 27-30).

Crossing the Jaboc, the Israelites pursued their victorious course into the Kingdom of Og. This prince having gathered his forces, resolved to encounter his enemies in Edrei (the modern Edhra), one of the most formidable strongholds of his dominion. Like the King of Hesebon, the King of Basan was utterly routed by Israel, and the result of this new victory of the Hebrews, was such a subjugation of the northern Amorrhite kingdom as to allow them to prepare freely for an invasion into Western Palestine [1] (Numb. xxi, 32-35; xxxii, 39, 41, 42; Deuter. iii, 1, sq.). For this purpose, they pitched their tents "in the plains of Moab, over against Jericho," that is in that part of Moabite territory which the Amorites had formerly wrested from Moab, and which Israel had recently conquered (Numb. xxii, 1). But whilst they were preparing to cross the Jordan at the fords nearly opposite Jericho, new and unexpected enemies arose on their rear.

These enemies were no other than Moab and Madian, tribes kindred indeed to Israel, but which now regretting that they allowed the Hebrews to pass unmolested on their borders, and fearing for their own independence so near a nation which had already conquered the mighty kings of the north, entered into an alliance against the Israelites. Their combined forces encamped on the heights of Abarim from which Israel's camp could be seen. Meantime Balac, the present King of Moab and a worshipper of Baal, wished to place his enemies under a divine curse, before attacking them. With this end in view, he sent elders both of Moab

---

[1] For a careful discussion of the difficulties concerning the historical character of the wars against Sehon and Og, see G. A. SMITH, Historical Geography of the Holy Land, pp. 560, sq., and also Appendix iii; see also R. KITTEL, A History of the Hebrews, vol. i, p. 228, sq. (English translation).

and Madian "with the price of divination in their hands" to Balaam, the most famous soothsayer of the time. This strange personage, whose real character has ever been a matter of discussion, and who, although living in Mesopotamia, had some knowledge of the one true God, refused at first to come and utter the curse required of him. Upon the reception of a second and more select embassy and of more brilliant promises, he, however, agreed to repair to Moab, with the express understanding that he should utter only what God would inspire him with. The episode of his ass's speaking to him, when on his way to Moab, is too well known to be detailed here; suffice it to say that the episode is clearly referred to as a historical event, in the Second Epistle of St. Peter (chap. ii, 16). After his arrival in Moabite territory, the famous soothsayer strove indeed by every means in his power to secure from Jehovah oracles against the chosen people, but, as it were, in spite of himself, he uttered a fourfold blessing upon Israel. (For the exact meaning and Messianic bearing of Balaam's prophetic utterances, see VIGOUROUX, Manuel Biblique, tome i; MEIGNAN, Prophéties Messianiques; TROCHON, Manuel d'Introduction à l'Ecriture Sainte, tome ii, p. 182, sq.)

After thus frustrating all the hopes of the King of Moab, Balaam withdrew without the promised honors and rewards, but not without giving to the enemies of the Israelites a counsel which proved most hurtful to the chosen people. Following his advice, the allied nations succeeded in seducing Israel to their impure and idolatrous rites, in punishment of which a plague broke out among the Hebrews and carried off upwards of 24,000 of them. Justice prompt and severe was meted out to the guilty Israelites, by Moses and the princes of the tribes, and especially by Phinees, the son of Eleazar, whose zeal was rewarded by the cessation of the pestilence and the promise of a perpetual priesthood in his family (Numb. xxii-xxv, 15; xxxi, 16).

And now a terrible vengeance was wreaked on the crafty Madianites; pursued into their own territory by 24,000 Israelites under the command of Phinees, they were utterly routed, their chiefs and all the male population were put to death; their cities were burned; their women and children taken captive; Balaam himself perished by the sword; and an immense booty divided between the combatants, the rest of the people and the sacred treasury in charge of the priests and Levites (Numb. xxv, 16-18, xxxi). In seducing the Israelites to idolatry, the Madianites had, in fact, instigated the people of God to rebellion against their lawful sovereign, and this is why they were so severely punished; that Moab was spared a like punishment, is probably due to the fact that Jehovah had already forbidden Israel to war against that nation, a prohibition not to be set aside so soon after it had been enjoined.

4. **Settlement in Eastern Palestine.** After these events, it was plain that no one could prevent the Israelites from settling quietly in the conquered kingdoms of Sehon and Og, if only Jehovah would permit them to do so. Accordingly, the pastoral tribes of Ruben and Gad — and afterwards the half-tribe of Manasses — asked of Moses, Eleazar and the elders that they might have for their possession the conquered land east of the Jordan, whose upland pastures were so desirable for their numerous flocks and cattle. To this petition Moses first strongly objected; but, on their promise of helping effectually their brethren in conquering Western Palestine, whilst their own families and flocks would settle east of the Jordan, the Jewish leader acceded to their request (Numb. xxxii; Deuter. iii, 18-20).

As might naturally be expected, the tribes of Israel which were allowed to occupy Eastern Palestine were destined to be greatly injured socially and religiously, because of their immediate contact with the pagan and wandering tribes of the great desert, and because of their separation from their brethren on the west of the Jordan. We see, for instance, that the children of the half-tribe of Manasses gave themselves up to idolatry, and that, together with Ruben and Gad, they were the first tribes transported into captivity (I Paralip. v, 23-26); but yet, for long centuries after their settlement, the Israelites who dwelt in the land of Galaad played an important part in the history of the Jewish nation (cfr. G. A. SMITH, Historical Geography of the Holy Land, p. 578, sq.).

§ *3. The Last Days of Moses. His Character.*

1. **The Last Days of Moses.** Whilst Israel encamped opposite Jericho, and as the time approached when the chosen people were to cross the Jordan to take possession of the land promised to the patriarchs of old, Moses was directed by God to ascend the Abarim mounts and to view from thence the Holy Land, into which he was never to penetrate. This direction, he understood, was the signal of his approaching death, and he accordingly prayed to God for a successor in his arduous office of leader of Israel. Josue was designated by Jehovah, and then presented by Moses himself to the whole nation as the one they should henceforth obey (Numb. xxvii, 12-23; Deuter. xxxi, 7, 8).

Another care of the Jewish lawgiver, conscious that his end was approaching, was to bid Israel by every means in his power to remain forever faithful to the worship of the one true God, and to observe all the ordinances of the law they had received through him, in order that they might enjoy the Divine blessings promised to faithfulness and avoid the terrible punishments wherewith disobedience was sure to be visited. This Moses did in three long discourses which are recorded in the first thirty chapters of Deuteronomy. In his first discourse he reminded the Israelites of God's past mercies to them since their departure from Sinai, and drew from this historical retrospect the practical conclusion that they should not forget their obligations to Jehovah, nor the great truths of His spirituality and perfect unity which they had been taught in Sinai. In his second address, Moses exposed the general Divine law which made of Israel a theocratic nation, together with a code of special laws which it was his particular object to expound and encourage Israel to obey; then he emphatically set forth the blessings and curses which Israel should expect according as it observed or violated these same Divine laws. The third discourse insists again upon the fundamental duty of loyalty to Jehovah and embraces (1) an appeal to Israel to accept the terms of the Divine Covenant together with a renewed warning of the disastrous consequences of a fall into idolatry; (2) a promise of restoration, even after the abandonment with which the nation had been threatened in the preceding discourse, provided Israel should sincerely repent; (3) the choice now set before the people between life and good on the one hand, and death and evil on the other (DRIVER, Deuteronomy, Introd., § 1).

After these pathetic exhortations the great lawgiver delivered the Book of the Law into the hands of the priests and elders of Israel, and next gave vent to his feelings in "an ode worthy of him who composed the hymn of triumph by the Red Sea" (Milman). Then having received the final summons for his departure, Moses pronounced a last prophetical blessing — similar in several ways to Jacob's parting blessing — after which he ascended Mount Nebo, from the summit of which his undimmed sight contemplated for the last time the vast territory so long promised by Jehovah as Israel's inheritance. There also he breathed his last, at the age of one hundred and twenty; but the place of his burial ever remained unknown, lest perhaps the Hebrews should be tempted to surround with Divine honors the sepulchre of their great liberator and lawgiver (Deuter. xxxi–xxxiv).

2. **Character of Moses.** It is no easy task briefly to point out even the salient features of the character of a man who, like Moses, appears in history in so many different capacities. Moses is at once the liberator, the lawgiver, the leader, the prophet, the historian of the Jewish nation, but above all he is the great "servant of Jehovah" (Deuter. xxxiv, 5; Numb. xii, 7; Exod. xiv, 31; etc.), for it was his unshaken fidelity to God which gave to his long and eventful life unity of purpose and firmness of action (cfr. Heb. iii, 5).

Because he is the obedient servant of God he undertakes the liberation of Israel, a work which he justly deemed so far above his natural abilities, and deals with Pharao precisely as bidden by Jehovah. As a faithful servant set over the house of his Divine Master, he is ever attentive to look up to Him for guidance and carries out constantly His least directions. As his sole object in life is to fulfil the great work intrusted to him — to train Israel to the pure belief in and faithful worship of the one true God, — he never courts popular favor, but represses every violation of the theocratic constitution with all promptness and energy, "and his leadership of the people is little less than a constant pleading to them of Jehovah's claims, of Jehovah's will to bless, and of Jehovah's power to punish" (RAWLINSON, Moses, p. 201). It is God's honor and glory that he has in view when he subdues his own quick temper so as to become the meekest of men, and when he loves the chosen people with such a fatherly affection as to offer himself a willing victim for their sins, and to intercede with God in their behalf when his own authority and devotion have been set at naught by Israel. He is not jealous of the prophetical gifts Jehovah may bestow upon others, and when the time has come he willingly passes over his sons, and assigns to a stranger his succession in the leadership of the Jewish nation.

In these, and other such respects, Moses was the beautiful

type of "a future prophet like unto him" (Deuter. xviii, 15, 18), of one who was to be the most faithful and meekest Servant of God, the Redeemer of the chosen people to whom He would give a higher law, train them during their journey through the wilderness of the present life for their future inheritance, and intrust the care of the Church He had founded to a visible shepherd.

As to the historical existence of Moses and his work, see KITTEL, History of the Hebrews, vol i, p. 238, sq., of English translation.

# SYNOPSIS OF CHAPTER XIII.

## Conquest of Western Palestine.

| | | | |
|---|---|---|---|
| I. THE INHABITANTS OF WESTERN PALESTINE: | 1. *Names and Origin.* | | |
| | 2. *Position in the Land* (probable extent of each tribe). | | |
| | 3. *Civilization:* | Arts of peace and war. — Social and moral life. | |
| | 4. *Religion:* | The worship of natural phenomena personified. | |
| | | Why so great a danger for the Israelites? | |
| | | Principal cause of order to exterminate. | |
| II. THE CONQUEST OF THE WEST OF THE JORDAN: | 1. *Invasion of Western Palestine:* | Crossing of the Jordan. | |
| | 2. *Successive Conquest of the* | A. Centre: | Jericho and Hai taken and destroyed. |
| | | | Scene at Sichem (Mounts Ebal and Garizim). |
| | | B. South: | The Gabaonites deceive Josue: their punishment. |
| | | | Victory over five confederate kings: (the sun and moon stand still). |
| | | | Various cities taken. |
| | | C. North: | Gathering of the other Chanaanæan kings. |
| | | | Their defeat at Merom; rapid conquest of their territories. |
| III. THE SETTLEMENT: | 1. *The Assignment of Land:* | Territories allotted to the twelve tribes. | |
| | 2. *Particular grants made to* | Caleb and Josue. | |
| | | The Levites (cities of Refuge). | |
| | 3. *The last days of Josue.* | | |

## CHAPTER XIII.

#### CONQUEST OF WESTERN PALESTINE.

§ *1. The Inhabitants of Western Palestine.*

1. **Names and Origin.** The aboriginal inhabitants of Western Palestine had long disappeared from that country when the Israelites invaded the Promised Land. They had given place to settlers, who, dwelling between the Jordan and the Great Sea, that is in a low country as compared with the high table-land beyond Jordan, were actually designated under the generic name of **Chanaanites** or **Lowlanders** (Exod. xiii, 11; Numb. xxi, 3). But besides this general name, the inhabitants of Western Palestine receive in various passages of Holy Writ referring to this period distinct names, which apparently correspond to the distinct tribes into which they were divided (cfr. Exod. xiii, 5; xxiii, 23; Deuter. vii, 1, etc.). Thus we read of the Hethites, the Hevites, the Amorrhites, the Jebusites, the Pherezites, the Gergezites, and the Chanaanites; whence it seems that this last name, besides being used in a wider sense to designate all the inhabitants of the country, was also applied, in a more limited sense, to a particular tribe west of the Jordan before the conquest.

Scholars agree generally that these distinct tribes were descendants of Cham, through Chanaan, as is apparently stated in Gen. x, 15-20 (cfr. also Gen. ix, 18, sq. and article **Chanaan**, in VIGOUROUX, Dictionnaire de la Bible). Some, however, have affirmed that they must have belonged to the Semitic stock, on the two following grounds: (1) they spoke a language very closely related to, if not identical with, Hebrew, since in all their intercourse with the Israelites there is no sign of the necessity of an interpreter (cfr. also Isai. xix, 18); (2) their chiefs, when overcome by Israel, found so easy a refuge among the Philistines, themselves a branch of the Semitic race, as to imply their common origin. It is easy to realize that these arguments are not necessarily conclusive against the Chamitic origin of the Chanaanites, who could acquire a knowledge of the Semitic language through their intermingling with the Semitic aborigines they had conquered, and who, in their own misfortune when defeated by Israel, could the more easily obtain a refuge among a nation of a different race, such as the Philistines, because Philistines and Chanaanites had lived long in amity and side by side in Western Palestine. Furthermore, the Chamitic origin of the Chanaanites seems well established by ancient traditions which affirm that they had migrated from the Chamitic settlements in the neighborhood of the Persian Gulf (cfr. HERODOTUS, History, book i, chap. i, § 1), and more particularly by the recently discovered "inscriptions which represent the Hethites as the dominant Scythic (and consequently Chamitic) race which gave way slowly before the Aramean Jews and the Phenician immigrants" (FAUSSET, Biblical Cyclopædia, art. Chanaan).

2. **Position in the Land.** As might naturally be expected, the seven Chanaanæan tribes mentioned above followed, to a large extent, the physical divisions of Western Palestine. A tribe or group of tribes dwelling in the lowlands of the country naturally received the name of Chanaanites, whilst the tribes occupying the highland districts were called Amorrhites, that is highlanders (cfr. Numb. xiii, 30).

Outside this general correspondence of the tribal divisions with the physical divisions of the land, little can be said with certainty about the exact position of the tribes of Chanaan at the time of the conquest of Western Palestine by Israel. One of the most important among those tribes were the **Amor-**

rhites, called **Amaru** on Egyptian monuments, and who, at this time, possessed probably all the mountain region on the southeast of Chanaan. They were a warlike tribe which some time before had made the conquest of the east of the Jordan, and which, a little later, were "to straiten the children of Dan in the mountain" (Judges, i, 34, 35). In the plains of Western Palestine, that is, in the valley of the Jordan, in a large portion of the plain of Esdrælon and also in the sea-coast, were the **Chanaanites**, whose name remains yet connected with one place to the southwest of Hebron (cfr. Numb. xiii, 30, and Josue xi, 3). Often named along with, yet as distinct from, the Chanaanites, are the **Pherezites**, who lived also in the plains, probably in the high plains under the range of Carmel (Josue xvii, 15, sq.). The **Hevites** formed apparently a confederacy of towns in the vicinity of Gabaon (Josue ix), and occupied the country under Mount Hermon (Josue xi, 3; Judges iii, 3). The **Jebusites** are best known in connection with the mountain fortress of Jebus, whilst of the **Gergesites** so little is known that some have assigned them a position in the west of Phenicia, and others, to the east of the Sea of Galilee. The last tribe of which we have to speak here is that of the **Hethites**, upon whom much light has been thrown by recent discoveries. In the most remote antiquity, they formed an immense empire whose chief towns were Cades on the Orontes and Charcamis on the Euphrates (Josue i, 4), and which for long centuries proved a most powerful rival of both Egypt and Assyria. It is not unlikely that the **Hethites** to whom Holy Writ refers were but a portion of this mighty people, which, after long conflicts with Egypt, had remained in Chanaan (cfr. SAYCE, Races of the Old Testament, chap. vii).

3. **Civilization.** We have only scanty data respecting the civilization of Chanaan at this time, but they all point in the same direction, that of a high development of material

prosperity. The tribes on the sea-coast were devoted to commerce, and became so well known in that line that in later days the name of "Chanaanites" was regarded as synonymous of "merchant." The report made by the twelve spies sent by Moses during Israel's first encampment at Cades (Numb. xiii, 18-34), together with the abundant crops which fell into the hands of the Hebrews at the time of the conquest (Josue xxiv, 13), gives us an insight into the fertility and culture of the soil at that time. On the other hand, the fact that one of their cities was called **Cariath-Sepher**, that is "the city of books" (Judges i, 11), joined to the numerous hieroglyphic inscriptions of the Hethites which have been recently discovered, proves that reading and writing were in use among them. They appear also as a warlike people dwelling in cities with walls and gates (Josue x, 20; etc.); they had fortresses upon the heights and their numerous iron chariots were irresistible (Josue xi, 4; xvii, 16; Judges i, 19; iv, 3). This view of their high civilization and prosperity is confirmed in a striking manner by the varied and lavished booty which the Egyptians took from the Hethites and represented on their own monuments, and by the triple list of the 118 towns of Chanaan lately found in an Egyptian temple at Karnak (cfr. GEIKIE, Hours with the Bible ii, p. 53, sq.).

Over the various Chanaanæan clans or tribes reigned many "kings," or sheiks, as we would say (Judges i, 7), and whose authority was probably limited by that of elders (Josue ix, 11). But whilst their material prosperity was so great and their social life apparently well organized, their moral condition had reached a frightful degree of corruption because immorality of every description was encouraged, fostered and even imposed by their idolatrous worship.

4. **Religion.** It was, in fact, the infamous worship of Baal and Astarthe, in which the Israelites had already so

lamentably shared when on the confines of Moab, that the chosen people were destined soon to witness in its lowest and worst forms on the west of the Jordan. In the eyes of the Chanaanites, Baal and Astarthe were the two divine personifications of the quickening and producing power of nature. The former represented this power in its active form, and was, therefore, considered as a male god, probably identical with the sun-god; the latter represented this same power in its passive character, and was accordingly considered as the necessary female counterpart of Baal. Both were deemed equally worthy of divine honors, and whilst Baal was worshipped on the mountain tops, Astarthe was adored in the sacred grove not far off. But, of course, as the worship of the mighty power of nature considered simply as the origin of the beneficent, or, on the contrary, of the crushing and painful phenomena of the world, did not recognize or impose morality, it had rapidly degenerated, and at the time of the conquest by Israel, it allowed, or even required, such cruel and licentious rites as sacred prostitution, self-mutilation, human sacrifices, and particularly the offering of children as the most precious and propitiatory sacrifices. (For details about the Chanaanæan religion, see VIGOUROUX, Bible et Découvertes Modernes, tome iii.)

This was indeed a most revolting worship; and yet, strange to say, it proved, almost immediately after the conquest of Chanaan, a very great danger for the Israelites, despite the clear and awful denunciations of their law against all idolatry. They had the greatest difficulty in remaining faithful to the exclusive worship of the invisible Jehovah, surrounded, as they were, on all sides by nations — even by peoples of their own stock, such as the Moabites and Edomites — which were addicted to the magnificent worship of Baal, the more so, because it was the common persuasion of the nations of antiquity that whilst invaders should, of course, retain their own ancestral worship, they should also conciliate the favor of the gods of the country they had conquered. It is certain also that the sensual rites of the worship of Baal and Astarthe must have been for Israel powerful enticements to idolatry after their long sufferings and privations in the desert (cfr. Numb. xxv), and that, in many cases, intermarriages with members of idolatrous tribes naturally betrayed them into sharing their religion (Judges iii, 6).

To prevent the Jews, as a nation, from sinking into such gross idolatry, and thus forsaking their glorious mission of keeping alive the belief in and worship of the one true God, Jehovah wished ever to be represented as a *jealous* God, who regarded the simultaneous practice of His religion and of idolatrous worship not indeed as a divorce, but as an adultery. He forbade not only intermarriages with the utterly corrupted races of Chanaan, he also repeatedly gave orders that the chosen people should do away with every temptation to idolatry by exterminating the Chanaanæan tribes (Exod. xxiii, 32, 33; xxxiv, 12–16; Numb. xxxiii, 51–56, etc.).

§ 2. *The Conquest of the West of the Jordan (Josue i–xii).*

1. **Invasion of Western Palestine.** Soon after the death of Moses, Josue, an Ephraimite of tried valor and the successor of Moses in command and his imitator in faithfulness to Divine guidance, received an order from Jehovah which he at once communicated to Israel. They were to be ready, after three days, to cross the Jordan and begin the conquest of Western Palestine. This was indeed no easy task, for the Jordan had no bridge, no ford that could give passage to nearly two and a half millions of people; and then beyond were the warlike tribes of Chanaan with their formidable chariots and well-disciplined armies. Trustful, however, in God's assistance, Josue did not shrink from undertaking this twofold task, and he at once sent spies across the river to reconnoitre "the land and the city of Jericho." On their

return, they brought back to the Jewish commander the comforting news of the extreme terror with which the glorious victories of Israel east of the Jordan had struck the inhabitants of Western Palestine (Josue i, ii).

It was apparently on the fourth day (the tenth day of the first month of the fortieth year after the departure from Egypt) that the Israelites crossed the Jordan in a manner which the Sacred Text plainly represents as miraculous (cfr., for instance, Josue iii, 13, 16, 17; iv, 7, 18, 22-25). After this wonderful event, Josue encamped at Galgal, about two miles east of Jericho, and where, after undergoing the rite of circumcision, the children of Israel celebrated the Pasch, eating bread made of the corn of the land, and not of the manna, whose supply ceased entirely on the next day (Josue v).

2. **The Conquest of Western Palestine.** The news of the miraculous crossing of the Jordan by the Hebrews soon spread far and wide, and deprived the inhabitants of Chanaan even of their lingering hope that the swollen waters of the river would detain the invaders some time longer on its eastern banks (Josue v, 1). The city of Jericho, so near the Israelite camp, although very strongly fortified, was particularly and justly affrighted, for it was supremely important for Josue to secure the possession of this stronghold before penetrating into Central Palestine. Nevertheless, its king and valiant soldiers resolved to oppose the fiercest resistance; and there is no doubt that they would have long set at naught the efforts of the besieging Israelites had not Jehovah once more intervened miraculously in behalf of His people. Despite the various attempts made to account for the fall of the walls of Jericho by mere natural causes, such as the undermining of the walls, an earthquake, etc., it remains beyond question that the sacred writer intends to describe an event supernaturally revealed to Josue before its

occurrence (Josue vi, 2, sq.), and regarded by all at the time as the result of positive Divine intervention.

The capture of Jericho opened to the Jewish leader the important passes into the central hills, and he at once determined to make the most of this advantage. He, therefore, sent a select body of troops against the strong town of Hai, about ten miles northwest of Jericho, but to his great dismay the Israelites were repulsed. This first defeat seemed in fact to imply that Jehovah had already forsaken His people, and was calculated to greatly encourage the Chanaanites in their resistance against Israel, but fortunately it was promptly made up for. By a clever stratagem, Hai was soon taken and destroyed, and the road to a broad plateau in the centre of the country fully secured (cfr. G. A. SMITH, Historical Geography of the Holy Land, p. 263, sq.). From Hai, Josue marched northward to Sichem, some twenty miles distant, and there held the solemn ceremony of the Blessing and the Curse on Mounts Garizim and Ebal, as prescribed in Deuteronomy, chap. xxvii. On his return from this solemn ratification of the Covenant, he doubtless left a force at Hai to secure the passes, but his main encampment continued in Galgal, in the valley of the Jordan (Josue vii, viii).

After this rapid conquest of the centre of Western Palestine, there was a general uprising against Israel, and only the Gabaonites obtained peace by their well-known stratagem; but in punishment for their deception, they were condemned to perpetual bondage "in the service of all the people and of the altar of Jehovah." The desertion of Gabaon, which was then the chief city of the Hevite confederation, from what seemed to be the common cause of the tribes of Chanaan, aroused the indignation of five powerful kings of the south, who resolved at once upon its destruction. But whilst they were encamped before Gabaon Josue marched by night from his camp at Galgal, and surprised and routed them. This was the memorable victory of Gabaon, or Beth-

Horon (about four miles distant from Gabaon), for the full completion of which the Hebrew commander obtained from God that the sun and moon should stand still in the midst of heaven, a miracle differently explained by Biblical scholars. Many, among whom are reckoned some Catholic scholars, looking upon this passage of Holy Writ (Josue x, 12-15) as an extract from the poetical book of *Yashar*, or "the Just," have thought that it should be considered as a poetical figure, which introduces Josue as commanding the sun and moon to stop their course, and even asserts that the sun and moon obeyed the mandate of a man, simply to convey the idea that the Hebrew chief most earnestly wished a prolongation of the day to complete the destruction of his enemies, and that he actually destroyed as many of them as if the day had been really lengthened. Much more common than this bold construction of the passage in question is the view which sees in the Biblical narrative the historical record of an actual astronomical miracle, which, being of course very easy to the Divine Power, was all the more opportune at that time, because it proved convincingly to both Israelites and Chanaanites the superiority of Jehovah over the sun and the moon, the two great deities of Chanaan. Perhaps the best way of meeting the various objections which are urged against this second view of the sacred narrative is to consider the lengthening of the day as the result of a miraculous deviation of the rays of the sun and the moon, because this would not entail either the stopping of the earth, or disturbances in the heavenly bodies. (For further information see VIGOUROUX, Manuel Biblique; DEANE, Joshua, his Life and Times, pp. 82-87; etc.)

Following up his victory, Josue took and destroyed the seven cities and kings of Maceda, Lebna, Gazer, Lachis, Eglon, Hebron, Dabir, and did not return to his camp in Galgal before he had completed in one rapid campaign the conquest of Southern Palestine (Josue x).

There still remained to subdue the kings of the north, who, hearing of the defeat of the south, had rallied round **Jabin** ("the Wise"), king of Azor, a strong city probably to the northwest of the lake of Merom. Their troops were very numerous and plentifully supplied with horses and chariots, but they proved unable to resist the sudden attack of Josue, who routed them by the waters of Merom and pursued them as far as Sidon to the northwest. After this victory Josue took and burned Azor and subdued numerous northern towns, so that at the end of his third campaign he found himself practically master of the whole country between Mount Halak, at the ascent of Mount Seir, on the south, and Baalgaad, under Mount Hermon, on the north. A much longer time, however, was required for the reduction of the numerous kings who still held each his own city, and it is well known that even then the old inhabitants maintained themselves in some parts of the land despite all the efforts of Israel (Josue xi).

§ *3. The Settlement (Josue xii–xxii).*

1. **The Assignment of Land.** The main part of Western Palestine being now subdued, Josue, with the help of the high priest Eleazar and of the heads of the tribes, divided it among the nine and one-half tribes which had yet to receive their settlements (Josue xiii, 7). Before detailing, however, their particular lots, the book of Josue reminds us of two facts: (1) that the sacerdotal tribe of Levi was not to share in the division of the land, because "Jehovah, the God of Israel, Himself is their possession"; (2) that Moses had already ascribed to Ruben, Gad and the half tribe of Manasses their territories on the east of the Jordan, and on the occasion of this second fact, the inspired writer gives briefly the limits of the possessions of the two and a half Transjordanic tribes. **Ruben** had the southern-

most territory extending from the Arnon River, on the south, to a little beyond Wady Heshban, on the north, where it reached the possessions of Gad; and from the Jordan, on the west, to the eastern desert. **Gad** was included between Ruben, on the south, and about the middle of the land of Galaad, on the north; whilst it stretched eastward from the Jordan to Aroer. The half tribe of **Manasses** embraced the territory between Gad, on the south, and Mount Hermon and Damascus, on the north; and between the Jordan, on the west, and the Arabian desert on the east.

The country west of the Jordan was now divided between the nine and a half remaining tribes by casting lots before the Tabernacle, and their territories may be better given under the threefold division of (*a*) the **South**, (*b*) the **Centre**, (*c*) the **North**.

(*a*) **The South.** The four southern tribes were Simeon, Juda, Benjamin and Dan. The most southerly district was assigned first to the tribe of Juda, but afterwards the southwestern portion of this territory was given to Simeon, which thus became the southernmost tribe. Next to Simeon, on the north, was Juda, which extended across the whole Western Palestine from the Dead Sea westward to the Mediterranean, and from the territory of Simeon and the River of Egypt, on the south, to an irregular line starting from a little to the southeast of Jericho, passing south of Jerusalem and reaching the Mediterranean some four miles below Joppe. To the northeast of Juda was the warlike little tribe of Benjamin, with a territory of about 25 miles in length by 12 in breadth, bounded on the north by Ephraim, on the east by the Jordan, on the south by Juda, and on the west by the tribe of Dan. The last tribe of the south was that of Dan, whose fertile territory was so compressed between the northwestern hills of Juda and the Mediterranean, that later on they had to seek another home in the north of Palestine.

(*b*) **The Centre.** The central portion of Chanaan was

allotted to the two brother tribes of the house of Joseph, **Ephraim and Manasses.** The tribe of Ephraim, to whom Josue belonged, received the more southerly portion of this large territory; its possessions, about 55 miles in length and about 30 in their greatest width, extended as far south as within a few miles of Jerusalem. The rest of Central Palestine was given to the half tribe of Manasses, which, differently from their fellow-tribesmen, had waited for sharing in the division of the country west of the Jordan, and now obtained a territory stretching westward to the Mediterranean and the slopes of Carmel, but not quite reaching the Jordan River on the east.

(*c*) **The North.** The northern part of Chanaan, extending from Mount Carmel to the chains of Lebanon, was assigned to the four tribes of **Issachar, Zabulon, Aser** and **Nephtali.** The tribe of Issachar possessed the great and most fertile plain of Esdrælon, and extended from Mount Carmel to the Jordan, and from Mount Thabor to Engannim. The territory of Zabulon lay immediately north of Issachar, to the south of Aser and Nephtali and between the Sea of Galilee and the Mediterranean. The territory allotted to Aser extended probably along the sea-shore from Carmel to Lebanon, about 60 miles long and 10 to 12 wide; it seems, however, that out of this extent the Phenicians kept possession of the plain by the sea, whilst Aser had to be satisfied with the mountains. Finally, to the east of Aser was Nephtali, which reached north to the Leontes River, and east to the Jordan, the lake of Merom and the Sea of Galilee.

2. **Particular Grants made at the Time.** Independently of this general division of the land, certain distinguished persons, as Caleb and Josue, received grant of the particular territory they asked for. Caleb claimed for his part that special portion of the land of Hebron which Moses had promised him upwards of forty years before, and he as-

sured at the same time that he would make the conquest of it. Josue assented to Caleb's request, and the courageous warrior secured for himself by force of arms the territory he had wished for (Josue xiv). Josue himself received as his personal inheritance the place he had asked, namely: Thamnath-Saraa, in Mount Ephraim, a town probably identical with the modern Tibnneh, some fifteen miles northeast of Lydda (Josue xix, 49, 50).

Another special grant was made to the Levitical tribe, which, as we have seen, did not share in this allotment of Chanaan. Besides the tithes of the produce of land and cattle, and other sacerdotal dues already granted by Moses for its maintenance, this tribe especially devoted to the ministry of Jehovah now received from each tribe four cities and suburban pasture-lands, or forty-eight in all (Josue xxi). Among these were included the *Six Cities of Refuge*, three on each side of the Jordan, which were so wisely set aside to check the barbarous custom of blood revenge, which still exists among the Arabic tribes, and in virtue of which the kinsmen of a man put to death consider it a duty to avenge him by the death of his intentional, or even unintentional, murderer. Any one who had shed human blood could find safety and protection in these cities of refuge, under conditions carefully laid down in the Mosaic law (cfr. Numb. xxxv; Josue, xx).

3. **The Last Days of Josue.** The great military leader of the Jews was well advanced in years when he proceeded to complete the division of the conquered land, and probably he did not survive long the dismissal of the Transjordanic tribes in peace to their homes (Josue xii). During the last days of his career Josue enjoyed in his own estate in the Promised Land the peaceful rest he had so well deserved by his military services to Israel and his constant faithfulness to Jehovah. Yet he could not forget that his conquests,

however extensive, had not brought about the utter destruction of the Chanaanites, which had been ordered by the God of Israel. Hence, gathering one day all those invested with some authority in Israel, he reminded them of God's past favors to His people, of God's willingness to do away entirely with the remains of the conquered races, and pointed out to them that the means to secure this all-desirable object was a grateful and persevering faithfulness to Jehovah.

Apparently soon afterwards Josue convoked in Sichem an assembly from all Israel, reviewed before them the history of God's dealings with the Jewish race, solemnly bade them choose between Jehovah and the idols of the land, and obtained from them a public renewal of the covenant with their God. Then, as a memorial of their sacred promise, he set up a stone pillar "under the oak that was in the sanctuary of Jehovah," that is, probably, under the sacred oak of Abraham and Jacob, "and wrote all these things in the volume of the Law of Jehovah." The dismissal of this assembly was soon followed by the death of Josue, at the age of 110 years, and by his burial in the border of his possession in Thamnathsare (Josue xxiii, xxiv). His death deprived Israel of one of its most successful and most pious warriors; his influence upon his countrymen did not, however, vanish altogether with him, for we read that "Israel served Jehovah all the days of Josue, and of the ancients that lived a long time after him, and that had known all the works of Jehovah which He had done in Israel" (Josue xxiv, 31; Judges ii, 10).

About the discovery of the tomb of Josue by V. Guérin, see VIGOUROUX, Bible et Découvertes Modernes, tome iii.

# SYNOPSIS OF CHAPTER XIV.

## THE TIME OF THE JUDGES.

I. LENGTH AND OBSCURITY OF THIS PERIOD.

II. SOCIAL CONDITION:

1. *Within:* A return in general to the patriarchal life:
   - Tribal independence;
   - Family life;
   - Justice;
   - War;
   - Etc.

2. *Without:*
   - A. Further conquests.
   - B. Cohabitation with the heathens; intermarriages.
   - C. Successive periods of oppression and freedom.

3. *The Judges:*
   - Meaning of the title.
   - How recognized as military leaders?
   - Nature and extent of their power.
   - Length of their rule.

III. RELIGIOUS LIFE:

1. *Religious Organization:*
   - Lack of powerful unity.
   - Poverty of Levites.
   - High priests without influence.

2. *Idolatry:* Successive falls of the Israelites.

# CHAPTER XIV.

### THE TIME OF THE JUDGES.

#### § 1. *Length and Obscurity of this Period.*

1. **Length of the Period of the Judges.** It would be a hopeless task to undertake the accurate reckoning of the number of years between the death of Josue and the beginning of the judgeship of Heli. Time and again the numbers given for the duration of the different judgeships appear to be only round figures; and in fact, some scholars look upon the whole chronology found in the book of Judges as a systematic chronology, in which a generation is regularly reckoned at forty years. This hypothesis is rendered all the more probable, because it removes the apparent discrepancy which would arise if the figures supplied by the book of Judges were taken strictly and their total of 410 years compared with III Kings vi, 1, where we are told that only 480 years elapsed between the exodus and the fourth year of Solomon's reign; whereas at least 600 years should be admitted for this same interval if the figures mentioned for the different judgeships are strictly accurate. There is another way, however, of getting rid of this difficulty: it is to suppose that some of the oppressions and deliverances were in part synchronous; and this view for which are adduced Judges iii, 31, compared with ix, 1, etc., has numerous supporters in the present day, although it can hardly be denied that the chronology of the period as presented in the book of Judges is on the face of it continuous (MOORE, Critical Commentary on Judges, p. xl).

But even though we should admit as probable the synchronism of several oppressions, judgeships, etc., falling within this period, it would still remain impossible to tell *which* oppressions or judgeships were actually synchronous, *how far* "rest" enjoyed by some tribes coincided with the oppression undergone by the others, and to determine how many years elapsed between the death of Josue and that of the ancients of Israel who outlived him (Josue xxiv, 31 ; Judges ii, 7, sq.).

These and other such difficulties ever made it impossible to determine, with anything like certainty, the duration of the period of the judges. The ancient Jews, followed in this by Eusebius, simply added the years of oppression to those of the different judgeships, and thereby obtained for this period only 219 years. Some Catholic scholars of this century have admitted a still shorter duration, chiefly because of certain synchronisms with the annals of Egypt, and have reduced this period to about 160 years, and it must be said that the many notes of time found in the several narratives of the book of Judges seem rather to favor this shorter duration (cfr. Speaker's Bible, vol. ii, p. 119). The most common view, however, holds that the period of the judges lasted upwards of 400 years (see VIGOUROUX, Manuel Biblique, tome ii).

2. **Obscurity of the Period of the Judges.** The obscurity just noticed about the length of the period of the judges extends also to its events. These events were recorded at a time not far removed from their occurrence, and hence numerous details which were then so well known both to the writer and his readers as not to require a distinct mention, are now altogether unknown to us. To this first cause of obscurity we may add another, derived from the fact that the writer of the book of Judges intended to compose much less a history of the period than a thesis in which he would

prove by some well-selected facts that Israel's apostasy from Jehovah invariably resulted in national misery, whereas its conversion was invariably followed by Divine rescue from oppression and by national prosperity (cfr. Judges ii, 11, sq.). Accordingly, the facts he sets forth are not presented in those historical circumstances of time, place, etc., which, however necessary for our good understanding of this period of Jewish history, were really foreign to his purpose. But the main cause of obscurity will ever be the very peculiar government of the Hebrew commonwealth during this same period, for whilst "kings, priests, heads of tribes, etc., offer points of comparison with the same functionaries in other nations, *the judges* stand alone in the history of the world; and when we think we found officers resembling them in other nations, the comparison soon breaks down in some point of importance," and becomes almost useless (KITTO, Cyclopædia of Biblical Literature, art. Judges).

It must be added, however, that this obscurity is being gradually removed by a careful study in the Eastern countries themselves of the archæology, topography, public and private, social and domestic customs of the Arabic tribes (cfr. VIGOUROUX, Bible et Découvertes Modernes, tome iii).

§ *2. Social Condition during the Time of the Judges.*

1. **Social Condition Within.** The settlement of the tribes in their respective territories and the death of Josue without a previously appointed successor, brought to an end even the appearance of that supreme power and central authority which had prevailed in Israel under Moses and Josue. The scattered tribes did not care to invest any member of a special tribe with an authority superior to that of their own local officers, and in preserving their independence within their own territories they naturally came back to that simple social condition of their ancestors, which we have

already described under the name of the **Patriarchal Life**, and which is substantially that of the Bedouin tribes of the present day; each tribe had probably its hereditary authorities whose power was very limited because there were no new laws to frame, no functionaries to appoint and pay, no taxes proper to fix or collect, etc.

This simplicity of organization was also noticeable in domestic life. The father of a family was ruler over his household and the eldest son inherited his authority, whilst the women attended to all the details of the household. All lived on the produce of the field and of the flock, which produce was also occasionally exchanged with the busy Phenicians, or with passing caravans, for some rich cloth or jewels, or for arms, etc.

The administration of justice was also of the simplest description, for there were neither judges to dispense justice, nor police to guard the laws, nor court-houses for the trial of offenders. Cases were decided at the gates of towns by the elders of each community, and the sentence was carried out by those interested in its execution. It was also at the gates of towns and villages that private business transactions were ratified in presence of the inhabitants who acted as witnesses (Ruth iv, 1-12). In case, however, the elders could not settle a dispute satisfactorily, the Mosaic law had provided that recourse should be had to the priests.

Naturally, there was no standing army, no militia, so that in the event of a war, each man armed himself as best he could, and following the head of his village, repaired to the common rendezvous of the tribe. There was likewise no provision made for any protracted campaign, and military tactics were practically limited to the art of swift marches and sudden attacks (cfr. VIGOUROUX, ibid ; and GEIKIE, vol. ii, chap. xiv, which is little more than a translation of the chapter of Vigouroux on this question).

Finally, during the whole period of the judges, we would

look in vain for the national commerce, the flourishing industry and the culture of arts which were to exist under the monarchy, that is, when the Jewish people became again a national unit, not only in belief, but also in public life.

2. **Social Condition Without.** The imperfect conquest of Chanaan by Josue had left powerful enemies of Israel, even within the limits of the territories assigned to the different tribes, and according to God's designs the Hebrews were to conquer and destroy them. In point of fact, the opening chapter of the book of Judges makes us acquainted with the wars of conquest waged by Juda, Benjamin, the House of Joseph (that is Ephraim and Western Manasses) against the Chanaanites, the Jebusites, etc., and with the remissness of which several tribes were guilty in not destroying the old cities and inhabitants of Chanaan, because they deemed it more advantageous simply to make them tributary. It tells us also that Juda was not successful when it attempted to expel the lowlanders from its own territory "because they had many chariots armed with scythes," and that the tribe of Dan was actually compelled by the Amorites to forsake the plain of the sea-coast and to take refuge into the mountains.

The immediate result of this lack of concerted action in pursuing to the end the war of extermination, was the cohabitation of the Israelites with the remnants of the conquered races, that is, the very social condition against which Moses and Josue had repeatedly and strongly warned the chosen people, because they foresaw that truce and leagues with the heathen Chanaanites, would soon lead to intermarriages and these again to their natural consequences: idolatry, moral and social degeneracy (Judges iii, 5, 6).

It is the same lack of concerted action in Israel against its enemies, which accounts, at least partially, for the many periods of oppression and freedom which are mentioned in the book of Judges. If, as granted on all hands, the oppressions befell only a part of the land at a time, it was because that part of the land had been left by the other tribes to fight alone against the enemies who had invaded its territory; and again, if the oppression was done away with, it was when all, or at least several, tribes, combined their efforts under the guidance of a common leader to throw off the yoke which had been gradually imposed upon them. It was then, naturally speaking, the lack of a central authority capable of keeping grouped together and of directing effectively all the forces of the nation, which made the Israelites liable to be subjugated by their surrounding enemies, and which ultimately led them to ask for a king (I Kings, viii, 19, 20).

3. **The Judges.** From the foregoing remarks it is easy to gather the probable meaning of the title of *Judges* in connection with this period of Jewish history. It did not mean primarily, as this title would naturally suggest to our minds, one in charge of administering justice, except in so far as supreme judicial authority in the East belongs invariably to the one invested with the highest power in the land, and in so far as it is the office of a judge to free those who appeal to him from their oppressors, and to secure the punishment of these same oppressors. Beyond this, it is impossible to point out a connection between the Judges of Israel and the peaceful magistrates to whom we ascribe this title; and this is important to bear in mind, in order to be able to realize the sense in which such personages as Samson, Jephte, etc., could be called Judges: they freed the Israelites from, and avenged them of, their oppressors (cfr. Luke xviii, 3, 5).

"In nearly all the instances recorded, the appointment of a *Judge* seems to have been by the free unsolicited choice of the people. The election of Jephte, who was nominated as the fittest man for the existing emergency, probably resembled that which was usually followed on such occasions; and probably, as in his case, the judge in accepting the office, took care to make such stipulations as he deemed necessary. The only cases of direct Divine appointment are those of Gedeon and Samson, and the last stood in the peculiar position of having been from before his birth ordained 'to begin to deliver Israel' " (KITTO, Cyclopædia of Biblical Literature, art. *Judges*). It was then most likely, when the oppression had become unbearable, that popular choice or direct Divine appointment led to the recognition of a man as a military leader.

Of course only those who were willing gathered around him, under the immediate leadership of their own chiefs of villages, clans and tribes. His military power over such volunteers, like that of an Arabic sheik of the present day, depended mostly on their own will, or on his skill in the management of men. "If victorious, he could speak as a master, but before the battle he could do little more than persuade. It must not be thought, moreover, that the Judges ruled over all the tribes, at least up to the time of Heli and Samuel. None of them, except Othoniel, seems to have ruled over Juda and Simeon; Debbora is the heroine and prophetess only of the northern tribes; Gedeon is the liberator of the centre of Palestine; Jephte, of the districts beyond Jordan, and Samson does not appear to have had authority over even his own tribe of Dan, and appears as judge only because of his personal exploits against the oppressors of the Israelites" (GEIKIE, Hours with the Bible, vol. ii, pp. 509, 511; EWALD, History of Israel, vol. ii, p. 365, English translation).

Freed from their oppressors, the volunteers who had gathered around the military leader, naturally returned to their homes, and the judge usually ceased to rule, although his fame continued to command respect and guarantee peace, and his well-known skill and wisdom caused him to be consulted in all important matters, a fact which explains how in Debbora and Gedeon we see the indications of a rule for life. In Gedeon we find, indeed, a successful attempt at a regular monarchical rule which he even passed to his son Abimelech; but in the other judges, it is most likely that little besides their reputation passed to their children.

### § 3. *Religious Life during the Period of the Judges.*

1. **Religious Organization.** One of the natural consequences of the precarious and temporarily active rule of each judge over a limited extent of territory was the utter powerlessness of those Hebrew leaders to establish and maintain the religious organization described in the law of Moses. They were selected for the almost exclusive purpose of freeing a section of the country from oppression; for this sole purpose they were followed by volunteers, and they apparently never did much else in behalf of their countrymen. Had they tried to enforce upon *all* Israel the perfect unity of belief and worship required by the Mosaic law, they would have signally failed in their attempt, because, on the one hand, not even their fellow-tribesmen would have helped them in bringing about this religious condition throughout the land; and, on the other hand, it does not seem that, like Moses and Josue, they could reckon, in the event of a general desertion, on the direct intervention of Jehovah to vindicate their authority.

It is true that the Tabernacle had been erected in *Silo*, and that this sanctuary should have been a great rallying-point for all the tribes; but this town "was remote from many of them, and lay in the territory of Ephraim, a tribe disliked for its pride and selfishness, so that, in the general anarchy of tribal division and patriarchal rule, private altars were erected by individuals" (GEIKIE, Hours with the Bible, ii, p. 519). Nor was this lack of powerful religious unity made up for by the influence of the ministers of the sanctuary, for during this long period of transition between the wandering life of the desert and the fully organized civilization of later days, the priests and Levites of Israel seem rather to have had a precarious mode of existence. If we look upon the story of Michas, in Judges xviii, 13 *b*, sq., as illustrative of the condition of the Levitical order during this period — and this character of the episode referred to can hardly be questioned — it is clear that the public teachers of religion were then so inadequately provided for that they had to wander in different places to secure a living.

Finally, the high priests of the period, those supreme heads of the Jewish priesthood, whose chief duty was to watch over the religious life of the theocratic nation and to exert the strongest and widest influence upon the direction of the national worship, are not mentioned in that connection before the time of Heli. It may, of course, be admitted that the new line of high priests — the line of Ithamar, the youngest son of Aaron — to which Heli belonged, had had the greatest difficulty in being recognized by the people at large, and, in point of fact, the high priesthood returned later to the line of Eleazar (I Kings ii, 30-36 ; III Kings ii, 26, 27); but whatever the cause, it is plain that the high priest possessed but little public authority during the period of the judges.

2. **Successive Falls of the Israelites into Idolatry.** The social and religious disconnection of the tribes, which is so prominent a feature in this period of Jewish history, afforded to the Israelites a good opportunity for indulging the idolatrous tendencies they had inherited from their ancestors, by freely yielding to the influence of the heathen nations with which they were surrounded, and hence we read that time and again "they forsook Jehovah and served Baal and Astaroth" (Judges ii, 11, sq.). At first they probably combined the worship of Jehovah with that of the Cha-

naanæan deities, but gradually they embraced fully an infamous worship, which, by its pompous and sensual rites, appealed powerfully to the low and idolatrous instincts of their nature. Divine Providence, however, watched over them, and by alternations of freedom and servitude following upon their faithfulness or unfaithfulness in the service of the true God, not only prevented them, as a nation, from settling down permanently in idolatry, but also led them to consider Him as the only God of the land He had promised to the patriarchs of old.

Of course, it is conceivable that both the punishment with which Jehovah visited the idolatry of the Israelites and the deliverance which He granted to their conversion might at times appear to us simply the outcome of natural events; but there is no doubt that in both sets of events the chosen people recognized the immediate working of an angered, or, on the contrary, of a forgiving God, and that they repeatedly fell away from His pure worship only because they gradually lost sight of their good resolves and of His merciful dealings with them.

# SYNOPSIS OF CHAPTER XV.

### HISTORY OF THE JUDGES.

I. THE FIRST THREE JUDGES:
- Othoniel,
- Aod,
- Samgar.

II. DEBBORA: (Judges iv, v.)
1. *Oppression of Israel by the Northern Chanaanites.*
2. *Debbora and Barac* (Personages; Exploits; Canticle).

III. GEDEON:
1. *His Call and Mission* (Judges vi).
2. *Successive Victories:* He refuses to reign. The ephod an occasion of idolatry.
3. *Abimelech:* his son (cruelty; reign; death.) (Judges ix.)

IV. JEPHTE: (Judges x–xii.)
1. *Why and How made a Ruler by Galaad?*
2. *His Vow:* Questions connected with the immolation of his daughter.
3. *Quarrel with Ephraim* (Sibboleth).

V. SAMSON: (Judges xiii–xvi.)
1. *Peculiar Character of his Judgeship.*
2. *Chief Facts of His Life:* their historical character.

VI. HELI: (I Kings I Samuel i–iv.)
1. *The Rise of Heli:* The change of the priesthood. Union of priest and judge.
2. *Israel's Defeat at Aphec:* its consequences.

VII. EPISODES CONNECTED WITH THE TIME OF THE JUDGES (Judges xvii–xxi; Ruth).

## CHAPTER XV.

#### HISTORY OF THE JUDGES.

1. **The First Three Judges** (Judges iii). The Biblical notices of **Othoniel, Aod** and **Samgar,** the first three judges of Israel, however short, are not altogether devoid of historical interest. What the sacred narrative tells us of Othoniel, for instance, is in perfect harmony with the natural desire of the rulers over Mesopotamia to subjugate the land of Chanaan; and, in particular, it makes us aware of the fact that very soon after the death of Josue Israel began to be unfaithful to God, since the deliverer from foreign oppression was no other than the younger brother of Caleb. Again, what we learn from Aod, the second judge in Israel, shows us that the Moabites, cowed for a time by the rapid and wonderful success of the Hebrews, were again anxious to weaken those dangerous neighbors of the Moabite territory, and that for this purpose they deemed it again necessary to secure the help of other tribes, namely, the Ammonites and Amalecites (cfr. Judges iii, 12, 13, with Numb. xxii, 2-4). Again, in Aod, who treacherously murdered the king of Moab during an audience he had obtained from that prince, we find a striking sample of the barbarity of the age. Finally, in the exploit of "Samgar, who slew of the Philistines six hundred men with a ploughshare," we have probably an instance of the manner in which the victory of a body of men is simply ascribed to their leader (see an instance of the same kind in I Kings, xviii, 7).

2. **Debbora** (Judges iv, v). Far more formidable than either the Mesopotamian invader, or the Moabites and their

allies, or the Philistines, was "Jabin, the northern king of Chanaan." His general, named Sisara, had not only invaded the territory of the Hebrews, but even for twenty long years he had grievously oppressed them, and from his oppression no deliverance could be expected, except from the mighty arm of Jehovah, for the Chanaanæan oppressor had a large army and no less than "nine hundred chariots set with scythes." Then it was that the God of Israel came to the rescue of His people by inspiring a woman, the celebrated Debbora, to secure the deliverance of her fellow-countrymen. As a prophetess, she spoke in the name of Jehovah, and directed Barac — manifestly a leading captain of the time — to assemble troops, promising him victory and the encouragement of her own presence.

The first battle between Israel and the Northern Chanaanites was fought in the plain of Mageddo, a ground unfavorable for the manœuvring of the Chanaanæan chariots, and it ended in a complete victory for the people of God. Sisara, in his rapid flight, confidently took refuge in the tent of Jahel — the wife of Haber the Cinite, then at peace with the Northern Chanaanites — but, having soon fallen asleep, he was treacherously put to death by her. This glorious victory of Barac was followed by many others which are not detailed in the Biblical narrative, but which resulted in the utter destruction of the northern oppressors of Israel (Judges iv).

This same glorious victory was celebrated by the triumphant Canticle of Debbora and Barac, one of the oldest and finest odes contained in the Bible (Judges v). Although this poem presents many obscurities which are probably due to the imperfect textual condition in which it has come down to us, it is substantially a natural and straightforward description, first, of Israel's situation before the rising of the Israelites at the voice of Debbora and Barac (verses 6–8); next, of the actual rising of the tribes against their oppressors

(12-18); finally, of the victory won by Israel, and of its sequel, the death of Sisara (19-27) (cfr. MOORE, Judges, p. 127, sq.).

3. **Gedeon** (Judges vi-ix). The next judge of Israel of whom we read in the sacred text is Gedeon, who was miraculously called by God to free His people from the repeated and plundering invasions of the Madianites and other Eastern nations. This was a hard task, even for a most valiant man like Gedeon, and this is why he pleaded the poverty of his family in the tribe of Manasses to which he belonged, and his own lowly position in his father's house, in order to be relieved from this responsible and dangerous mission. As, however, he was promised Divine assistance, and received what he considered to be miraculous signs of his mission, he resisted no longer, overthrew by night the altar of Baal, which had been erected in his own village of Ephra, probably near Dothain, and gave bravely the signal of war against the oppressors of the land.

Thereupon, Madianites, Amalecites and other tribes crossed the Jordan, and encamped in the plain of Jezrael, an offshoot of the great plain of Esdrælon; and Gedeon, followed by numerous warriors of the tribes of Manasses, Aser, Zabulon and Nephtali, took position not far from the enemy. It was not, however, by means of these numerous troops that Jehovah wished to secure victory to His people, and by Divine command Gedeon put aside three hundred men only, whom he armed with trumpets, and with torches enclosed in pitchers which they broke, crying out, "The sword of Jehovah and Gedeon!" Surprised and panic-stricken, the enemies of Israel attack each other, and make in all speed for the fords of the Jordan, pursued by the rest of the troops of Gedeon. But before all the Madianites and Amalecites could cross the river, the inhabitants of Mount Ephraim took possession of the fords, and in a hard-fought battle defeated them.

They also made prisoners two leaders of Màdian, called Oreb and Zeb, whose heads they sent to the great Hebrew leader, rebuking him at the same time for not having called upon the men of Ephraim to fight the common enemies of the country. Gedeon appeased them "by one of those proverbial phrases which in the East serve for conclusive arguments" (SMITH, Old Testament History), and then pursued beyond Jordan the rest of the invading army under the leadership of Zebee and Salmana. Passing by Soccoth and Phanuel, places celebrated by their connection with the old patriarch Jacob, he met with a cruel refusal of supplies for his fainting soldiers, and threatened both places with signal vengeance at his return. A third victory crowned his arms, and Zebee and Salmana, overtaken in their flight, were made prisoners. Soccoth and Phanuel experienced the terrible vengeance of Gedeon, and Zebee and Salmana were put to death.

Grateful for this glorious deliverance, the Israelites offered to Gedeon the dignity of a hereditary king, which he refused with these noble words: "I will not rule over you, neither shall my son rule over you, but Jehovah shall rule over you." But whilst satisfied with the rank of judge, Gedeon asked of his soldiers the rings and other ornaments they had taken from the enemy, and he made with this spoil what seems to have soon become an object of idolatrous worship in Israel.

After the death of Gedeon, his half-Chanaanite son, Abimelech, persuaded his fellow-townsmen of Sichem, that, in place of the divided rule of his numerous brothers, he, *their bone* and *their flesh*, should have the supreme authority. To this the Sichemites agreed, and with the seventy pieces of silver they lent him from the treasury of the temple of Baal-Berith he recruited a band of outlaws, by whose means he did away with all his brothers — except the youngest, named Joatham — and was then crowned king in Sichem. His rule was marked by an attempt at a regular royal organization in

Sichem and the neighboring towns, and also by a cruelty which rendered him odious to his subjects. After a reign of three years, a rebellion, headed by Gaal, the son of Obed — a man otherwise unknown — broke out, and threatened Abimelech with a speedy death. The tyrant, however, was victorious in a battle against the Sichemites, took and destroyed their city and killed its inhabitants; he also set on fire the citadel of Sichem, suffocating and burning those who had taken refuge therein. But his cruelty was soon to come to an end, for if he was again successful in capturing Thebes, one of the neighboring towns, he met with an ignominious death when he attempted to set on fire its tower.

Thus perished the first man invested with the royal authority over a part of Israel; his cruel deeds were well calculated to make the nation at large hesitate before granting the same rank to any other man, and, in point of fact, Thola and Jair, who are represented in the Bible as his immediate successors, had only the title of judges, and they apparently did nothing great for their country, which might have secured for them an authority which Abimelech had reached with such cleverness and exercised with such cruelty (Judges x, 1-5).

4. **Jephte** (Judges x, 6-xii). The history of few judges is more generally known than that of Jephte, whose judgeship is next described in the sacred narrative. If his illegitimate birth and actual life of a freebooter commended him but little for the important function of a ruler in Israel, his well-known valor, joined to the awful straits to which his fellow-tribesmen were then reduced, prompted the tribes east of the Jordan to offer him the military leadership in the fight they were about to wage against the Ammonites. Jephte consented, but under the condition that, in the event of success, he should retain the supreme command, a condition which the inhabitants of Galaad joyfully accepted, for they

had already groaned eighteen long years under the most grievous oppression. His first step in assuming the command was to send an embassy to the King of Ammon, urging the Divine right of Israel to the land of Galaad. Of course these negotiations failed, and the only thing now to be done was to prepare for war. With this end in view, Jephte speedily gathered troops, and when on the point of beginning the campaign made a solemn vow to Jehovah, saying: "If Thou wilt deliver the children of Ammon into my hands, whosoever shall first come forth out of the doors of my house and shall meet me, when I return in peace from the children of Ammon, the same shall be Jehovah's, and I will offer him as a holocaust" (Judges xi, 30, 31).

Two principal questions have been agitated in connection with this vow, which Jehovah apparently ratified by granting to Jephte the greatest advantages over the Ammonites and the actual freedom of his country. The first question concerns the precise nature of Jephte's vow and of its fulfilment.

Since the Middle Ages, many Jewish rabbis and Catholic and Protestant interpreters have thought that Jephte never intended to offer a human sacrifice, but used, whilst making his vow, the word "holocaust" in a kind of spiritual sense, as denoting the completeness of consecration to God's special and perpetual service to which he would devote the first person of his household he should meet on his return. It so happened that it was his only daughter who was first to meet him, and, in virtue of his vow, he consigned her to a life of perpetual celibacy. Many plausible arguments drawn from the Mosaic law, which so expressly forbids human sacrifices, and of which Jephte must have been aware, from the manner in which the vow and its fulfilment are recorded, etc., have been set forth in favor of this opinion; yet it must be said that the plain meaning of the words used by this judge of Israel whilst making his vow and the unquestionable fact that a vow of perpetual virginity was then unknown to the Hebrews, prove that both the Jewish and Christian traditions, which were unanimous in this regard down to the twelfth century, admitted rightly that Jephte actually immolated his daughter in fulfilment of his vow; and this view is supported in the present day by many able scholars (cfr. for a good discussion, VIGOUROUX, Manuel Biblique, tome ii).

The second question connected with the vow of Jephte has been suggested by Rationalists, who have appealed to the actual immolation of his daughter by a judge of Israel as one of the many facts in Jewish history which would prove that human sacrifices in honor of Jehovah were a part of Hebrew worship from the time of Abraham (Gen. xxii) down to the time of Josias, in the seventh century before Christ. Whatever may be thought of the other Biblical passages which Rationalists adduce as proving their position — and which indeed are far from proving it — it is certain that a conclusive argument in their favor cannot be drawn from the present instance. We should far less consider Jephte as a representative worshipper of Jehovah in his quality of judge of Israel than as a freebooter who had suddenly become a Hebrew general, and had accordingly lost nothing of his barbarous and heathen ideas and feelings, so that it is only natural that, under the excitement of immediate preparation for battle, he should have imagined he would honor Jehovah by promising Him what he was wont to consider as most welcome to the gods, a human victim. It is only natural also, that success having crowned his efforts, he should feel in duty bound to immolate his daughter, a fact which from the tenor of the narrative was plainly an extraordinary event (cfr. JAS. ROBERTSON, Early Religion of Israel, 3d edit., p. 255), and should not consequently be regarded as a usual practice commanded, or even tolerated, in Hebrew worship (cfr. CHAS. ROBERT, Réponse à "l'Encyclique et les Catholiques Anglais et Américains," p. 41).

Like Gedeon, Jephte had to listen to the loud complaints of the Ephraimites for not having called upon them to fight against the Ammonites, but returned a very different answer. A war ensued, in which the men of Ephraim were entirely routed in a great battle east of the Jordan. All those who rushed to cross the fords of the Jordan found them guarded by the soldiers of Jephte, and were unmercifully put to death whenever they failed in uttering the correct sound of *sh* in the word *Shibboleth*, and thus betrayed their Ephraimite origin.

Jephte continued to "judge Israel" up to the end of his life, and was succeeded by three judges, of whom the Bible has preserved little besides their names (Judges xii, 7-15).

5. **Samson** (Judges xiii–xvi). The most formidable oppressors of the Israelites towards the close of this period were the Philistines, who, apparently, had been recently reinforced by immigrants from the island of Crete (cfr. PELT, vol. i, p. 326, footnote 2), and who, in their efforts to enlarge their territory eastward, had gradually reduced a part of Israel to servitude. Long years elapsed before the deliverance of God's people from their powerful oppressors was even begun by Samson, a man whose adventures, as recorded in the Bible, differ so much from the facts which are narrated respecting the other judges of Israel, and bear, apparently, so close a resemblance to the deeds of the mythological heroes of Greece and Rome. Differently from all the judges of Israel already mentioned, his birth and special mission were distinctly foretold to his parents, and differently from Aod, Debbora and Barac, Gedeon and Jephte, he never appears as a military leader who puts to flight the armies of the oppressors of Israel, but is rather "a solitary hero endowed with prodigious strength, who in his own quarrel, single-handed, makes havoc among the Philistines," so that

it is not easy to see "in what sense he can be called a judge at all" (MOORE, Judges, p. 313).

Samson belonged to the tribe of Dan, and was a **Nazarite** from his birth, that is, he was bound by vow not to use either wine or strong drink, and to refrain from cutting his hair; in point of fact, the extraordinary strength with which he was endowed — and which soon appeared in his tearing a lion "as he would have torn a kid in pieces" (Judges xiv, 6) — was dependent on his fulfilment of the conditions of this vow, and particularly on his care that his hair should never be cut. In his youth, he married a Philistine woman, a fact which soon became the occasion of his intense hatred against the oppressors of his people, as also of some of his famous exploits, namely, the killing of thirty Philistines at Ascalon, the catching of three hundred jackals, ordinarily called foxes, and setting fire by their means to the splendid harvest of his enemies, and finally the slaying of one thousand men with the jaw-bone of an ass. His second marriage with another Philistine woman named Dalila, who proved still more treacherous to Samson than his first wife, was also the occasion of deeds of prodigious strength — such as, for instance, the carrying of the enormous gates of Gaza "up to the top of the hill, which looketh towards Hebron"; and also ultimately of his deliverance into the power of his enemies and of the destruction both of himself and of the temple and princes of the Philistines, by pulling down the pillars of the house whither he had been brought when taken from his prison.

These leading facts of Samson's life are more than sufficient to make us realize why the sacred narrative speaks of Samson as a judge of Israel (Judges xv, 20; xvi, 31 *b*), and describes his mission as that of one who "shall *begin* to deliver Israel from the hands of the Philistines" (Judges xiii, 5). For since, on the one hand, he did all in his power to avenge his people of their enemies he can justly be regarded as one of the *judges* of God's people; and since, on the other hand, he did not succeed fully in shaking off the foreign yoke which was still long to weigh on the Israelites after his death, but simply humbled and weakened the Philistines, it is plain that he only began the great work of Israel's deliverance.

It is true that the whole history of Samson is treated as purely fabulous by thorough-going unbelievers, who see in this part of the Biblical narrative nothing but legends derived from *solar* myths (cfr. H. OORT, The Bible for Learners, vol. i, p. 411, sq.). To substantiate their position, they remind us first of the many *solar* myths which underlie the mythology of the old Pagan nations; next, of the fact that the Hebrews were at that time perfectly acquainted with sun-worship; and, finally, of the derivation of the name of *Samson* from a Hebrew word meaning "Sun." Of course, it cannot well be doubted that in the time of the judges the Israelites were acquainted with sun-worship, also that the history of Samson has a close analogy with that of Hercules, and, finally, that the word Samson *may* be derived from the Hebrew for "Sun." But even granting all this, it does not follow all at once that the principal deeds of Samson are pure fiction, that even the substance of the Biblical narrative has no real basis on real events. The history of Samson, as it is recorded in the book of Judges, will ever appear to the unprejudiced reader better accounted for by admitting as its basis the actual existence of a hero of great physical strength and lawless life, who distinguished himself in the defence of his nation against the Philistines by such exploits as those of which records have been preserved to us, than by going back to a *possible* derivation of the word Samson, and to solar myths of which there is not the least actual trace in the Biblical narrative. The first explanation fits naturally in the circumstances of time and place to which the life of Samson is referred by the sacred writer; the second is a mere hypothesis, almost entirely unconnected with the actual conditions of Israel during that period of Jewish history. (For interesting and valuable details going to show the historical character of the principal facts of Samson's life, see VIGOUROUX, Bible et Découvertes Modernes, tome iii; cfr. also GEIKIE, Hours with the Bible, vol. iii, chap. i.)

**6. Heli** (I Kings called also I Samuel, i-iv). The time of the judges was practically brought to a close by the judgeship of Heli, whose rise to the high priesthood is shrouded in obscurity, for the sacred text tells us nowhere how this dignity passed from the line of Eleazar into that of Ithamar, to which Heli belonged. It is also unknown by what series of events this head of the sacerdotal body succeeded in joining in his person the twofold dignity of judge and high priest; perhaps we should look upon this union of functions heretofore separated as a temporary experiment of a form of government, which, without being monarchical, would yet place in the hands of one single individual a power sufficient to effect the union of all the tribes against the long and cruel oppression of the Philistines, and which, failing signally to attain its object, prepared all minds for the near setting up of the monarchy in Israel.

However this may be, when we read of Heli in the Bible he appears to us a good but weak old man, equally incapable of leading the Israelites to victory and of checking the perversity of his own children, who profaned the sacred place at Silo and caused all the people to murmur by their sacrilegious exactions. In vain did Jehovah warn repeatedly this unworthy head of the civil and sacerdotal power; the weakness of Heli prevented him from stopping effectively abuses which were soon to be punished in the most exemplary manner. The Philistines, always ambitious, always ready to enlarge their conquests, profited by this weakness of the Hebrew Government to gather troops and march to Aphec, a place which cannot be identified at the present day, and where the Israelites were defeated with the loss of about four thousand men. Alarmed at this reverse, the ancients of Israel had the Ark of the Covenant brought into the camp, borne by the two sons of Heli, Ophni and Phinees, and its presence inspired the Hebrew warriors with the greatest confidence in the future success of their arms, but their hopes were severely disappointed. A battle was fought in which they were utterly routed and sustained the loss of thirty thousand men, of the two sons of the high priest, and even of the Ark of the Covenant. This awful calamity was soon followed by the death of Heli, who, hearing of the capture of the Ark, fell from his seat, broke his neck and died; and by the practical fall of Silo as the ecclesiastical centre of the nation, for this town, being now deprived of the Ark of Jehovah, gradually sank into insignificance (cfr. DEANE, Samuel and Saul, p. 40, sq.).

7. **Episodes of the Time of the Judges** (Judges xvii-xxi; Ruth i-iv). Intimately connected with the history of this period are two episodes, which are recorded at the end of the book of Judges, and the charming idyl of the book of Ruth.

The first episode, contained in Judges, chaps. xvii, xviii, presents a sad illustration, chiefly of the religious decay of Israel during the period of the judges. It relates how an Ephraimite, named Michas, owning a shrine with an image and oracle, and having a Levite as his priest, was robbed of his image and priest by a considerable portion of the tribe of Dan when on their way northward in search of new settlements; and how the Danites, after having ruthlessly murdered the former inhabitants of the district at the sources of the Jordan, set up Michas' image in a sanctuary at which ministered a priesthood claiming actual descent from Moses. The second episode, found in Judges, chaps. xix-xxi, and whose historical character has been very seriously questioned, gives the story of the causes and consequences of a war between the tribe of Benjamin and the other tribes of Israel. The episode is briefly as follows: The wife of a Levite having been frightfully abused by the inhabitants of a Benjamite town, called Gabaa, the other tribes of Israel arose to avenge the outrage, and asked of the tribe of Benjamin the surrender of the men of Gabaa. The Benjamites refused, and, after having been successful in two encounters, were so utterly defeated that only six hundred men survived the battle. In order, however, that the tribe of Benjamin should not entirely disappear from Israel, force and deceit were successfully resorted to in order to supply wives to the surviving Benjamites, after which the Israelites dispersed to their homes.

In striking contrast with these wild scenes, alas, too much in harmony with a period when "every one did as he pleased" (Judges xvii, 6; xxi, 24), stands the charming idyl known as the book of Ruth, and the substance of which is as follows: To escape a famine which had happened in Western Palestine, Elimelech, a man from Bethlehem-Juda, had migrated with his family to Moab, where he died, leaving a widow, Noemi, and two sons who married Moabite women, called Orpha and Ruth. After a lapse of about ten years, his two sons also died, and Noemi now prepared to return to her native town. Ruth devotedly followed her, and, arrived at Bethlehem, went out to glean in the fields of Booz, a wealthy kinsman of Elimelech, and who ultimately married Ruth, with whose filial devotion he had become acquainted. It is from this union that sprang Obed, the grandfather of David.

The history of Ruth furnishes a natural transition between the tribal period and the period of the monarchy. It belongs to the time of the judges, and shows how in the calmer intervals of this disturbed period the practical working of the

Mosaic law can secure the peace and prosperity of the Jewish home, and at the same time it prepares for the Royal Period of Jewish history by tracing back the genealogy of David, the real founder of the Hebrew monarchy, to one of the purest characters with which the Bible makes us acquainted. For the numerous illustrations of Oriental life calculated to give to the book of Ruth vividness and reality, see the various commentaries, and also, SMITH, Bible Dictionary, article Ruth, vol. iv, p. 2756, sq.

# SYNOPSIS OF CHAPTER XVI.

## THE BEGINNING OF THE MONARCHY.

### (I Kings i–xii.)

I. SAMUEL, THE LAST JUDGE:
- A. *His Early Life:* Birth; Youth; Early vision.
- B. *His Judgeship:*
  1. Favor and influence with the people. { Cariathiarim. Masphath. }
  2. Miraculous victory over the Philistines; Subsequent peace.
  3. Residence at Ramatha; Yearly circuits.
  4. Popular demand for a King: { Why made? How considered by { Samuel? God? } }

II. SAUL, THE FIRST KING:
1. *His Election:* (I Kings ix, x.) { By God (Anointment of Samuel). By the People (The Law of the Kingdom Proclaimed). }
2. *His first Victory over the Ammonites* (I Kings xl, 1–11).
3. *Second Inauguration of the Monarchy at Galgal* (I Kings xi, 12–15).
4. *Samuel's last Appeal to the People; he withdraws* (I Kings xii).

# THIRD OR ROYAL PERIOD.

## FROM THE INSTITUTION OF THE MONARCHY TO THE BABYLONIAN CAPTIVITY.

### CHAPTER XVI.

#### THE BEGINNING OF THE MONARCHY.

§ *1. Samuel, the Last Judge.*

1. **Samuel's Early Life** (I Kings i–iii). It was during the high priesthood and judgeship of Heli that Samuel, the future introducer of the monarchy into Israel, was born in Ramathaim, a town which cannot be identified at the present day. His father, Elcana, was an Ephraimite of Levitical descent, who, despairing of offspring from Anna, his first wife, had — as allowed by Oriental customs — taken Phenenna for his second wife, and had become by her the father of numerous children. As usual in such cases, the wife not blessed with children had to bear the taunts of her more fortunate rival, and, despite the tender affection which Elcana evinced on all occasions for his first wife, Anna, in her ardent desire to obtain a son from Jehovah, vowed solemnly that her future child should be devoted to the Divine service, as a Nazarite, all the days of his life. Her prayer was heard, and her child, to whom she gave the name of Samuel, was accepted, when still in tender years, by the old high priest Heli for the service of the sanctuary.

In the midst of the general corruption of the time, the child grew in simplicity and innocence under the loving care of the pious women who had regular duties to perform in connection with the Tabernacle (cfr. Exod. xxxviii, 8; I Kings ii, 22), of his mother, who visited him at stated times, and especially of Heli, who found in Samuel a devotion to his well being, and a readiness to follow his advice which the aged high priest had long looked for in vain in his own wicked children. Samuel's work was naturally divided between such offices as his strength allowed him to discharge in connection with the sanctuary at Silo and the services he rendered to Heli, whom dimness of sight and increasing infirmities made largely dependent upon the help of others; apparently, the high priest slept in a chamber near the Tabernacle, and Samuel was ever within call during the night.

While Samuel was thus "advancing, growing on and pleasing both Jehovah and men" (I Kings ii, 26), it became more and more necessary that the wickedness of the two sons of Heli and the weakness of their father should be visited by a signal punishment, and the young Samuel was selected by God to announce to the old high priest the awful calamities now near at hand. In a vision during the night Jehovah, having called Samuel three times, revealed to him the terrible fate that awaited Heli and his house. Early the next morning Samuel complied with the positive injunction of Heli, that he should tell him his vision, and the defeat of Aphec together with its disastrous consequences soon proved to all Israel that Samuel was the chosen prophet of Jehovah, that is, one to whom He was pleased to manifest His will and to reveal Himself time and again (I Kings ii, iii).

2. **Samuel's Judgeship** (I Kings vii, viii). For twenty years after the crushing defeat of the Israelites at Aphec the Philistines severely oppressed the people of God, and during this time Samuel passed from youth to manhood and acquired

an ever-increasing favor with the people at large. At length, the time came when the young prophet thought he could speak with authority and point out to Israel that the reason why its enemies, although they had long before been compelled to restore the Ark of the Covenant (I Kings v-vii, 2), had ever since been allowed to dominate, was because the Hebrews had not served Jehovah *only*. He therefore bade them put away the idols of Chanaan, which divided their allegiance to the true God, and promised victory in the event of an attack. These words of Samuel, which were probably addressed to the people on the occasion of a religious meeting at Cariathiarim, where the Ark had been deposited, met with such success that Israel gave up openly all idolatrous worship and "served Jehovah *only*" (I Kings vii, 3, 4). Samuel profited by these generous dispositions to convene a general assembly of the nation at Masphath, probably about "five miles north by west of Jerusalem" (HENDERSON, Palestine, its Historical Geography, p. 113). The people solemnly pledged themselves to the exclusive worship of Jehovah, and not unlikely proclaimed Samuel as their *judge*, that is, as the leader now in charge of securing the deliverance he had promised to them (I Kings vii, 5, 6).

Naturally enough, the Philistines understood that the convention of Israel at Masphath was a direct menace to the continuance of their tyranny and accordingly they gathered their whole force to crush the Israelite insurrection. Great was the dismay of the Hebrews when contemplating the formidable attack now impending; yet they had confidence in Samuel's power with God, and their trust in Jehovah and His prophet was rewarded by a victory which the sacred writer represents as miraculous. The results of this triumph were very great, for besides the actual loss of men sustained by the Philistines, these oppressors of the Israelites were so "humbled that they did not come any more into the borders of Israel," and were gradually compelled to restore to the

Hebrews the cities which they had taken from them. It seems also that the Amorrhites who had taken part with the Philistines hastened to make peace with Israel, and that this auspicious beginning of Samuel's judgeship was followed by long years of national freedom and prestige (I Kings vii, 7-15).

During these long years of public prosperity Samuel resided at Ramatha, where he built an altar to Jehovah, and continued to be considered as the judge of Israel. Unlike those who had preceded him in the office of judge, he not only gave the example of personal faithfulness to the service of the true God, but also took it to heart to ensure a like faithfulness in the Divine service on the part of all those who recognized his authority. With this end in view, he made it his business to visit every year some of the spots consecrated by hallowed memories, there to offer sacrifice to Jehovah. The names of three of these venerated spots are mentioned in the sacred text, namely, Bethel, Galgal and Masphath; but besides "he often betook himself to other places at uncertain intervals to redress grievances, or to punish wrong doing, or to offer Divine worship" (see I Kings xvi, 2, sq.; DEANE, Samuel and Saul, p. 69).[1] It was also to secure more effectively national faithfulness to Jehovah, that Samuel established those "*Schools of the Prophets,*" which have become so famous, and in which young men were especially trained for the prophetical mission, that is, for becoming the direct representatives of the God of Israel and promoting by every means in their power, purity of morals and of Divine worship throughout the land.

[1] Although not a priest, but only a simple Levite, Samuel offers freely sacrifices to Jehovah. To account for this apparent violation of the Mosaic law, two principal suppositions have been made: (1) as a *prophet*, Samuel was allowed by a special permission of God to perform priestly acts; (2) at that time a strict distinction between the duties of the priests and those of the simple Levites had not yet been drawn. Perhaps it might be admitted that in so doing Samuel simply exercised one of the functions which were then connected with the supreme power in Israel (cfr. for instance I Kings x, 8; xiii, 9, 12, 13).

It was in this peaceful, and at the same time most useful, manner that the last judge of Israel spent the best years of his life, respected alike by the Israelites whom he governed with firmness and justice, and by the Philistines who remembered their former defeats. But as time went on and as he advanced in years, Samuel felt unable to support alone the whole weight of the administration, and accordingly appointed his two sons as *judges* over a part of the territory which recognized his authority. He placed them as his substitutes at Bersabee, on the extreme southern frontier of Palestine, with the sincere hope that by their services in that part of the land they would endear themselves to the people at large, and thus deserve a continuance in office after his death. Great indeed must have been his disappointment when the ancients of Israel came to the old judge and complained that, differently from him, his sons had proved greedy and rapacious men, had perverted justice and taken bribes; keener still must have been his grief when these same elders of Israel, voicing the actual feeling of the Jewish nation, asked for a king, saying, "Make us a king to judge us, as all nations have." This popular demand for a king was no mere passing desire of only a section of the country; it was rather the natural outcome of a long and steadily growing tendency of the people at large towards a form of government capable of imparting unity and strength to the long-divided forces of the Jewish nation. It was also the natural outcome of the circumstances of the time: the Philistines, profiting by the weakness of the aged judge of Israel, had gradually recovered confidence in their arms and had succeeded in establishing strong garrisons in the very heart of the country (I Kings ix, 16; x, 5; xiii, 3); and the Ammonites, formerly subdued by Jephte, threatened again the region east of the Jordan (I Kings xii, 12). In presence of such enemies, the Israelites saw only one means of securing victory: it was to discard both Samuel, too old to be their general, and his two sons, plainly unworthy of the command, and to ask for a king.

However natural this petition of the Hebrews may now appear to us, it greatly displeased the old judge of Israel, whose former victories and lifelong services seemed to him undervalued by this bald request: "Make us a king to judge us." Yet he did not reject their request at once, but, as was his wont, he prayed to Jehovah for guidance. In His answer God bade Samuel to hearken to the voice of the people, although by asking for a king to judge them, *as all nations had*, the Israelites had plainly shown how little they understood their glorious privilege to be different from other nations, and to have no other king but Jehovah. Before, however, granting the petition of his fellow-countrymen, the aged prophet drew for them a picture which embraced the principal features of the government of Eastern monarchs, and which was indeed calculated to make them pause before giving up the freedom and quiet and exemption from taxes, etc., which they had hitherto enjoyed, but which were to be sacrificed before the will of their future king. This remonstrance was of course useless, and the people having renewed their petition for a king, nothing else remained to be done but to select the one who was to be the first monarch of Israel; as this choice, however, was of the greatest importance, Samuel sent the people away, and waited for some further direction from Jehovah.

§ 2. *Saul the First King.*

1. **The Election of Saul** (I Kings ix, x). The Biblical narrative does not tell us how long after granting the petition of the Jewish people for a king God made known to Samuel that on a certain day he would meet the man of the land of Benjamin, whom He destined to be the first King of Israel (I Kings ix, 15, 16); but we are told in detail by what

succession of apparently trivial events this meeting was actually brought about. It makes us acquainted with the loss of the asses of Cis, a man of Benjamin; with the useless efforts of his son, named Saul, a man of goodly stature, to track them; with the happy suggestion of Saul's companion to consult the seer — that is the prophet — of the land of Suph, a man famous for his correct predictions, and who had just come into the city to offer a public sacrifice in the high place; and finally, with the actual meeting of Samuel and Saul, when the latter, addressing the former, said, "Tell me, I pray thee, where is the house of the seer?" Samuel, inwardly made aware that his questioner was the future King of Israel, answered that he himself was the seer and that the asses vainly sought after by Saul had been found. Then he announced to the son of Cis the exalted dignity to which Jehovah had called him. In vain did Saul plead the smallness of his tribe in Israel and the insignificancy of his own family, the prophet gave him the first place at the sacrificial meal, welcomed him to his own house, and the next morning accompanied him to the end of the town. There, the servant having been bidden to pass on, the last judge of Israel taking a little vial of oil, poured it upon the head of Saul, and thus anointed him the first king of the chosen people.

These were, of course, wonderful events in the eyes of Saul, and Samuel, to enable him gradually to feel that they were glorious realities, gave to Saul three signs which soon met with their perfect fulfilment. Nothing indeed was better calculated than this fulfilment to confirm Saul in his actual belief that he was the chosen of Jehovah for the Jewish throne, nothing, also, should have convinced him more firmly that the mysterious recommendation the old prophet made to him just before parting, namely, that he should wait for Samuel at Galgal seven days, and should not offer victims to God before his actual arrival, must be complied with to its fullest extent; and yet, we shall soon see that Saul discarded this parting recommendation of the prophet.

After returning home, the **Anointed of Jehovah** — as the Jewish kings are called in Holy Writ — preserved a prudent silence concerning what had taken place between Samuel and himself till his election should be ratified by the people. This ratification was effected in a general assembly which Samuel had convened in Masphath, and in which the old judge invited all to leave the selection of the king in the hands of Jehovah by the casting of lots. The lot fell upon Saul, and accordingly the son of Cis was presented to the people, who, struck with admiration for his kingly appearance, cried and said: "God save the king!" Before dismissing the assembly, Samuel told the people the **Law of the Kingdom**, whereby were probably meant some such limitations to the royal power as those which we read in the book of Deuteronomy (xvii, 14-20; cfr. JAHN, Hebrew Commonwealth, p. 64, sq.), and having "written it in a book, laid it up before Jehovah."

The ceremony ended, the people withdrew to their homes, and Saul returned to his little town of Gabaa — a place which has been identified with the modern **Tell El Ful**, about three miles north of Jerusalem — where he resumed his former humble duties (I Kings xi, 5). In thus acting, the new King of Israel evinced a consummate prudence, for under the circumstances of the time, when numerous and powerful opponents belonging probably to the great tribes of Juda and Ephraim openly derided him as wanting in military means for his office, he could do little more than to dissemble his resentment, and retire to private life till events should vindicate his election.

2. **Saul's First Victory over the Ammonites** (I Kings xi, 1-11). A month had scarcely elapsed when a favorable opportunity arose for proving how mistaken the

opponents of the new king were in their estimation of his warlike abilities. The children of Ammon, long recovered from the severe defeat inflicted upon them by Jephte, had invaded the territory of the Transjordanic tribes, and actually besieged the capital of Galaad, Jabes, which occupied a commanding position on the top of an isolated hill, and which is now identified with the ruins of Ed Deir, about six miles south of Pella, on the north of the Wady El Yabis. Despairing of a victorious resistance, the inhabitants of Jabes offered to surrender; but Naas, the Ammonite king, in his desire to avenge upon them the former defeat of his nation by the Galaadite, Jephte, refused to accept the surrender, unless the defenders of Jabes should consent to lose their right eyes, and thus become unfit for further military service. Naas agreed, however, to a respite of seven days, during which the inhabitants of the besieged city could implore the help of the other tribes of Israel. Their messengers, probably aware of the new royal office in Israel, went straight to Gabaa, and all the people, who heard their tale of woe, "lifted up their voices, and wept." When in the evening Saul came back from the field, "behind the oxen with which he had been working" (EDERSHEIM, Bible History, iv, p. 52), he found his own town lamenting over the future fate of Jabes Galaad. At this news, "the spirit of God came upon him," and cutting in pieces the oxen he was driving, Saul sent them to the various districts of Israel by messengers, saying, "Whosoever shall not come forth, and follow Saul and Samuel, so shall it be done to his oxen." The whole people obeyed the summons, and thus surrounded by spirited warriors whom he numbered in Bezec — the modern Ibzik on the hills opposite Jabes Galaad — Saul promised to the besieged town the most prompt relief. On the morrow, at break of day, the forces of Israel skilfully divided into three companies, attacked, routed the enemy, and rescued Jabes.

3. **Second Inauguration of the Monarchy in Galgal** (I Kings xi, 12-15). Nothing could have better vindicated in the eyes of the nation Saul's Divine appointment as king over Israel than his short and glorious campaign against the Ammonites. In point of fact, the popular feeling ran so high that, in their enthusiasm, the Hebrews would have put to death, on the very evening of their victory, those who had at first refused to recognize Saul, had not the Jewish monarch intervened lest such excesses should stain that glorious day; "for to-day," said he, ascribing all the glory to the invisible King of Israel, "Jehovah hath wrought salvation in Israel."

After this moderate answer, which must have won to Saul the grateful admiration of his former opponents, Samuel thought it most opportune to confirm, in a most solemn manner, the sovereignty of the Jewish king. Obeying his summons, all the people met at Galgal, "the famous Benjamite sanctuary in the Jordan valley" (DEANE, Samuel and Saul, p. 108), "and there they made Saul king before Jehovah, . . . and Saul and all the men of Israel rejoiced exceedingly."[1]

4. **Samuel's Last Appeal to the People: his Withdrawal** (I Kings xii). And now the time had come for the aged prophet to give up his *official* work, as *judge* of Israel. He therefore profited by the general meeting at Galgal to address a last appeal to the people at large. In a skilful discourse, he first challenged any charge against his own administration, and next insisted on the great truth, that national prosperity or adversity would depend in the future, as in the past, on the faithfulness or unfaithfulness of the people to the exclusive worship of Jehovah. Then, to give more weight to his parting words, he asked a miracle from the Almighty. It was then the time of the wheat-harvest (May-June), when rain is almost unknown in Palestine; yet,

[1] For a different view of all that regards the election and coronation of Saul, see DRIVER, Notes on the Hebrew Text of the Books of Samuel, p. 67, sq.

at the prayer of His prophet, God "sent thunder and rain." This wonderful event led the people to a sincere confession of their distrust of Jehovah in asking for a king, and to an earnest entreaty to Samuel that he should pray for the public welfare. In his answer, the former judge of Israel promised never to forget the interests of his fellow-countrymen in his prayers to God, and again reminded the people that Jehovah would mete out to them recompense or punishment according to their faithfulness or unfaithfulness in His service.

And so the assembly parted, Israel to their tents, Saul to the work of the kingdom, and Samuel — no longer a judge, but still a prophet — to the difficult task of acting as the inspired instructor and guide of both king and people.

# SYNOPSIS OF CHAPTER XVII.

## THE REIGN OF SAUL AND YOUTH OF DAVID.

(I Kings xiii–xxx; I Paralip. x; xii.)

---

**I. THE REIGN OF SAUL:**
1. *His Military Achievements and Rejection by God.*
2. *His Character:*
   - A. Chief traits
     - Before reaching the throne.
     - Once on the throne.
   - B. Contrasted with that of Jonathan.
3. *His end at Gelboe.* Condition of Israel at his death.

---

**II. THE YOUTH OF DAVID:**
1. *Origin and Early Life:* the chosen of God.
2. *Relations with Saul:*
   - A. The first introduction of David to Saul.
   - B. Saul treats David successively as a
     - Favorite.
     - Dangerous rival.
     - Deadly enemy.
   - C. David remains invariably and deeply attached to Saul: his lamentation over the death of Saul and Jonathan.
3. *His Wanderings:*
   - Principal places of refuge and chief incidents.
   - Effects of his wanderings.

## CHAPTER XVII.

### THE REIGN OF SAUL AND YOUTH OF DAVID.

### § *1. The Reign of Saul.*

1. **Saul's Military Achievements and Rejection by God.** The history of the reign of Saul commences with the second inauguration of the monarchy at Galgal, after which Samuel ceased to be considered as a ruler together with the Jewish king (I Kings xi, 7, 12, 14). It is now impossible to determine the exact age of Saul at this time, for the figures which formerly indicated it in the sacred text (cfr. I Kings xiii, 1, with II Kings ii, 10; v, 4, etc.) have been altered (cfr. HUMMELAUER, in Libros Samuel is, p. 132, sq.); but it is probable that this monarch was between thirty-five and forty years old at his accession, since immediately afterwards, Jonathan, his son, had the command of a part of the army, a position which the young prince would hardly have held if much less than twenty years of age (I Kings xiii, 2).

Thus, then, the first King of Israel was in full possession of his physical and mental powers when, taking the reins of government, he assumed the hard task of liberating his subjects from their enemies (I Kings ix, 16, etc.), and, in point of fact, the sacred narrative tells us that he was victorious in all the wars he waged against them (I Kings xiv, 46). Of these wars, however, only two are detailed in the Bible, because they illustrate what absolute obedience to His orders Jehovah expected of the Jewish kings, and because they show with what justice Saul having repeatedly denied this obedience, God selected another man, "a man according to

His own heart," that is, willing to rule over Israel in perfect dependence on the guidance of the invisible yet supreme King of the chosen people (cfr. I Kings xiii, 13, 14).

The first of these wars was conducted against the Philistines, the old oppressors of the land (I Kings ix, 16), and it began with a quick and successful attack against the garrison of Gabaa by Jonathan, to whom Saul had intrusted the command of 1,000 men. To avenge this defeat, the Philistines invaded the country with so large an army that its very sight struck with terror the Israelites who had gathered around Saul at Galgal. And now the time had come when the Jewish monarch should show himself perfectly obedient to Jehovah. It was his duty not to offer sacrifice before the arrival of Samuel, the authorized messenger of God near the King of Israel (I Kings x, 8). Impatient and distrustful — he indeed saw the people gradually slipping from him — Saul did not wait until the actual coming of the prophet, but offered the holocaust to appease Jehovah before the battle. Scarcely was the sacrifice over, when Samuel appeared, and declared that in punishment of his disobedience Saul would not be the head of a dynasty in Israel, a severe but necessary sentence against the first Jewish king, who by his disobedience had set openly the example of a violation of that primary condition of Jewish national life and prosperity, which ever consisted in a perfect compliance with the directions of Jehovah (I Kings xiii). Despite this first disobedience of their king, the Israelites obtained a signal victory at Machmas, a place about eight miles north of Jerusalem; in fact, the loss of the Philistines would have been much greater had it not been for a rash and foolish curse under which Saul laid the people, and to which he would actually have made Jonathan a victim if the army had not strongly objected to the death of one "who had wrought this great salvation in Israel" (I Kings xiv, 1–46).

The second war detailed in the Biblical narrative was directed against the Amalecites, that nomad race which formerly had "opposed the Israelites in their way when they came up out of Egypt," and which but recently had made predatory raids on the southern districts of the Hebrews, whilst the latter were engaged in war against the Philistines (cfr. I Kings xv, 2; xiv, 48). In the name of Jehovah, Samuel had put the Amalecites under the ban, and Saul was now commissioned by him to utterly destroy everything they possessed, and "slay both man and woman, child and suckling, ox and sheep, camel and ass." Accordingly, placing himself at the head of a very large army, Saul undertook apparently to carry out strictly this frightful sentence; but when victorious, he reserved the best part of the spoil, and spared the life of Agag, the Amalecite king. This second violation of God's command proved to evidence that Saul would never be a theocratic king, punctual in his conformity to Jehovah's orders; and in consequence Samuel was directed by the God of Israel to proclaim Saul's disqualification for being king over the chosen people. This the prophet did, despite his own attachment to a man whom he had himself anointed; and, notwithstanding the excuses alleged by the monarch, he announced to Saul the transfer of the royal dignity to one of a neighboring tribe. This was to be the last meeting between Samuel and Saul, and the unfortunate King of Israel, fearing the effects of this sentence of rejection upon his subjects, begged the prophet not to break openly from him, but to offer sacrifice together with him before parting. To this Samuel finally consented, and then he withdrew to mourn over the rejection of the first Jewish king by the Supreme Ruler of Israel (I Kings xv). (For reasons tending to justify the sentence of extermination against Amalec, see DEANE, Samuel and Saul, p. 148).

2. **The Character of Saul.** The man whose posterity and person had thus been, the one after the other, excluded

from the Jewish throne, had formerly displayed qualities which apparently rendered him worthy of being the first to wear the crown in Israel. Before reaching the throne, he had shown himself a model of delicate feelings (I Kings ix, '5); rare modesty and humility (ix, 21; x, 22); genuine docility (ix, 22, 25; x, 1, etc.); great self-restraint and wise forbearance (x, 27; xi, 12–15); great simplicity and disinterestedness (xi, 5, sq.); in a word, of all the virtues best calculated to make all hope that, once on the throne, he would prove himself a king ever ready to carry out faithfully all the directions which Jehovah would give him through Samuel, His accredited ambassador. Unfortunately it was not to be so, for soon after reaching the crown Saul actually showed himself a very different man. Worldly wisdom betrayed him into his first disobedience (I Kings xiii, 7–13); preoccupation for his own satisfaction rather than for God's glory caused him to utter oaths no less contrary to prudence than to justice and humanity (xiv, 24, sq.); his self-will appeared so manifestly in his second disobedience when fighting against Amalec that Samuel himself could not help contrasting Saul's inward dispositions before reaching the throne with those he displayed later on (xv, 17); his own excuses, on this same occasion, proved clearly that he had set popularity above duty (xv, 20, sq.), and finally, if he confessed his sin (xv, 24, 30) it was not so much because of his sorrow for his offence against God, as because of its political consequences present and future (xv, 25, 30). It is not even improbable that his lack of disinterestedness was not foreign to his saving Agag, and the best of the spoil under pretence of offering them to Jehovah, and it is well known that his disappointed ambition and base jealousy gradually led him to madness which bordered on demoniacal possession, and to a fierce and relentless persecution of David (I Kings xvi, 14; xviii, 8, sq.; cfr. also HUMMELAUER, in Libros Samuelis, p. 168).

The character of Saul after his accession, stands also in

striking contrast with that of his son, Jonathan. This young prince, a type of military valor (I Kings xiii, 2, sq.; xiv, 1, sq.), was also a pattern of submission to the Almighty (xiv. 10) and of noble self-sacrifice (xiv, 43). "Jealousy and every mean or low feeling were strangers to the generous heart of this eldest son of Saul. Valiant and accomplished himself, none knew better how to acknowledge valor and accomplishments in others. In the intensity of his admiration and love for David, he not only risked his life to preserve him from harm, but even shrank not to think of him as his destined king and master, and of himself as one with him in friendship, but next to him in place and council" (KITTO, Cyclopædia of Biblical Knowledge, art. Jonathan).

3. **The End of Saul at Gelboe.** All his life Saul waged war against the Philistines (I Kings xiv, 52), for naturally enough these inveterate enemies of Israel profited by the wretched condition of the Jewish king to invade repeatedly a country whose defence from foreign foes lay apparently much less close to the heart of Saul than the extermination of his personal opponents within. Furthermore, the land of Israel had gradually been deserted by some of its most valiant soldiers, who, despairing of the fortunes of Saul, had joined themselves to David (I Paralip., or Chronicles, xii, 1, sq.); so that it was with great hope of success that, some time after the death of Samuel, they marched northwards along the sea-coast, entered the plain of Esdraelon with numerous troops, and pitched their camp on the slope of the Little Hermon — now called Jebel Duhy — which bounds the Great Plain on the east, at a place called Sunam — the present Sulem — three and one-half miles north of Jezrahel. Saul, having gathered whatever troops he could collect, encamped on Mount Gelboe, which bounds the plain of Esdraelon on the south, that is, in an extremely perilous position, for he was in imminent danger of being surrounded

by the Philistines who had also marched a strong body of troops to Aphec (I Kings xxix, 1), in the rear of the Jewish army (DEANE, Samuel and Saul, p. 201).

Sorely afraid, and feeling forsaken by Jehovah, whom he consulted in vain about the future, the unfortunate king fell back upon one of those soothsayers he had formerly tried to banish from the Holy Land. At night and in disguise he made the seven miles which separate Gelboe from Endor, and there wished that the witch of the place would evoke the spirit of Samuel, the former guide of his life. It seems plain, from the wording of his narrative, that the sacred writer intends to describe a personal apparition of the old prophet, and to record his prediction of the awful fate which soon awaited Saul and his army (see on this question, CLAIR, Livres des Rois, p. 75, sq.; and HUMMELAUER, in Libros Samuelis, p. 248, sq.), and there is no doubt that this distinct knowledge of his ruin, now so near at hand, destroyed effectively every hope of escape which might still linger in the mind of the king. Soon afterwards the battle was fought; it ended with the rout of the Israelites, the death of Saul and of three of his sons (I Kings xxviii; xxxi; cfr. also II Kings i).

"This victory of the Philistines gave them possession of a long tract of country; the north submitted to them without a blow, and many of the Israelite cities between the plain of Esdrælon and the Jordan were deserted by the inhabitants and occupied by the enemy" (DEANE, David, p. 81). This was indeed a very sad condition of affairs for Israel, but God had long been preparing in David a truly theocratic king fully able to repair the fallen fortunes of the chosen people.

§ 2. *The Youth of David.*

1. **Origin and Early Life.** David, the man chosen by Jehovah to be the successor of Saul on the Jewish throne,

belonged to the tribe of Juda, and through some of his immediate ancestresses he was allied to the foreign races of Moab and Chanaan (cfr. Ruth iv, 18, sq.; Matt. i, 5; Luke iii, 32). He was the youngest son of Isai, a small proprietor of Bethlehem, concerning whom very little else is known.

The early life of the future king, poet and prophet of Israel was that of an humble shepherd in charge of the flocks of his father which were pastured on the neighboring hills. This was an arduous life in the unenclosed country around Bethlehem, but it proved a valuable training for his future destiny. "His bodily powers were exercised and braced by a hardy life in the open air; courage and self-reliance became habitual in the presence of constant danger and responsibility; dexterity in the use of rustic weapons, the bow and the sling, were acquired. . . . In his lonely hours, as he watched his father's sheep, he attained that skill in minstrelsy which early attracted the notice of his contemporaries" (DEANE, David, pp. 4, 5).

One day as he was tending his flock, he was hurriedly summoned home before Samuel the great judge and prophet of Israel. This venerable old man, after weeping long over the rejection of Saul by God, had lately arrived in Bethlehem, there to anoint as king that one of the sons of Isai whom Jehovah would point out to him. In vain had he seen, one after the other, the seven brothers of David, who had remained at home. Jehovah had chosen none among them to be the successor of Saul, and now he was waiting for the youngest of the sons of Isai, for, had said the aged prophet, "We will not sit down [at the sacrificial meal] till he come hither." When David appeared, "ruddy and beautiful to behold, and of a comely face," Jehovah said to Samuel: "Arise, and anoint him, for this is he." Then it was that the introducer of the monarchy into Israel carried out in favor of this new chosen of God the ceremony of the anointment which he had formerly performed in behalf of the first Jewish king (I Kings xvi, 1-13).

2. **Relations of David with Saul.** It is indeed difficult at the present day to say on what exact occasion David was first introduced to Saul, for there seem to be two different representations of this event in the present Hebrew text (cfr. Kings xvi, 14-23, with I Kings xvii, xviii), and several theories are still held to do away with the apparent discrepancies which are noticeable between the two representations. The core of the difficulty is briefly as follows: in chapter xvi, the first introduction of David to Saul is connected with the sending of Saul to Isai for his youngest son, in order that by his musical skill David may appease the fits of madness to which the Jewish king is subject; in chapter xvii, on the contrary, David seems to be introduced to Saul for the first time, in connection with his successful fight against Goliath. Of the many theories which have been advanced to meet this difficulty, only two appear to account fully for its presence in the Hebrew text. The first theory takes notice that the *Septuagint*, or oldest Greek translation of the Hebrew, does not contain in chapters xvii and xviii of the first book of Kings those verses the presence of which in the Hebrew text makes the whole difficulty, and then it suggests that these verses did not exist in the primitive Hebrew text of the first book of Kings, but are glosses of a later date, so that the first introduction of David to Saul would have really happened as it is recorded in I Kings, xvi, 14-23 (cfr. MARTIN, Critique de l'Ancien Testament, tome i, p. 62). The second theory holds that the first book of Kings being made up of earlier documents (cfr. HUMMELAUER, in Libros Samuelis, p. 184), the compiler of the book adopted various documents, some connected with the life of Saul, others with that of David, and containing already the discrepancy in question, and simply embodied them in his

work without harmonizing their contents, so that, at the present day, it is impossible for us to tell which of the two representations is the correct one (cfr. LOISY, La Questior Biblique et l'Inspiration des Ecritures, p. 14; cfr. also LAGRANGE, Revue Biblique, Octobre, 1896, p. 512; DRIVER, Notes on Hebrew Text of the Books of Samuel, p. 116, 117).

Be this as it may, it is unquestionable that either representation of this event pictures to us the early relations of Saul with David as very friendly, for we are told that he loved David exceedingly (I Kings, xvi, 21; cfr. xviii, 9); kept him constantly near his person (xvi, 22; xviii, 2); made him his armor-bearer, and perhaps also captain of his body-guard (xvi, 21; xviii, 5); in a word, it was plain to all that David was the favorite of Saul, and this is why the courtiers of the latter exhibited towards the former a special respect and devotion (xviii, 5). But this period of favor did not last long: the public rejoicings at the triumphant return of the army from the campaign against the Philistines provoked the jealousy of Saul, for the chief praise in the songs of the women was given to David (I Kings xviii, 6-9); and twice in his madness the unfortunate king attempted to kill (xviii, 11) one whose presence he could bear no longer (xviii, 12) and whose conduct he watched as that of a dangerous rival (xviii, 15). Not satisfied with removing David to a distant post of command, Saul went so far as to endanger his life in a conflict with the Philistines by a perfidious promise of the hand of his second daughter, named Michol (I Kings xviii, 20-25); but, discomfited by the success of the valiant David, he henceforth considered him as a deadly enemy (xviii, 29), sent to arrest him in his house (xix), and began against him a relentless persecution which caused the shedding of much innocent blood (xxii).

While thus cruelly pursued with the hatred of Saul, David never exhibited in return any other feeling than that of faithfulness and compassion towards the unfortunate monarch, who was his father-in-law, and in whom he ever contemplated the anointed of Jehovah (I Kings xxiv, 7, 11). He knew, moreover, that however fierce and unjust was the persecution he had to suffer, only the invisible and supreme Master of the chosen people could dispose of the throne (xxiv, 13), and accordingly spared Saul's life in several occurrences (xxiv; xxvi). It is impossible to read the long chapters which detail this period of David's life as an outlaw without feeling that he remained invariably and deeply attached to Saul, and that his touching lamentation over the death of the first king of Israel, and Jonathan the beloved friend of David, was the natural outpouring of the sincerest affection for both (II Kings i, 18-27). (For a careful rendering of this beautiful elegy, see in *The New World*, the article "The Historical David," by B. W. Bacon, vol. iv, p. 559).

3. **The Wanderings of David.** Unwilling to start a rebellion against Saul, although this would have been easy to one who, like him, had enjoyed so much favor with the army and people of Israel, David began that wandering life with which the Biblical narrative makes us acquainted, and for which his former shepherd life had well prepared him, notably by a perfect familiarity with all the glens and numerous caves of the limestone district around Bethlehem.

Having escaped from his own house — whither Saul had sent to arrest him — by a stratagem of his wife, Michol, he fled first to Samuel, at Naioth in Ramatha (I Kings xix, 11, sq.), who probably advised him to make sure by means of Jonathan whether a reconciliation with the king would not be possible. Convinced by a short interview with this young prince that Saul's enmity was no mere transient passion (xx), he withdrew to Nobe, a place which cannot be identified at the present day and where his duplicity cost the priest Achimelech his life (xxi, 1-9; xxii, 6-19), and thence to the court of Achis, the King of Geth (some fifteen miles south of Ramleh), where he escaped the revengeful feelings of the Philistines by simulating madness (xxi, 10-15).

Returning into the territory of Juda, he became the leader of a band of about 400 men with whom he maintained himself in different places, sometimes hiding in caves, as in that of Odollam, some miles south of Bethlehem (xxii, 1); sometimes occupying a town, as that of Ceila (xxiii), the modern Khurbet Kila, south of Odollam; sometimes in the wilderness (the deserts of Ziph (xxiii, 15), of Engaddi (xxiv), etc.). It was probably during his stay in the cave of Odollam that occurred the memorable exploit of three of David's men risking their lives to procure him some water from the well of Bethlehem (II Kings xxiii, 13-17; I Paralip. xi, 15-19); and whilst at Celia he was joined by Abiathar, who had become high priest on the murder of Achimelech, his father (xxii, 20; xxiii, 4), and by various warriors (I Paralip. xii, 8-18). To this same period of David's wanderings belong the adventure with Nabal and David's marriage with Abigail, his sparing the life of Saul on two occasions (xxiv; xxvi), and also his second residence with Achis, who gave him Siceleg, in the neighborhood of Bersabee. Many plausible reasons have indeed been advanced to justify the conduct of David at this time, when he laid waste the country of his allies, the Philistines, and gave Achis to understand that he simply fought against the tribes dependent on Juda (cfr. CLAIR, Livres des Rois, p. 399, sq.; and DEANE, David, p. 70, sq.), but all these reasons are hardly sufficient to exonerate him (xxvii, 6-12). He also followed the army of Achis when marching to the battle of Gelboe against the Jewish forces under the orders of Saul, but was dismissed from the expedition because of the loud complaints of the princes of the Philistines (xxviii, 1, sq.; xxix).

Returning to Siceleg, he found it burnt by the Amalecites, but he soon recovered all plunder they had taken, and even obtained greater spoil, which he politicly sent to his friends in Juda (xxx), and very soon after the death of Saul he repaired into Juda, by which event David's life as an outlaw was brought to a close (AYRE, Treasury of Bible Knowledge, art. David).

There is no doubt that this checkered period of his life produced a deep and lasting impression upon the successor of Saul. It was naturally calculated to increase his courage and self-reliance, to train him to public government and administration, especially whilst acting as the petty king of Siceleg, and to inspire him with many of those feelings and descriptions which we find in the canticles of "the excellent Psalmist of Israel" (II Kings xxiii, 1). This period of proscription had the further result of endearing him to the Jewish nation, who saw in him a skilful commander and faithful patriot, and a man whom Jehovah manifestly preserved to restore to pristine grandeur Israel, now so low under the rule of an impotent and maddened king (cfr. STANLEY, Jewish Church, lecture xxii; DEANE, David, p. 82).

# SYNOPSIS OF CHAPTER XVIII.

## The Reign of David.

(II Kings–III Kings ii, 11; I Paralip xi-xxix).

---

**I. First Years at Hebron:**
1. *Rapid Consolidation of his Power.*
2. *Final Recognition by all Israel.*

---

**II. Glorious Rule at Jerusalem:**
1. *His Capital and Court:* Comparison with Eastern princes.
2. *Political Administration:*
   - Military organization.
   - Social institutions.
3. *Ecclesiastical Arrangements:*
   - The Ark on Mount Sion.
   - Great religious functionaries.
   - Priestly and Levitical organization.
4. *Outward Relations:*
   - His wars: their character.
   - Pacific relations: their happy results.
5. *Extension and Prosperity of his Empire.*

---

**III. Fall and Last Years:**
1. *His Fall and its Punishment.*
2. *His Restoration,* — subsequent faults, — death.
3. *Character of David.*

## CHAPTER XVIII.

#### THE REIGN OF DAVID.

§ *1. First Years at Hebron.*

1. **Rapid Consolidation of the Power of David.** It was only at God's bidding that after the death of Saul David removed with his band of men and his family from Siceleg to Hebron (II Kings ii, 1-3). This ancient city, the burial-place of the patriarchs, situated among the hills of Juda, some twenty miles southwest of Jerusalem, was well fitted for the capital of the kingdom soon to be started by David. For, as long as his pretensions to the Jewish crown were recognized only by the men of his tribe, Hebron was the most central as well as the strongest city of his dominions. Here the chiefs of Juda, who had probably opposed from the first the accession of a Benjamite to the throne, gathered around him, and at once elected him as their king, an election which David hastened to publish to the country not yet invaded by the Philistines (II Kings ii, 4-7).

Meanwhile, Abner, the general, and uncle of Saul, had proclaimed Isboseth king, at Mahanain, on the east of the Jordan — the modern Mukkumah, between Phanuel and Es Salt — where, after the defeat of Gelboe, the broken remnants of the Israelite army had probably gathered. From this place, celebrated in the history of Jacob (Gen. xxxii, 2, 10), Abner crossed the Jordan, and gradually succeeded in clearing the country from the Philistines and in subjecting it, with the exception of the territory of Juda, to the rule of

Isboseth (II Kings ii, 8, 9). He then endeavored to conquer Juda ; hence a civil war, or rather a protracted series of skirmishes, the general result of which is described as "the house of Saul decaying daily, but David prospering and growing always stronger and stronger." In point of fact, whilst David felt strong enough to secure to himself alliance through marriage with powerful families in the land, Isboseth became so weak and so entirely under the power of Abner that this all-powerful general finally took a public step which, in those days, was regarded as implying an open claim to the throne (cfr. II Kings xii, 21 ; III Kings ii, 21); and when rebuked for it by his master, swore that he would henceforth join David's party and insure its success (II Kings ii, 10–iii, 11).

2. **David Recognized by all Israel.** After his irretrievable rupture with Isboseth, Abner opened negotiations with David, who accepted with joy his first advances and simply required, for a league between them, that Michol should be given back to her first husband. This was, of course, promptly done, and Abner and his companions were soon welcomed into David's camp. Then rapidly followed, though without the consent of the King of Juda, the successive murders of Abner and Isboseth (II Kings iii, 12–30 ; iv).

The death of the latter made David's way to the throne over all Israel absolutely clear, for the sole direct surviving heir of Saul was Miphiboseth, the infirm and young son of Jonathan, who could not be seriously thought of as a competitor for the crown. All things pointed to David as the only possible head of the nation. The Philistines were restless and disunion at this moment might be fatal. A leader was naturally found in David, a man of common descent, a tried and well-approved commander, the chosen of Jehovah. The ancients of Israel, who had long wished to make him king (cfr. II Kings iii, 17), with their followers in very large numbers assembled at Hebron and "anointed David to be king over all Israel" (II Kings, v, 1-3): he had reigned seven and one-half years in Hebron (cfr. DEANE, David, p. 94, sq.).

### § 2. *Glorious Rule of David in Jerusalem.*

1. **His Capital and His Court.** David's first care upon coming to the possession of the entire kingdom was to secure a capital which could not excite the jealousy of any tribe in Israel and yet would be worthy of this glorious destiny. This capital he found in Jerusalem, the strong city of the Jebusites, which, as it lay on the confines of the tribes of Juda and Benjamin, had never belonged to either (cfr. Judges xix, 12), and of which he took possession through the heroic exertions of his men and of Joab in particular (II Kings v, 6-8; I Paralip. xi, 4-6).

At the time of its conquest by David, Jerusalem was but a very small town, the exact site of which has been only recently determined by a close examination of Scriptural passages (notably of Nehemias iii, 1, sq.), and by careful excavations conducted in the Holy City itself. These recent investigations seem to prove conclusively that the fortress-town captured by David's troops and enlarged by him — hence it was called "the City of David" — occupied only the hill between the Cedron and Tyropœon valleys, to the south of Mount Moriah, from which it was separated by a ravine which was filled up somewhat later on (cfr. PELT, Histoire de l'Ancien Testament, tome ii, p. 28, sq). On this hill — which is properly Mount Sion — David built himself a palace with the aid of the Phenician artists whom Hiram, King of Tyre, supplied to him. He then surrounded himself with a royal estate hitherto unknown to Israel, but resembling in many ways that of the great Eastern monarchs of the time. He conformed to Oriental opinion, which regarded the multiplication of wives as a necessary proof of the magnificence of the ruler, and hence to the several wives he had already taken in Hebron he added others after his settling down in Jerusalem. By thus acting, he indeed satisfied his own pleasure or political interests and added to the magnificence of his court (for each wife had a separate splendid establishment), but he also prepared for himself much family sorrow and trouble, and at the same time introduced into his palace a luxury and worldliness tending to assimilate the habits of his court and the sentiments of the courtiers to those of other Oriental potentates. In point of fact, he had his own royal mule especially known as such (III Kings i, 33), and his royal seat or throne in a separate chamber or gateway in the palace (III Kings i, 35). The highest officers of the court, even the Prophets, did not venture into his presence without previous announcement, and when they did enter it was with the profoundest obeisance and prostration (II Kings ix, 6; xiv, 4, 22, 23; III Kings i, 16, 23, etc). His followers who, up to the time of his accession, had been called his "young men," "his companions," henceforth became his "servants," "his slaves" (II Kings x, 2, etc). Finally, all used in addressing him magnificent titles which bear a striking resemblance to those we find applied to the Egyptian monarchs in the Tell el-Amarna tablets; compare for instance III Kings, i, 24, 36, with *Records of the Past*, new series, vol. v, p. 66, sq. (see STANLEY, Lectures on the Jewish Church, vol. ii).

2. **Political Administration.** Although David thus introduced into Israel a royal estate absolutely unknown under his predecessor, yet he did not change the predominant feature of the Jewish monarchy; his reign, as that of Saul, was to be spent in defending the country against its various enemies (III Kings v, 3), and this is why one of the principal cares of his administration was to keep a standing

army on an excellent footing. For this purpose, he divided the national forces into 12 divisions of 24,000 men, each division being liable to be called on to serve in their respective months (I Paralip, xxvii, 1-15), and placed the whole army under the command of Joab, who had obtained this most important dignity under the walls of Jerusalem. He no doubt realized that for the defence of a hilly country like Palestine, cavalry and numerous chariots would be of little avail; and hence, differently from the armies of the other nations, that of Israel remained under him made up exclusively of infantry and supplied with only a few chariots (cfr. II Kings viii, 14). He, of course, maintained the body-guard, which had been instituted by Saul, and gave its command to the distinguished Levite, Banaias, son of Joiada (II Kings xxiii, 19, sq.). To this he added a kind of military order composed of 600 select men with the special title of *Gibborim*, heroes, or mighty men, under the command of Abisai, his nephew (II Kings xxiii, 8-39; I Paralip. xi, 9-47).

Side by side with this military organization, David created or developed several social institutions. While he himself was the head of all government, civil and military, he did not supersede the time-honored authority of the heads and elders of tribes, but "he extended and improved it, especially by distributing a large portion of the Levites through the country, of whom no fewer than 6,000 were made officers and judges (I Paralip. xxiii, 4). For developing the material resources of the country, he had storehouses in the fields, in the cities, in the villages and in the castles; there were vineyards and wine-cellars, and cellars of oil, superintended each by appointed officers; in different valleys herds and flocks grazed under the care of royal herdsmen and shepherds; an officer, skilled in agriculture, presided over the tillage of the fields; the sycamore and olive trees were under the eye of skilful foresters," etc. (I Paralip. xxvii, 25-31. BLAIKIE, Manual of Bible History, p. 254).

3. **Ecclesiastical Arrangements.** As David had made Jerusalem the centre of social and political life in Israel, so he resolved to make it the centre of religious worship by removing to Mount Sion the Ark of the Covenant, which was then at Cariathiarim. For this purpose he held a consultation with the Jewish elders, who readily approved his design. His first attempt met indeed with a mortifying defeat, when the priest Oza was smitten with instantaneous death for having even unwittingly touched the Ark (II Kings vi, 1-11; I Paralip. xiii); but three months afterwards he succeeded in carrying this symbol of Jehovah's favor and presence, in solemn procession and amidst hymns of triumph, into the Jewish capital. Perhaps, even at this time, he cherished the project of erecting a magnificent temple to the God of Israel, and thereby completing the work of religious centralization; it is only later on, however, when he had done with his various wars, that he saw his way to submit this undertaking to the approval of the prophet Nathan. At first the prophet encouraged, but afterwards, in God's name, objected to David's project, and told him that this glorious work was reserved for his son and successor. It is in connection with this announcement that Nathan revealed to David the great future which awaited his race. His house, he was told, should reign forever over Israel, and his seed would erect to Jehovah a temple and would be raised to Divine sonship. In this glorious announcement, Jewish and Christian traditions have ever seen a prediction of the Messias, the greatest Son of David, and the eternal Ruler over the house of Jacob; and St. Peter declares that David, being "a prophet," understood it of Christ (Acts ii, 30, 31). No wonder then that the Jewish monarch found in it an ample compensation for his disappointment at not being allowed to build a temple to Jehovah, and that his prayer before the Ark on this occasion expresses so fervently his thanks for the promise, and his desire for its fulfilment (II Kings vii; xxiii, 1, sq.; I Paralip. xvii).

Having thus provided, as far as it lay in his power, for the unity of government and worship, David surrounded himself with four great religious dignitaries whose principal duty was to guide him in all ecclesiastical matters of importance. These were the prophets Gad and Nathan, his constant advisers, and the two high priests Abiathar and Sadoc, who represented the two rival houses descending from Aaron. These latter were especially charged to superintend Divine worship, the former in Jerusalem, where the Ark now rested, the latter in Gabaon, an ancient place of worship where the Tabernacle was still preserved. Naturally enough, there were in Israel at this time other religious functionaries inferior in rank to these four great dignitaries of David, and working under their direction; they probably formed two great classes: (1) that of *prophets* especially instructed in singing and music under Asaph, Heman the grandson of Samuel, and Idithun (I Paralip. xxv); (2) that of *Levites* or attendants on the sanctuary, who divided among themselves the functions directly connected with Divine worship. As a matter of fact, it is to this period of Jewish history that the first book of Chronicles refers the introduction of that system of *courses* further elaborated later on, whereby the whole *sacerdotal* body was divided into classes, named after their respective chiefs and presided over by them. They carried out their functions week by week, their particular duties being apportioned by lot. The rest of the Levites, to the number of 38,000, ranging from twenty years of age and upwards, received also a special organization (I Paralip. xxiv; cfr. also II Paralip. xxxi, 2).

4. **Outward Relations.** Whilst thus engaged at home in introducing into every department of administration something like system and order, David did not lose sight of what the circumstances of the time required of him in connection with the various surrounding nations. It was his mission to

pursue and bring to a successful issue the great work of liberating his people from their enemies which had been begun by Saul; and, in point of fact, almost his entire life was spent in wars along all the borders of Israel. On the southwest, he fought against the Philistines, and took from these inveterate enemies of the Jews the town of Geth and a great part of their dominion. On the southeast, he conquered and established garrisons in the territory of Edom. On the east of the Jordan, he attacked and well-nigh exterminated the Moabites, whilst on the northeast, he overthrew the Syrians of Soba as well as those of Damascus who had marched to the defence of their kindred. Finally, he waged a protracted war against the Ammonites, who had entered into a defensive alliance with several of the Syrian princes, and wreaked upon them a frightful vengeance. Of course, of all these wars the Biblical narrative gives us little more than a brief mention; yet it is sufficient to make us feel how severe was the treatment which David inflicted upon the conquered. Thus we read of the Moabite prisoners that he put two-thirds to death, and granted life to only one-third (II Kings viii, 2), and of the Ammonite cities compelled to surrender, that "bringing forth the people thereof he sawed them, and drove over them chariots armed with iron, and divided them with knives and made them pass through brickkilns" (II Kings xii, 31). Efforts have been made in various ways to account for the peculiar barbarity of such treatment; it has been said, for instance, that David belonged to a barbarous age, that cruelty has ever been a part of Oriental tactics to strike enemies with terror, that in the case of Ammonites (and possibly also in the case of the Moabites), these cruelties were a retaliation for a gross provocation (II Kings x, 2-4; I Paralip. xix, 1, sq.), etc. It seems, however, that these excuses, either separately or collectively, do not cover the whole ground, and leave David's character in regard to his treatment of the conquered, stained with unjustifiable atrocities (II Kings viii, 1, sq.; I Paralip. xviii, 1, sq.).

It is only to the northwest of Palestine, that we find David keeping up carefully pacific relations. It seems that the Phenicians, having helped the Philistines in their first wars against him, soon reversed their policy and showed themselves anxious to be on friendly terms with the young and growing nation of the Jews; and it is certain that the Jewish monarch was no less anxious to cultivate the friendship of a people whose aid as to materials and workmen he needed so much for the various buildings the erection of which he either carried out or contemplated. This contact with the heathen outside Jewish territory, which David was not so prone to seek as his son and successor, led to good results. The Israelites learned therefrom something of the useful and ornamental arts, and this prepared the way for the positive achievements of the age of Solomon (I Paralip. xxii).

5. **Extension and Prosperity of the Empire.** As the outcome of his successful wars, David had succeeded in extending the frontiers of Israel's dominions to the very limits promised to Abraham long centuries before (Gen. xv, 18). His empire included besides Eastern and Western Palestine several tributary kingdoms, and extended from the Great Sea to the Euphrates and from the mountains of Lebanon to the eastern arm of the Red Sea. Its area was about 60,000 square miles, and its population nearly 5,000,-000. This was probably the largest empire in the Oriental world at the time, and it had been obtained by faithfulness to theocratic principles, as is suggested by what we read in II Kings vii, 9, that Jehovah "made him (David) a great name, like unto the name of the great men that are in the earth." David's own feelings of gratitude to God for so much glory are expressed in that noble psalm of thanksgiv-

ing, which is found in both the second book of Kings (chap. xxii) and the book of Psalms (Ps. xvii).

As might naturally be expected, the nation at large felt proud of the numerous conquests which had been achieved by its leader, but more particularly did it feel grateful for the unexampled prosperity which prevailed throughout the land before the great crime of David with Bethsabee. Up to that fatal moment, the public mind was united in promoting the welfare of the country, and under the wise direction of a strong, centralized government, agriculture and industry soon reached a flourishing condition.

### § 3. *Fall and Last Years of David.*

1. **His Fall and its Punishment.** It was during the war with the Ammonites that David fell into those most aggravated sins of adultery and murder, which compromised almost entirely the unity and prosperity of his empire because of the long series of family, personal and public calamities with which God visited him (II Kings vi-xii, 14).

The first disgraceful transaction which followed in the line of judgment upon *David's house*, was the incest of Amnon, followed two years later, by the death of that worthless prince, through the agency of Absalom (II Kings xiii, 1-29). For this offence, Absalom himself so tenderly loved by the king, was obliged to take to flight, and actually spent three years with the Syrian king of Gessur (II Kings xiii, 30-39).

The next punishment fell heavily upon the *entire kingdom*. Absalom, having been recalled and restored to favor, started a rebellion and usurped the throne. Accordingly, David flying from his capital, passed east of the Jordan, where he made a stand against his unnatural son, whilst the latter entered Jerusalem in triumph (II Kings xiv, xv. HIBBARD. Palestine, p. 258, sq.).

2. **David's Restoration, Subsequent Faults and Death.** It can hardly be doubted that if Absalom had not followed the insidious advice of a secret friend of David, — thereby wasting precious time in striving to collect a large army from the whole nation, — but had at once pursued his "weary and weak-handed father" with a comparatively small body of men, he would have secured the final success of his revolt. Absalom's delay saved David, around whom a powerful army soon assembled, east of the Jordan. A severe battle was fought which resulted in Absalom's defeat and death, in the break up of his insurrection and in the restoration of his father (II Kings xvi–xviii).

Scarcely was David restored when a new revolt broke out. The northern tribes took it ill that the men of Juda should have presumed to reinstate the king without their concurrence. In consequence there followed an insurrection headed by Seba, a Benjamite, which for some time threatened more evil to David than even the revolt of Absalom, but which was ultimately quelled by the valiant, though most unscrupulous Joab (II Kings xix, xx).

After a long famine and a severe war with the Philistines which followed soon afterwards (II Kings xxi), David, moved probably by some ambitious design contrary to the theocratic character of a Jewish king, had a military census taken by his officers. This was a serious and public fault against the essential character of the Constitution of Israel, and was therefore punished by a fearful pestilence which carried away no less than 70,000 Israelites. At length the prayer of the humbled monarch arrested the destroyer (II Kings xxiv; I Paralip. xxi).

The declining years of David were also marked by factions, which on the question of the royal succession soon to be opened, divided the army, the royal household and even the priesthood. Adonias, the eldest surviving son of David, upheld by Joab and Abiathar, took measures to procure for himself the right of succession, and caused a powerful diversion in the public mind in his favor. This roused Bethsabee, the mother of Solomon, and Nathan, the prophet, who immediately induced David to have Solomon inaugurated king and successor with due form and solemnity (III Kings i). To him alone, the aged monarch intrusted the charge of building a house to Jehovah (I Paralip. xxii), the materials of which he had himself gathered in great quantity during the last ten years (I Paralip. xxvii, xxix). After Solomon's coronation David lived but a short time: his rule had lasted forty years, thirty-three of which were spent in Jerusalem (III Kings ii, 11).

3. **Character of David.** Few rulers have been more sincerely admired and more universally praised than David the great founder of the Jewish monarchy. It is, indeed, impossible to justify all his acts or to regard him as a perfect character, for even a brief study of his life as described in the Biblical narrative discloses faults numerous and considerable, in truth those very faults which one might naturally expect to find in the chieftain of an Eastern and comparatively barbarous people. Thus, in his exile from the court of Saul, he appeared at times not much better than a freebooter, who had recourse, when he deemed it expedient, to craft or even falsehood. In Hebron and in Jerusalem he had his harem, like other Eastern kings. He waged war and revenged himself on his foreign enemies with merciless cruelty, like other warriors of his age and country. Adultery and murder and the unlawful numbering of his people were three deep stains on his character and memory, and his parting advice to his son not to spare Joab and Semei is not perhaps absolutely excusable.

These are so many dark shadows which can be noticed in the Biblical picture of David's reign, because Holy Writ presents to us not the panegyric, but the truthful record of the deeds of an Oriental monarch. But they should not make us lose sight for a moment of the bright and lovely and holy features of the character of David as drawn in the inspired narrative. Before he reaches the throne he stands before us adorned with the perfect innocence of his lonely shepherd life, with that bravery and trust in Jehovah which makes him meet Goliath with his rustic weapons; with that deep respect for the anointed of the Lord which causes him to spare time and again the life of Saul, his unjust and fierce persecutor. Called to the throne by the will of God and the free choice of his nation, he assumes the reins of government with a vigor which contrasts with the long years of weakness of the preceding ruler, and which soon introduces system and order into all the branches of public administration. Never any complaint is heard against his manner of rendering justice; and he is remarkable by his valor in an age of warriors, no less than by his piety and constant adherence to the exclusive worship of God in a time and nation whose bent was towards sensual idolatry. His inspired canticles — for he composed many psalms despite the negations of destructive critics — whilst revealing his poetical genius, make us acquainted with the inward feelings of his soul, and have caused Jewish and Christian traditions to consider him as the royal prophet of Israel. His lamentable falls he more than expiated by the depth of his sorrow and the humility of his resignation under God's punishments. In a word, he was the great man of his age, and in almost all respects, the model of a theocratic ruler, "an example worthy of the imitation of his successors, and according as these appear on comparison with him, the sacred writers estimate their characters" (JAHN, Hebrew Commonwealth, p. 76; cfr. also III Kings xv, 3, 11; IV Kings xiv, 3; xvi, 2; xviii, 3, etc.).

Finally, through almost "all the circumstances of his life, David has been regarded as typical of his great Son. His birth at Bethlehem, his private unction there, his victory over the giant foe who had defied the army of the living God, his sweet music which put to flight the evil spirit, the persecutions that he endured, the compassion and forgiveness which he exhibited, his zeal for the House of God, his wars and triumphs over heathen nations, his rejection by his own people, the treachery of his tried comrade, his final victory over all opposition — all these and such like details have a prophetic and typical import and speak to the Christian of the love and sufferings and triumphs of Jesus" (DEANE, David, p. 221).

# SYNOPSIS OF CHAPTER XIX.

## The Kingdom of Solomon.

*Section I. Its Beginning and Prosperous Period.*

I. Its Beginning:
1. *How Solomon was Prepared and Called to succeed David.*
2. *His Accession and First Acts.*

II. Commercial Relations:
- By Land with: Egypt. Arabia. Tyre.
- By Sea: How brought about. With what countries. (Ophir.)

III. Internal Prosperity:
1. *Intellectual Life of Solomon and his Times.*
2. *Military and Political Organization of his Empire.*
3. *Extension and Peaceful Condition of his States.*

IV. Public Works:
- *In Jerusalem:*
  - A. The temple (building; description; dedication).
  - B. His own palace; wall of city.
- *In the Provinces:* cities built by him.

## CHAPTER XIX.

### THE KINGDOM OF SOLOMON.

#### SECTION I. ITS BEGINNING AND PROSPEROUS PERIOD.

§ *1. Beginning of Solomon's Kingdom.*

1. **How Solomon was Prepared and Called to Succeed David.** Unlike the first two kings of Israel, Solomon, the second son of David by Bethsabee, was born in the Jewish capital and brought up in the midst of such state and luxury as belonged to his father's court. Three persons especially had much to do with his early training: his father, his mother and the prophet Nathan. The influence of his father was no doubt of the happiest kind. Matured by years and chastened by sorrow and misfortune, David must have watched over this child of his beloved wife with a special care and set before him examples of personal love and devotion to Jehovah, of strict and constant attention to public affairs. Furthermore, as he knew that Solomon was destined to rule over Israel, he no doubt initiated him gradually into the many details of political government and into his great project of erecting a temple to the Lord.

"But the boy would be also with Bethsabee, his mother — in his childhood almost entirely so; and that must have been a very different influence. The mother's influence in an Eastern court is almost always bad, for she is not trained to think of anything higher for her child than the merest self-indulgence" (WINTERBOTHAM, Life and Reign of Solomon, p. 14), and in this particular case, a happy motherly influence could hardly be expected on the part of one who had consented to share in a royal adultery, and whose main concern was apparently to secure the throne to her beloved child. Fortunately, therefore, for Solomon, he found in Nathan, the faithful prophet of Jehovah, and a man of great influence with both David and Bethsabee, examples and precepts that would counteract to some extent the softness of his early training by his mother, add considerably to the power of the good example and advice of his father, and prepare him gradually for the great future before him.

Thus Solomon grew up destined to the throne not only by the peculiar love of David and Bethsabee, but also and principally by the solemn decree which Nathan had uttered in his favor on the part of Jehovah (II Kings vii, 12, 15; III Kings ii, 15, 24). It was most likely in consequence of this Divine decree that David had secretly promised to Bethsabee that her son Solomon would succeed to the kingdom (III Kings i, 17), and that when Adonias, his eldest surviving son, put up a claim to the throne and was not thereupon rebuked by him, Nathan intervened and requested that the royal dignity should belong to the one chosen by the Supreme King of Israel. It is also probable that the prophet profited by this occasion to make David sensible of the great evils which might arise for his family and nation should he die before the actual coronation of his successor, and this accounts for the fact that the aged monarch lost no time in having Solomon inaugurated King of Israel, and expressed his great joy at seeing the ceremony over (III Kings i, 48; cfr. also III Kings ii, 22).

2. **Accession and First Acts of Solomon.** A few months elapsed when, by the death of his father, Solomon became the sole occupant of the Jewish throne. He was still very young — probably between sixteen and twenty — and whilst he knew he possessed the affectionate loyalty of

the nation at large, he could not forget that very near his throne he had several bold and designing enemies. "The pretensions of his own elder brother Adonias still commanded a powerful party; Abiathar swayed the priesthood; Joab the army. The singular connection in public opinion between the title to the crown and the possession of the deceased monarch's harem has been already noticed. Adonias, in making request for Abisag, a youthful concubine taken by David in his old age, was considered as insidiously renewing his claims to the sovereignty. Solomon saw at once the wisdom of his father's dying admonition (III Kings ii, 5-9; he seized the opportunity of crushing all future opposition, and all danger of a civil war. He caused Adonias to be put to death, suspended Abiathar from his office and banished him from Jerusalem, and commanded that Joab, though he had fled to the altar, be slain for two murders of which he had been guilty, those of Abner and Amasa. Semei, another dangerous character, was commanded to reside in Jerusalem, on pain of death if he should quit the city. Three years afterwards, he was detected in a suspicious journey to Geth, on the Philistine border, and having violated the compact, he suffered the penalty" (MILMAN, History of the Jews).

Thus secured, according to the advice of his father, from internal enemies, Solomon married Pharao's daughter. This was clearly a political alliance, the chief aim of which was probably to flatter the national pride of the Israelites by making them more fully realize the high standing they actually possessed among the greatest monarchies of the world. Although this alliance with a heathen woman must have appeared contrary to the religious traditions of the people of Jehovah, yet its irregularity was not objected to at the time. Another thing contributed towards rendering this alliance acceptable to the Jewish nation, namely, the splendid and costly sacrifice which the young monarch hastened after his accession to offer on "*the great high place*" in Gabaon, where the Tabernacle still remained, and which was calculated to prove to all his sincere devotion to the worship of the God of Israel. The sacred writer informs us that this sacrifice was so pleasing to Jehovah that He appeared to Solomon, offered him whatever gift he might choose, and bestowed upon him "an understanding heart to judge his people." An illustration is then given of the wonderful judicial wisdom of the king in the memorable incident of the two women who contested the right to a child (III Kings, iii).

### § 2. *Commercial Relations.*

1. **Commerce by Land.** Solomon is the first Jewish ruler who, having in his hands the great military and commercial roads between the Euphrates and the Nile, felt free enough from foreign foes to start and carry on an active commerce with the nations which surrounded Israel. His principal traffic by land was with *Egypt* for the horses and chariots for which this country had become famous. He needed them to keep up his own large supply, for he himself possessed horsemen and chariots in great numbers after the manner of the Egyptian and Hittite kings, and more particularly to satisfy the incessant demands for such warlike or splendid equipages by the Hittite and Aramean warriors (III Kings x, 28, 29). To transport them across his territory he naturally put in good repair the old caravan roads which long centuries of war and confusion had allowed to fall into a miserable condition, and "after a system long established in Egypt, he built towns at suitable points as centres of commerce and depots of goods for sale" (GEIKIE, Hours with the Bible, vol. iii, p. 422). That the Jewish king kept the monopoly of this lucrative trade, as indeed of all his commerce, is most likely from what we know of the customs of Oriental monarchs.

Solomon's commercial relations with **Arabia** are less accurately known to us than those he had with Egypt. It is from Arabia that he must have mainly derived the spices which were extensively used during his reign (cfr. III Kings x, 25; Prov. vii, 17; Cant. iii, 6; iv, 10, 14, 16, etc.); for although they might have been brought to him by sea, yet they have ever been transported by caravans throughout the East. From the same country he may also have imported many of his precious stones (cfr. III Kings x, 2, 10; II Paralip. ix, 1, 9, 10).

The last country with which Solomon maintained direct commercial relations by land was PHENICIA. His traffic with Hiram, King of Tyre, was chiefly required by his own numerous architectural undertakings; for without the friendly transactions with this pagan prince, Solomon would never have been able to carry out the building of the Temple of Jerusalem and of his various palaces. Phenicia was ever famous in antiquity for its skilled wood-carvers and metal-casters, and the Israelites, at least at this time, were far from having acquired the knowledge in the useful and fine arts which such public constructions required. It may be added in passing that if the Jewish king vanquished many a time his royal brother of Tyre in their contests of wit (JOSEPHUS, Against Apion, i, 17), the Phenician monarch certainly got the better of the son of David in their business transactions (III Kings v; vii; 13, sq.; ix, 1, sq; II Paralip. ii; viii, 2).

2. **Commerce by Sea.** It was his intercourse with Phenicia which suggested to Solomon maritime enterprises which departed entirely from the old traditions of the Jewish people, never much acquainted with the sea. Whilst the Tyrians covered the Mediterranean Sea with their ships, founding numerous colonies, opening trading ports — the chief of which was Tarsis, probably on the southern coast

of Spain, then abounding in gold and silver mines — David secured the possession of Asiongaber at the northern end of the eastern arm of the Red Sea and his son and successor, Solomon, bethought himself of procuring a fleet which would cross the Red Sea and trade with the eastern ports of India. This was a bold conception, for to carry it out Solomon could not reckon either on native ship-builders or native sailors. Yet by means of his friendly alliance with Hiram he was able to secure ships which he manned partly with Phenician sailors, partly with his own subjects from Dan and Zabulon, who were somewhat familiar with the sea by their residence near the coast.

It is hardly probable that the ships of Solomon sailed in company with those of Hiram and shared in their profits. The Phenicians most likely kept the monopoly and the "Tarsis navy" spoken of in the Hebrew text of III Kings x, 22; II Paralip. ix, 21, was a generic term simply to designate ships of a particular build, just as Englishmen might talk of an "Indiaman" without necessarily implying that the ship sailed only to India (FARRAR, Solomon, his Life and Times, p. 122).

Whatever may be thought of Solomon's maritime partnership with the King of Tyre in the commerce of the Mediterranean, there is no doubt that he attempted the navigation of the Red Sea, for which Hiram and his Tyrians could feel no sort of jealousy. Sailing from Asiongaber, the Jewish navy went to Ophir, a place the exact site of which has been the subject matter of endless discussions. Some have identified it with the ancient gold mines and extensive ruins recently discovered in Southern Africa; others with a place called El Ophir in the southern part of Arabia (Gen. x, 29); others again with a place at the mouth of the Indus, etc., etc. The last opinion just given seems, on the whole, very probable on the following grounds: (1) all the imports mentioned in the Bible are of Indian origin; (2) the names given them (except of course of gold, silver and precious stones for which there were already Hebrew words) are Sanscrit words; (3) the place at the mouth of the Indus, is named by Ptolemy **Abiria**, and by Hindu geographers **Abhira**, a name practically identical with that of Ophir; (4) finally, in the Septuagint, or oldest Greek translation of the Old Testament, Ophir is translated *Sophir*, which in Coptic means *India*, and this rendering is adopted by the Arabic versions; the Vulgate itself renders Ophir by India in Job xxviii, 16 (cfr. VIGOUROUX, Bible et Découvertes Modernes, tome iii; FARRAR, Solomon, pp. 123-126).

The principal products brought from Ophir were, besides gold and silver, ivory, precious stones, sandalwood, apes and peacocks, the last of which caused the greatest wonder among the Jewish population (III Kings ix, 28; x, 11, 22; II Paralip. viii, 18; ix, 10).

§ *3. Internal Prosperity.*

1. **Intellectual Life of Solomon and his Times.** The prosperous period of Solomon's reign was not only the best epoch for the development of Jewish industry and commerce, it was also the most favorable time for the development of national intellectual life. In this respect, as in every other, the King of Israel took the lead, and he became very widely known as the "*wisest* man of his time," whereby it was probably meant that he was endowed with an extraordinary "faculty of acute observation, shrewdness in discovery or device, cleverness of invention " (DRIVER, Introduction to Old Testament Literature, chapter viii; cfr. also III Kings iii, 2, 3). Solomon's wisdom thus understood allowed him to cultivate with great success that *gnomic* poetry which "consists of acute observations on human life and society, or generalizations respecting conduct and character " (DRIVER, chapter vii); and in fact no less than 3,000 prov-

erbs are ascribed to him (III Kings iv, 32). Of all these proverbs of the Jewish monarch, only a very small number has come down to us embodied in a general collection known as our canonical "Book of Proverbs." Many times his proverbs assumed the form of "parables from nature," that is, of shrewd sayings which men could verify for themselves by ordinary observation of natural facts and which contained important lessons. As these sayings were often suggested by a close observation either of animals, such as the lizard, the ant, the lion, the bear, etc. ; or of plants, such as the cedar, the hyssop, etc., we find it stated that Solomon "treated about trees from the cedar that is in the Lebanon, unto the hyssop that cometh out of the wall, and discoursed of beasts and of fowls, and of creeping things and of fishes" (III Kings iv, 33).

We are further told that he composed "a thousand and five poems" (III Kings iv, 32), whence it follows that Solomon also cultivated *lyric* poetry assiduously; but of all the lyric compositions of the Bible, only a few have been ascribed to him, namely: Psalm LXXII in the Hebrew (LXXI in the Vulgate), Psalm CXVII in the Hebrew (CXVI in the Vulgate), the Canticle of Canticles, and Ecclesiastes.

Perhaps to this same period of the **Golden Age** of the Hebrew literature must be ascribed the remarkable poem known under the name of the Book of Job, in which case, it would be necessary to admit that some of the deepest problems offered to the human mind by our mortal existence greatly agitated already the *wise men* of Solomon's time (cfr. PELT, Histoire de l'Ancien Testament, tome ii, p. 65-92).

Besides these various inspired poems, it can hardly be doubted, that in Israel, as in any nation which has reached a high literary development, other poetical compositions were written bearing on topics which had no religious or sacred character. Finally, as forming a part of the intellectual activity of the time, we must mention the public and private diaries which were later utilized by the compilers of our books of Kings and Chronicles (III Kings iv, 3; xi, 41; II Paralip. ix, 29).

2. **Military and Political Organization.** As might naturally be expected from a monarch who had set before himself the ideal of peaceful wealth and literary culture instead of that of military glory, Solomon left practically untouched the military organization introduced by his father. Like David, he had his standing army, now commanded by Banaias, the son of Joiada; his military order of 600 men, and his body-guard under the command of a captain whose power extended over the king's household. To these he simply added a comparatively large number of cavalry and charioteers.

The political organization underwent more considerable changes. Having surrounded himself with wise and respected counsellors (III Kings iv, 2), the king did away with the time-honored division of Israel into tribes, and put taxation on a new basis. He preserved indeed the old number of *twelve* in his new division of the land, but his twelve provinces were made according to population and resources, and over each of these he himself appointed a governor. His aim was clearly to deal a fatal blow at the old tribal jealousies and divisions which he remembered had so terribly shaken the kingdom during the last years of his father, and at the same time to regulate taxation more easily. The financial administration which was intrusted to the provincial governors was in fact of the simplest kind; apparently no direct taxes were levied, but all that was requisite for Solomon's court and government had to be provided, each province supplying in turn what was required for a month (III Kings iv).

3. **Extension and Peaceful Condition of his States.** With such excellent financial organization, it should have been easy for the Jewish king to meet the yearly expenses of his reign, the more so because the various tributary nations — Philistines, Edomites, Moabites, Ammonites, Arabians of the desert and Syrians of Damascus — showed themselves faithful in paying him whatever dues had been imposed on them by David (III Kings iv, 21). Solomon's passion for building soon betrayed him, however, into enormous expenses which he felt unable to cover except by alienating a part of his dominions. So that had the King of Tyre been pleased with the twenty cities on the border of Phenicia, which his royal brother had given him, the kingdom of Solomon would have been actually less extensive than that of his father (III Kings ix, 10, sq.). The only city which was added to Solomon's dominions, during his long reign, was that of Gazer, which the King of Egypt took from the Philistines and bestowed upon his daughter as a dowry at the time of her marriage with the Jewish monarch.

But if the territory of Israel was not increased during the rule of Solomon, there is hardly any doubt that the population increased rapidly owing to the actual cessation of war, and to the growing material prosperity which the nation enjoyed for many years (III Kings iv, 20). This was indeed a time of peace and plenty "when Juda and Israel dwelt without any fear, every one under his vine and under his fig-tree" (III Kings iv, 25). It was the time of that lavish expenditure of those great architectural and commercial undertakings which at first naturally tended to increase the well-being of the country "by making money more plentiful, by providing employment, creating large demands and arousing ambitions hitherto unknown" (WINTERBOTHAM, Solomon, p. 34). National pride and interest were gratified not only by the most precious and most abundant treasures which foreign nations and chieftains offered to the Jewish king and which were then mostly spent among the people ; but also by Solomon's care to bestow only upon Israelites the posts of honor and profit. It is not therefore to be wondered at that the sacred writers of the books of Kings and Paralipomenon describe with a special delight the riches and glory of the son of David, and the peace and prosperity which the whole nation "from Dan to Bersabee" enjoyed under his rule. Indeed this period of peace, of prosperity and of glory contrasted so strongly with the insecurity of the time of the judges and even of the reigns of Saul and David, and with the misfortunes of later ages, that this glorious period of Solomon's reign gradually came to be considered as the type of that kingdom of course more prosperous, more lasting than that of Solomon, yet like unto it, which the Messias, the greatest Son of David, would introduce into the world for "the glory of the Jews and the revelation of the Gentiles" (III King iv; II Paralip. viii, ix; Matt. vi, 29; Luke ii, 25, 32).

§ *4. Public Works.*

1. **Public Works in Jerusalem.** Among the many wonders of Solomon's reign which struck the imagination of the Jewish people and made them long remember the splendor of his rule, were the public buildings wherewith he embellished the capital of his empire. The first, and by far the most important of these great buildings, was the **Temple.** Towards the construction of this sanctuary David had gathered great treasures, quantities of brass, iron, stone, timber, etc. (I Paralip. xxii), and had matured a detailed plan which he explained to his son with the solemn charge that he should carry it out with ardor and perseverance (I Paralip. xxviii). On coming to the throne Solomon lost no time in taking up a work so dear to his father and to the nation

at large. For this purpose he entered into a regular treaty with Hiram, by which he bound himself to supply the Tyrians with large quantities of corn, oil and wine, and received in return their timber which was floated down to Joppe, and a large number of artificers. Besides, Solomon ordered a levy out of Israel, which furnished him with 30,000 workmen, 10,000 of whom were employed at a time to cut timber in Libanus, and he compelled 150,000 strangers, chiefly of Chanaanite descent, to carry burdens and hew stones (III Kings v; I Paralip. ii).

These preparations completed, the work was begun on the site bought by David from Ornan the Jesubite, on Mount Moriah, an eminence near Jerusalem, at once rendered sacred as the spot where Abraham had offered up Isaac, and where the plague had been stayed during the last reign. The rugged top of Moriah was levelled with great labor; its sides, which to the east and south were precipitous, were faced with walls of great stones, built up on the sloping sides, the interval between being occupied by vaults or filled up with earth. The lower, bevelled stones of the wall remain, the relics of the eastern wall alone being Solomon's. They bear Phenician red marks on their bottom rows, at the depth of 90 feet, where the foundations rest on the rock itself. No sound of hammer or of axe, or of any tool of iron, was heard as the structure arose (III Kings vi, 7); every beam already cut and squared before being floated down to Joppe, every stone already hewn and bevelled in the quarries recently discovered under the present city of Jerusalem, near the Damascus gate, was laid silently in its appointed place (MACLEAR, Old Testament History, p. 356).

Like the Tabernacle, on the general model of which it was built, the Temple faced the east. It consisted of the "*House of Jehovah*" or Temple proper, erected on the top of the sacred mount, and of two concentrated enclosures or

"*Courts of Jehovah's House*" surrounding the Temple proper in such a manner that the inner court stood upon higher ground than the outer one, and the House of Jehovah upon a position highest of all.

The Temple proper was but a small building, a shrine erected to the God of Israel that He might dwell in the midst of His people, not in our sense a church freely open to all. It had three distinct parts: (1) the **Vestibule**, about 30 feet wide and 15 feet deep, within which arose two pillars of brass, their capitals ornamented with network, chainwork and pomegranates; (2) the **Holy Place**, the dimensions of which were exactly double those of the Tabernacle, was 60 feet long from east to west, by 30 wide, and 45 high. It was entered from the Vestibule by folding-doors made of cypress overlaid with gold and richly embossed. Every part of this wonderful room was overlaid with gold, and the walls of hewn stone panelled with cedar, were further adorned with beautiful carvings representing cherubim, fruits and flowers. It contained the golden Altar of Incense, on either side of which were five golden tables for the " loaves of proposition " and five golden candlesticks, each seven-branched. (3) the **Holy of Holies** or *Most Holy Place* was a perfect cube of 30 feet. The entrance was from the Holy Place through folding-doors which were probably always open, though the opening was concealed by a rich veil of the brightest colors. Like the Holy Place, the Holy of Holies was most richly decorated, overlaid with gold in all its parts. It contained but one object, the original Ark of the Covenant overshadowed by two gigantic cherubim likewise overlaid with gold. On three sides of the Temple proper there were side buildings three stories high and so arranged that the Temple proper rose above them like a clerestory rising above aisles, the window-openings being fitted with fixed lattices of boards; the Most Holy Place, however, was apparently without any light or ventilation from the outside. (On the resemblance of Solomon's Temple to those of Egypt, cfr. VIGOUROUX, Bible et Découvertes Modernes, tome iii.)

Descending from the Vestibule, one would come to the "*Inner*" (III Kings vi, 36) or "*Court of the Priests*" (II Paralip. iv, 9) within which — as within the Court of the Tabernacle — was the Altar of Holocausts, 30 feet long and 15 high, and standing on the exact site of the threshing floor of Ornan. In the same court, were also found a great tank or "sea" of molten brass used for the ablutions of the priests, ten lesser movable vessels of brass for the washing of entrails, and all the other utensils necessary for the various Jewish sacrifices. This court was paved with great stones, and enclosed by a low wall of polished stones and a row of beams of cedar. Only the priests and those who offered sacrifices were allowed into the inner court, a part of which — the nearest to the Temple — was actually reserved for the exclusive use of the priests.

From this Inner Court, steps led down to the "*Outer Court*" where the people gathered to attend the various sacrifices and ceremonies of the Mosaic Ritual (cfr. Jerem. xxxvi, 10). This outer court was probably left unfinished by Solomon, but when completed it was surrounded by a strong wall, supplied with four massive gates of brass, and contained within together with colonnades, chambers and rooms used for various purposes. From this court, steps led down to a wide esplanade destined to become later the *Court of the Gentiles* (cfr. PELT, Histoire de l'Ancien Testament, tome ii, p. 24, sq.; EDERSHEIM, Bible History, vol. v, p. 75, sq.).

As soon as the Jewish monarch had finished the House of Jehovah and the Inner Court (which was indeed necessary for carrying on the Divine service), he dedicated his work to the worship of God in a splendid festival the details of which have been preserved to us by the sacred writers (III Kings viii ; II Paralip. v-vii).

Before the Temple was thus completed and dedicated Solomon had begun the erection of his own magnificent palace, to which he devoted thirteen years of labor. It was most likely made up of several different buildings after the manner of the Assyrian palaces, and of these buildings little more than the names has come down to us. The principal building was probably the **House of the Forest of Libanus**; next in importance was the **Porch of Judgment**, and finally the **Porch of Pillars**. He also made a house for the daughter of Pharao, whom he had taken to wife (III Kings vii, 1-12). Solomon's magnificent palace, for the splendor of which nothing was spared, was below the platform of the Temple, for "he constructed an ascent from his own house to that of Jehovah, that is, a subterranean passage 250 feet long by 42 feet wide, of which the remains may still be traced" (Smith, Old Testament History, p. 491).

About the same time Solomon supplied Jerusalem with water by means of reservoirs and aqueducts, and completed or simply repaired the fortification of his capital (III Kings xi, 27).

2. **Public Works in the Provinces.** The public works carried out by the son of David outside Jerusalem regarded chiefly fortresses which he either strengthened or rebuilt with a view to prevent invasion or protect his own caravan-roads. Thus he fortified Baalath, Gazer and the two Bethorons to command the pass which led from the coast-plain to the highlands of Benjamin; the post of Heser to defend the northern entrance of Israel's territory from Syria and Assyria; Mageddo to guard the plain of Esdrælon. Lastly, at some 250 miles northeast of Jerusalem, half-way between Damascus and the Euphrates, he built Tadmor, afterwards called Palmyra, in an oasis of the Syrian wilderness, wherefrom he could overawe the predatory tribes of

the desert, and secure his communication with the outlying post of Thapsacus on the Euphrates (WINTERBOTHAM, Solomon, p. 63, sq.).

Besides these fortresses, the names of which are given in the Bible, the king strengthened many other towns, and in particular he provided magazine cities for his chariots and his cavalry (III Kings ix, 19).

# SYNOPSIS OF CHAPTER XX.

### The Kingdom of Solomon.

*Section II. Its Decline and Disruption.*

**I. Its Decline:**

1. *Causes:*
   - In general: The adoption by Solomon of the ways of Eastern monarchs
   - In particular:
     - Despotism; enormous expenditure; enforcement of compulsory labor.
     - Sensual life; multiplication of wives and concubines, *hence*
     - Idolatry admitted, practised.

2. *Signs:*
   - A. Abroad: Rebellions of Edom and Syria.
   - B. At home:
     - Dissatisfaction of people and prophets.
     - Rapid fortune of Jeroboam.

3. *The End of Solomon.* Judgments passed on him.

**II. Its Disruption:**

1. *How Brought About?*
   - Old jealouses between the tribes of Juda and Israel.
   - Conduct of Roboam at his coronation.

2. *Its Consequences:*
   - Mutual rivalry of Juda and Ephraim.
   - Religious separation.
   - Greater weakness against more formidable invasions.

3. *The Two Kingdoms Compared:*
   - Their extent.
   - Political and religious life.
   - Duration.

[228]

## CHAPTER XX.

### THE KINGDOM OF SOLOMON.

SECTION II. ITS DECLINE AND DISRUPTION

§ *1. Decline of Solomon's Kingdom.*

1. **Causes of Decline.** The prosperous period of Solomon's reign was unquestionably the golden age of the Jewish nation. Under his wise and vigorous rule commerce and literature made gigantic strides, peace and plenty prevailed throughout the country. Nor was there any apparent reason why this splendor and prosperity should not last till the death of the monarch and be handed down intact to his successors, for he was surrounded by the confidence, admiration and love of his subjects, by a numerous family and powerful alliances through marriage at home and abroad. And yet "Solomon in his old age was about to bequeath to his heir an insecure throne, a discontented people, formidable enemies on the frontiers, and perhaps a contested succession" (MILMAN, History of the Jews). The general cause of this sad and rapid decline of the Jewish king is to be found in his complete adoption of the ways of Eastern monarchs, however at variance this might be with the spirit and actual requirements of a theocratic government. His evident desire had been even to outdo in their splendor and luxury all neighboring courts; and in consequence, he had gradually made everything around him purely Asiatic, entirely foreign to the ideal of a monarchy as sketched in Deuteronomy (xvii, 16, 17), since in direct defiance of it he had multiplied horses

in the land, accumulated gold and silver, and contracted marriage with foreign wives (III Kings x, 10, sq.; xi, 1, 2; II Paralip. ix, 13, sq.).

From this general adoption by Solomon of the ways of Eastern potentates and his efforts to surpass them all in magnificence, naturally followed the first particular cause of his decline, namely, his despotism (III Kings xii, 4). To gratify his worldly ostentation he demanded from his subjects enormous sacrifices, which they supported willingly at first, but soon regarded as unbearable burdens. The temples and palaces, cities and fortresses with the construction of which he gratified his passion for building "in Jerusalem and in Libanus and in all the land of his dominion" (II Paralip. viii) were rendered possible only by the exaction of forced labor even on the part of his own subjects (III Kings xi, 27, 28; xii, 14), and by the imposition of taxes the rate and burden of which naturally increased as time went on. If we add to this the enormous expenditure entailed by the maintenance of a large standing army, of a numerous and magnificent court, both apparently out of proportion with the resources at his disposal, it will be easy for us to understand how on the one hand, Solomon's treasury gradually became so exhausted that the vicegerent of Jehovah was driven to cede a portion of God's own Holy Land to the pagan king Hiram, in order to pay the debts he had contracted; and how on the other hand, the Jewish people were gradually led to consider the rule of the son of David as a despotic yoke from which they long and intensely yearned to be relieved (III Kings xi, 28; xii, 1-6).

A second special cause of the decline of Solomon's kingdom consists in his multiplication of wives and concubines. Like other Eastern despots, he freely indulged his passions, and in this — if the enormous figures of 700 wives and 300 concubines given in III Kings xi, 3, be admitted as correct (with which compare Canticle vi, 7) — he even seems to have gone much beyond them all, most likely with a view to give evidence to his contemporaries of his superior wealth and power. Of course, this sensual life of the king, besides involving necessarily his own physical and spiritual decay, remained a source of constant scandal for his subjects at large, and for the grandees of his court in particular; and as we have already noticed, it betrayed him into connections by marriage with foreign nations, that is, into alliances contrary at least to the spirit of the law (III Kings xi, 2).

The last particular cause of the decline of the kingdom of Solomon, and one which resulted naturally from his love for and marriage with foreign wives, was the idolatry which he tolerated, encouraged and not unlikely practised himself (III Kings xi, 1-34). To please them he not only allowed them to practise their idolatrous and abominable rites within his dominions, but actually built high places "for Chamos the idol of Moab, and for Moloch the idol of the children of Ammon, on the hill that is over-against Jerusalem," that is probably that part of the Mount of Olives which faced directly the august temple of Jehovah. He apparently went further and actually "worshipped Astarthe, the goddess of the Sidonians, and Moloch, the idol of the Ammonites" (III Kings xi, 5, 33). This was, of course, a most heinous crime on the part of a king of Israel to whom "Jehovah had appeared twice," and whose perverse example could not but exercise the most disastrous influence upon the minds and hearts of the Jewish people, hardly weaned, so to speak, from those idolatrous and licentious rites in which their ancestors had freely and repeatedly indulged. In point of fact, people and courtiers followed him in his worship of Astarthe, of Chamos and Moloch (III Kings xi, 33), and although Asa, Josaphat, Joas and Ezechias put an end to idolatry throughout all the rest of their dominions, yet they did not feel powerful enough to fight against the popular feeling in favor of the high places which Solomon had built to the gods of his foreign wives in the vicinity of Jerusalem and which subsisted up to the great religious reforms effected by Josias (III Kings xxiii, 13).

2. **Signs of Decline.** It was chiefly during the "old age" of Solomon, as the third book of Kings takes notice — the parallel narrative of his reign in the second book of Paralipomenon has no reference to the idolatry of this prince — that the son of David "had his heart turned away by women to follow strange gods." As he advanced in years the weakness of his will betrayed itself more and more, and his application to public affairs proportionately relaxed. It is therefore during this period that the signs of decline became more apparent. Among these, we may mention with the sacred writer (III Kings xi, 14–26) the fact that Hadad, one of the royal blood of the Edomite princes, began to organize a revolt against Solomon's supremacy in Edom, a province on which Jewish maritime commerce depended so much; and that an adventurer, named Razon, seized Damascus and set up what seems to have been an independent sovereignty (MILMAN, History of the Jews).

These rebellions of powerful tributary States against the Jewish suzerainty over the east of Jordan were also calculated to increase the dissatisfaction experienced at home by both people and prophets against the infamous and despotic rule of their king. By this time, the people at large had long ceased to be dazzled by the splendor of Solomon's court, by the greatness of his fame for wisdom in all he said and did, and as years went on and no relief from compulsory labor or enormous taxation was in view, they grew tired of his unbearable yoke and contemplated his death in a near future as an occasion of bettering their sad condition. Nor is it improbable that the true patriotic spirit of the bulk of the people resented more and more the ever-increasing moral and religious corruption of the capital of Israel. "The old men who had been Solomon's advisers in his days of greatness — the sons of Nathan and Sadoc and others — cannot have regarded these proceedings without alarm. Some of them, probably in concert with the prophets of the time, Semeias, Addo and Ahias, must have remonstrated with the king on his folly so contrary to the real interests of the theocratic government. But their remonstrances were uttered in vain" (SIME, The Kingdom of All-Israel, p. 571). Solomon was therefore well aware of the growing and but too well-founded dissatisfaction of his people, yet he blindly went on, and despised even the Divine sentence of which the prophet Ahias was most likely the bearer, and which announced to Solomon the rending of the kingdom after his death (III Kings xi, 9–13 ; 29, sq.).

This general dissatisfaction explains the rapid fortune of Jeroboam, whom Solomon intrusted with one of the most important posts of the kingdom. It was because of the increasing difficulty in raising taxes in the district of Ephraim, a tribe ever opposed to the influence of Juda, that the king, "seeing him a young man ingenious and industrious, made him chief over the tributes of all the house of Joseph." It was because in this post of trust and power, Jeroboam could realize how widespread and deep seated was the dissatisfaction of the people with the existing order of things that he foresaw the day when, according to the prediction of Ahias, the prophet of Silo, he would successfully take possession of the throne of at least the northern tribes. It was finally because of the desire of the people to get rid of Solomon's hated yoke, that on the occasion of the fresh compulsory labor entailed by the repairing or strengthening of the walls of Jerusalem, Jeroboam dared " lift up his hand (that is, start an open rebellion) against the king," and that although unsuccessful in his premature attempt against Solomon, he was not forgotten by the people during his sojourn in Egypt, whither he withdrew till the death of the Jewish monarch (III Kings xi, 26–xii, 3).

3. **The End of Solomon.** Amid these unmistakable signs of the decline of his kingdom Solomon died, when about sixty years of age. His rule of forty years had been divided into two parts of nearly equal duration, but of a very different character. The first period, marked by glory, power and righteousness, had been succeeded by another of degradation, of weakness and of unfaithfulness to the God of Israel. The very brief manner in which the sacred writers record his demise (III Kings xi, 41, sq.; II Paralip. ix, 29, sq.) offers a striking contrast with the fulness of details they supply concerning the last days of David. Differently from his dying father, Solomon could not speak to his successor of a prosperity near at hand, for he knew with full certainty from Jehovah that the large States he had inherited from David would be soon divided, and that only the much smaller portion would belong to his son and successor; nor could he most likely address to this same son words of earnest, loving entreaty that he should serve faithfully the God of Israel, seeing that he himself had not only been long unfaithful to Jehovah's worship, but also died without those feelings of repentance which had secured to David his pardon. Hence we are simply told that "Solomon slept with his father, and was buried in the city of David his father, and Roboam reigned in his stead."

It is true that ecclesiastical writers have ever been divided on the question of the salvation of Solomon, and that great names like those of St. Irenæus, St. Hilary, St. Cyril of Jerusalem, St. Ambrose and St. Jerome, who believe that the son of David is among the saved, can be opposed to those of Tertullian, St. Cyprian, St. Augustine and St. Gregory the Great, who number him among the lost; nor can it be denied that this is a question which no one will ever be able to solve, since Holy Writ tells us nothing about it; yet it seems that this very silence of the sacred writers — if it points to anything — points rather to the final impenitence of Solomon.

### § 2. *Disruption of Solomon's Kingdom.*

1. **Manner in which it was Brought About.** The disruption of the kingdom of Solomon, which occurred so soon after his death, although apparently sudden, had been gradually prepared by the old mutual jealousies of the powerful tribes of Juda and Ephraim. For upwards of 400 years the leadership of the nation had been practically in the hands of Ephraim, for whilst great Jewish leaders like Josue, Samuel, and in some manner Saul — because of the manifold connection of Benjamin with the house of Joseph — belonged to it, it had within its boundaries Silo and Sichem, the one the religious, and the other the civil capital of Israel. Hence the readiness of the Ephraimites to complain whenever any important national event took place without their concurrence (cfr. Judges viii, 1–3; xii, 1–7); hence also their efforts during seven long years for supporting Isboseth, the son of Saul, against David who had been proclaimed king by the tribe of Juda. They indeed submitted to the inevitable when David was recognized as king by all Israel, but felt deeply the wound he inflicted on their pride when he made Jerusalem the religious and civil capital of the country, instead of the old centres of Silo and Sichem. In vain, therefore, did the Jewish monarch strive to calm their resentment by bestowing high favors upon many Ephraimites. His restoration by Juda without the concurrence of Ephraim so vexed the house of Joseph that the rebellion it occasioned well-nigh precipitated a disruption (II Kings xx, 1, the expressions of which should be compared with III Kings xii, 16). Again, the Ephraimites felt keenly what must have appeared

on the part of Solomon an attempt to do away with the glorious past of their tribe, when this prince divided the whole kingdom into twelve provinces simply in accordance with the actual resources and population of the various districts; and they became gradually so exasperated by his oppressive taxation that to keep them under subjection he felt the need of appointing over them Jeroboam, a man of great valor, and one on whose faithfulness he could apparently depend, through gratitude for this rapid elevation. Finally, feelings of insubordination to Solomon's rule were such in Ephraim that Jeroboam, thinking the time had come to seize the Jewish throne, raised the standard of revolt against the king: he was indeed defeated, but not lost sight of during his exile in Egypt.

Thus, then, at the death of Solomon everything had long been tending towards a separation of Ephraim — and indeed of the northern tribes which had ever been very much under its influence — from Juda, its rival and oppressor; and only a favorable occasion was required for securing a disruption.

This favorable occasion soon offered itself when stubborn and haughty Roboam, the son of the deceased monarch, not only refused to comply with the just requests of the representatives of the tribes that he should lighten the heavy yoke put upon them by Solomon, but even dared to say, "My father made your yoke heavy, but I will add to your yoke; my father beat you with whips, but I will beat you with scorpions." This was the crowning insult; it was addressed to both the Ephraimites and the other tribes of the north; and it at once met with the old revolutionary cry of Seba: "Go home to your dwellings, O Israel!" and with these words announcing that the disruption was an accomplished fact: "Now, David, see to thy own house" (III Kings xii, 1-16).

2. **Consequences of the Disruption.** The disruption so long prepared and so suddenly accomplished was a

momentous event in the history of the Jewish nation. As might naturally be expected, its first consequence was the perpetuation of the old rivalry between northern and southern tribes. In point of fact, if we except the short period of about thirty years, during which vain attempts were made to establish friendly relations between them by the intermarriage of the royal families, the kingdoms of Juda and Israel, which arose from the disruption, were ever at war.

A second natural consequence of the disruption was a religious separation between the southern kingdom, or kingdom of Juda, and the northern kingdom, or kingdom of Israel. The unity of the Jewish people was essentially religious, and the first king of the ten separated tribes felt that he must break it or see his kingdom soon wrested from his hands (III Kings xii, 26, sq.). "Humanly speaking, Jeroboam's fear was well-founded. If Jerusalem continued to be the centre of religious unity, if the Levites from all parts of Palestine went up in their turns to conduct the Temple service, and if the people continued to flock to the Holy Place three times a year, as the law commanded them, there could not but have been great danger of a reaction setting in and a desire for reunion manifesting itself. It was natural, therefore, that the king should cast about for some means of avoiding this consummation, which not only threatened his royalty, but even his life. The later history shows how effectual were his measures for counteracting the tendency to reunion with Juda. They prevented all healing of the breach between the two kingdoms, and made the separation final. They produced the result that not only no reunion took place, but no symptoms of an inclination to reunite ever manifested themselves during the whole period of the double kingdom" (Speaker's Commentary, vol. ii, p. 559).

The third natural consequence following the disruption was the greater weakness of the chosen people at the very time when even its existence would soon be threatened by much more formidable invasions than in the past. Up to this moment the Jewish monarchs had fought against comparatively weak enemies, namely, the small nations and tribes which surrounded the Holy Land; but, henceforth, they will have to cope with much more powerful enemies. At first, Egyptian forces will invade Southern Palestine, capture the Holy City and plunder the House of Jehovah. Next, the Assyrians — termed the Romans of Asia on account of their military power and skill — will invade the country, and succeed ultimately in destroying utterly the northern kingdom. Finally, the kingdom of Juda, after having withstood longer the repeated invasions of Assyria, will fall a prey to another Eastern power, the great Babylonian Empire.

3. **The Two Kingdoms Compared.** Thus, then, from a very powerful empire in Western Asia, the Jewish nation had been reduced by the disruption to two comparatively small and defenceless kingdoms. Of these, the northern kingdom, known as that of Samaria, Ephraim, or Israel, greatly surpassed the southern or kingdom of Juda in extent and population. The area of the former is estimated at about 9,000 square miles (about that of New Hampshire), with a population of about four or five millions. It included eight tribes: namely, on the west of the Jordan, Ephraim, one-half Manasses, Issachar, Zabulon, Aser, Nephtali, with the coast-line between Acre and Joppe; on the east of the Jordan, Ruben, Gad and one-half Manasses. Its vassal States were Moab and so much of Syria as had remained subject to Solomon (IV Kings iii, 4; III Kings xi, 24). The kingdom of Juda included that tribe itself together with Benjamin, and at least eventually, a part, if not the whole, of Simeon and Dan. Its area is estimated at 3,400 square miles, with a population of about one million and

three-quarters. Besides this, Edom continued faithful to Juda for a time, and the ports of the Red Sea furnished an outlet for its commerce.

But whilst the northern kingdom greatly surpassed the southern in population, extent and fertility, contained several important cities and was superior to Juda in military power, it was unquestionably inferior to the southern kingdom when considered from a political and religious standpoint. "If Israel had ten tribes, it had the fatal heritage of disunion. Juda as, virtually, a single tribe, had the priceless blessing of national and religious unity. Its kings, to the last, traced their descent in an unbroken line from David, the national hero. Whereas Israel was to have its capital successively in Sichem, Thersa and Samaria, that of Juda was always Jerusalem; while rival temples at Dan and Bethel invited the subjects of the northern kingdom, there was only one sanctuary for its southern rival" (GEIKIE, Hours with the Bible, vol. iv, p. 8).

These and other such advantages of the smaller kingdom, that of Juda, over the kingdom of Israel account for the fact that it outlived its rival by more than one hundred and thirty years, for whilst the northern kingdom was destroyed in 721 B. C., the southern subsisted till 588 B. C.

# SYNOPSIS OF CHAPTER XXI.

## The Kingdom of Israel.

**I. Jeroboam I and his Immediate Successors:**
1. *Their Characters and Aims.*
2. *Political and Religious Organization of the Kingdom.*

**II. The House of Amri:**
1. *Amri* (Accession; foundation of Samaria).
2. *Achab:*
   - Public works.
   - The Phenician worship of Baal; persecution of the prophets.
   - Elias; the man; his mission and miracles.
   - Syrian wars — alliance with Juda.
3. *After the Death of Achab:*
   - Revolt of Moab (the Moabite stone).
   - Translation of Elias. Eliseus succeeds him in the prophetical office.

**III. Dynasty of Jehu:**
1. *The Accession of Jehu* (IV Kings ix-x, 28).
2. *Relations of Jehu with Syria and Assyria.*
3. *Glorious Rule of Jeroboam II:*
   - The Northern Empire of Solomon restored.
   - Prophets of the Time (Jonas, Amos, Osee).

**IV. Closing Reigns:**
1. *The Kings:* Murderers and profligates.
2. *Final Overthrow of Israel:*
   - The Assyrian invasions.
   - The Ten Tribes led captive to Assyria.

[240]

# CHAPTER XXI.

### THE KINGDOM OF ISRAEL.

§ *1. Jeroboam and His Immediate Successors (Nadab, Baasa and Ela).*

1. **Their Characters and Aims.** Although the Biblical narrative gives us only few details concerning the reign of the founder of the northern kingdom and of his immediate successors on the throne, yet it allows us a sufficient insight into the character and aims of these princes. Now that he is on the throne, Jeroboam shows himself what he ever was, namely, an active, shrewd, ambitious, unscrupulous man. His distinct object is to maintain his kingdom separate from that of Juda (III Kings xii, 26, 27), and he deems good every means conducive to this great aim of his reign. For this purpose, he strengthens his frontiers by building the fortresses of Sichem (west of the Jordan) and Phanuel (east of the Jordan), cultivates the devotion of Ephraim, the most powerful tribe of his realm, by selecting Sichem, one of its cities, for his capital, introduces into his States a religious worship and organization entirely opposed to the pure worship of Jehovah, and actually calls upon the King of Egypt to invade the Holy Land and protect him against the rival kingdom of Juda. Despite the protestations of the prophets of the time, he perseveres to the end in his impious line of action, and sets thereby an example of reckless ambition but too closely followed by his successors on the throne of Israel (III Kings xii, 20–xv).

Thus of Nadab, Jeroboam's son and successor, we read that "he walked in the ways of his father and in his sins, wherewith he made Israel to sin" (III Kings xv, 26); and of Baasa we are told, that having reached the throne by the murder of Nadab, he slew all the members of the house of Jeroboam to secure his own throne against any competitor, began the building of Rama, on the extreme southern frontier of his States, "that no man might go out or come in of the side of Asa, King of Juda," and persevered to the end in the impious line of conduct of Jeroboam (III Kings xv, 17-21; 27-34; xvi, 1-6). Finally, Ela, the third successor of Jeroboam, having imitated the unworthy examples of his predecessors on the throne of Israel, was slain, together with all the members of his family, by an ambitious officer named Zambri who occupied the throne only seven days.

2. **Political and Religious Organization of the Kingdom.** Whilst they were clearly anxious to prevent Israel from reuniting with Juda, Jeroboam and his immediate successors were no less careful to connect the new condition of things with the past history of the Jewish nation. Naturally enough, the division of the country by Solomon into twelve provinces which had been swept away by the very fact of the disruption, was not re-established; but the older division of the nation into tribes appeared again such as it had existed under the first kings, Saul and David. The northern kingdom assumed also the old military character of the original monarchy, and the captain of the army became a personage who at times played no less important a part than either Abner or Joab. Of course, the same general divisions of the army continued, and if the chariots and horses were multiplied and are now so far organized that we read of two divisions of cavalry, each with its distinct commander (III Kings xvi, 9), this was but the continuation of what had been partially established by Solomon. As formerly in the court of

David there were civil officers destined to increase the prestige of the monarch, so now in the court of Jeroboam and of his successors; and the prophets of Jehovah continue to hold intercourse with the northern kings.

Even in what concerns the religious organization into which the greatest changes were introduced, Jeroboam was anxious that these changes should be connected in the mind of the people with the past history of the nation. The two golden calves he set up at both extremities of the land, in Dan and Bethel, although probably made after the pattern of the calves worshipped in Egypt, were publicly given by him as symbols of the Divine Presence watching over the whole country, and artfully connected with the worship of the golden calf by the nation assembled at the foot of Mount Sinai. Deserted by the Levites who courageously forsook his States, he established a priesthood which, as in olden times, was not confined to any particular tribe, and which would depend on the king as the chief priest, as the Levites and priests had depended on Moses and Josue — and apparently, also, at least to a large extent, on David. Of course, all the rest of the Jewish ritual he preserved most carefully; and if he introduced any change, it was, as in connection with the Feast of Tabernacles (the celebration of which he prescribed should take place one month later than in Juda), because of some special reason acceptable to the people at large.

This religious organization of the kingdom of Israel was indeed a clever piece of work. Its innovations were not such as to shock the bulk of the nation ever hankering after a more sensuous form of worship than that offered by the pure worship of Jehovah; and they were calculated to render easier to the subjects of the northern kingdom the satisfaction of their religious instincts by reviving two ancient places of worship within their own borders. Hence it is, that in whatever else his successors differed, they one and all agreed n upholding the new form of worship, which, once established, appeared essential to their national unity.

### § 2. *The House of Amri.*

1. **Amri, his Accession, Foundation of Samaria.**
After the death of Ela, Zambri his murderer was at once recognized as his successor by the court and a part of the people, whilst Amri, the captain of the host, was proclaimed king by the army of Israel. A few days were sufficient for Amri to get rid of this competitor, but it took him no less than four years to subdue Thebri, the rival whom a large party in Israel had elected as successor to Zambri. At length he triumphed, and became the head of a powerful dynasty.

One of his first cares seems to have been to give up Thersa, the city which had for some time taken the place of Sichem as the capital of the northern kingdom, and to select for his own residence a city which would not be stained with so much royal blood. This he found in the " hill of Semer," about thirty-five miles in a straight line northwest of Jerusalem and six miles northwest of Sichem, which he purchased and on which he built a town called *Samaria* after the former owner of the site. This was a fine location for a capital; it combined the advantages of "a strong position, rich environs, a central situation and an elevation sufficient to catch untainted the cool healthy breezes of the Mediterranean" (MURRAY's Handbook), and this is why Samaria ever remained an important city through the various fortunes of the country and its people.

It has also been inferred from passing statements in the sacred narrative that this skilful monarch secured much greater advantages to his people by making peace with the Kings of Juda and Syria (cfr. III Kings xx, 34). Unfortunately, he was wedded to the religious policy of Jeroboam, and in this direction he seems to have gone even much farther than his predecessors (III Kings xvi, 15-27).

2. **Achab.** As a natural consequence of the peace obtained by Amri, security and prosperity prevailed throughout the northern kingdom during the greater part of the reign of Achab, his son and successor. The new monarch, anxious to signalize his rule by the culture of the arts of peace, built new cities in various parts of his kingdom (III Kings xxii, 39), one of which is especially named in the Biblical narrative. This was Jericho, probably raised by Achab from its ruins, in defiance of the curse of Josue (Josue vi, 26). To rival Solomon in his outward display, the son of Amri looked about for another royal residence, not to supersede by it Samaria, but in order that no part of the embellishments he contemplated should be ascribed to his father. The city thus favored was Jezrael, which "was planted on a gentle eminence, in the very centre of a rich plain, and commanded the view of Carmel on the west, and the valley of the Jordan on the east" (STANLEY, Lectures on the Jewish Church). There he erected a magnificent palace hard by the city wall and built of ivory (III Kings xxii, 39), a style of architecture which was soon imitated by the Israelite aristocracy (Amos iii, 15; vi, 4).

Having thus followed the example of Solomon in his outward display, Achab imitated him also in his practice of polygamy (III Kings xx, 5), and more unfortunately still in his alliance with the heathen. He was the first northern king whose chief wife was one of the old accursed Chanaanite race. He married Jezabel, the daughter of Ethbaal who had gained the crown of Tyre and Sidon by the murder of his brother, and who united to the royal dignity his former office of high priest of Astarthe (cfr. JOSEPHUS, Antiquities of the Jews, book viii, chapter xiii, § 1).

"The immediate consequence of this ill-fated union was

that the religion of Jezabel became the worship of the northern kingdom, Achab built in Samaria a temple to "**Baal**"— the Sun-god (the producing principle in Nature)—in which he erected not only an altar, but, as we gather from IV Kings iii, 2 ; x, 27, also one of those pillars which were distinctive of its vile services. As usual, where these rites were fully carried out, he also "made the Ascherah"— Astarthe, the Moon-goddess (the receptive principle in Nature)— so that the Phenician worship was now established in its entirety. As we infer from later notices, there was a "vestry" attached to these temples, where special festive garments, worn on great occasions, were kept (IV Kings x, 22). Achab — or perhaps Jezabel — appointed not less than 450 priests of Baal and 400 of Astarthe, who were supported by the bounty of the queen (III Kings xviii, 19 ; xxii, 6). The forced introduction of this new worship led to a systematic persecution of the prophets and even of the openly professed worshippers of Jehovah which had their complete extermination for its object (III Kings xviii, 13 ; xix, 10 ; IV Kings ix, 7). These measures were wholly due to the absolute power which Jezabel exercised over Achab, whose undeniable good qualities were sadly marred by fatal weakness, selfishness, uncontrolled self-indulgence, an utter want of religion, and especially the influence of his wife" (III Kings xxi, 25) (EDERSHEIM, Bible History, vol. v, pp. 179, 180).

It was at this juncture so critical for the very existence of Jehovah's worship in the kingdom of Israel, that Elias, one of the most wonderful men of Jewish history, appeared on the scene. Besides the fact that he was born in Thesbi, a town spoken of in the book of Tobias (i, 2 in the Septuagint) as belonging to the tribe of Nephtali, we know nothing of the early years of this great prophet of Israel. When we meet him first in the sacred narrative he stands before Achab arrayed in a garment of black camel's hair and girt about his loins with a leathern girdle. With that strong faith and fearless courage which will accompany him everywhere, he has come to begin his great mission of recalling to the king and to his people that Jehovah is the only true God. He announces that for several years "there shall not be dew nor rain, but according to the words of his mouth," and then he wandered far from the face of the angered monarch, first to the brook Carith, and next to the Phenician town of Sarephta, experiencing in both places those unmistakable marks of Divine providence in his favor which are recorded in III Kings xvii (cfr. also III Kings xviii, 9, 10).

After a lapse of three years, when drought and famine have become well-nigh unbearable, Elias reappears boldly before Achab, and obtains from him that sacrifices should be publicly offered on Mount Carmel for the purpose of determining whether Jehovah or Baal was the true God. The test proved so clearly in favor of Jehovah that the assembled multitude proclaimed with one voice " Jehovah is God, Jehovah is God," a solemn act of faith which was rewarded by the cessation of the drought, and the effect of which Elias endeavored at once to render permanent by the extermination of the priests of Baal (III Kings xviii). Notwithstanding his heavy blow at Baal-worship in Israel, idolatry soon flourished again in the northern kingdom owing to the supreme influence of Jezabel in religious affairs, and the faithful prophet of Jehovah soon took to flight to escape her revengeful feelings. He therefore went southward to Bersabee, then to Mount Sinai, and his steps were ever accompanied by miraculous proofs of Divine providence in his behalf (III Kings xix).

Here it should be noticed that the miraculous powers ascribed to Elias by the sacred writer were no less necessary to this great champion of Jehovah in face of the State idolatry of the northern kingdom, than they had been to Moses in his fight against the idolatry of ancient Egypt. Nor were the wonders of which Elias was himself the object less necessary to him than similar miracles had formerly been to Moses, to preserve his life amidst the countless dangers which surrounded him, and to keep up his courage in an almost desperate struggle. Indeed, it seems that under the influence of such Divine intervention in behalf of the person and work of this prophet of Jehovah, Achab relaxed at times the persecution he had started in Israel, and even allowed himself to be guided by the advice of prophets faithful to the true God, as this occurred in the two defensive wars the king had to sustain against Ben-Adad, the King of Syria, and out of which he came victorious. Not so, however, with Jezabel, who ever considered Elias as her own personal enemy, and who never stopped at a crime which might secure the end she had in view, as is clearly evidenced in the well-known story of Naboth and his vine. It was after the murder of this God-fearing man under the false charge of blasphemy, that Elias warned Achab of the violent death which awaited him, and which soon occurred in the third war which the King of Israel, then allied with Josaphat, King of Juda, waged against Syria (III Kings xx–xxii, 40).

3. **After the Death of Achab.** The inglorious death of Achab produced an immediate rupture of peaceful relations with Moab, on the southeastern frontier of Israel (IV Kings i, 1 ; iii, 4, sq.). The fact of this rupture is confirmed by the independent testimony of an inscription discovered east of the Jordan in 1868, and now known as the stele of Mesa or the Moabite stone. This inscription is written in the Phenician or old Hebrew character, and speaks not only of Mesa as revolting against the King of Israel, but also of his conquest of several towns east of the Jordan which Ochozias, the son and successor of Achab, was then powerless to defend (IV Kings i, 2, sq.). We learn, indeed, from the Bible that the war against Moab was actively pursued by Joram, the brother and successor of Ochozias, but neither

in the sacred narrative nor in the Moabite record are we told the precise manner in which it ended (IV Kings iii, 6–27). For a translation of the Moabite inscription, see *Records of the Past*, new series, vol ii.)

It was apparently but a short time before the death of Ochozias that Elias, who had foretold the death of that prince (IV Kings i, 2, sq.), left this world in the mysterious manner which is described in IV Kings ii, for it was Eliseus, his successor in the prophetical office, who guided Joram in his expedition against the Moabites, and a little later in his wars against Syria (IV Kings vi, vii). As the dearest disciple of his master, Eliseus inherited "a double portion of his spirit" and also his wonderful power of working miracles, many of which have found place in the inspired record (IV Kings ii, 13–viii).

§ *3. Dynasty of Jehu.*

1. **Accession of Jehu.** Whilst Joram lay critically ill in Jezrael from the severe wounds he had received during the siege of Ramoth Galaad, Eliseus, who knew that the time had come for the long-predicted destruction of the family of Achab, sent "one of the sons of the prophets" to Jehu the captain of the host of Israel still gathered before Ramoth Galaad. The messenger thus despatched was to anoint Jehu in the most secret recess of his house, to announce to him that he was chosen to be Jehovah's instrument to destroy the house of Achab, and then to fly with all speed. The young prophet discharged perfectly his mission, and the newly-anointed monarch made known without delay to his fellow-officers all that had taken place. These in turn, catching something of the enthusiasm which lighted up the countenance of Jehu, proclaimed him king at once, and leaving strict orders that no one should go out of the camp who was not fully devoted to him, they escorted him on his way to Jezrael.

As the cortege approached the city Joram, King of Israel, and Ochozias, King of Juda (then also in Jezrael) drove out, each in his chariot, to meet Jehu. A few brief words exchanged revealed to Joram the extent of his danger and that of his royal companion, and he at once gave the signal of flight. It was too late. The Israelite monarch, shot to the heart by an arrow from Jehu's own hand, was flung into Naboth's vineyard, and the King of Juda overtaken in his flight towards Beth-gan (the modern Jenin) wounded in his chariot, but escaped to Mageddo, some twenty miles distant, where he expired.

These murders were but the prelude of horrible massacres. "Jezabel was flung down from a window in Jezrael and was devoured by dogs. Seventy sons of Achab were put to death in Samaria. The brothers of Ochozias were put to death in the same place. The priests and the worshippers of Baal were enticed into his temple at Samaria, the doors were then blockaded, and the inmates were killed to a man. Thus finished the mighty house of Achab, and the fabric of Phenician idolatry, reared with such care and at such cost, was utterly overthrown" (BLAIKIE, Manual of Bible History, p. 290. IV Kings ix-x, 28).

2. **Relations with Syria and Assyria.** Of the comparatively long government of Israel by Jehu — he reigned twenty-eight years — the sacred writer gives us but a short record, which stands in striking contrast with his lengthy account of the incidents which accompanied the accession of that prince. He simply tells us that at home, Jehu did not forsake the worship of the golden calves started by Jeroboam, and that abroad, he was unfortunate in his war against the Syrian king, Hazael, who ravaged all the possessions of Israel east of the Jordan (IV Kings x, 29-34). To this scanty information of the Biblical narrative, recent discoveries have added an interesting detail: Jehu is the first

Israelite king whose name is distinctly mentioned in an Assyrian inscription. From the obelisk of black marble which Salmanasar II erected at Kouyounjik (near Mosoul), we learn that Jehu paid to the Assyrian monarch a tribute of "silver, gold, bowls of gold, chalices of gold," etc. (cfr. *Records of the Past*, new series, vol. iv, p. 52). We are not indeed told the reason for which the King of Israel had to pay this heavy tribute, but it is not improbable that it was because, not feeling able to withstand alone the forces of Hazael, he had summoned to his help Salmanasar II, whose victories against the King of Syria, Hazael, are expressly mentioned on the same obelisk (cfr. *Records of the Past*, ibid., pp. 44, 45).

3. **Glorious Rule of Jeroboam II.** Perhaps the most prosperous of all the reigns which the northern kingdom ever knew was that of Jeroboam II, the third successor of Jehu. That prince was indeed the deliverer of Israel from the Syrian yoke whom Jehovah had promised to His people (IV Kings xiii, 5), for he not only fought bravely against Syrian invaders, as his father Joas and his grandfather Joachaz had done, but actually carried the war into their own country and took Damascus their capital. He next turned his arms against Moab and Ammon and conquered their territory, so that a short time after his accession the dominions of Israel extended again from the source of the Orontes on the north to the Dead Sea on the south.

The whole northern empire of Solomon was thus practically restored, a wonderful result which had been foretold by one of the prophets of the time, *Jonas*, whose well-known mission to the great city of Ninive is described in the inspired book which bears his name.

Peace and security naturally followed on this territorial extension of Israel (IV Kings viii, 5) and together with them a rapid artistic and commercial development set in, as we readily infer from the passing allusions to it which we find in the book of *Amos*, another prophet of this period (cfr. for instance Amos iii, 11, 12, 15; v, 11; vi, 4, 5, etc.). Unfortunately, "the prosperity of the people passed, in the metropolis of Samaria and in many other parts of the country, into debauchery and excess and then again into pampered effeminacy of morals (Amos ii, 7; iv, 1-8; viii, 13). . . . Again, the freer intercourse of the people with heathen nations, who had either been conquered or were distinguished by commerce and art, together with the general spread of looseness and intemperance of life, caused an extensive introduction of heathen religions" (EWALD, History of Israel, vol. iv, pp. 125, 126, English translation). All this was, of course, sternly rebuked by Amos, who foretold the destruction of the house of Jeroboam by the sword (Amos vii, 9), together with severe punishments upon Israel and, indeed, with the approaching ruin of the northern kingdom (Amos vii, 11, 17, etc.). All this is more particularly described, more sternly rebuked by **Osee**, who probably prophesied during the latter part of Jeroboam's rule, that is, when the worst effects of a merely material prosperity had become apparent in a generally prevalent drunkenness, debauchery and idolatry (cfr. Osee iv, 1, 12, 13, etc.). No wonder that he also threatens the existing dynasty with speedy extinction and the kingdom itself with near destruction (Osee i, 4, sq., etc.).

### § 4. *Closing Reigns.*

1. **The Kings: Murderers and Profligates.** After the death of Jeroboam II, the kingdom of Israel hastened to its ruin under the rule of murderers and profligates. His son and successor, Zacharias, was murdered after a reign of only six months. His murderer, Sellum, had occupied the throne hardly one month, when he met with the same fate at the hands of one Manahem, who came from Thersa, and who,

having committed the most revolting cruelties against his opponents, reigned ten years in Samaria. His son and successor, Phaceia, reigned but two years, after which he was slain by Phacee, one of his captains. Phacee occupied the throne for the comparatively long period of twenty years, but was at length put to death by Osee, the nineteenth and last King of Israel (BLAIKIE, Manual of Bible History, p. 296).

2. **Final Overthrow of the Northern Kingdom.** It was in the midst of these rapid and bloody changes of rulers that the northern kingdom was repeatedly invaded by such powerful warriors as the Assyrians. The first Israelite king who had to suffer from these terrible enemies was Manahem, whose kingdom was actually invaded by *Phul*, a prince who is probably identical with Teglathphalasar, and to whom Manahem hastened to proffer submission and tribute to preserve his crown (IV Kings xv, 19, 20; I Paralip. v, 26; cfr. also VIGOUROUX, Bible et Découvertes Modernes, vol. iv). The next Israelite king whose territory was invaded by Teglathphalasar was Phacee, who had leagued himself with Syria against the kingdom of Juda. In his distress Achaz, King of Juda, had called upon the Assyrian monarch, and in consequence, instead of the easy victory the allied kings of Israel and Syria had hoped for, they were utterly defeated: the northern part of the kingdom of Israel west of the Jordan was laid waste by the conqueror, and a large number of Israelites carried into captivity (IV Kings xv, 29; xvi, 7, sq.; I Paralip. v, 26).

Upon the death of Teglathphalasar, Osee, who had succeeded Phacee on the throne of Isreal, thought it an opportune time for withholding the tribute he had hitherto paid to Assyria. Then it was that Salmanasar IV invaded the territory of Israel and received from Osee the solemn promise of an annual tribute. After a time, however, Salmanasar found out that Osee was negotiating with Sua, the King of Egypt, to get rid of his tribute to Assyria, whereupon the Assyrian monarch invaded and ravaged the kingdom of Israel, cast Osee into prison, and laid siege to Samaria. It was during this siege, which lasted upwards of two years, that Salmanasar died, so that it was only under his successor Sargon II (although the Biblical narrative apparently suggests the reverse (IV Kings xvii, 4-6) that Samaria was captured, and the Israelites carried in large numbers into Assyria. The captives were chiefly placed " in the cities of the Medes," that is, in one of the easternmost districts of Assyria, and strangers from various parts of Babylonia were brought in to occupy the deserted land of Israel. These new settlers soon joined the worship of Jehovah, "the God of the land," to that of their own idols, and gradually formed a mongrel race, which was ever hated by the Jews, but more especially in the time of Our Lord (IV Kings xvii; John iv, 9, 27; viii, 48).

Thus ended the kingdom of Israel in 721 B. C. Its destruction should have indeed been a warning to the Jews of the south that they should serve Jehovah with perfect faithfulness and thereby escape a similar fate. But, as we shall see in the next chapter, the people of Juda never clearly realized that Jehovah could forsake Juda as He had done Israel, and they therefore went on their evil ways provoking God to anger, till the Babylonian Captivity came on and made forever of the Jews a monotheistic nation.

# SYNOPSIS OF CHAPTER XXII.

## THE KINGDOM OF JUDA.

I. THE FIRST KINGS OF JUDA:
- A. *Animosity against Israel:*
  1. Vain attempts to re-establish the power of Juda over the ten tribes.
  2. The foreign invasions during this period.
  3. Religious life of Juda.
- B. *Alliance with Israel:*
  1. Josaphat: His reforms; alliance with Achab; his wars.
  2. Athalia: Her influence over Joram and Ochozias. Her personal rule.
  3. Joas: His accession; his reign before and after the death of Joiada.

II. FROM AMAZIAS TO EZECHIAS:
1. *Kings Previous to Achaz:* Internal condition of Juda. Outward relations.
2. *Achaz:* Depths reached by his idolatry and iniquity: *Isaias.* Various Invasions; The aid of Assyria secured.
3. *Ezechias:* His Reforms; Invasions of Sennacherib (Nineveh monuments).

III. MANASSES AND JOSIAS:
1. *Manasses:* Idolatry — fearful persecution. A captive in Babylon — his restoration. History of Judith.
2. *Josias:* Religious Reforms: Discovery of the Book of the Law — *Jeremias.* The Invasion of Nechao.

IV. THE FALL OF JUDA:
1. *Political Parties among the Jews at the Beginning of this Period.*
2. *The Invasions of Nabuchodonosor and the Last Kings of Juda.*
3. *Destruction of Jerusalem. Subsequent Condition of the Country.*

CHRONOLOGY OF THE ROYAL PERIOD.

# CHAPTER XXII.

### THE KINGDOM OF JUDA.

§ *1. The First Kings of Juda.*

1. **Animosity against Israel.** The sudden formation of the northern kingdom upon the death of Solomon was naturally considered by Roboam his son, and by the two following kings of Juda, Abiam and Asa, as a revolt against lawful authority. This explains how for sixty long years these princes cherished a great animosity against Israel, and attempted repeatedly to re-establish the power of Juda over the ten tribes (III Kings xii, 19, 21 ; II Paralip. xiii, 5). It was for this purpose that Roboam gathered a numerous army from Juda and Benjamin, and that although these large forces disbanded by order of Jehovah, the King of Juda kept up an armed hostility against Jeroboam "all the time of his life" (III Kings xii, 21–24 ; xiv, 30 ; xv, 6). For this same purpose, Abiam, the son and successor of Roboam, collected a large number of troops, with which he defeated Jeroboam in a pitched battle and secured a temporary accession of territory to Juda (II Paralip. xiii, 2–20). It was apparently for the same purpose that Asa, the third successor of Roboam, not only warred against Israel (IV Kings xv, 16), but also gave so powerful an impetus to the migration of religious Israelites to Jerusalem that King Baasa of Israel began the fortifications of Rama, on his southern frontier, with the view of checking a movement which tended immediately towards religious, and ultimately towards political reunion (II Paralip. xv, 9 ; xvi, 1).

What contributed most to foster the animosity of Juda against Israel were the two foreign invasions, which the intrigues of Jeroboam and his second successor, Baasa, most likely brought about against the southern kingdom. The first invasion was carried out by Sesac, King of Egypt, and it proved most disastrous for Juda, whose capital was captured and temple plundered. Of this memorable event we have an independent confirmation in a bas-relief which was found in 1828, by Champollion, on the south side of the great temple of Karnak, at Thebes. There we see Sesac (Sheshang, in Egyptian) represented together with a large number of prisoners of war, among whom one with Jewish features is designated as " *Iutah Malek*," which means either *Kingdom of Juda* or *King* of Juda (VIGOUROUX, Bible et Découvertes Modernes). The second invasion, due most likely to the intrigues of Baasa, was carried out by " Zara, the Ethiopian," who is identified as Osarken I, son and successor of Sesac, and king of both Egypt and Ethiopia. Differently from the first, this second invasion ended with a very brilliant victory of Asa, King of Juda (III Kings xiv, 25, sq.; II Paralip. xiv, 9, sq.).

It is then easy to understand that the kings of Juda were greatly provoked against the Israelite monarchs whom they knew to be the underhand cause of these formidable invasions, and that when Asa found himself hard pressed by Baasa he did not hesitate to call upon the foreign help of Benadad, the ruler of Syria, against the King of Israel, as we read in III Kings xv, 17, sq.

During this period of animosity of Juda against Israel, the religious life of the southern kingdom rapidly developed at first on the lines started by Solomon. Idolatry and its sensual rites spread to a fearful extent, so that false gods had soon "altars and statues and groves upon every high hill and under every green tree, and that the most infamous rites of the Chanaanites were revived (III Kings xiv, 22-24). Indeed, the king himself forsaking the law of Jehovah, gave the example, and *all* the people trod in his footsteps (II Paralip. xii, 1).

God, however, watched over this select portion of the Jewish nation, and did not allow Juda to sink down quietly and long into such depths of religious corruption. By means of external punishments and still more effectively by the efforts of His prophets, He gradually prepared a reaction against idolatry. Things went on, it is true, pretty much the same under Abiam as they had under Roboam. But Abiam ruled only three years, and at the accession of Asa, the reaction was already so strong that at the very outset of his reign, the new king felt free to deprive Maacha, his grandmother and the prime-mover of the idolatrous worship in Juda, of all authority and influence at court (III Kings xv, 11, sq.; II Paralip. xiv, 2, sq.). A little later he went further still, and did almost entirely away with idolatrous rites, altars, statues, etc. (II Paralip. xv, 1–16); yet even then he allowed the high places where Jehovah was worshipped to subsist, because the nation at large was not yet prepared for a complete centralization of Divine worship in Jerusalem (II Paralip. xv, 17; cfr. also xx, 33).

2. **Alliance with Israel.** Asa was succeeded on the throne by Josaphat, whose religious policy was not only modelled on that of his father, but actually more thoroughgoing against all idolatrous worship, for he did his best to destroy whatever remains of it still existed in the kingdom of Juda (II Paralip. xvii, 3; III Kings xxii, 42–47). Furthermore, he soon understood that to render these religious reforms permanent, it behooved him to remedy the extreme religious ignorance which prevailed in many parts of the land. He therefore appointed a sort of roving commission especially charged to impart to the people a more precise knowledge of the religion of Jehovah and of the law of Moses (II Paralip. xvii, 7, sq.).

Other important reforms were carried out by this wise prince, such as the reorganization of justice, the strengthening of his kingdom by the erection of walled cities and the maintenance of a powerful army. The result of them all was that under him, Juda was feared by all its neighbors, and that in some cases, friendly overtures were made either to accept a position of dependence on the Jewish king, or to secure his favor by valuable presents (II Paralip. xvii, 10, sq.; xix).

The great mistake of Josaphat was that he joined affinity with Achab, King of Israel, who most willingly gave his daughter, Athalia, in marriage to Joram, the eldest son of the King of Juda. This political alliance had, in time, the most disastrous consequences, although its immediate results do not seem to have interfered considerably with the prosperity of Josaphat's kingdom (II Paralip. xvii, 2, sq.). It is true that this alliance betrayed him into an expedition against Syria from which he narrowly escaped with his life (III Kings xxiii; II Paralip. xviii), and that this unsuccessful campaign itself soon brought about a confederacy of Ammonites, Moabites, and others, who invaded the territory of Juda in countless numbers, but the final result was a great victory, which more than made up for the loss of prestige suffered in the war against Syria (II Paralip. xx). Later on, he was also involved together with Joram, the second son of Achab, in an expedition against Moab; his arms were also crowned with success, and if he withdrew from the siege of a Moabite city into his own land, it was for a reason the precise nature of which does not appear from the Biblical narrative (IV Kings ii).

The successor of Josaphat on the throne of Juda was his son *Joram*, whose reign was marked by many disasters which are recorded in IV Kings viii, 20, 22; II Paralip. xxi, 16, 17, and are ascribed to Divine judgments upon the people for their irreligion (IV Kings viii, 18, sq., II Paralip. xxi, 10).

This unfaithfulness of the nation to Jehovah so soon after the vigorous reforms effected by Asa and Josaphat was the result of the influence which **Athalia**, the daughter of Jezabel, exercised in favor of Baal and Astarthe worship during the reign of Joram her husband. Her influence was still greater during the reign of her son Ochozias, and on the murder of the latter by Jehu, she rose up, killed all the royal family of the house of Joram (IV Kings xi, 1; II Paralip. xxii, 10) with the exception, however, of Joas, concealed by his nurse, and established her personal rule over the land.

The main efforts of this first queen of God's people during the six years of her tyrannical reign were centred in the establishment and spread of the infamous worship which her mother had implanted in the northern kingdom. She cleverly abstained from all violent measures, such as suppressing altogether the ancient religion, shutting up the ancient temple or hindering its rites, and persecuting the worshippers of Jehovah. But short of these extreme methods, she left nothing untried to make of her religion the religion of the State. "In Jerusalem itself a rival fane rose up, dedicated to the Phenician god, adorned with altars and images (IV Kings xi, 18) and continually enriched with spoils from the neighboring temple of Jehovah, nay, in part built of stones, transferred by the queen's orders, from the old sanctuary to the new (II Paralip. xxiv, 7). The temple of Solomon was left to decay and ruin; that of Baal constantly increased in size and magnificence. Its services were conducted by a high priest of Baal, the counterpart of the Aaronic high priest, who still maintained, albeit with shorn splendor, the rites of the Levitical worship in the old edifice" (RAWLINSON, Kings of Israel and Juda, p. 115).

It was therefore high time that an effective reaction should set in, as it actually did in the seventh year of Athalia's reign. Under the auspices of Joiada, the high priest of Jehovah, the young *Joas*, who had escaped from the massacre of the royal family of Joram, was proclaimed king and Athalia was put to death, together with Mathan the high priest of Baal (IV Kings xi, 4-21; II Paralip. xxiii). Thus at the tender age of seven, Joas began a reign of forty years, the first part of which was marked by a strong revival of the worship of Jehovah, and by a careful restoration of the temple of Solomon and its sacred furniture (IV Kings xi, 17-xii, 16; II Paralip. xxiv, 1-14). Unfortunately, the second part of the reign of Joas, which began soon after the death of Joiada, was very unlike to the first. To the good influence of the priesthood in the person of Joiada which had hitherto prevailed near Joas, succeeded the perverse influence of the heads of the Jewish aristocracy who by means of flattery secured the toleration of idolatrous worship in Juda. Once under this accursed influence, Joas refused to listen to the solemn warnings of priests and prophets, and even went so far as to order the death of the son of his benefactor Joiada, called Zacharias, who had predicted national calamities in punishment of national apostasy. The blood of Zacharias shed in the Temple court was soon avenged, first by the defeats which were inflicted on the King of Juda by the Syrians, and next, by the murder of Joas by his own officers (IV Kings xii, 17-21; II Paralip. xxiv, 17-27).

§ 2. *From Amasias to Ezechias.*

1. **Kings previous to Achaz.** Between Joas and Achaz, three kings — Amasias, Azarias (called Ozias in Paralip.), and Joatham — occupied the throne of Juda, and during their reigns, the internal condition of the kingdom was generally prosperous. This is particularly true of the condition of Juda during the long reign of Azarias, a prince equally remarkable as an administrator, an agriculturalist and an engineer, and whose material improvements were, to a large extent, continued by his son, Joatham. It seems also that

on the whole, the worship of Jehovah fared pretty well under these three monarchs. We see, however, that the first was in his later days betrayed into idolatry, that the second, also in his later days, dared to intrude into strictly priestly functions, and that the third had not the courage of working at the reformation of the sad prevailing condition of morals and religion, which is described in the opening chapter of Isaias, and which paved the way for the open idolatry of Achaz.

In their outward relations, the immediate predecessors of Achaz were always successful (with the sole exception of the disgraceful defeat of Amazias by Joas, King of Israel); even under Azarias, the greatest of these kings, the southern kingdom arose to its former military renown, and had again a name terrible to the surrounding nations (IV Kings xiv, xv; II Paralip. xxv-xxvii).

2. **Achaz** (IV Kings xvi; II Paralip. xxviii; Isai. vii-xii). The son and successor of Joatham was Achaz, who, during his short rule of sixteen years, proved himself a prince far worse than any of his predecessors. Early in his reign he delighted in the abominable practices of Phenician and Ammonite worship, and we read that he went even so far as to "make his son pass through the fire" in honor of Moloch. A little later, in Damascus, he apostatized publicly from the national faith and, in consequence, on his return to Juda he desecrated the Temple of Jehovah in various ways, shut up its great doors and discontinued the offering of its sacrifices. He, moreover, erected "in all the corners of Jerusalem and in all the cities of Juda" altars whereon to burn incense to other gods. Gold and silver statues glittered throughout the country, and soothsayers come from the East, wizards, etc., were freely consulted by its inhabitants (Isai. ii, 6, 8, 20; viii, 19).

The great opponent for this frightful idolatry was Isaias,

whose prophetic voice was never willingly heard by Achaz, although from a mere human standpoint, past history and clear insight into the future should have convinced the king and his heathen counsellors that the policy of adherence to the national faith he advocated was the only means to secure the prosperity and independence of the Jewish State. Achaz was bent on his idolatrous course, and all the warnings, offering of signs, and threats of the prophet availed nothing. No wonder then that Jehovah delivered the king into the hands of his enemies, and that the wretched prince was unable to withstand the combined efforts of Israel and Syria, the invasions of the Edomites into the southern district of Juda, and those of the Philistines on the west and southwest. It is also at this critical juncture, that, hard pressed in every direction and unwilling to have recourse to Jehovah, Achaz called on the help of the powerful king of Assyria. Teglathphalasar delivered, it is true, the Jewish monarch from his various enemies, but it was at an enormous cost. Juda became tributary to Assyria, as recorded in the Bible and confirmed by the Nimrud inscription of Teglathphalasar (*Records of the Past*, new series, vol. vi, p. 126), and Achaz appeared in Damascus before the Assyrian monarch as his vassal. (For the Messianic bearing of Isaias vii–xii, see CORLUY, Spicilegium Dogmatico-Biblicum, vol. i; VIGOUROUX, Manuel Biblique, vol ii, § 924, sq.; CHARLES ELLIOTT, Old Testament Prophecy, etc.)

3. **Ezechias** [727–698 B. C.] (IV Kings xviii–xx; II Paralip. xxix–xxxii; Isai. xxxvi–xxxix). The very depths of impiety reached by Achaz, together with the condition of political degradation to which this worthless prince reduced the kingdom of Juda, brought about a strong reaction against both idolatrous worship and vassalage to Assyria. The religious reforms of Ezechias, his son and successor, were at once thorough and far-reaching. Not only he

opened the doors of the Temple of Jehovah and restored to its purity and order Divine worship, but he also did away with all things contrary to the law, such as images, groves, high places, even the brazen serpent formerly erected by Moses and which had become an object of superstitious reverence, and actually made an attempt at securing the conversion of "the remnant of Israel that had escaped the hand of the King of the Assyrians " (II Paralip. xxx).

To these religious changes, Ezechias added several material improvements, and then, perhaps confident in the help of Egypt, threw off the Assyrian yoke. Sennacherib reigned at the time in Assyria, and as soon as his own condition of affairs in Babylonia allowed it, he turned his arms towards Western Asia. In his first invasion of Palestine, of which we have his own account (cfr. *Records of the Past*, new series, vol. vi, p. 90, sq.), he took the fenced cities of Juda, blockaded Jerusalem and laid siege before Lachis, a town of the maritime plain and now identified with Tel El Hesy. Then it was that Ezechias sent to Lachis promising submission. Sennacherib accepted it under the condition of an enormous tribute and withdrew to Nineveh (IV Kings xviii, 13-16).

Soon, however, he was made aware of proceedings between Egypt and Juda against his authority and therefore invaded Palestine for the second time, with an immense army (RAWLINSON, Kings of Israel and Juda, p. 192). Whilst besieging Lachis, he sent three of his officers to frighten Jerusalem into surrender. Neither their summons, nor the threatening letter sent a little later to Ezechias by the Assyrian monarch, who after having taken Lachis was now besieging the neighboring town of Lobna, could shake the confidence of the Jewish king in the help of Jehovah, for Isaias had promised deliverance to him in the certain and precise following terms: " the King of the Assyrians shall not come into this city, nor shoot an arrow into it, nor come before it with shield, nor cast a trench about it. By the way he came, he shall return, and into this city he shall not come, saith Jehovah."

The fulfilment of this prediction is well known. The angel of Jehovah destroyed during the night the bulk of the Assyrian army, and the rest fled with Sennacherib towards Nineveh. Of this wonderful deliverance there is of course no record in the Assyrian annals, but for a striking confirmation of the Biblical narrative we may appeal to the Egyptian account of this miracle preserved by Herodotus (History, book ii, chapter 141), as he learned it from the priests of Egypt, that is, disfigured in order that they might ascribe it to the power of their own gods (IV Kings xviii, 17–xix).

After this glorious deliverance of Juda, only a few events are recorded of the reign of Ezechias. These are (1) his recovery from a severe illness together with the promise of fifteen years more of life; (2) the visit he received from the Babylonian king **Merodach Baladan**, to whose envoys he showed all his riches with great ostentation, whereupon Isaias predicted the Captivity of Babylon; (3) the birth of a long-desired son, to whom he gave the name of Manasses.

### § 3. *Manasses and Josias.*

1. **Manasses** [698–644 B. C.] (IV Kings xxi; II Paralip. xxxiii). Soon after the death of Ezechias the heathenizing party in Juda started a powerful reaction in favor of idolatry, and when Manasses took the reins of government he set his heart on undoing the good his father had done. For this purpose, he not only re-established all the forms of idolatrous worship which Achaz had formerly started in the kingdom, and like him made his sons pass through fire, surrounded himself with soothsayers, etc.; but he went even so far as to set a pillar of Astarthe in the

House of Jehovah. His impiety was only equalled by his tyranny, and the blood of those who refused to join him in his idolatry ran like water through the streets of Jerusalem. A Jewish tradition — perhaps alluded to in Heb. xi, 37 — reckons Isaias among the victims of the tyrant and represents him as sawn asunder. In vain did the prophets of the time predict that the future fate of Jerusalem would be like that of Samaria; threats and remonstrances were useless, and actual punishment could alone bring back the king to his senses, and prevent Juda from becoming an altogether heathen nation. Risings of the Philistines, Moabites and Ammonites were speedily followed by an Assyrian invasion.

The captains of Asarhaddon, the son and successor of Sennacherib and who had lately added Babylonia to the Assyrian empire, invaded Juda, besieged Jerusalem, took Manasses captive and carried him off to Babylon. There, Manasses repented sincerely, and the King of Babylon allowed him to return to Jerusalem as a tributary king. In so acting, Asarhaddon wished most likely that this city naturally so strong and moreover situated so near the Egyptian frontier should be held by one whom he could trust implicitly in the event of the struggle with Egypt which he was contemplating. Thus restored, Manasses set himself to work to undo the mischief he had wrought, but this was no easy task and his son **Amon** [643-642 B. C.], for two years, imitated after him, his first and worst practices.

From a comparison between the text of the book of Judith, as it has come down to us, with Assyrian inscriptions recently discovered, it seems probable that the condition of things described in this inspired book corresponds best with the time of the captivity of Manasses, and that the expedition of Holophernes it records took place under Assurbanipal, the son of Asarhaddon. (As to the *historical* character of the book of Judith, see PELT, vol. ii, p. 283, sq.; VIGOUROUX, Bible et Découvertes Modernes.)

2. Josias [641-610 B. C.] (IV Kings xxii-xxiii, 30; II Paralip. xxxiv, xxxv). Fortunately for Juda, Josias, the son and successor of Amon proved a king most sincerely and constantly devoted to the worship of the true God. When sixteen years old, the young prince started himself an energetic reform not only in Jerusalem, but also through Juda and indeed through the territory which had formed the kingdom of Israel. Not satisfied with doing away with every trace of idolatry, he also destroyed the high places where Jehovah worship had been so far practised, and started on a positive re-establishment of the pure national religion. A special commission was empowered to restore the Temple and to levy contributions for this purpose. In the course of the repairs, Helcias, the high priest, found a roll which contained the *Book of the Law* whereby is not meant most likely the whole Pentateuch known as "*the Law*" in later times, but only Deuteronomy or a part thereof (cfr. CHARLES ROBERT, Réponse à "The Encyclical and the English and American Catholics," p. 52, sq.; DRIVER, International Critical Commentary on Deuteronomy). The *Book of the Law*, newly discovered, was read to the king and the threats it contained against idolatry, and the national punishments it foretold against national apostasy struck Josias with terror; hence his care to have the whole nation renew the solemn covenant with the God of Israel, and to celebrate the Pasch with a ritual accuracy never surpassed since the establishment of the monarchy.

It was early in the reign of Josias that the ever-celebrated patriot and prophet Jeremias received his prophetical call from Jehovah. From his writings we learn that unfortunately the conversion of many in Juda was more apparent than sincere (Jerem. iv, 14; vi, 19, 20; vii, 8-10, etc.).

The virtues of Josias could only delay the fate of a kingdom naturally doomed to destruction between the two mighty rival empires of Egypt and Chaldæa. As a faithful vassal of the latter, Josias opposed Nechao, when this Egyptian king attempted to profit by the stir and conflict then prevailing on the banks of the Euphrates and in the adjacent countries. The Jewish monarch was defeated at Mageddo and mortally wounded, and Nechao succeeded in establishing his authority over the territory west of the Euphrates.

§ *4. The Fall of Juda.*

1. **Political Parties among the Jews at the Beginning of this Period.** No one lamented more sorrowfully the demise of Josias than the prophet Jeremias (IV Kings xxxv, 24, 25), and this indeed most justly. To him the death of the king was the death of a personal friend; it was also the deathblow of the policy he was long still to advocate of a faithful alliance with Chaldæa as the only means to preserve the Jewish kingdom from utter destruction. Despite the protestations of the prophet and of his friends who formed still, it is true, a powerful Assyrian party in Juda, the kings who succeeded to Josias, together with their noblemen, the false prophets and the bulk of the nation ever regarded Egypt as their only chance of salvation, provoked repeatedly the invasion of the Holy Land by the Chaldeans, and thus hastened blindly the ruin of the Jewish polity so plainly and so often foretold by Jeremias (cfr. art. Jeremiah, in SMITH, Bible Dictionary).

2. **The Invasions of Nabuchodonosor and the Last Kings of Juda** (IV Kings xxiii, 31–xxiv; II Paralip. xxxvi). For some unknown reason — probably because he did not owe his elevation to the King of Egypt — Joachaz, the son and successor of Josias, was dethroned by Nechao after three months of rule, and replaced on the throne of Juda by the eldest son of Josias, called Eliacim, but who, on his accession, took the name of Joakim [610–599 B. C.]. It was

under this wicked successor of Josias, that Nabuchodonosor, then acting as lieutenant of his father Nabopolassar, King of Babylon, on his victorious march to Egypt through the territory west of the Euphrates, invaded Juda for the first time, and bound the Jewish king in fetters to carry him to Babylon (cfr. II Paralip. xxxvi, 6, in the Hebrew). We learn however from IV Kings xxiv, 1, that Joakim was allowed to stay in Jerusalem as a tributary king, and that for three years he showed himself a faithful vassal, after which he threw off the yoke. The time chosen by Joakim to vindicate his freedom was well chosen, for Nabuchodonosor was apparently long unable to come in person to re-establish his authority; nevertheless, the Babylonian troops overran the territory of Juda and reduced it to the lowest degree of misery. Joachim, the son and successor of Joakim, reigned but about three months, for the Babylonian king having at length invaded the country, took the Holy City and carried the Jewish king to Babylon together with a very large number of captives belonging to the leading classes. **Matthanias** [599-588 B. C.] (who exchanged his name for that of **Sedecias**), the uncle of the captive king, was now set on the throne of Juda, but notwithstanding the advice of Jeremias, he courted an alliance with Egypt and, in consequence, soon saw his States overrun by the Babylonian armies. Under him, perhaps, more than even under his predecessors, the Jews were addicted to the grossest idolatry, so that the measure of iniquity being at length filled up, "the wrath of Jehovah arose against His people and there was no remedy," for he delivered them into the hands of Nabuchodonosor, who invaded the country for the last time.

3. **Destruction of Jerusalem. Subsequent Condition of the Country.** Whilst the army of the Babylonian king ravaged the Holy Land far and wide, he himself with his best troops, laid siege to Jerusalem. The attack was

skilfully and vigorously conducted, and resistance already began to appear useless when suddenly the news spread of the departure of the Babylonian king to meet an Egyptian army which was advancing to the rescue of the Jewish capital. The news proved true, and many thought that the siege was at an end. Not so, however, with Jeremias who predicted the speedy return of Nebuchodonosor. The prediction was fulfilled, and after a siege of nearly eighteen months, during which all the horrors of famine and pestilence preyed on the unfortunate city (cfr. the description of these horrors in the Lamentations of Jeremias), the Babylonian army penetrated into Jerusalem by the north side.

Whilst the victors pillaged the Holy City and spared neither age nor sex, Sedecias with his family and a few of his troops effected his escape towards Jericho, but he was overtaken and led bound before the Babylonian monarch, who had his eyes put out after they had seen the death of his attendants and of his sons.

Then followed the destruction of Jerusalem: the Temple of Jehovah, the palace of the king and the houses of the wealthy were set on fire; the walls of the city were thrown down, the sacred vessels plundered; the chief priests put to death, and most of the inhabitants carried into captivity (588 B. C.).

After this frightful disaster, Godolias, a friend of Jeremias, was appointed governor of the miserable Jewish remnant which was allowed to stay in the land. Jerusalem being now in ruins, Godolias fixed his residence at Masphath, but he was soon treacherously murdered by Ismahel, whereupon the little remnant of the Jews, fearing the vengeance of Nabuchodonosor, fled into Egypt whither Jeremias accompanied them (Jeremias xxxvii–xliv).

## Chronology of the Royal Period.

Perhaps the reader has been surprised to find that no dates have been supplied in those parts of the preceding chapters which relate the history of the monarchy before the capture of Samaria. Of course, it would have been easy to adopt the chronology commonly received for that period of Jewish history. From this, however, we refrained because recent investigations have proved that the chronological data supplied by the books of Kings before the destruction of the kingdom of Israel, not only are at variance with the dates furnished by Assyro-Babylonian chronology which are held as fully ascertained, but also do not agree with the chronological data which are met with in the parallel narratives of the books of Paralipomenon. The first event, the date of which is perfectly established by synchronous facts, is the capture of Samaria, in 721 B. C. The reign of Saul extended approximately from 1050 to 1010 B. C.; that of David, from 1010 B. C. to 970 B. C., and the disruption of Solomon's kingdom occurred about 930 B. C. (cfr. PELT, Histoire de l'Ancien Testament, vol. ii, p. 126, sq.).

# SYNOPSIS OF CHAPTER XXIII.

## The Prophetical Office in the Old Testament.

*Section I. Nature and History.*

---

**I. NATURE:**
1. *Meaning of the Words:* Prophet; prophecy.
2. *Prophetical Mission:* Its proper object essentially religious.
3. *Prophetical Inspiration:*
   - Described in its main features.
   - Contrasted with heathen divination.
4. *Prophetical Training* (the schools of the prophets).

---

**II. HISTORY:** (Three Principal Periods.)

1. *Before Samuel:*
   - Prophets and prophetical utterances
     - Before Moses; from Moses to Samuel.
   - The Mosaic law "a prophecy" (Matt. xi, 13).

2. *From Samuel to the Babylonian Captivity:*
   - Rise of the prophetical order.
   - Oral and literary work of the chief prophets in Israel, Juda.
   - Attitude of the prophets towards
     - The Jewish law and priesthood.
     - Idolatry and "calf-worship."

3. *Prophets of the Captivity and the Restoration:*
   - Special mission of Ezechiel and Daniel during the exile.
   - Old Testament prophecy closed with the announcement of "the angel of the covenant" (Mal. iii, 1).

# CHAPTER XXIII.

### THE PROPHETICAL OFFICE IN THE OLD TESTAMENT.

#### SECTION I. NATURE AND HISTORY.

§ *1. Nature of the Prophetical Office.*

1. **Meaning of the Words: Prophet; Prophecy.**
It is impossible to peruse the historical records of the Old Testament without noticing that, chiefly during the Royal Period, there existed in the Jewish State a powerful element for the guidance of both rulers and people in the person of the **Prophets** of Jehovah and in their **Prophecies** or prophetical utterances. The *Seer* or *Prophet* of that period — as indeed of any period in Jewish history — was neither necessarily nor exclusively a man endowed with supernatural insight into the future, and hence able to foretell far distant events, although to be considered as a *true* prophet, predictions, if made by him, had to be verified by the event. He was rather, according to the constant meaning of the Hebrew word rendered by "Prophet," the man who had been selected by Jehovah to receive and communicate to others knowledge of the Divine will and purposes. The prophet was thus the mouthpiece of the God of Israel, and his prophecy a Divine message (cfr. PELT, vol. ii, p. 136; CHARLES ELLIOTT, Old Testament Prophecy, p. 21, sq.).

2. **Prophetical Mission.** No one, of course, could lawfully call himself a prophet of Jehovah and claim to give utterance to a Divine message, who had not been

selected and called by the Almighty for the exalted mission of being his messenger and speaking in his name. This prophetical mission, when actually intrusted to a man, was ever in harmony with the essentially theocratic character of the Jewish people, and its proper object was not so much the political or material well-being of the nation, as its moral and religious advantage. The true prophet had stood in the secret counsel of Jehovah, the God and King of Israel, and when he came forth he spoke the words he had heard from his mouth. His was the mission of declaring God's will, of denouncing God's judgments, of defending truth and righteousness and innocence, of keeping alive the constant intercourse been God and his chosen people, of making of Israel's religion a moral and spiritual religion, of opposing sternly idolatry and promoting energetically public compliance with the Divine law and ultimately of preparing by all this the nation at large, for the coming of the Messias who was "the end of the law" (Rom. x, 4).

3. **Prophetical Inspiration.** To fulfil this most important and most difficult mission, the true prophets of Israel received a wonderful gift, known under the name of prophetical inspiration. This inspiration did not find its origin in the unassisted intelligence of man, in his natural parts and powers however great, but was the result of a special and higher supernatural working of the Spirit of God. Thus Holy Writ teaches repeatedly that the prophets received their communication by the agency of the Divine Spirit (Numb. xi, 17, 25 ; I Kings x, 6, etc.), whilst it describes the false prophets as men who "spoke out of their own heart, and not out of the mouth of Jehovah" (Jerem. xxiii, 16).

The ordinary mode of communication between God and His prophets was what may be called a direct manifestation of His will by *word*. It usually consisted of ideas distinctly suggested to the understanding of the prophets without any articulate sound (for cases of articulate speech, see I Kings iii, 4, 10, sq.; Exod. iii, 4, etc.). God revealed also His will and purposes in *visions*, and this is the very title of the prophesies of Isaias, for instance; but the precise nature of these visions cannot well be defined. It is probable, however, that ordinarily pictures familiar to the prophets were presented to their imagination without any external corresponding object, and that in some cases actual apparitions are described, as, for instance, in Daniel viii, 16, sq. Finally, God's communications were made, but more rarely in *dreams* sent during the sleep of the prophets.

The principal difference between the two latter modes of Divine revelation and the former seems to consist in this: when God spoke to the prophets, they retained the use of their external senses and the normal exercise of their intelligence and freedom; when, on the contrary, Divine communications were imparted in visions or dreams, the prophets were in what has been called *ecstasy*. Their external senses were at rest; their soul was inactive, passive, powerless to react against what they perceived, whilst on the contrary, their power of intuition was raised to its highest degree and enabled the prophets to understand and behold everything with the greatest distinctness (cfr. Daniel viii, 18, sq.; x, 9, sq. See also VIGOUROUX, Manuel Biblique, vol. ii, PELT, vol. ii, p. 140, sq.).

This state of ecstasy stands in very great contrast with *heathen divination*. Whilst the higher faculties of the Jewish prophet are the medium of communication with Jehovah, the spiritual God of Israel, the lower powers of human nature in the pagan diviner were ever conceived as the means whereby he had access to his god (cfr. W. R. SMITH, Old Testament in the Jewish Church, second edit., p. 285, sq.). Again, whilst heathen diviners uttered their oracles when in paroxysms of delirium and frenzy, the prophets of the Old Testament when making their announcements were always in full possession of themselves, knowing that they had a Divine commission and prefacing their prophetical utterances accordingly (cfr. HANNEBERG, Histoire de la Révélation Biblique, vol. i, p. 294, sq.).

4. **Prophetical Training.** It was only natural that men, who felt some attraction for the exalted and difficult functions of the prophetical office, should be gradually prepared by a special training for those parts of their future work which depended upon religious and literary culture. In point of fact, schools in which promising young men were gathered and trained in view of the prophetical mission existed among the Jews during the whole Royal Period, and their institution is generally referred to Samuel, the introducer of the monarchy into Israel. One of these existed in his lifetime at Ramatha, where his house was (I Kings xix, 19, 20; vii, 17); others flourished in various places, such as Bethel, Jericho, Galgal, etc.

These schools, now known as the *Schools of the Prophets*, appear to have consisted of students different in numbers; at the head of each there was an elderly or leading prophet, who acted as president (I Kings xix, 20; IV Kings iv, 38) and to whom the young men gave the name of "Father" or "Master" (IV Kings ii, 3; I Kings x, 12). The *Sons of the Prophets*, as these students were called, lived together in distinct communities (IV Kings iv, 38), and were, no doubt, instructed in the knowledge and interpretation of the Divine law. Subsidiary subjects of instruction were music and sacred poetry (I Kings x, 5; IV Kings iii, 15; I Paralip. xxv, 3, sq., etc.). In this way, they prepared by recollection, study and prayer to receive from God a call and inspiration, which He often bestowed upon students so instructed, and which were necessary in order that men however well trained might undertake the prophetical ministry.

## § 2. History of the Prophetical Office.

1. **First Period: Before Samuel.** Long centuries before the institution of the monarchy, the sacred records speak of prophets and prophetical utterances among the chosen people. During the Patriarchal Age, however, Abraham, the great ancestor of the Jews, is the only man called a "prophet" in Holy Writ (Gen. xx, 7), and outside Divine communications made to individuals by oracles and visions, even the great patriarchs of Israel were inspired to prophesy only upon the occasion of some great event, such for instance as their parting blessing. In Moses, on the contrary, we find the type of the prophet of Jehovah so perfectly realized in his close intimacy with the God of Israel, and in his prophetical utterances, that Jewish tradition has ever considered him as the greatest prophet of the Old Covenant (Deuter. xxxiv, 10). Around him, we notice a few persons moved at times by the spirit of prophecy, but as the prophetical gift had been granted to Moses for the fulfilment of his mission as Liberator and Lawgiver of the Jews, it passed to his successor only in so far as Josue needed it to complete the work of Moses by introducing the Hebrews into the Promised Land. At times also, the judges were endowed with the spirit of prophecy (Judges iv, 4) for a work similar to that of Moses and Josue, and here and there we even catch a glimpse of a man sent on a special prophetical mission by Jehovah (Judges vi, 8; I Kings ii, 27, sq.) or favored with some Divine communication (Judges xiii, 2, sq.; I Kings iii, 1). It remains true, however, that the prophetical order was simply foretold by Moses, and that his prediction was not fulfilled before the time of Samuel (Deuter. xviii, 15-22; for the interpretation of this passage of Deuteronomy see PELT, Histoire de l'Ancien Testament, vol. ii, p. 137, footnote 6).

But if Moses did not leave after him an order of men intended to carry on his prophetical work or discharge the prophetic mission such as it was intrusted to the prophets of later days, he at least had supplied the chosen people with a constant "*prophecy*" in the law he had given to them (Matt. xi, 13). The whole purpose of the Mosaic law was clearly to ward off idolatry from the Jewish nation, to promote an ever-closer intercourse between Israel and Jehovah, and prepare effectively the chosen race for the coming of Him who is the "end of the law," and these various objects were, as we have seen, the very objects of the prophetical mission. In another sense, the Mosaic law was also a *prophecy*, to wit, inasmuch as its various elements (priesthood, sacrifices, etc.) were but the figure of those of the Christian dispensation for which they were preordained (see Epistle to the Hebrews, *passim*).

2. **Second Period : From Samuel to the Babylonian Captivity.** The introduction of the monarchy into Israel opened a new and particularly critical period in the religious life of the Jews. The establishment of kings among the Jews naturally tended to diminish the feeling of the people that they were a *theocratic* nation, the *peculiar people of Jehovah*. In like manner, one may well conceive that Jewish kings would aim at becoming gradually independent of all religious supremacy, and that some of them could prove so entirely unfaithful to the spiritual worship of Jehovah as to use the whole weight of their power in the State in favor of idolatrous religions. Add to these difficulties against the survival of pure monotheism in Israel under the monarchy, the constant proneness of the bulk of the nation to idolatry, and it will be readily seen that the rise of the prophetical order at the beginning of this period was a new means of faithfulness provided by God in view of new dangers. He wished to have henceforth direct and official representatives to plead his cause with the people of His choice, to oppose fearlessly all national tendencies towards idolatry, and to

remind at each step, both kings and subjects, of their essential dependence on Him the invisible and supreme Lord of Israel.

This the first prophets of the Royal Period did only by word of mouth, speaking to their own generation of the blessings of various kinds promised by God to his chosen people if faithful; of the manifold punishments that awaited its unfaithfulness; and finally, of God's renewed favor to those who repent (ANDREWS, God's Revelations of Himself to Men, p. 86). Several of these prophets limited their action to watching sedulously over the spiritual and religious interests of the nation; others added to this the literary work of theocratic writers of history (cfr. for instance, I Paralip. xxix, 29). It may also be noticed that after the disruption of Solomon's empire, the oral work seems to have been more active and more effective in the northern, than in the southern, kingdom. This difference is perhaps sufficiently accounted for by the fact, that in the former there were numerous prophetic societies helping on the mission of the prophets; whilst in the latter, individual prophets had to meet almost entirely unseconded, at least equal, if not greater, obstacles (cfr. art. Prophetic Office in *Schaff-Herzog*, Encyclopædia of Religious Knowledge, vol. iii).

However this may be, it is beyond doubt that the earliest written prophecies, those of Jonas in the kingdom of Israel, and of Joel, and perhaps Abdias, in the kingdom of Juda, are to be placed about the middle of the ninth century B. C. In thus writing down their prophecies, the Divine messengers had naturally among other objects, that of proving to future generations the truth of their predictions (cfr. Isai. xxx, 8; Jerem. xxx, 2, 3). If we reckon Baruch with Jeremias as one book, the Old Testament comprises the books of eleven prophets who wrote before the Babylonian exile, three of whom belong to the northern kingdom, namely, Amos, Osee and Jonas; and eight to the southern kingdom, namely, Isaias, Jeremias, Joel, Abdias, Micheas, Nahum, Habacuc and Sophonias. Of course, it may readily be admitted, that some literary productions of the Jewish prophets are now lost, as may be inferred from references to older sources, such for instance, as Isai. ii, 2-4; Mich. iv, 1-4, etc., and that some of those which are still extant present considerable deviations from their original form, as we know is the case with the prophecies of Jeremias.

It is particularly in connection with the prophets of the Royal Period, that critics of our century have affirmed the existence of an antagonism on the part of these messengers of Jehovah to the Jewish law and priesthood. The prophets, we are told, are exclusively concerned with the moral and spiritual duties of Jehovah's worship, and are in opposition to the priests and the ritual enactments of the written law. Hence it is inferred that the legislation of the Pentateuch did not exist in the days of those prophets and that the Jewish hierarchy did not attain to full power until prophecy ceased.

All this, however, seems very much at variance with the facts of the case. The prophets of the royal period presuppose the existence of a law and of a covenant like that described in the Pentateuch (cfr. Amos iii, 2; Joel i, 9, sq.; Osee ix, 3, 15, etc.); they know of a ritual complied with by their contemporaries and they object to this compliance only in so far as the people remain satisfied with a mere observance of outward rites without regard for the fulfilment of higher moral and spiritual duties (Isai. i, 11, sq., etc.). In like manner, the prophets know of the Jewish priests of their time as the ministers of Jehovah, and as intercessors in behalf of the people (Joel i, 9, 13, 14; ii, 15-17). True it is, sometimes priests of Juda are rebuked for their sins, but so are also the prophets unfaithful to their calling (Isai. xxviii, 7), and if the priesthood of the northern kingdom is upbraided by Osee, it is because of its non-Levitical origin and calf-worship.

Thus, then, the attitude of the prophets towards the Jewish law and priesthood is perfectly in harmony with the exalted character of their calling; they must promote in Israel that inward piety which seems to have ever been greatly wanting in the Jewish nation, raise the standard of morality as high as possible and spare no one, high or low, in their censures of evil. Nor is their attitude less easily understood with regard to idolatry and "calf-worship." Naturally enough they were the deadly opponents of idolatrous worship, and when we bear in mind the most severe enactments of the Mosaic law against idolaters (cfr. Exod. xxii, 20; Deut. xviii, 20, etc.), it is not difficult to understand that extreme measures, like those of Elias against the false prophets for instance, must have appeared to them as the fulfilment of a duty. The conduct of some early prophets of the northern kingdom regarding the "calf-worship" introduced by Jeroboam can be justified still more easily; we have no record of opposition by these prophets to calf-worship in Israel; if, in reality, they raised none, it may be supposed that they thought it better to make all their efforts bear on the destruction of Baal worship, which had already become the official worship of the northern kingdom, and which, if not soon overthrown, threatened with permanent extinction the religion of Jehovah in Israel (cfr. CHARLES ELLIOTT, Old Testament Prophecy, p. 152, sq.; p. 144, sq.).

3. **The Prophets of the Captivity and the Restoration.** With the Babylonian captivity opened for the Jews a new era fraught with new and special dangers for the religion of Jehovah among the chosen people. It is only natural, therefore, to find that the mission intrusted to Ezechiel and Daniel, the two great prophets of the exile, exhibited special features worthy of notice.

Ezechiel had been carried to Babylon at the same time as King Jechonias, in 598 B.C., that is, ten years before the destruction of Jerusalem. His mission during this short period was to prepare his fellow-captives for the near coming but unexpected ruin of the Holy City; and after this event had taken place according to his prediction, he had to make the most of his influence as a recognized prophet of Jehovah, to comfort the Jews, to prevent them from considering the victory of the Babylonians over God's chosen people as a victory of heathenism over the true theocracy. Heathenism, with all its actual might and glory, was doomed to destruction, and the people of Jehovah would be restored to the Holy Land.

Daniel also had the mission of comforting the exiled Jews and of strengthening them in their faith, but this he did not so much by his exhortations as by the whole tenor of his life. He was an exemplar of holy living, of perfect faithfulness to Jehovah in the very midst of the seductions of a corrupt and heathen court; his miracles and prophecies, and more particularly the wonders granted to him for his own preservation, were to all the Jews manifest proofs that Jehovah had not forsaken His people, but rather watched lovingly over them in the land of exile. But besides this indirect mission to his own, Daniel had a direct one to the heathen. It was given him to prove to them that Jehovah is the sole God deserving worship, because He alone revealed the most hidden secrets (Daniel ii), inflicted exemplary punishments on those who opposed His designs (iv; v), protected against all harm His faithful worshippers (iii) and was the sole living God, all the others being lifeless idols utterly unable even to defend themselves against assailants (xiv).

After the return from the exile, the main object of Aggeus, Zacharias and Malachias, the prophets of the time of the restoration, was "to remove the hindrances among the people to the fulfilment of God's promises, and to direct their eyes to the dawning of the Messianic salvation" (CHAS. ELLIOTT, p. 185). The last of these prophets, who is also the last of the prophets of the Old Testament, is especially remarkable for the clearness of his predictions concerning the work, the sacrifice and the person of the Messias, so that the Old Testament prophecy may be said to close with the announcement *of the Lord whom the Jews sought and of the Angel of the Covenant whom they desired* (Malach. iii, 1).

# SYNOPSIS OF CHAPTER XXIV.

## The Prophetical Office in the Old Testament.

*Section II. Predictions and Influence.*

---

**I. Predictions of the Prophets:**

1. *Their Supernatural Character:*
   - On what principal grounds questioned in our century?
     - Utterly inadequate.
   - These rationalistic grounds Clearly opposed to
     - Veracity of prophets.
     - Statements of Our Lord and New Testament writers.

2. *Their Manifold Object:*
   - The Jewish people; the heathen nations.
   - The Messias and His kingdom.

3. *Their Chief Characteristics:*
   - Moral and religious import.
   - Lack of ambiguity.
   - Obscurity (its principal causes).
   - Conditional fulfilment.

---

**II. Influence of the Prophets:**

1. *Obstacles to be Overcome:*
   - Popular religious degeneracy (sensual idolatry; mere formalism).
   - Opposition of kings and princes.
   - Conditional character of prophetical predictions.

2. *Means of Success:*
   - Certain features of the prophetical institution.
   - Personal moral qualities of the prophets.
   - Preternatural powers.

3. *General Results* (Moral — political — religious).

# CHAPTER XXIV.

## THE PROPHETICAL OFFICE IN THE OLD TESTAMENT.

### SECTION II. PREDICTIONS AND INFLUENCE.

#### § *1. The Predictions of the Prophets.*

1. **Their Supernatural Character.** Up to recent times, it was universally held that the predictions of the prophets of the Old Testament were proofs of their Divine mission, and a real preparation to the Gospel. Contemporary Rationalists, however, and even many outside this radical school, either reject entirely the supernatural character of the predictive element in the Old Testament prophecies, or regard it as something secondary in comparison with the doctrinal teachings and the historical data which are contained in the prophetical writings. They do not indeed deny altogether that the Hebrew prophets foretold the future and that many of their predictions had a striking fulfilment; but according to them, the agreement between the prediction and the event may be referred to merely natural causes. We are told, for instance, that the power of foreseeing events in the near future may be quite natural to the human soul in some peculiar physical and mental states, when dormant and otherwise unknown powers are suddenly aroused to activity. Again, it is said that the prophets were wonderfully acute discerners of the signs of the times, and that reasoning from the analogy of history, from the well-known unchanging char-

acter of God's moral government, they might make a prediction regarding the distant future which would be fulfilled, the more so because the prediction itself would exercise a considerable influence on the dispositions and actions of those who became acquainted with it (cfr. KUENEN, Prophets and Prophecy in Israel, p. 277, English Translation; STACKPOLE, Prophecy, chap. v).

These, and other such appeals to mere natural causes to account for all the predictions of the prophets, will ever appear at best inadequate to the unprejudiced reader of Jewish history and prophecy. A large number of the predictions of the prophets related to remote events and were given out in an age when the causes to which they owed their origin either did not exist, or were so obscure and latent as to be concealed from the observation of the most perspicacious men, especially as these predictions were not merely general in their character, but strongly marked by the addition of many circumstances of the events which they foretold. Nor could the analogy of history enable men to make conjectures like the predictions which foretold not only the exile of the Hebrews, but also their return to their country and their subsequent prosperity, the burning and devastation of Jerusalem, the empire of the Chaldeans and the seventy years' captivity in Babylonia, etc. (cfr. Amos ii, 5; ix, 4, 14; Osee ii, 15-23; viii, 14; xiv, 5-9; Mich. iii, 12, iv, 1, sq.; vii, 8-17; Jerem. xxv, 11, sq.). Since such clear predictions could not be made by men of the greatest sagacity, and must necessarily have proceeded from God Himself, we may conclude that others agreeing with these in nature and design, and attributed to the same God, have Him also for their especial author (JAHN, Introduction to the Old Testament, p. 299, English Translation).

Again, all rationalistic attempts at explaining away the supernatural character of the prophetical predictions must fail before the well-known attitude of the prophets themselves regarding their own predictions. They claimed openly the gift of Divine illumination respecting the future (cfr. for instance, IV Kings i, 3, sq.), clearly distinguished between those predictions they could have made through their own unassisted powers and those which they owed to special communications from Jehovah (III Kings xxii, 14, sq.; Jerem. xxviii, 9; Isai. xx, 1, sq., etc.), and in a variety of ways succeeded in making their contemporaries believe that this was the great difference between the predictions they uttered and those which were made by the false prophets. Whence it plainly follows that the veracity of the prophets requires that we should admit that they received from God a distinct foreknowledge of the future near or distant; and indeed, had they not actually possessed this supernatural foresight, they would have soon lost their great influence upon the various classes of Jewish society.

It should also be noticed in this connection that to deny the supernatural character of the predictions of the prophets of the Old Testament is to run directly counter to the statements of Our Lord (cfr. for instance, Luke xxiv, 25, 26, 44, 46), and of the inspired writers of the New Testament (cfr. in particular, II Peter i, 19–21).

2. **Manifold Objects of the Predictions of the Prophets.** Amidst the great variety of topics about which the Jewish prophets uttered predictions, some deserve special attention because of their greater prominence in the prophetical writings.

Naturally enough, the chosen people themselves are the object of numerous predictions on the part of the prophets. It was of the special benefit of the Jews that Jehovah called men to the prophetical office, and that He made known the future to His select messengers. Because the Jews were His "peculiar people," that is, the theocratic nation of antiquity, prosperity was to be foretold to them as a reward for faithfulness, public calamities as chastisements for unfaithfulness, restoration to favor as a return for sincere repentance, and final rejection as the awful punishment of perseverance in apostasy. Such were the general purposes for which the prophets of Israel were allowed distinct insight into the future of the Jewish nation, and were directed to utter predictions which, under a variety of forms, corresponded to the special needs of the people of God in the various periods of its national existence.

It was also because of the chosen people that we find in many of the Jewish prophets predictions which regard the heathen nations. There we find foretold the manner in which Jehovah intended to use them as instruments of His retributive justice to Israel, and next to punish them for their own pride and cruelty whilst inflicting upon the Jews chastisements which the chosen people had but too well deserved. There, also, we find predicted the future call of the nations of the world to become in their turn the chosen people of God, in place of the ungrateful nation, which, despite promises and favors, threats and punishments, was ultimately to lose that glorious privilege.

Whilst contemplating the future restoration of the Jews to the Land of Promise, and the future call of the nations to the worship of the true God, the prophets of Israel are induced to foretell another kingdom which will begin with the theocratic people, perpetuate the glorious rule of David, the faithful theocratic king of the Jews, and extend its sway over all the nations of the world. This is the Messianic kingdom which the prophets of Israel describe in its ideal perfection, under the glorious images of an ideal earthly prosperity. At the head of that kingdom — the true continuation of the Jewish theocracy — there will be a descendant of David, born in Bethlehem, and who will prove the ideal King long expected to start a universal and eternal rule of happiness in the faithful service of Jehovah. It is for this glorious rule of the Messias that the Jews are bidden to prepare by the practice not only of outward but also of inward righteousness. Unfortunately, under the misleading guidance of the *Scribes*, who to a large extent succeeded the prophets in the office of keeping alive the true religion in Israel, the ancient people of God, as a nation, will lose sight of the inward righteousness which alone could fit the Jews for entering the Messianic kingdom at its coming. No less unfortunately for them, both the leaders and the people of Israel will take to the letter the glorious descriptions of worldly peace, plenty, victory, etc., which they will notice in the prophetical writings, and miss altogether the meaning of other traits of the Messianic picture drawn before their eyes, so that when the Messias comes and sets up His kingdom they will not be able to recognize in Him and in His work the many traits of the prophetical predictions which pointed to a kingdom "not of this world" and to a suffering Messias, and in consequence they will be excluded from the Kingdom of God.

3. **Chief Characteristics of the Predictions of the Prophets.** From the foregoing remarks, it is clear that, unlike the oracles of the heathens, the predictions of the Jewish prophets were not uttered "to support the tottering interests of States or kings, to satisfy mere curiosity about the future, or to incline the people to the wishes of their rulers. They all tended to one object, worthy of a Divine intervention, the proof of the Divine mission of the prophets, and, by consequence, of the true doctrine concerning God, namely, that the one only God who sent the prophets is the omniscient Ruler of the universe (Isai. xli, 21, sq.); and particularly that He was governing the Hebrews in such a manner that they should preserve the knowledge of Him until the period when it should be propagated to all nations by a great Messenger who was to arise from the posterity of David" (JAHN, Introduction, p. 297, English Translation). It may also be

noticed that the predictions of the prophets are usually bound up with further instructions, warnings, etc., which had a religious or moral bearing for their direct purpose.

A second manner in which the predictions of the prophets offer a striking contrast with the heathen oracles is their lack of ambiguity. This is particularly true in connection with very near events, when oracles and soothsayers carefully selected ambiguous expressions in order that in any result their credit might be preserved. Not so with the Hebrew prophets who, whether they used external symbols, elevated or even poetical style, parabolic or allegorical descriptions, invariably made it clear what they foretold the event would be, and spoke with great definiteness, although they knew full well that, should their predictions remain unfulfilled, a prompt death awaited them from the hands of powerful enemies in the Jewish State.

This does not mean, of course, that all the predictions of the Jewish prophets are perfectly clear, for, in point of fact, whilst some of them present this perfect clearness, most are surrounded with considerable obscurity. But they are not ambiguous in the strict sense of the expression, and when they have been transmitted to us complete they are clear enough to enable us to discern the historical event to which they refer.

The obscurity of the prophetical predictions is not simply due to the poetical style in which they are written, or to the fact that they refer to very ancient events, with which we are but imperfectly acquainted, it is due also to the purpose of the predictions themselves. It stands to reason that if the prophecies had had from the beginning the same degree of clearness as that which history requires, they would have sometimes been a positive obstacle to their own fulfilment, by suggesting to those on whose free agency this fulfilment depended so to act as to prevent the occurrence of the event foretold. In consequence, many of them when uttered or written down were so obscure as to leave the event, or rather its main circumstances, unintelligible before its fulfilment, and so clear as to be intelligible after it. Another natural cause of obscurity in the prophetical predictions is to be found in the unquestionable fact that the prophets usually beheld things not as we are accustomed to see objects near at hand, but as we see things at a distance, that is, all at once, with different degrees of distinctness for the various objects according to their nearness, and without giving an accurate idea of the distance which may intervene between them. The prophets had therefore at times but an imperfect knowledge particularly of the intervals of time which separated the events which they foretold, and in consequence these same events are often predicted without that chronological order which would be necessary for perfect clearness.

The last characteristic of the predictions of the prophets to be noticed here is their conditional fulfilment. Many predictions were of the nature of a promise or a threat with regard to persons or cities and countries, as we find it stated in Jeremias xviii, 7-10 and Ezechiel xxxiii, 13-16. This is, of course, in perfect harmony with the moral government of a just and holy God, and should be distinctly borne in mind because it explains why many predictions have been unfulfilled, and from the nature of the case will never be fulfilled: the actual retribution of the predicted evil or good things was dependent on the continuance of the same moral attitude of the people concerned, and as this moral attitude was actually changed, the promised reward or denounced punishment were necessarily withheld.

### § 2. *Influence of the Prophets.*

1. **Obstacles to be Overcome.** As might naturally be expected, the influence of the prophets of the Old Testa-

ment varied considerably in the different periods of Jewish history, according to the greater or lesser obstacles which these various periods opposed to the successful discharge of the prophetical mission. To prove faithful messengers of the God of Israel, the prophets had, first of all, to resist with all their energy the religious degeneracy of the nation at large. Instead of feeling naturally attracted towards the pure and ennobling worship of the one true God, the bulk of the chosen people ever felt a wellnigh irresistible tendency towards an impure and degrading polytheism. It was therefore a hard task for the defenders of the exclusive worship of Jehovah and preachers of inward righteousness, such as the prophets were, to produce in the minds and feelings of the people a reaction against sensual idolatry, a harder task still to prevent its inherited and inveterate craving for impure rites from getting the upperhand and betraying the nation into lower and worse forms of idolatry than those they had but recently renounced. Further, even when the Jewish race kept aloof for some time from the shameful excesses of Baäl or Moloch worship, there usually crept in another form of religious decay, that of mere formalism in the practice of the religion of Jehovah. Time and again, we hear, therefore, the prophets, those men favored with special intercourse with the living God, lifting up their voices and protesting energetically against the soulless form of worship which was ever compatible with moral corruption. It must be said, however, that if the action of the prophets of Jehovah had been seconded by the political leaders of the Jews, by the kings and princes, the faithful messengers of God would have found it far less difficult to purify and elevate the religious tone of the nation; but, unfortunately, most of the kings of Juda and Israel, together with the larger number of their courtiers, opposed the influence of the prophets by every means in their power. Through personal inclination towards idolatry, those kings and princes practised, encouraged idolatry, and when rebuked for it by the prophets, they resented this interference, persecuted and put to death those troublesome opponents of whom they spoke as the enemies of the State. Thus was the whole weight of political and social influence usually brought to play right against the noble but limited efforts of the prophets and their disciples.

As a last obstacle against which the true prophets of Jehovah had to struggle in order to preserve their influence upon their contemporaries, we may mention the conditional character of their prophetical predictions. The non-fulfilment of these conditional predictions, which, as stated above, was ever possible, and which at times occurred actually, was calculated to cause them to be considered as false prophets, unworthy of credence, and, therefore, to turn against them both friends and foes of Jehovah worship.

2. **Means of Success.** To face these general obstacles, together probably with many others arising from the particular circumstances of their time, the prophets of Israel had at their disposal powerful means of success. First of all, certain features of the prophetic institution, such as the special training which many of them had undergone in the prophetical schools, the direct Divine call and sometimes personal intercourse with Jehovah, the miracles oftentimes performed for their preservation, the public and private services which they rendered to their contemporaries, and even the elevation of their moral and religious teachings, etc., were so many things which procured for them the deep reverence and grateful affection of many of their fellow countrymen, sometimes of the kings and leaders of the nation.

Another means of success for the prophets in the discharge of their difficult mission was found in their personal moral qualities. We have, it is true, details concerning the life and work of only a few prophets of Israel, but it can hardly be doubted that the other prophets trod in the footsteps of those who are best known to us, that they were men of genuine singleness of purpose, ardent zeal, persevering energy, men ever ready to make the most of every opportunity either to win back king and people to the pure worship of Jehovah, or to render closer the union of the Jews with their invisible king. Their disinterestedness was beyond question, and stood in striking contrast with the greedy selfishness of the soothsayers and false prophets in the land. They were indeed "men of God," as they were called, and their examples of holy living no less than their ardent exhortations contributed powerfully to increase the influence they exercised upon their contemporaries.

It remains true, however, that the wonders it was given to the prophets to perform and the true predictions they uttered were their greatest means of success. These preternatural powers were justly considered by the nation at large as unquestionable proofs of a Divine mission; they contributed much to secure to the prophets enthusiastic and grateful followers, and caused them to be publicly consulted, even by several of the worst kings, in cases of pressing national danger.

3. **General Results.** When after this rapid survey of the work and history of the prophetical office in the Old Testament, we try to sum up the general results produced by this great institution among the Jewish people, we find first of all that even when the severe rebukes of the prophets did not succeed in effecting the moral reformation they were urging upon king and people, they yet secured to Israel over the other nations the advantage that the moral precepts should not be violated without protest. By thus inveighing fearlessly against public corruption, the prophets kept alive among the chosen people a distinct knowledge of what was right, and prevented the Jews from sinking down quietly or

permanently to the low moral level of the surrounding pagan nations. Of course, their holy examples and fervent exhortations had also the precious result of communicating to the minds and hearts of many of their contemporaries something of the generous piety which they themselves possessed.

In the second place, it is easy to realize that from a political standpoint the Hebrew prophets were of great advantage to their nation. In exercising fearlessly their mission of rebuking the Jewish monarchs, they ever reminded the kings that they were not, that they could not be, absolute rulers over the Holy Land in the same manner as the kings of the neighboring tribes. By their opposition to the unjust or irreligious enactments of the royal power, they also taught the people not to bow down too easily before the will of a mortal monarch.

Finally, from a religious point of view, the mission of the prophets of Israel had the best and most faithful results. They prevented idolatry, even when imposed by despotic kings, from taking such root in the people as to preclude all return to Jehovah; they kept alive the precious remembrance among the Jews of their covenant with the one true God, and repeatedly promoted religious reforms. More particularly did they bring out the spiritual element of Judaism, and direct the eyes of the nation towards the coming of the Messias and the setting up of His kingdom.

# SYNOPSIS OF CHAPTER XXV.

## The Babylonian Captivity.

I. THE BABYLONIAN EMPIRE:
- 1. *Geography* (Extent; principal provinces; splendid capital).
- 2. *History:*
  - Beginning of the new Babylonian or Chaldean Empire (606 B.C.).
  - Rapid consolidation and wonderful prosperity under Nabuchodonosor.
  - Decline and fall (a comparatively easy prey to Cyrus).
- 3. *Civilization:*
  - Manners and customs.
  - Arts of peace and war.
  - Religion.

II. THE JEWS IN EXILE:
- 1. *Number and Quality of the Captives.*
- 2. *Social Condition in Babylonia:*
  - At first, cruel slavery inflicted.
  - Prompt organization as colonists.
  - Share in the commerce of the conquerors.
  - Final attachment to Babylonia as to a mother country.
- 3. *Religious Life:*
  - General reaction against idolatry.
  - Religious
    - practices faithfully kept up.
    - beliefs confirmed and developed.
  - Origin of synagogues as places for religious meetings.

THE BOOK OF TOBIAS.

# FOURTH PERIOD.

## THE RESTORATION: FROM THE BABYLONIAN CAPTIVITY TO OUR LORD.

### CHAPTER XXV.

#### THE BABYLONIAN CAPTIVITY.

§ *1. The Babylonian Empire.*

1. **Geography.** Babylonia is the name which the Greeks and the Romans gave to "the land of the Chaldeans" (Jerem. xxiv, 5; Ezech. xii, 13) into which the Jews were carried captive by Nabuchodonosor. The Babylonian empire proper comprised the region along the lower course of the Euphrates and the Tigris, from the point where they approach each other near the modern Baghdad, to their mouth in the Persian Gulf and from Elam on the east to Arabia on the west. As a worthy successor to the immense Assyrian empire, the new Babylonian or Chaldean empire controlled all the southern and western portions of the former Assyrian dominions, and included such important provinces as Susiana, Elam, Mesopotamia, Syria, Phenicia, Palestine, Idumæa, Northern Arabia and probably Lower Egypt.

The great cities found in this vast extent of territory were very numerous, and among them we may notice Borsippa, Sippara, Erech, Susa, Carcamis, Haran, Emath, Damascus, Jerusalem, Sidon, etc. Prominent among them all was Babylon, the capital of the empire, and commonly believed to have occupied the site of the ancient Babel (Gen. xi, 4, 5, 9). It was situated in a flat, fertile plain on both sides of the Euphrates, some 200 miles above its junction with the Tigris. Its extent, strength and beauty are detailed by Herodotus (History, book i, chap. 178, sq.), according to whom Babylon was 200 square miles in extent, cut into squares by straight streets, and enclosed by a double line of walls. The Greek historian speaks also (1) of the houses as being mostly three and four stories high, (2) of the splendid temple of Bel, a tower 600 feet square, having eight stories, 480 feet high, with a winding ascent passing around it, and the chapel of a god at the top, (3) of an immense palace of the kings, the ruins of which are identified with the Kasr, an enormous pile of bricks, tiles and fragments of stone, (4) of the fine quays of Babylon. Berosus, a Babylonian priest and historian, who lived a little later than Herodotus, has also left an account of the famous hanging gardens of the great Babylon (cfr. JOSEPHUS, Antiq. of the Jews, book x, chap. xi, § 1).

It must be said, however, that whilst a few explorers of the ruins of that splendid city accept the enormous figure given for its extent by Herodotus, most, and apparently on very good grounds, reject it and think that Babylon was about eight miles in circuit.

2. History. The founder of the new Babylonian or Chaldean empire, the position and extent of which have been just described, was Nabopolassar (Nabu-pal-usur in Assyrian), a general of great ability, who was made first governor and next king of Babylonia when that country was still only a province of the Assyrian empire. Nabopolassar proving disloyal to his suzerain, the last Assyrian king, Asaraddon II, attacked and destroyed Ninive in union with Cyaxares, King of Media, and started a new empire with Babylon for its capital (606 B. C.).

The son and successor of Nabopolassar in 604 B. C., was Nabuchodonosor (Nabu-kudur-usur in the Assyrian inscriptions), to whom the new Babylonian empire owed chiefly its rapid consolidation and wonderful prosperity. During a long reign of forty-three years, this great warrior recovered Syria and Palestine, destroyed Jerusalem and carried away the Jews to Babylon, reduced Phenicia, ravaged and probably conquered Egypt. Then laden with spoils and glory, he utilized to its utmost limit the physical strength of his numerous captives — Jews, Phenicians, Syrians and Egyptians — to cover his whole territory with gigantic works, the remains of which excite admiration even to the present day. He fortified his capital with the greatest care, not only repairing the old wall around the city, but adding to it another less thick but almost as strong. He raised the walls of a huge palace in the incredibly short time of fifteen days, as we read in his large inscription and in the history of Berosus, and dug a canal the remains of which Rawlinson traced for a distance of from 400 to 500 miles. "He built or rebuilt almost all the cities of Upper Babylonia, Babylon itself, upon the bricks of which scarcely any other name is found, Sippara, Borsippa, Cutha, Teredon, Chilmad, etc.; he formed aqueducts and constructed the wonderful hanging gardens at Babylon; he raised the huge pyramidal temples at Borsippa and Akkerkuf, together with a vast number of other shrines," etc. (RAWLINSON's edition of *Herodotus*, History, vol. i, p. 413; cfr. also LENORMANT, Manual of the Ancient History of the East, vol. i, pp. 476-486).

The wealth, power and general prosperity of the Babylonian empire under Nabuchodonosor are nowhere better illustrated than in the opening chapters of the book of Daniel (cfr. especially, ii, 37, 38; iii, 1, sq.; iv, 17-19). There we read also of his excessive pride, which made him consider himself as more than a mortal man (cfr. inscription quoted by LENORMANT, loc. cit.) and required divine honors from his subjects

(Daniel iii; iv, 27). After a long punishment in that strange form of madness which the Greeks called *Lycanthropy*, the Babylonian monarch was restored to health and to his former grandeur. Soon afterwards he died predicting, says Abydenus, the ruin of the Chaldean empire (EUSEBIUS, Præpar. Evang., book ix, chap. 41).

The prediction was soon to be fulfilled; the Babylonians owed their rapid success to their hordes of cavalry, rather than to their energy of character or to their knowledge of military tactics, and both were most desirable in view of conflicts with the Persians in a near future. Furthermore, the immediate successors of Nabuchodonosor, Evil-Merodach and Neriglissar, besides being men unworthy of the throne, were no match, from a military standpoint, for the young Cyrus who had already conquered Media. The only ruler worthy of Nabuchodonosor's throne was the last King of Babylon, named Nabonahid, who reigned seventeen years. This prince was formerly, although wrongly, identified with King Baltassar, who is spoken of in the book of Daniel (chap. v) as the son of Nabuchodonosor and apparently as the last King of Babylon, for, from the inscription which has a reference to Baltassar, it seems well established that he was really the son of Nabonahid and had been associated by him to the empire. After the defeat of Nabonahid by Cyrus, Babylon was taken during a royal banquet given by Baltassar, and its capture put an end to the Babylonian empire (cfr. *Records of the Past*, new series, vols. iii, p. 125, sq.; v, p. 160, sq.; WALLIS BUDGE, Babylonian Life and History, chap. vi; VIGOUROUX, Bible et Découvertes Modernes, vol. iv; DEANE, Daniel, chap. viii).

3. **Civilization.** The civilization of Babylon, in the midst of which the Jews lived during the Exile, resembled very closely that of Ninive, its former rival. In Babylonia as in Assyria, the upper classes wore a long sleeveless robe

adorned with fringes and bound around the waist with a belt, a mantle over their shoulders, a tiara or fillet on their heads and sandals on their feet. The dress of the soldiers and lower classes was much more simple: it consisted in a linen tunic which did not quite reach the knees, and which was fastened round the waist by a girdle or sword-belt; sometimes even a simple kilt seems to have taken the place of this tunic, more frequently the kilt was worn under it. They all curled their hair and beard, used staves and a seal usually in the form of a cylinder.

The diet of the poorer class was simple, consisting almost exclusively of dates, which were perhaps pressed into cakes, as usual in the country at the present day. To this were probably added some vegetables, such as gourds, melons, etc., and in the marshy regions of the south, fish. The diet of the rich was more varied and pleasing to the taste. Wheaten bread, meats of various kinds, luscious fruits, fish, game appeared on their table, and wine imported from abroad was the usual drink. A festival banquet was magnificent and generally ended in drunkenness. Music, instrumental and vocal, entertained the guests, a rich odor of perfumes floated around, and there was great display of gold and silver plate. The splendid dresses of the guests, the exquisite carpets and hangings, the numerous attendants gave an air of grandeur to the scene (RAWLINSON, Ancient Monarchies, vol. iii, p. 19).

Marriages were made once a year at a public festival, when the maidens of age to marry were put up at public auction. Polygamy was permitted, but probably practised only by very wealthy men. The dress of the women consisted of a long tunic and mantle, and a fillet for confining the hair, and their seclusion seems scarcely to have been practised in Babylonia with as much strictness as in most Oriental countries.

All deeds and contracts stamped on tablets of clay were

signed and sealed in presence of several witnesses, who attached their seals, or at least their nail marks, to the document. It was then enclosed in an outer coating of clay on which an abstract of the contents was given. These tablets, of varied shapes and colors, make us acquainted with all kinds of topics. Papyrus was, of course, one of the writing materials, but it had long been reserved for what we would call "éditions de luxe," and the usual material was the clay, on which, whilst still wet, cuneiform or "wedge-shaped" characters were impressed by means of a metal stylus with a square head: then the clay was dried in the sun. In all the great cities of the empire there were regular libraries well supplied with books in papyrus and clay, and the decipherment of such writings and inscriptions as have been recently discovered in Assyria and Babylonia has proved a source of invaluable information. (Many of those old texts will be found correctly rendered into English in the six volumes of the *Records of the Past*, new series, published under the editorship of PROFESSOR SAYCE.)

In architecture, painting and sculpture, the Babylonians were inferior to the Assyrians, but it was not so in commerce, both foreign and domestic. Great numbers engaged in the manufacture of textile fabrics, particularly carpets and muslins, and many more excelled as lapidaries. But it is chiefly in agriculture that the bulk of the people was engaged, with such success that on many points modern nations have, as it were, re-invented, but not improved on Babylonian methods. It seems also that in the days of Nabuchodonosor there was a firm of bankers whose special business it was to carry on the commerce of Babylon.

If we except the physical sciences, it can easily be proved that the various branches of human learning were cultivated with intelligence and success by the Babylonians. (For details, see WALLIS BUDGE, Babylonian Life and History, chap. viii.)

The Babylonians were armed with swords, bows and arrows, and staves; and in later days they used helmets and shields. Their battles, in which horses and chariots besides infantry were used, were little more than sudden surprises and skirmishes. In besieging cities, they employed scaling ladders, and men were set under cover to dig out the stones from the foundations, that the city walls might fall. On the taking of a city they ruthlessly destroyed everything, so that only a few kings took captives as working bondmen.

However monotheistic may have been the primitive religion of Babylonia, it is beyond doubt that in the time of the Exile they had long worshipped gods without number. From Ilu (El) the fountain-head of all divinity, a first triad of gods known as Anu, Ea and Bel (with three female counterparts) was supposed to have emanated. These three gods represented time, intelligence and creation, and from them had originated a second triad, made up of Sin, Samas and Rimmon (with, of course, three corresponding female deities) and representing the moon, the sun and the evening star. Next in order of succession came the five planets: Adar, Merodach, Nergel, Istar and Nebo, whose names appear so often in Assyrian proper names.

To these great gods, and to a countless host of minor deities, the Babylonians addressed prayers, sung hymns and litanies, some specimens of which have come down to us. But what is far more important to notice, is the Chaldean account of the creation of the world, and a legend respecting the Tower of Babel and the Flood, which have been discovered and which are in close agreement with the inspired account in Genesis (cfr. SMITH, Chaldean Account of Genesis).

The splendid worship of Babylon was conducted by priests, through whom the worshippers made offerings, sometimes of the most costly kind, and sacrifices of oxen and goats. The priests were married and lived with their families, either within the sacred enclosures of the temples or in their immediate neighborhood. They were supported either by lands belonging to the temple to which they were attached, or by the offerings of the Babylonian worshippers.

Notions of legal cleanness and uncleanness akin to those prevalent among the Jews were found in the religious system of the Babylonians, and like the Jews also, the Chaldeans kept the seventh day. Let us mention finally their belief in demons, in a future life, and also the immoral character of some of their religious practices. (In connection with this idolatrous system of the Babylonians, chapter vi of Baruch and chapter xiv of Daniel should be read.)

### § 2. *The Jews in Exile.*

1. **Number and Quality of the Captives.** It is impossible in the present day to give even the approximate number of the Jewish captives whom Nabuchodonosor carried to Babylon in his various invasions. Even though we should suppose that the figures supplied in the Bible (in the books of Kings, of Jeremias, and Ezechiel) have not been tampered with, it would remain very probable that these official figures represent only the number of the men of rank whose influence was feared, if left in Judæa, and of those whose technical skill or physical strength made particularly desirable for the numerous and gigantic works of the King of Babylon (cfr. IV Kings xxiv, 14). But of course the members of the families of those exiles followed them into captivity, and only a very small remnant of Jews, and these of the poorest sort, remained in the land.

2. **Social Organization in Babylonia.** The bitter sense of bereavement experienced by the Jews thus torn away from their country can be more easily imagined than described. It is this feeling which is suggested by the

Hebrew word "Guloth," by which they designated the Captivity; it is also this feeling which we find so touchingly expressed in the well-known Psalm, *Super flumina Babylonis*. Nor is this to be wondered at, when we bear in mind the barbarous treatment which the bulk of them had most likely to undergo at the beginning of the Exile. They were the bondmen of Nabuchodonosor, and despite all their efforts to execute speedily and well the hard task daily exacted from them, they could say in all truth, "The plowers (the overseers) plowed upon my back; they made long their furrows" (Psalm cxxviii, 3, in Vulgate). To the sufferings inflicted by the lash were, no doubt, joined in many cases those of the dungeon, of hunger and of nakedness; hence we hear the captives complaining that they are "devoured" and "broken in pieces," and repeating that wish inspired by revengeful hatred: "O daughter of Babylon, miserable; blessed shall he be who shall repay thee thy payment thou hast paid us. Blessed he that shall take and dash thy little ones against the rock!"

Soon, however, their condition became less unbearable, for, owing to the high influence of Daniel at court, his three Jewish companions, Sidrach, Misach and Abdenago were "appointed over the works of the province of Babylon" (Daniel ii, 48, 49). Henceforth they enjoyed the rights which Babylonian civilization ever recognized in slaves of whatever origin: they had, for instance, a right to compensation for their labor, and the faculty of redeeming themselves from bondage. Nay, more, they seem to have been allowed to settle in colonies here and there over the land, and to organize themselves pretty much in the same way as in Judæa (Ezechiel xx, 1).

This they actually did, when, giving up their foolish hope of an immediate restoration to the Holy Land, they complied with the wise counsel of Jeremias, that they should build houses, plant orchards, marry their sons and daughters, work and pray for the peace and prosperity of Babylon (Jeremias, xxix, 4-7). In point of fact, the history of Suzanna and the two elders narrated in the book of Daniel (chap. xiii) gives us positive information about an extent of self-government which we would have hardly supposed granted to the Jews in their exile. It allows us also an insight into the material prosperity which many among them were doubtless able to secure to themselves by sharing in the industrial and commercial life of their conquerors. Indeed, it has been supposed, and with some probability, that the great banker of Babylon, Egibi, was of Jewish origin.

Thus the Jews gradually became attached to this foreign country, and in proportion as they enjoyed material prosperity, religious freedom, satisfaction of commercial instincts and genuine consideration from the heathens, in the same proportion, also, their enthusiasm for the desolate land of Palestine abated, especially in the minds of the new generation born in Babylonia. A striking proof of this is found in the fact that when permission to return to the Holy Land was granted to the exiles only a small number availed themselves of it, and the rest preferred to continue to live in a country in which they had a comfortable home. Henceforth, and for long centuries to come, Babylon was to be a great centre of Jewish population, a great seat of Jewish learning.

3. **Religious Life.** As might naturally be expected, idolatry, to which the Jews had long been accustomed in Palestine, flourished at first among them in Babylonia, the more so because, by the destruction of Jerusalem and its temple, Jehovah had proved inferior in the eyes of many to the idols of the nations. Soon, however, it became a conviction with a large number that these great evils were, after all, nothing but the just punishment of their wicked deeds, and under the influence of the prophets, priests and Levites of Jehovah this better frame of mind spread daily. Again,

the fulfilment of the predictions concerning the fall of Jerusalem and Ninive, the courage and patronage of Daniel, together with the miracles granted to him and the spectacle of many heathens embracing Hebrew worship, brought about a strong reaction against idolatry. In fact, Divine Providence intervened so repeatedly and powerfully during the seventy years of the Exile, both in favor of the worshippers of Jehovah and against their opponents, that this reaction proved a lasting one, and that the descendants of the exiles remained, as a body, invariably faithful to national monotheism.

Of course, in Babylon the Levitical worship could not be carried out in its fulness. The sacrificial rites of the Temple, for instance, were naturally stopped during the period of the Exile, but this made it all the more desirable that the rest of the religion of Jehovah, which could be observed outside Palestine, should be faithfully adhered to by the Jews. During that time they no doubt read with great reverence whatever sacred books were in their possession, eager to find in them prospects of a brighter condition for their religion and commonwealth. It is also during this same period that the practice of lifting up their hearts to God in prayer at the regular time of the morning and evening incense-offering spread among the exiles; to these sacred times for supplication they seem even to have added the hour of noon (Daniel vi, 10).

Whilst the religious practices of the Jews were thus faithfully kept up in Babylon, and even improved upon, their religious beliefs were also confirmed and developed. The unity of God and inanity of idols became daily more evident truths to their minds; the power of prayer and of good works was also emphasized in various ways, whilst the great dogma of the resurrection of the dead was formulated with a distinctness which could hardly be surpassed (Ezech. xxxvii; Dan. xii, 1–3). At the same time, the Messianic belief was developed into the idea of a Divine Messenger, of a great King, who would found, not a transient and limited kingdom like unto the great empires of the world, but a universal and everlasting theocracy. Finally, Jewish theology respecting the holy angels was developed and completed; henceforth they were clearly conceived as constituting a hierarchy of spirits, who under God, have a great power over men and demons, and are busied about the interests of individuals and empires.

A last, but very important feature of the religious life of the Jews during their exile, is to be found in the institution of the *Synagogues* as places for religious meetings. We have, it is true, no definite statement in the inspired records to the effect that this is the period of Jewish history to which we must trace back the origin of those synagogues, which we find so multiplied in the time of Our Lord and His apostles, but the circumstances of time and place were such as would naturally lead the Jews to start such an institution; and they were no sooner restored to their own land, than something very much akin to the synagogal worship in its most developed form is observable in the Biblical records (cfr. Nehemias viii).

### *The Book of Tobias.*

Intimately connected with the period of the Exile, although not with the captives of Babylon, is the inspired book of *Tobias*, the text of which has reached us only in translations which present many important variations. Naturally enough, the historical character of this book had long remained unquestioned among Catholics, for all the details it contains are presented in the form of a narrative. A few Catholic scholars, however, especially because of alleged historical inaccuracies, and the peculiar character of the miracles it describes, have, of late, departed from this time-honored position. They prefer to look upon it as an inspired story based on facts and therefore, even from a historical standpoint, very useful to Biblical students. There is no doubt, that it supplies many interesting data concerning the material, moral and religious condition of those Jews of the northern kingdom who were spread through the Assyrian empire (cfr. PELT, vol. ii, p. 296-300).

# SYNOPSIS OF CHAPTER XXVI.
### RETURN FROM THE EXILE.

**I. ZOROBABEL AND THE SECOND TEMPLE:**

1. *The New Exodus:*
   - The decree of Cyrus (its motives).
   - The first departure under Zorobabel.
   - The route followed.

2. *The "Old Country":*
   - State of Palestine on the arrival of the exiles.
   - Political organization.
   - Religious concerns:
     - The sacrifices begun at once.
     - The second temple:
       - Beginning—interruption.
       - Dedication—description.
   - The rebuilding of the city-walls forbidden by Assuerus (The Book of Esther).

**II. NEHEMIAS AND ESDRAS:**

1. *Nehemias:*
   - First visit to Jerusalem (445–433 B. C.):
     - His mission.
     - Solemn promulgation of the law.
   - Second visit to Jerusalem:
     - His reforms.
     - The Samaritan Temple on Mount Garizim.

2. *Esdras:*
   - The second departure under Esdras (398 B. C.).
   - His reforms in Jerusalem.
   - Other works ascribed to him:
     - The Great Synagogue (canon of the Old Testament).
     - Authorship of several books of Holy Writ.
     - Local synagogues (scribes and traditions).

GENERAL CONDITION OF PALESTINE UNDER PERSIAN RULE.

## CHAPTER XXVI.

### RETURN FROM THE EXILE.

#### § *1. Zorobabel and the Second Temple.*

1. **The New Exodus.** The Babylonian Captivity was brought to a close in B. C. 536, by the decree of Cyrus which has been preserved to us in Esdras i, 1-4 (cfr. also II Paralip. xxxvi, 22, 23). From the wording of this decree — which speaks of Jehovah as the God of heaven, as the bestower of kingdoms, as He who commanded Cyrus to build Him a temple in Jerusalem — it was formerly inferred that being a Persian, the conqueror of Babylon was a strict monotheist, and was thereby led to grant to the Jews, because they also were monotheists, the long-desired permission to return to the Holy Land. But the cylinder inscription of Cyrus discovered in 1879 (cfr. *Records of the Past*, new series, vol. v) makes it plain that "he was no strict monotheist, and that political, and not religious, motives prompted him to set the Jews free. It was a part of his general policy to allow perfect freedom to all religions, and it was with the same indifference that he allowed the Jews to build their temple that he rebuilt the temples of the Babylonian gods" (DEANE, Daniel, p. 161). Cyrus was also aware that the Jews of Babylon looked upon him as the deliverer promised to their race by their sacred books, and he realized how great a help it would be for his new empire if this friendly people were established under its protection, between its territories and Egypt, the ancient rival for dominion over Western Asia. Hence, he not only issued a decree which secured full free-

dom to the Jews to return, but even added to this the grant of the sacred vessels of Jehovah's temple, which Nabuchodonosor had carried into Babylon (Esdras i, 7, sq.).

Although a comparatively small number of Babylonian exiles availed themselves of the royal favor extended to them, yet the decree of Cyrus was considered as an event of national importance by the many, who feeling unable or disinclined to return, contributed largely of their wealth towards the well-being of their returning brethren and the prospective erection of a second temple to Jehovah. The "new Exodus" was carried out under the leadership of Zorobabel (whose Chaldean name of *Sassabasar* is also given in the sacred text), "the prince of Juda." This courageous descendant of David and worthy ancestor of Our Lord, having received from the Persian officers the sacred vessels, the restoration of which had been enjoined by Cyrus, and having made everything ready for the departure of the exiles who had gathered around him, set out for the Holy Land (Esdras i, 4–ii, 67).

We are not told the route followed by his joyous caravan. Not unlikely "it was the great trade-road along the Tigris and past the ruins of Ninive; then across Mesopotamia to Haran, the home of their first father; from there to Carcamis, the ancient Hittite stronghold at the fords of the Euphrates, and from thence south by Aleppo, Emath and Damascus to Jerusalem" (A. B. DAVIDSON, The Exile and the Restoration, p. 76). It was a long and fatiguing journey of at least four months, for we know that the much less numerous caravan headed later on by Esdras took between three and four months to reach Jerusalem, but their courage was kept up by their ardent desire to contemplate the holy mountains of Juda.

2. **The "Old Country."** At length they reached Palestine, the actual state of which was indeed far from

cheering. It is true that the northern part of the Holy Land had been already resettled by numerous exiles who had gradually returned from the captivity of the ten tribes, but the central part of the territory was occupied by the descendants of the mixed races settled in it by the Assyrian kings after the destruction of Samaria. The condition of southern Palestine was still more lamentable. The Edomites had seized Hebron and all Juda, together with the eastern part of Benjamin, and of this most sacred territory they were bound to give up to the returning Jews but a small part, by the express command of the Persian monarch.

But however straitened on all sides by other races, the returned exiles considered as sacred the territory which had been surrendered to them and began at once to settle in it. Part of them occupied Jerusalem and its surrounding villages, whilst others repaired to the towns in Juda and Benjamin, from which they or their fathers had been torn away (cfr. Nehemias xi, xii, 28, 29). They formed a small community, which, of course, did not require any complex political organization. Its civil head was Zorobabel, with the Persian titles of "Athersata" (Esdras ii, 63), and "Pasha" (Aggeus i, 1), which were equivalent to that of "governor" of Juda, whilst Josue, the son of Josedech, filled the position of high priest. Under them, and apparently associated with them in the government of the colony, were ten selected men known as "the chief of the fathers" (Esdras iv, 2; viii, 1). These twelve men formed a council which represented the whole nation: hence their number of twelve plainly fixed after the number of the tribes of Israel. They attended to all the affairs, social, religious, etc., of the returned exiles; but yet recognized the supremacy of the Persian monarch, whose superior power over all Palestine was represented by an officer with the title of "Chancellor." Under these councillors, and working harmoniously with them, there were also secondary officers, whose duties and powers cannot be defined strictly at the present day (cfr. Nehemias x, 29; Esdras iii, 12).

It may be noticed in this connection that no attempt was made to re-establish the Jewish monarchy, although so prominent a descendant of David as Zorobabel was already at the head of the government. Perhaps this was owing to the fact that the Jews were not anxious to see restored a form of government which had contributed so much to make the nation unfaithful to Jehovah, and to bring about the ruin of the Jewish commonwealth. Besides, of course, the governor of the Jews had not received the title of King from the Persian monarch, and, under the circumstances, an attempt at restoring the monarchy would have been objected to by this suzerain of Palestine.

Another restoration, that of Divine worship, lay infinitely closer to the heart of the returned exiles than the restoration of the monarchy. Their return had been clearly prompted by a religious impulse, and this is why, soon after they had effected their settlement, the religious and civil authorities of the nation gathered the people to witness the setting up of an altar to the God of Israel and the renewed offering of the morning and evening sacrifices on the first day of the seventh month. The great Festival of the Tabernacles was also celebrated with due solemnity, and the various legal holidays were henceforth observed with strict faithfulness (Esdras iii, 1-6). A step towards the restoration of the Temple had already been taken in the form of generous contributions towards the rebuilding of the House of Jehovah on its former site (Esdras i, 68-79). It was not, however, before "the second month of the second year of their coming" that the first stone of the "second" temple — called also the Temple of Zorobabel — was laid, amidst the sound of the priestly trumpets, the sacred hymns of the Levites and the joyful acclamations of the people. Yet this glorious day for Israel was also marked by the loud sobs of "many of the priests and Levites, and the chief of the fathers and of the ancients of the people who had seen the former temple" and remembered its past glories (Esdras iii, 6 b–13).

The work of reconstruction was not, however, to proceed without interruption. The mixed races which dwelt in Samaria made overtures to the supreme council of the Jews, that they also might be allowed to share in the great work of rebuilding the Temple of Jehovah; but they were refused, lest friendly relations should lead to intermarriages between the Jews and the Samaritans and to familiarity with their impure worship of the God of Israel (cfr. IV Kings xvii, 24–41; Esdras iv, 1–3). Whereupon the Samaritans resorted to every means to prevent the progress of the national temple of their neighbors. Not satisfied with interfering directly with the workmen of Juda, they exerted all their influence with the King of Persia, and in consequence, "the work of the House of Jehovah, in Jerusalem, was interrupted" until the reign of Darius I (Esdras iv, 4, 5, 24). The rule of this prince (521–485 B. C.), much milder than his immediate predecessors, Cambyses (529–522 B. C.) and Smerdis (522–521 B. C.), was deemed by the heads of the Jewish colony a favorable opportunity to resume the great work so long suspended, and in compliance with the stirring exhortations of the prophets Aggeus and Zacharias the Jews actually resumed the building of the second temple. The report of the Pasha of Palestine to the court of Persia about this resumption of the work served only to prove that Cyrus had indeed allowed the rebuilding of the Temple of Jehovah, as was affirmed by the Jewish authorities, and to procure for them greater resources and full security to complete their sacred undertaking. The Temple thus finished (B. C. 515) was dedicated with the greatest solemnity: numerous victims were offered in thanksgiving, and "twelve he-goats as a sin-offering for all Israel, according to the number of the tribes of Israel." For the service of this second House of Jehovah, the priests and Levites were distributed again into courses; and we read that soon afterwards the Passover was celebrated within its courts by all the Jews who had undergone the purifications required by the Mosaic law (Esdras v-vi).

"This second temple, though inferior in many respects to the first, having no ark, no mercy-seat, no visible revelation of the Divine glory, no Urim and Thummim, still was in breadth and height, in almost every dimension, one-third larger than that of Solomon. In three particulars the general arrangements differed from those of the ancient sanctuary: (1) there were no trees in the courts; (2) at the northwest corner was a fortress-tower, the residence of the Persian, afterward of the Roman, governor; (3) the court of the worshippers was divided into two compartments, of which the outer enclosure was known as the *Court of the Gentiles* or *Heathens*. This temple furnished a fixed place of worship for the nation, and ultimately became the theatre of far more glorious illustrations of the Divine attributes than the first temple ever witnessed" (STANLEY, Lectures on the History of the Jewish Church, lecture xliii, and SCHAFF, Bible Dictionary, art. Temple).

The Temple once finished, the Jewish leaders started on the rebuilding of the walls of Jerusalem, although apparently they had never received any permission from the Persian king to that effect; this afforded the Samaritans a natural opportunity for denouncing the Jews again to the court of Persia and they availed themselves of it. It does not seem, however, that their complaints were favorably received by the Persian king Xerxes I (485-465 B. C.), whom the Bible calls Assuerus. But they were most successful under Artaxerxes I (465-424), who strictly forbade the Jews to proceed with the rebuilding of the walls of the Holy City (Esdras iv, 6-23).

It is most probably an episode of the reign of Xerxes I that we find described in *the Book of Esther*, the form of which is more complete in the Greek translation which has reached us than in the original text such as it is found in the Hebrew Bible. The contents of this sacred book are briefly as follows: The Jews who had remained scattered through the Persian empire were threatened with utter destruction by the hatred of Aman, the prime minister of King Assuerus. The time and manner of this butchery had already been fixed, when Esther a young Jewess, who had but recently become the favorite wife of Assuerus, acting upon the counsel of her uncle Mardochai, intervened successfully in behalf of her own nation. The Jews thus rescued from death instituted in memory of their deliverance the annual festival of Purim. The book of Esther has generally been considered as historical in the Church, and there is no doubt that the events it narrates fit in very well with all the data supplied by other sources of information concerning Persian history (cfr. TROCHON, Introduction à l'Ecriture Sainte, vol. ii, p. 331, sq.). The recent discoveries made by DIEULAFOY in the Acropolis of Susa, where King Assuerus held his court, have proved how accurate are the descriptions contained in the book of Esther (cfr. VIGOUROUX, Manuel Biblique, vol. ii, chap. viii; F. LENORMANT et ERNEST BABÉLON, Histoire Ancienne de l'Orient, vol. vi, ninth edit.; RAWLINSON, Ezra and Nehemiah, p. 76, sq.).

§ *2. Nehemias and Esdras.*[1]

1. **Nehemias.** For some time already, the rebuilding of the walls of the Holy City had been stopped by order of

[1] Writers on Jewish history have admitted so far that the mission of Esdras preceded that of Nehemias. For reasons which it would be too long to detail here, we consider it as certain that in reality the mission of Nehemias preceded that of Esdras, and as this order of events allows a much more satisfactory arrangement of the facts recorded in the Bible, we adopt it here, after such Catholic writers as Van Hoonacker, Meignan, Lagrange and Pelt (cfr. LAGRANGE, Revue Biblique Internationale, 1894, p. 561, sq., and PELT vol. ii, p. 366, sq.).

Artaxerxes I (surnamed Longimanus), when some Jews come from Palestine to Susa told Nehemias, a Jewish cup-bearer to the Persian king, the wretched condition of the Holy Land, of its inhabitants and in particular of Jerusalem "the ancient wall of which," they said, "is broken down and the gates thereof are burnt with fire." Whereupon Nehemias resolved that he would avail himself of the affection and confidence Artaxerxes had towards him to secure the permission of rebuilding the wall of Jerusalem. Nehemias succeeded in his design; he was appointed governor of Juda for twelve years, and obtained from the king, together with an escort to accompany him to Palestine, letters for "the governors of the country beyond the Euphrates" and for the "keeper of the king's forest" in the Holy Land (445 B. C.).

After a rest of three days in Jerusalem, Nehemias inspected the state of the wall for himself, by night, accompanied only by a few, and revealing to no one his further designs. He next assembled the Jews, and making known to them the great work he had come to accomplish with them, he secured their coöperation. Many difficulties he had to overcome on the part of Sanaballat, the Horonite, and his friends; many traps laid for him in the country and in Jerusalem he had to escape; but excited by his confidence in Jehovah, and guided by his counsels, the Jews finished the walls, and hung up the gates, fifty-two days after the work had been resumed (Nehemias i-vi).

The next concern of Nehemias was that of repeopling "Jerusalem, the Holy City," with Jews of the purest descent (for these only could be fully depended upon for its defence), and for this purpose he made a census of the whole Jewish population with the help of a former census of Zorobabel and other documents. He carefully excluded all foreign elements and ordered that every tenth man should dwell in the capital, whilst the rest were allowed to remain in the other cities (Nehemias vii, xi).

Nor did Nehemias forget what was supremely important for the reorganization of the Jewish State, namely, the public renewal of the covenant with Jehovah. On the first day of the seventh month (probably 444 B. C.) all the people assembled in the broad place beside the Water Gate, and the scribe Esdras, acting simply as the secretary of Nehemias himself (for the name of Esdras is not found among the signatories of the covenant), read to them out of the *Book of the Law*. The portion he read the next day gave instructions for keeping the Feast of Tabernacles, and this festival was accordingly celebrated on the fifteenth day with strict compliance with all the requirements of the law. The twenty-fourth was kept as a day of fasting and confession, the people solemnly acknowledging that national forgetfulness of the law of Jehovah had been the cause of all their national calamities. The new covenant was written down and signed by the princes, priests and Levites of Israel, headed by Nehemias, the " Athersatha " or governor of Juda. The special legal ordinances to which the Jews pledged themselves on this occasion were of particular importance at the time; they were, abstinence from marriage with the heathen, keeping holy the Sabbath, the contribution of the third of a sicle by each Israelite (the sicle or shekel was equivalent to about fifty-five cents of our money) for the maintenance of God's temple and altar, the tithes, first-fruits and other dues to the priests and Levites (A. B. DAVIDSON, The Exile and the Restoration, p. 107, sq.).

We are not told how long after this promulgation of the law the solemn dedication of the city-wall took place. It is not improbable, however, that this solemn ceremony was carried out as one of the last acts of the first govenorship of Nehemias, after which he entrusted the care of the city to the high priest Eliasib, and returned to Persia (Nehemias viii, ix, x, xii, 26–xiii, 6).

Somewhat later on — how long after the end of his first

mission it is impossible to say — Nehemias came back to the Holy City with full powers from Artaxerxes I. There he found that grave abuses had crept in; he did not hesitate, therefore, to have recourse even to armed force to punish the violators of the law, those in particular who had intermarried with foreigners. He notably expelled from Jerusalem Joiada, the son of the Jewish high priest Eliasib, who had so far set the bad example to the people as to marry the daughter of a certain Sanaballat, who was apparently the governor of Samaria. This affront was so keenly resented by Sanaballat that soon afterwards he erected for his son-in-law a temple on Mount Garizim. Thus began the schismatic worship of the Samaritans, which continued to be maintained on that mountain up to the time of Our Lord (Nehemias xiii, 6-31; John iv, 20; JOSEPHUS, Antiq. of the Jews, book xi, chap. viii).

2. **Esdras.** It was most probably in 398 B. C. — the year which corresponds with "the seventh year" of the Persian King Artaxerxes II (Mnemon) — that a second departure of the exiled Jews took place under the leadership of Esdras. This man of priestly descent, of whom we spoke already as secretary to Nehemias, had apparently succeeded him in the royal favor, and had just received from Artaxerxes, together with the most valuable gifts for the Temple of Jehovah, the greatest powers to secure the full compliance of all the Jews with the law of God. A few thousand Jews had gathered around him, "among whom were many of the priesthood, both of the higher and lower orders" (MACLEAR, p. 476). After a solemn fast by the river Ahava (whereby is possibly meant the modern *Hit*, a famous ford of the Euphrates) to obtain the blessing of Jehovah on their journey, they set out and arrived unmolested at Jerusalem. After a three days' rest the gifts, with which the priests and Levites who had accompanied Esdras were laden, were deposited in the Temple treasury, and numerous victims were

offered, "all for a holocaust to Jehovah" (Esdras, vii, viii).

Having exhibited his credentials, Esdras was told the full extent of an old abuse against the Mosaic law: "the people of Israel and the priests and Levites had mingled their seed with the people of the lands; and the hand of the princes and magistrates had been first in this transgression." Whereupon, by public mourning and prayer, he impressed the people with the enormity of their sin, and after a short time obtained "of the chiefs of the priests and of the Levites, and all Israel," a solemn oath "that they would do according to his word." The extreme measure proposed by Sechenias, a Jewish zealot, that the foreign wives and children born from them should be dismissed, was accepted by the multitude in solemn assembly, at the bidding of Esdras. As, however, the rainy season had already set in, the putting away of the foreign wives was carried out only gradually, under the direction of Esdras and the magistrates whom he appointed to assist him in his investigations through the land of Juda and Benjamin (Esdras ix, x).

This is all that the sacred text tells us of the mission of Esdras to the Jews of the Holy Land, for the book which bears his name and makes us acquainted with his mission ends abruptly with the list of the names of those Israelites whom he compelled to put away their wives. But as he is spoken of in this sacred book as "a *scribe* instructed in the words and commandments of Jehovah, and His ceremonies in Israel," as the man "who had prepared his heart to *teach* in Israel the commandments and judgment" (Esdras vii, 10, 11), it is not surprising to find that Jewish traditions have ascribed to him numerous other works. Among these may be mentioned here: (1) the institution of the **Great Synagogue**, made up, we are told, of 120 men, who, under the presidency of Esdras, completed the collection or canon of Holy Scripture, revised and rewrote the sacred books of the

Old Testament in the Chaldee character; (2) the authorship of several of those books: Paralipomenon, Esdras, Nehemias, Ezechiel, Daniel, etc.; (3) the establishment of local synagogues in which men called "scribes" would, after the example of Esdras, interpret in the vernacular those portions of the sacred text which were publicly read in Hebrew, a language but imperfectly understood by the bulk of the worshippers; (4) the beginning of oral traditions claiming to give the correct meaning of the text of the Holy Scriptures, but which ultimately did away with its real spirit.

3. **General Condition of Palestine under Persian Rule.** From what we know of Jewish history during the Persian rule, it is plain that the mission of Zorobabel, Nehemias and Esdras was that of *Restorers* of the Jewish theocracy. Their main efforts were centred in reorganizing the commonwealth of the Jews on a religious basis, and in checking every tendency which might betray the nation into unfaithfulness to the God of Israel. Under their influence, Juda and Benjamin renewed several times their covenant with Jehovah, and the high priest of the Jews, that is, the natural representative of God, obtained a prominent part in the government. Especially during the intervals between Zorobabel and Nehemias, between the governorships of Nehemias, between Nehemias and Esdras, it is clear that under the satraps of Cœle-Syria, the action of the high priesthood had a very considerable influence upon religious and civil matters alike. Thus then, during the Persian rule the government of the high priests was gradually inaugurated in Israel and, of course, it continued with about the same powers during the short time which elapsed between the death of Esdras (the exact date and place of which are unknown) and the overthrow of the Persian domination in Syria (B. C. 332). During the same period the country seems to have enjoyed a steadily increasing prosperity.

# SYNOPSIS OF CHAPTER XXVII.

## RULE OF THE HIGH PRIESTS.

I.

FROM
JADDUS TO
ELEAZAR:

1. *Visit of Alexander the Great:* His favors to the Jews of { Jerusalem. Alexandria.
2. *Rapid Changes of Foreign Rulers.*
3. *Prosperous Rule of Simon I and Eleazar:* { Public works of Simon the Just. The Septuagint.
4. *Rise of Hellenism.*

II.

ONIAS II
AND
SIMON II:

1. *Onias II* (250–226 B. C.): { His difficulties with Ptolemy III, Euergetes. Power of the "Son of Tobias."
2. *Simon II* (226–198, B. C.): { His personal courage against Ptolemy IV, Philopator. Palestine finally subjected to Antiochus III, the Great.

III.

ONIAS III,
JASON
AND MENELAUS:

1. *Onias III* (198–175 B. C.): { Prosperous beginning of his pontificate (II Mach. iii, 1–3). Episode of Heliodorus (II Mach. iii, 4–iv, 6); Onias in Antioch.
2. *Jason and Menelaus:* { Rapid growth of Hellenism in Jerusalem under Jason. Accession and tyranny of Menelaus. Plunder of Jerusalem and profanation of the temple by Antiochus IV, Epiphanes.

# CHAPTER XXVII.

### RULE OF THE HIGH PRIESTS.

#### § *1. From Jaddus to Eleazar.*

1. **Visit and Favors of Alexander the Great.** The religious freedom and material prosperity which the Jews had so long enjoyed under the Persian suzerainty explain how, after the rapid overthrow of the Persian domination in Syria by Alexander the Great, the Jewish high priest Jaddus refused to transfer to the Greek conqueror the allegiance which the nation had vowed to the Persian monarchs. The capture of Tyre by Alexander and the report of his cruelties to its inhabitants overawed, however, the Jews, and to appease the victorious king, now on his march towards Jerusalem through the plain of Saron, they sent him ambassadors. As he approached the Holy City, a long procession of priests and elders, headed by Jaddus, clad in his pontifical robes, went out to meet him on the plateau of Scopus, the high ridge to the north of Jerusalem.

Following a wise policy of conciliation, the Greek monarch accepted the proffered submission of the Jews and entering their city, displayed the greatest reverence for the worship of Jehovah. Having offered sacrifices in the Temple, he was shown in the prophecies of Daniel the prediction that a Greek would overthrow the Persian empire; whereupon, he granted to the Jews the free enjoyment of their religious and civil liberties for themselves and for their brethren in Media and Babylonia, together with the exemption of tribute during the Sabbatical years.

These great favors of Alexander to the Jews of Jerusalem so attached the nation to his cause that many among them enlisted in his army and followed him in his march to Egypt. In return for the valuable services of this Jewish contingent, the Macedonian conqueror of the land of the Pharaos granted to the Jews who settled in the new Egyptian city he had founded, and which — after his own name — he had called Alexandria, equal civic rights with the Macedonians (331 B. C.).

The visit of Alexander to Jerusalem, just recorded, is known to us only by the testimony of Josephus, and as in this testimony marvellous circumstances are mingled with natural events, the whole story has been rejected by several writers. Many things, however, stated by Josephus in this connection, fit in so well with the general history of the time that his narrative must be admitted as grounded on fact (Antiquities of the Jews, book xi, chap. 8; cfr. also SMITH, New Testament History, p. 16, sq.).

2. **Rapid Changes of Foreign Rulers.** Upon the death of Alexander (323 B. C.), his vast empire was divided among his generals: Egypt was assigned to Ptolemy I, son of Lagus (323-285 B. C.), whilst Palestine, as a part of Cœle-Syria, passed into the possession of Laomedon. Between these two rivals a war soon broke out, and for fifteen years the Holy Land was alternately a province of Egypt, or a province of Syria, according to the varying fortunes of war. At the beginning of this conflict, Onias I, the Jewish high priest, having refused to transfer the allegiance of the nation to the ruler of Egypt, saw Jerusalem taken by a large Egyptian army, which entered it under the pretence of offering sacrifice, on a Sabbath-day, when religious scruples prevented the Jews from offering any resistance (320 B. C.). A few years later, Palestine fell into the hands of Antigonus, one of the most successful generals of Alexander (314 B. C.),

but two years later it became again a possession of Egypt. Once more Palestine was reconquered by Antigonus, who gave orders that all its fortresses should be dismantled, but ultimately in 301 B. C., after the decisive battle of Ipsus, in Phrygia, whilst Upper Syria was adjudged to Seleucus I, Judæa and Samaria were annexed to Egypt, and remained so during a whole century (301-202 B. C.).

3. **Prosperous Rule of Simon the Just and Eleazar.** The successor of Onias I, in the high priesthood, was Simon, surnamed the Just (310-291 B. C.), who is the last of "the men of renown" praised in the book of Ecclesiasticus, chapter l. From this inspired book we learn that Simon I repaired and fortified Jerusalem and its Temple with strong and lofty walls, made a spacious reservoir of water, and maintained the Divine service in the greatest splendor (l, 1-23). Jewish tradition has ever regarded this great pontiff as the last member of the Great Synagogue, and its rule as "the best period of the restored theocracy" (SMITH, New Testament History, page 20).

Simon I was succeeded by his brother Eleazar II, whose rule from 291 to 276 B. C. seems to have been blessed with profound peace under the mild government of the first two Ptolemies, Soter (son of Lagus) and Philadelphus (B. C. 285-247). It is under the reign of this latter king that a portion of the Hebrew sacred Scriptures was rendered into Greek for the first time. This fact is made known to us by a legend, the substance of which is briefly as follows: The King of Egypt, Ptolemy Philadelphus, we are told, had recently established a library in Alexandria, his capital, and at the suggestion of his head librarian, Demetrius Phalereus, he determined to enrich it with a copy in Greek of the Sacred Writings of the Jews. Thereupon, he was advised by one of his distinguished officers, Aristeas by name, to set free the thousands of Jewish slaves who were in the various parts of the kingdom, in order that he might thereby secure the good-will and help of the Jewish authorities at Jerusalem to carry out his design. This he did with royal liberality; and a long procession of these freed men started for the Holy City, bearing with them most costly presents for the Temple, together with a letter from the king, requesting Eleazar, the high priest, to send a copy of the Law, and Jewish scholars capable of translating it.

In compliance with the request, Eleazar sends down to Egypt fine parchment manuscripts of the Pentateuch written in golden letters, and six learned men out of each tribe, *seventy-two* in all (hence the version received the name of the **Septuagint**, which is a round figure for seventy-two), to carry out the great work of the translation. During seven days the interpreters have audiences of the king and excite the admiration of all by the wisdom with which they answer seventy-two questions, after which lodgings are assigned to them in the island of Pharos, away from the bustle of the capital. There they complete their work in seventy-two days, and it obtains the formal approval of the Jews of Alexandria. Finally, King Ptolemy receives the translation of the Law with great reverence, and sends the interpreters home laden with rich gifts for themselves and for the high priest.

Whatever may be thought of the marvellous details of this legend, which was accepted by Josephus (Antiquities of the Jews, book xii, chapter ii) and by many writers after him, it seems beyond doubt (1) that it refers to a time when the numerous Jews, who had settled in Egypt, had ceased to be familiar with the Hebrew language, and therefore desired a Greek translation of the Law for public reading in the synagogues; (2) that a translation of the Pentateuch was made in Alexandria about the middle of the third century before Christ; (3) that the King of Egypt, Ptolemy Philadelphus, probably showed some interest in the work, and obtained a copy of the translation for his royal library of Alexandria;

(4) that friendly relations existed between Ptolemy Philadelphus and the Jewish high priest Eleazar. (For fuller information, see article "The Septuagint" in American Ecclesiastical Review, August, 1896, by the present writer.)

4. **Rise of Hellenism.** It is to the vast conquests of Alexander the Great that we must refer the origin of those influences which are designated under the general name of *Hellenism*. "It had been his fond dream to found a universal empire which would be held together not merely by the unity of government, but also by the unity of language, customs and civilization. All the Oriental nations were to be saturated with Hellenic (that is Greek) culture, and to be bound together with one great whole by means of this intellectual force. He therefore took care that always Greek colonists should directly follow in the steps of his army. New cities were founded, inhabited only by Greeks, and also in the old cities Greek colonists were settled. Thus over one-half of Asia a network of Greek culture was stretched, which had as its object the reducing under its influence of the whole of the surrounding regions. The successors of Alexander the Great continued his work; and it is a striking testimony to the power of Greek culture that it fulfilled in large measure the mission which Alexander had assigned to it. All Western Asia, in fact, if not among the wide masses of the population, yet certainly among the higher ranks of society, became thoroughly Hellenized" (SCHURER, The Jewish People in the Time of Jesus Christ, first division, vol. i, page 194, sq., English Translation). Of course, this steady advance of Greek civilization all through Western Asia meant the spread of ideas and customs, moral, social and religious antagonistic to the religious and national traditions and customs of the theocracy but lately restored and enforced in Israel. It is therefore important to notice the rise and early developments of influ-

ences which from the very beginning were an abiding danger for the Jews who resided outside Palestine because of their daily contact with Hellenic culture, and which very soon constituted a real danger for the faith and morals of the Jews of the Holy Land, because many cities in the neighborhood of Juda and Benjamin offered to them, together with advantages of a material and intellectual kind, numerous and powerful allurements to foreign customs and pagan rites.

### § 2. *Onias II and Simon II.*

1. **Onias II** (250–226 B. C.). For some unknown reason, Onias II, the son of Simon the Just, entered on the high priesthood only after the successive rules of his uncles Eleazar and Manasses. He proved a ruler very much unlike his father of glorious memory. Whilst Simon I was an active and liberal prince, ever faithful to Egyptian suzerainty, Onias, on the contrary, showed himself an indolent ruler who probably through avarice and through compliance with Syrian influence withheld for several years from Ptolemy III, *Euergetes* (247–222 B. C.), the annual tribute of twenty talents. Notwithstanding his well-known good-will towards the Jews, the King of Egypt threatened Palestine with invasion should Onias refuse longer to obey the summons to answer for his conduct. The threatened invasion was however averted owing to the singular cleverness of the high-priest's nephew, Joseph, "the son of Tobias" as he is called, who paid the arrears, and so ingratiated himself with the Egyptian monarch that for twenty-two years he held the office of collector of the tribute of Phenicia, Palestine and Cœle-Syria. Unfortunately, the power which the son of Tobias had started in the Holy Land was soon to prove "a source of evils as great as the danger from which he had delivered it" (SMITH, New Testament History, p. 22 ; cfr. JOSEPHUS, Antiq. of the Jews, book xii, chap. iv, § 1–6).

2. **Simon II** (226-198 B. C.). The son and successor of Onias II was Simon II, who became high priest four years before Ptolemy IV, **Philopator** (222-204 B. C.), ascended the throne of Egypt, and five years before Antiochus III, *the Great*, ascended that of Syria. Between these two great rivals, Judæa was indeed in a precarious condition; yet, it clung at first to its allegiance to Egypt, and after his great victory at Raphia, near Gaza (B. C. 217), Philopator paid a friendly visit to Jerusalem, offered sacrifices and made rich presents to the Temple. Impelled, however, by curiosity, the Egyptian king wished to enter the sanctuary and penetrate into the Most Holy Place, as indeed he would have been at perfect liberty to do in any Egyptian temple. To this the high priest objected with great courage and firmness, but apparently in vain, until a preternatural terror seized the king and prevented him from violating the innermost sanctuary of the living God.

This mortifying event seems to have marked the end of the kind disposition of the Egyptian ruler towards the Jews, and we are told, that upon his return to Alexandria he started a violent persecution against the Jewish element of that city. At his death, his son and successor Ptolemy V, **Epiphanes**, was but a child five years old, and Antiochus III availed himself of this opportunity for attacking the Egyptian dominions. In 203 B. C. the Syrian monarch seized Cœle-Syria and Judæa, but in 199 B. C. Scopas, the Egyptian general, recovered Judæa, garrisoned Jerusalem and ruled over it with an iron hand. Finally, in the following year, Antiochus defeated the Egyptian forces in a decisive battle at the foot of Mount Panium — thus named after a cave sacred to Pan — near the sources of the Jordan, and obtained thereby full mastery over the territory of Cœle-Syria and Judæa. The Syrian conqueror was welcomed as a deliverer into the Holy City, and he, on his part, anxious to attach the Jews to his cause, issued a decree whereby he granted them full freedom of worship, "forbade the intrusion of strangers into the Temple and contributed liberally towards the regular celebration of its services. At the same time, imitating the examples of Alexander and Seleucus, he gave orders to Zeuxis, the general of his forces, to remove 2,000 Jewish families from Babylon into Phrygia and Lydia, where they were to be permitted to use their own laws, to have lands assigned to them, and to be exempted from all tribute for ten years" (MACLEAR, New Testament History, p. 15; cfr. JOSEPHUS, Antiq. of the Jews, book xii, chap. iii, §§ 3, 4).

### § 3. Onias III, Jason and Menelaus.

1. **Onias III.** The same year in which Antiochus III showed himself so favorable to the Jewish people and religion, the son of Simon II succeeded his father in the high priesthood under the title of Onias III (198-175 B. C.). Of the beginning of this new pontificate, the second book of Machabees (iii, 1-3) gives us a short but laudatory description: peace and order prevailed in the Holy City, and royal gifts were bestowed in abundance upon the Temple of Jehovah, and in particular, King Seleucus IV, **Philopator** (187-175 B. C.), the successor of Antiochus the Great, defrayed liberally all the expenses entailed by the offering of the Jewish sacrifices.

The peace and prosperity of Onias's godly rule were soon disturbed, however, by the disgraceful contests among the members of the family of Joseph, the successful collector of revenue already spoken of under a preceding high priest. However just, the intervention of Onias III simply resulted in arousing against him the revengeful feelings of Simon, apparently a member of that powerful family and now governor of the Temple and collector of the royal revenue for Seleucus IV. In consequence, Simon fled to Apollonius, the royal governor of Cœle-Syria, and told him of enormous treasures laid up in the Jewish temple. Upon this unexpected but most welcome news for the thoroughly exhausted treasury of the Syrian king, Heliodorus the royal treasurer was immediately dispatched to Jerusalem to seize this most alluring treasure. The inspired writer of the second book of Machabees has left a most graphic account of the interview between the Syrian envoy and the Jewish high priest; of the intense agony of both priest and people when Heliodorus, on the very day he had fixed for the purpose, advanced to pillage the Temple of Jehovah; of the terrible manner in which the royal officer was prevented by heavenly messengers from carrying out his work of profanation and plunder, and finally of the manner in which he was restored to health and vigor by the prayers of Onias in his behalf, and then withdrew to Seleucus testifying openly to his master that "He who hath His dwelling in the heavens, is the Visitor and Protector of that place" (II Mach. iii, 4-40).

Naturally enough, Simon was enraged at this ill-success of Heliodorus's expedition, and he openly accused Onias of imposture, whilst his partisans in Jerusalem felt so sure of his influence with the governor of Cœle-Syria that they did not hesitate to defy the authority of the High priest by committing several murders in the Holy City itself. Under such circumstances, Onias understood that the only means to set all things right was to go up to Antioch, and to request the direct interposition of the sovereign, and he therefore repaired to the great capital of the Syrian empire (II Mach. iv, 1-6).

2. **Jason and Menelaus.** Not long after the arrival of the Jewish high priest at Antioch, Seleucus was succeeded on the throne of Syria by his brother Antiochus IV, surnamed *Epiphanes* "the Illustrious," or *Epimanes* "the Madman," from whom, instead of the vindication he had come to claim, Onias soon met with deposition from the high priesthood. This deposition purchased at very great price by an

unworthy brother of Onias, who became high priest, was the real triumph of Hellenism in Jerusalem. Long before this, Greek customs and manners had gradually crept into the Holy City from the surrounding Greek cities, and had been favored by leading men among the Jews; but the accession to the high priesthood of a man whose very name — he had changed his Hebrew name of *Josue* into the Greek name of *Jason* — was a pledge to Hellenism, was an event of great significance in Israel (I Mach. i, 12, sq.; II Mach, iv, 13). In point of fact, the new high priest had hardly entered on his government when his true character became manifest to all. Nothing was omitted by him to wean the Jewish population from all the customs and religious views and practices of their fathers; and during the three years of his rule, he succeeded but too well in corrupting the faith and morals of the youth of Jerusalem. (For details see II Mach. iv, 9-22; cfr. also SCHURER, vol. i, p. 202, sq.)

His successor was another Hellenizing leader, who purchased the deposition of the incumbent high priest by offering to the crown of Syria 300 talents of silver over and above the amount already paid by Jason. Of this new high priest — who also exchanged his Hebrew name of *Onias*, for a Greek name, namely, that of *Menelaus* — Holy Writ speaks as "having the mind of a cruel tyrant, and the rage of a wild beast" (II Mach. iv, 25). In fact, all that we know of him, points to one of the worst tyrants that ever lived. To pay the enormous sum of money he had promised to Antiochus, he stole several sacred vessels of gold, and when rebuked for this crime by the venerable Onias III, "his gold all-powerful among the officers of the Syrian court" (Milman) secured the murder of the old man. Nor was his gold less powerful on another occasion, when the most serious charges against his cruel rule were brought by Jewish ambassadors before King Antiochus who was then in Tyre; for as we are told by the sacred text "Menelaus who was guilty of all the evil, was acquitted by the king of the accusations, and those poor men, who, if they had pleaded their cause even before Scythians (the most barbarous nation in the estimation of the time), should have been judged innocent, were condemned to death " (II Mach. iv, 23-50).

Meantime, Jason had not given up all hope of recovering the high priesthood, and when the following year the false rumor that Antiochus IV had perished in his expedition against Egypt, reached Palestine, he rebelled against Menelaus, his brother, took the Holy City and exercised the most frightful revenge against his opponents. He did not, however, succeed in securing again the high dignity he so ardently coveted, for his extreme cruelties caused a powerful reaction which compelled him to fly beyond the Jordan. At the news of the insurrection, which was probably reported to Antiochus as a deliberate revolt of the whole nation, the Syrian monarch most successful against Egypt, "left that country with a furious mind, and took Jerusalem by force of arms." A three days' massacre followed, during which 40,000 inhabitants were slaughtered and as many more sold as slaves. To complete the humiliation of the Jews, Antiochus next entered every part of the Temple under the guidance of Menelaus "that traitor to the laws and to his country," took possession of all the sacred vessels and hidden treasures which he found, after which he departed into his own country leaving Menelaus in charge of the high priesthood, whilst two foreign officers, Phillip and Andronicus, became governors of Jerusalem and Samaria respectively (170 B. C.; cfr. I Mach. i, 17-29; II Mach. v, 1-23).

# SYNOPSIS OF CHAPTER XXVIII.

## THE NATIONAL INDEPENDENCE RECONQUERED.

### (168–135 B. C.)

I. REVOLT AGAINST SYRIA:
  1. *Dreadful Persecution of the Jews by Antiochus:*
     - Motive.
     - Incidents.
     - Results.
  2. *Mathathias* (167–166 B. C.):
     - His retreat at Modin; His five sons.
     - Revolt against Antiochus Epiphanes.
     - His victories and death.

II. RELIGIOUS AND POLITICAL RESTORATION:
  1. *Judas Machabeus* (166–161 B. C.):
     - His name of Machabee; His victories.
     - Rededication of the Temple.
     - The War of Independence pursued with varying success.
     - Alliance with Rome secured; defeat and death of Judas.
  2. *Jonathan* (161–143 B. C.):
     - His election as the successor of Judas Machabeus.
     - Gradual restoration of the Jewish State:
       - Decline of the Hellenistic party.
       - Prestige of Jonathan at home and abroad.
       - Alliance with Rome and Sparta.
     - The captivity of Jonathan.

III. JUDÆA AN INDEPENDENT KINGDOM:
  1. *Election and First Acts of Simon Machabeus.*
  2. *National Independence Secured* (Beginning of a new era).
  3. *Prosperous Administration of Simon:* He becomes hereditary sovereign of the Jews.
  4. *Successful War against Antiochus VII:* Tragic end of Simon (135 B. C.).

# CHAPTER XXVIII.

### THE NATIONAL INDEPENDENCE RECONQUERED.

§ *1. Revolt against Syria.*

1. **Dreadful Persecution of the Jews by Antiochus Epiphanes.** Two years after his victorious expedition against Egypt spoken of in the preceding chapter, Antiochus IV, bent on taking Alexandria the sole Egyptian city which had withstood successfully the power of his arms, reappeared before its walls with a large army. There, however, he was soon confronted with the Roman envoys who commanded him to leave Egypt. This positive injunction, with which Antiochus Epiphanes had to comply at once, threw him into a paroxysm of rage which he vented upon the Jews whilst returning to his States through Palestine. He dispatched Apollonius, one of his generals, with a body of 22,000 men to inflict upon Jerusalem the treatment he had intended for Alexandria, and his orders were but too faithfully complied with (cfr. I Mach. i, 30–42 ; II Mach. v, 24–26). It seems, however, that in thus acting, Antiochus had a further purpose. He wished "to Hellenize Jerusalem thoroughly. The Jewish population which would not yield, was treated with great barbarity; the men were killed, and the women and children sold into slavery. Whoever was able escaped from the city. In place of the Jewish population thus destroyed, strangers were brought in as colonists. Jerusalem was henceforth to be a Greek city. In order that such measures might have enduring effect, the walls of the city were thrown down, but the old city of David was forti-

fied anew and made into a powerful stronghold, in which a Syrian garrison was placed " and from which the pagan soldiers could effectively prevent any one from stealing into Jerusalem and offering sacrifice in the Temple (SCHURER, The Jewish People in the Time of Christ, division 1, vol. i, p. 206, English Translation).

It was this Hellenizing policy which soon afterwards caused Antiochus, the fervent worshipper of Zeus Olympius, to issue from Antioch a decree enjoining upon all his subjects the worship of his gods and of no other. This decree was readily complied with by the nations around Palestine, but not so with the bulk of the Jewish population (I Mach. i, 43, sq.); whereupon, royal letters were sent by messengers to Jerusalem and to all the cities of Juda ordering explicitly the utter destruction of Judaism and the introduction of Greek idolatry. This strict prohibition of whatever was peculiar to or characteristic of Jewish civilization and religion, was extended to all the cities of the Syrian dominions and special commissioners were sent in every direction to enforce the will of the persecutor (I Mach. i, 53).

The royal commissioner sent to Samaria and Judæa was an old man named Athenæus, who neglected nothing to root out Jewish worship from Jerusalem and the country around. The Temple of Jehovah became the Temple of Zeus Olympius. An altar to that god was erected on the Jewish Altar of Holocausts, swine's flesh sacrificed on it, and the most impure practices of heathen worship carried on in the sanctuary of the living God. In like manner, in all the cities of Juda pagan altars were set up and heathen sacrifices offered. The observance of all Jewish rites, notably of circumcision and of the Sabbath, was punishable with death. Once a month, a rigorous search was made, and if a copy of the law was discovered in the possession of any one, the copy was torn to pieces or burnt and the owner put to death. Every month, also, in honor of the king's birthday, the people all had to offer sacrifices and eat swine's flesh, and in the annual celebrations in honor of Bacchus they were compelled to crown themselves with ivy and join in the procession (I Mach. i, 54-64; II Mach. vi, 1-9).

During this dreadful persecution many fled from the cities and hid themselves in the numerous caves of the country, or in the wilderness, "where they lived amongst wild beasts." Of those who remained in the towns of Juda, a large number apostatized through fear or ambition, whilst many endured martyrdom with heroic courage. Of this last category only a few samples were put down on record, or at least have been preserved to us. Two women who were accused of having circumcised their children were led about through the city with the infants hanging to their breasts, and then thrown down headlong from the walls. A gathering of worshippers were burned alive in a cave, to which they had fled to keep the Sabbath. Eleazar, an old man ninety years of age, and "one of the chief of the scribes," chose to be beaten to death rather than to let it be believed that he had eaten swine's flesh, and a mother with her seven sons underwent for the same offence a death preceded by the most revolting and most excruciating torments (I Mach. i, 65-67; II Mach. vi, 10; vii).

This cruel and systematic persecution — like every subsequent persecution of the true religion — was a fearful ordeal in which the chosen people were searched and their unworthy elements cast away, whilst many waverers between Judaism and Hellenism compelled to declare themselves selected death with the faith of Jehovah rather than life with the pollutions of heathenism. But under the circumstances of the time, this persecution had a further result. It prevented the Jews, as a nation, from passing quietly, and, as it were, imperceptibly from their national customs and religion to those of their masters, for it put a stop to the insidious manner in which Hellenism was being gradually introduced by unworthy high priests into the Jewish State.

2. **Mathathias** (167-166 B. C.). Whilst Antiochus and his officers were thus doing their utmost to stamp all trace of Judaism out of Palestine, Divine Providence was preparing in Mathathias and his family the religious and political restoration of Israel. In the beginning of the persecution, this aged priest had removed with his five sons, John, Simon, Judas, Eleazar and Jonathan, from Jerusalem to the mountain town of Modin, some twenty miles distant. There he had watched with religious and patriotic anxiety the fearful inroads of persecution into his country, and every new outrage against Jehovah's religion and people was a cause of renewed mourning for him and his sons. At length, the royal envoy reached the out-of-the-way town of Modin, and, having succeeded in winning over to idolatry several of its Jewish inhabitants, urged on Mathathias as "the great man in that city" to set the example of compliance with the royal decree, and promised to him and his sons the king's favor together "with gold and silver and many presents."

Of course, the venerable priest rejected every offer for him and his family, and when "a certain Jew came in the sight of all to sacrifice to the idols upon the altar of Modin," in a moment of holy zeal, he slew him upon the altar together with the royal envoy, and pulled down the altar. Then with religious and patriotic enthusiasm he invited all to shake off the heathen yoke, saying, "Every one that hath zeal for the law and maintaineth the Testament, let him follow me." He then fled with his sons into the mountains south of Jerusalem, whither he was soon followed by numerous Israelites zealous for the worship of Jehovah. The news of this growing revolt soon reached the heathen authorities of Jerusalem, and they at once resolved to crush it by attacking the rebels on the Sabbath, when the Jews, through religious scruple, would not offer any resistance. This plan at first succeeded but too well, and on one single occasion 1,000 Jews were thus slaughtered on a Sabbath day, but at the news of this butchery, Mathathias and his friends wisely resolved that henceforth they should defend themselves on the Sabbath, "lest they should be quickly rooted out of the earth" (I Math. ii, 1-41).

Soon the Jewish patriots were joined by "the congregation of the *Assideans*" (that is most likely that party which had been long organized among the Jews to oppose and defeat the efforts of the partisans of idolatry), and also by a number of persecuted worshippers of Jehovah. Thus an army was formed, and under the leadership of Mathathias it carried on a guerilla warfare with the greatest success (I Mach. ii, 42-48). Soon, however, the fatigues of an active campaign proved too severe a task for the physical strength of the venerable Jewish priest, and he succumbed, exhorting his sons to pursue the great work of liberation under Judas as their military leader, and Simon as their prudent adviser (I Mach. ii, 49-70).

§ *2. Religious and Political Restoration.*

1. **Judas Machabeus** (167-161 B. C.). Judas, the new Jewish commander, proved worthy of the leadership to which he had been appointed by his dying father. Bold and valiant in action, yet prudent and discreet in counsel, he soon struck with terror the enemies of Israel, and thereby deserved the surname of **Machabeus**, the more probable meaning of which is the *Hammer*, like that of Charles *Martel*, the hero of the Francs. Confident in the help of Jehovah and the valor of his followers, he first surprised by night many towns which held out for the enemies of Israel, and set them on fire; and when next regular armies advanced to put a stop to his ravages, he did not refuse to meet them in the field (II Mach. viii, 1-7). The sacred writer details with manifest delight the manner in which Judas imparted to his warriors his own confidence in Jehovah and his hope of victory, and also the manner in which he proved himself a skilful tactician in presence of outnumbering enemies. He tells us how

Apollonius, the late plunderer of Jerusalem, having been defeated and slain by Judas, the deputy-governor of Syria, a man named Seron, and extremely anxious to acquire military renown, was ignominiously routed at Bethoron, a place already famous by the victory of Josue over the southern Chanaanites (I Mach. iii, 10-24; cfr. in the present work, pp. 138, 139). He records also how Judas was victorious in his encounters with large armies headed by the best Syrian generals of the time: Gorgias and Nicanor, and Timotheus, and Bacchides and Lysias (I Mach. iii, 10-iv, 35; II Mach. viii, 9-36).

After these glorious exploits, Judas and his fellow-warriors profited by a moment of respite to enter the ruined city of Jerusalem. The wretched condition of the Temple of Jehovah especially claimed their attention: "the sanctuary was desolate and the altar profaned, and the gates burned, and shrubs growing up in the courts as in a forest or on the mountains, and the chambers joining the Temple thrown down." After lamentation and prayer, the military leader appointed a body of armed men to keep in check the Syrian garrison in the citadel, and then the work of cleansing began. With the help of priests perfectly faithful to Jehovah, the holy places were purified, the great altar of burnt-offering which had been profaned was demolished and gave place to another worthy of God's worship, new vessels and new furniture were brought into the purified sanctuary, the lamps lighted up, and finally the offering of sacrifice was resumed on the 25th day of the ninth month (Casleu; 165 B.C.). The feast of the re-dedication lasted eight days, and it was decreed that an annual festival, also of eight days, should henceforth commemorate this great event (I Mach. iv, 36-59; II Mach. x, 1-8; John x, 22).

To consolidate this work of restoration, there remained to Judas a twofold work. The first, which he carried through with great vigor and success, was the submission of the neighboring tribes, which, alarmed at the progress of the Jews, had taken arms against them (164 B. C.). The second one, of course much more difficult, was the bringing to a successful issue of the war of independence against Syria. For three years Judas pursued this patriotic work with rare energy and perseverance, though with varying success, as might naturally be expected on the part of a general who had constantly to meet such outnumbering enemies. The first year (163 B. C.) was marked by a treaty which granted to the Jews the free use of their own laws and religion under Syrian supremacy, and by the recognition of Judas "as governor of Palestine; and from this year, his accession to the principality is usually dated" (MACLEAR, New Testament History, p. 39).

The next year was less fortunate; hostilities were resumed by the Syrians, and the Assideans in large numbers, deceived by a certain Alcimus, who had secured an appointment to the high priesthood from the Syrian authorities, separated from Judas Machabeus. The position of the latter was therefore very precarious in presence of the large army which had invaded the Jewish territory. Soon, however, after his instalment as high priest, Alcimus revealed his true character and showed himself the leader of the Hellenizing party; whereupon the Assideans joined again the cause of Judas. This re-enforcement allowed the Jewish commander to take the field again against the Syrian general Nicanor, whom he utterly defeated at Bethoron, early in 161 B. C.

It is at this juncture that Judas, anxious to secure the protection of the Romans against the ill-will of the kings of Syria, sent messengers to Rome. The Jewish ambassadors were well received, an alliance offensive and defensive was concluded, and a letter sent by the Roman Senate to the King of Syria, that he should desist from all attacks upon the Jews. Before, however, these transactions could be known in the East, Judas had been defeated and slain on the battlefield at Laisa, and his few faithful soldiers routed (B. C. 161; cfr. I Mach. iv, 60–ix, 18; II Mach. x–xv).

2. **Jonathan** (161–143 B. C.). The much lamented death of Judas Machabeus left the Nationalist or **Machabean** party in a very precarious condition. Throughout the land "the wicked men," that is, the Hellenists, showed themselves again, were appointed to posts of honor and power, and betrayed the partisans of Judas into the hands of the Syrian general Bacchides. At length, the partisans of Judas understood that their salvation required absolutely the choice of a skilful leader, and in consequence they selected Jonathan as their "prince and captain." It is evidence to the weakness of the Machabean party at that time, that its valiant commander and his followers found it necessary to withdraw at once east of the Jordan; but fortunately, upon the death of the unworthy high priest Alcimus, Bacchides returned to Syria and gave to the Jews a respite of two years.

After this truce, the Syrian general reappeared in the field upon the promise of the Hellenistic leaders of an easy victory; the reverse took place, however, to the confusion and destruction of these wicked men, and the outcome of a short campaign skilfully conducted by Jonathan was a treaty of peace which left Jonathan practically master of Judæa, "although Jerusalem and many of the stronger towns occupied by garrisons, either of Syrians or apostate Jews, defied his authority" (MILMAN; cfr. I Mach. ix, 19–73).

This state of things lasted for six years, during which the Hellenistic party became steadily less influential, whilst on the contrary, the Machabeans grew so powerful that at the end of this period their alliance was most carefully courted by Alexander Bales and Demetrius, the two competitors for the Syrian throne. Of the offers of Demetrius, Jonathan accepted the power of entering, repairing and fortifying the

Holy City; of those of Alexander, in favor of whom he declared himself, he accepted the title of *High Priest.* Alexander came victorious out of the conflict for the Syrian throne, and granted to the Jewish high priest the title of *Strategus* of his country and that of *Ruler of a part of the Syrian empire* (I Mach. x, 1-66).

Jonathan in return " remained faithful to his patron even against a new claimant to the crown of Syria. And such was his influence that the latter, on gaining possession of the throne, not only forgave the resistance of Jonathan, but confirmed him in the Pontificate and even remitted the taxation of Palestine on a tribute (probably annual) of 300 talents. But the faithlessness and ingratitude of the Syrian king (Demetrius II) led Jonathan soon afterwards to take the side of another Syrian pretender, an infant whose claims were ostensibly defended by his general, Tryphon " (EDERSHEIM, Life and Times of Jesus the Messiah, vol. ii, pp 572, 573), and who was crowned in Antioch under the title of Antiochus VI (I Mach. x, 67-xi, 58).

Soon after this event and several military exploits (I Mach. xi, 59-74) Jonathan sent ambassadors to Rome, who renewed the former treaty between Judas and the Roman Senate; he entered also into alliance with the Spartans (I Mach. xii, 1-23). New victories crowned his arms, and it seemed at the time as if he was destined to restore his country to complete independence. Soon, however, Tryphon, who was anxious to procure for himself the throne of Syria, considered Jonathan as the chief obstacle to his ambition, secured through treachery his person in Ptolemais and consigned him to a dungeon (I Mach. xii, 24-54).

§ *3. Judæa, an Independent Kingdom.*

1. **Election and First Acts of Simon Machabeus.** There was but one voice in the assembly which gathered in

Jerusalem at the invitation of Simon Machabeus, to nominate him as the military leader of the nation, and vow to him perfect compliance with his orders. Simon, therefore, lost no time in completing the fortifications of Jerusalem, and in taking possession of Joppe, the principal harbor on the coast of Palestine. Then he advanced in person with a large army against Tryphon, who had invaded the Holy Land. Thereupon, the crafty Tryphon opened negotiations: "Jonathan was detained for a sum of money he owed to the king; if one hundred talents of silver were sent and his two sons as hostages for his peaceable conduct, he would be released." Simon knew that Tryphon's words were not to be trusted; yet to make it evident to all he sent the money and the hostages, and Tryphon, as Simon had foreseen, did not surrender Jonathan. He even soon put him to death, and did the same with the young king Antiochus, after which he seized the throne (I Mach. xiii, 1-32).

Whilst Tryphon made himself very unpopular by his cruelty, Simon strengthened his fortresses for fear of a further attack and then sent to Demetrius II an offer to recognize him as king, provided he exempted Judæa from all taxation. Demetrius granted this with the greatest readiness, and from this moment a new era began in Israel, that of national independence, so long unknown to the Jewish people. This great work was soon afterwards completed by the capture of the citadel of Jerusalem, that great symbol and stronghold of foreign domination; after which Simon organized fully the Jewish army, placing at its head "John, his son, a valiant man for war" (I Mach. xiii, 32-54).

Under the wise rule of this great high priest, the Holy Land enjoyed all the advantages of peace and security. He executed the law with great vigor and impartiality; he repaired the Temple and multiplied its sacred vessels; he kept the fortresses of the land well supplied with provisions and ammunitions, and under his prudent administration the wasted country soon recovered its ancient fertility. The writer of the first book of Machabees speaks with enthusiasm of this prosperous period, the fame of which reached Sparta and Rome, and which secured to Simon such gratitude from the nation at large, that "the Jews and their priests consented that he should be their prince and high priest forever," with this significant restriction, however, "till there should arise a faithful prophet." Thus had Simon Machabeus become by popular choice the hereditary sovereign of the Jews, and to all this power, Antiochus Sidetes, eager to secure the favor of Simon in his attempt at recovering his father's dominions, added the "leave to coin money of his own," promising him at the same time further favors when he would have reached the Syrian throne (I Mach. xiv-xv, 9).

Despite, however, the generous manner in which the Jewish prince helped Antiochus to overcome Tryphon, the Syrian monarch proved untrue to his word, and this entailed a war between Syria and Judæa which resulted in the defeat of the Syrian troops (I Mach. xv, 10-xvi, 10).

Simon did not live long after this victory of his arms, for during a tour of inspection through the country, Ptolemy, his son-in-law, and governor of Jericho, caused him to be murdered with his two younger sons towards the close of a splendid banquet to which he had treacherously invited them (I Mach. xvi, 14-17).

# SYNOPSIS OF CHAPTER XXIX.

## THE LAST JEWISH DYNASTY.

### (135–37 B. C.)

I. JUDÆA BEFORE THE ADVENT OF POMPEY:
- 1. *Outward Relations:*
  - 1. Friendly intercourse with Rome carefully kept up.
  - 2. Samaritan hatred increased by the destruction of the Temple on Mount Garizim.
  - 3. Wars with Syria and surrounding nations.
- 2. *Inner Condition:*
  - 1. Literary activity of the period (Psalms; historical writings; the Book of Enoch).
  - 2. Jewish sects: { Pharisees. Sadducees. Essenes. } Origin and manifold importance.
  - 3. Political and judicial organization (the Sanhedrim).

II. ADVENT OF POMPEY:
- A. *How brought about:*
  - Lengthened strife between Hyrcanus II and Aristobulus II.
  - Their appeals to Scaurus.
  - The policy of Pompey.
- B. *Action of Pompey in Jerusalem:*
  - Conduct of Aristobulus at this juncture.
  - Siege and profanation of the Temple.
  - Judæa tributary to Rome.

III. HEROD THE GREAT:
- 1. *Origin and Rapid Fortune of the Herodian Family.*
- 2. *Early Relations of Herod with* { the Romans. the Asmoneans. }
- 3. *Herod, King of Judæa:* End of the Asmonean dynasty (B. C. 37).

[347]

# CHAPTER XXIX.

### THE LAST JEWISH DYNASTY.

For the interval between the death of Simon Machabeus and the time of Herod the Great the authentic records of events hitherto found in the Bible fail us altogether, for the last fact mentioned in the books of Machabees is the accession of John, surnamed Hyrcanus, the sole surviving son of Simon Machabeus (I Mach. xvi, 18-24). Our main, not to say our exclusive, source of information about this important period of Jewish history consists in the extant writings of Josephus, which betray too often a lack of discrimination between mere legend and actual fact. From his writings, however, and from traditions preserved elsewhere, it is possible to draw a sufficiently reliable sketch of the principal events of the period which preceded immediately the coming of Our Lord.

§ *1. Judæa before the Advent of Pompey.*

1. **Outward Relations.** The successors of Simon Machabeus who ruled over Judæa before the intervention of Pompey in Jewish affairs were (1) his son John Hyrcanus, whose rule lasted thirty years (135-105 B. C.); (2) Aristobulus I (whose Hebrew name was Judas), who was the first Machabean ruler who assumed the royal title and who reigned but one year; (3) Alexander Jannæus (Hebrew name, Jonathan), the brother of Aristobulus I (104-78 B. C.); and (4) Alexandra (Hebrew name, Salome), the widow of the late king (78-69 B. C.).

These various princes, whatever their differences of character, seem to have followed the same line of policy in their outward relations. In Rome, they saw a powerful ally whose friendship was to be carefully kept up and skilfully made use of. It appears, for instance, that after a very disadvantageous treaty between John Hyrcanus and Antiochus VII, *Sidetes*, the Jewish high priest, "was desirous to renew that league of friendship which the Jews had with the Romans" and that through his ambassadors, he asked from the Senate a declaration to the effect that the treaty was null and void, as a violation of the freedom guaranteed by Rome to the Jewish nation (JOSEPHUS, Antiq. of the Jews, book xiii, chaps. viii, ix). It is under the same Machabean prince that Samaria was invaded by Jewish forces, Sichem captured and the temple on Mount Garizim levelled to the ground (128 B. C.), an event which was, of course, very gratifying to his nation, but which intensified the long standing hatred of the Samaritans against the Jews. Twenty years later, Samaria itself was taken and entirely demolished (JOSEPHUS, book xiii, chap. x, §§ 2, 3).

The most powerful, if not the most hateful, enemy of Judæa was Syria, which in the early part of the rule of Hyrcanus succeeded in obtaining a tribute from him for the fortresses he held outside Judæa, and in having the walls of Jerusalem demolished. It is true that a little later the Syrian armies which came to the rescue of Samaria were twice defeated by the Jews, but it is most likely that if they had not feared the armed intervention of Rome and had not been hampered by the distracted state of their affairs at home, the Syrian monarchs would have easily recovered their supremacy over the Jewish people. Be this as it may, it is certain that the princes of Juda took advantage of the disordered condition of Syria to turn their arms against their neighboring enemies: Moab, Galaad, Ammon, Arabia Petræa, etc. Prominent among these expeditions was that of John Hyrcanus against the Idumeans, who for more than four centuries had been masters of the southern part of Juda. He defeated them and ordered them either to become Jews or to be driven out of their country. They chose the former alternative, received circumcision and submitted so thoroughly to the Jewish laws that they became completely identified with their conquerors and never after reappeared as an independent nation (JOSEPHUS, Antiq. of the Jews, book xiii, chap. ix, § 1).

2. **Inner Condition.** It has been affirmed by several contemporary writers that whilst the rule of the Machabees gave back to the Holy Land peace and security, industry and fertility, new hymns were composed and added to the book of Psalms, the date of which as a final collection of inspired hymns should be brought down to the reign of John Hyrcanus or Alexander Jannæus (cfr. II Mach. ii, 14; I Mach. xiii, 51). Whilst admitting the possibility of this view, it seems better to appeal to less questionable arguments in favor of Jewish literary activity during the rule of the first Machabean princes. It is beyond doubt, for instance, that public records were then kept of the deeds of the high priests (cfr. I Mach. xiii, 42) and that our first book of Machabees was compiled from them towards or soon after the close of the Pontificate of John Hyrcanus (I Mach. xvi, 23, 24). Again, as evidence in favor of the literary activity of that same period, we may appeal to the large historical work written by a certain Jason of Cyrene, and of which our second book of Machabees professes to be an abridgment (II Mach. ii, 24, 27), for both the work of Jason and that of the inspired writer of the second book of Machabees were most likely composed in the first half of the second century before Christ. To the same conclusion points that fragmentary survival of an entire literature which once circulated under the name of the *Book of Enoch*, and the various parts of which date back to the period between 170 and 95 B. C.

Of much more importance than these literary compositions

in the inner history of this period is the definite appearance of two Jewish sects which henceforth played a great part in the political and religious history of their nation. These were the *Pharisees* and the *Sadducees*. These sects were the slow outcome of the twofold movement noticed several times already, the one against, the other in favor of, Hellenism, and this is why it is impossible now to assign their origin to any particular individual or date in Jewish history. The Pharisees continued, although of course in a modified form, after the triumph of the Machabees, the traditions of the *Assideans* (I Mach. ii, 42) or strenuous opponents of all leanings towards Greek customs and modes of thought. As their name indicates, the Pharisees were champions of the *separateness* of the Jewish people from other nations; and, in point of fact, under their influence, as early as the beginning of John Hyrcanus's rule, popular feeling ran high against "associating with foreigners or conversing with them" (JOSEPHUS, Antiq. of the Jews, book xiii, chap. viii, § 3). As the public inheritors and defenders of traditions which they deemed necessary for the perfect fulfilment of the Mosaic law, they had steadily urged on the Jewish rulers and finally secured the passage and enforcement of several laws. They actually wielded such a power in the State that John Hyrcanus felt it necessary to set himself against them and join their opponents, the Sadducees (JOSEPHUS, ibid, chap. x, § 6). The time soon came, however, when the Machabean princes Alexander and Alexandra realized how far the bulk of the nation was alienated from them through the opposition of the Pharisaic party, and in consequence found it necessary to give them ample share in the government of the country (JOSEPHUS, ibid, chap. xv, § 5; xvi, §1, sq.). After these concessions on the part of the royal power, the Pharisees developed freely the tenets and customs peculiar to their party, and impressed them powerfully upon the nation at large. They contributed greatly to keep alive among the Jews in the century which preceded the coming of Our Lord the distinctive beliefs of the Jewish race, as, for instance, the hope of a great national deliverer in the person of a Messias, the doctrine of the immortality of the soul, of a Divine Providence, of an *oral* tradition at least equal in authority with the written *law*. Nor were they less successful in imparting to the Jewish multitudes their zeal in carrying out the external observances of their ancestors, such as fasts, prayers, tithes, washings, sacrifices, etc. Ardent patriots themselves, they made of their followers men ever willing to lay down their lives for the national faith and independence, and as the bulk of the nation adhered zealously to a party so intensely national in politics and orthodox in religion, the Sadducees themselves in their public acts found it necessary "to conform to the notions of the Pharisees" (JOSEPHUS, Antiq. of the Jews, book xviii, chap. i, § 4).

The Sadducees were in reality opposed to the Pharisees almost in every thing. They were the inheritors of the Hellenistic tendencies, for which, as we have seen, the high priests were so largely responsible among the Jews. As a party, the Sadducees seem ever to have possessed in the Jewish commonwealth a fair amount of influence, but this was much more because of their wealth or high station in society than because of the number and enthusiasm of their followers. Contact with pagan thought and culture did not excite in them anything like the horror it produced in the Pharisees and their partisans, and whilst they wished to maintain their priestly position on the basis of the Mosaic law, they unhesitatingly rejected customs and traditions that would have interfered materially with the worldly spirit which animated them. Their tenets were chiefly of a negative kind: they denied, among other points of the Pharisaic belief, the existence of angels and the immortality of the soul. In politics, the Sadducees were ever in close alliance with the ruling power.

Besides the two great sects of the Pharisees and the Sadducees, Josephus mentioned a third one, namely, that of the Essenes, whose origin has been connected on more or less plausible grounds with the separatist tendencies of the Pharisees. It is not unlikely that their later organization into small colonies or villages at long distances from the towns was due to their desire of a greater separation from whatever might have interfered with the perfect purity of soul which was the main object of their lives, and it seems well established that the "differences between them and the Pharisees lay mainly in rigor of practice and not in articles of belief" (WESTCOTT, in SMITH, Bible Dictionary, art. Essenes; cfr. also the description of the life of the Essenes by JOSEPHUS, Antiquities of the Jews, book xviii, chap. i, § 5).

A last feature to be noticed in connection with the inner condition of Judæa under the first Machabean (called the *Asmonean*, from one of the ancestors of Mathathias, named Hasmon) rulers regards the political and judicial organization of the country. It seems that the power of the Machabeans became stronger and more absolute only gradually in the Jewish State, and that at first, whilst recognized as *high priests* and even *princes*, they had to reckon considerably with the *elders* of the nation. In fact, the occasion of the rupture between John Hyrcanus and the Pharisees already mentioned was their well-known opposition to his tendency to concentrate all public powers in his hands. It was only the second successor of Simon Machabeus who ventured to assume the royal title, because he felt strongly upheld by the Sadducees; and even then, it is not unlikely that his conduct was disapproved of by a large part of the nation which spoke of him as "a lover of the Greeks." Ultimately, however, the royal power got the better of the opposition, "and during the last period of Alexander Jannæus's reign the eldership ceased as a ruling power, and became transformed into a *Sanhedrim*, or ecclesiastical authority, although the latter endeavored, with more or less success, to exercise civil jurisdiction, at least in ecclesiastical matters" (EDERSHEIM, Life and Times of Jesus, the Messiah, vol. ii, p. 677).

Such is most likely the origin of the **Sanhedrim** or highest council of the Jews, made up of chief priests, elders and scribes presided over by the high priest. It counted seventy-one members, perhaps in remembrance of the seventy elders who assisted Moses in the administration of justice and to whom Jewish rabbis delight to trace back the origin of the Sanhedrim. The members were to be of pure Israelite descent and were governed by a president and two vice-presidents; besides, there were secretaries and other officers. Of course, the powers possessed by the Sanhedrim at its origin cannot be defined in the present day; but there is no doubt that it took advantage of the rapid decline of the Machabean dynasty to increase its jurisdiction, and that immediately before Our Lord's time it superintended the ritual of public worship, regulated the Jewish calendar, enforced the exact fulfilment of the law, punished false prophets and even exercised judicial control over the high priests (cfr. SCHURER, division ii, vol. ii, pp. 165-195).

### § 2. *The Advent of Pompey.*

1. **How Brought About?** At the death of Queen Alexandra (B. C. 69), the party of the Pharisees, who had been all powerful in the State under her name, immediately placed Hyrcanus II, her elder son, on the Jewish throne, although the late queen had destined the royal dignity for Aristobulus, her younger son. Thereupon, Aristobulus, at the head of the Sadducees and of the army, compelled his brother to resign, and took the title of Aristobulus II.

Here would have ended the strife between the two brothers, had it not been for the ambition of a man who then appeared upon the scene. This man was Antipater (the father of Herod the Great), an Idumean by birth, but a Jew by religion. Antipater, brought up in the court, had contracted a close friendship with Hyrcanus, the heir-apparent to the throne. The withdrawal of the latter to private life defeated his ambitious schemes; he therefore persuaded Hyrcanus that his life was in danger and ultimately prevailed on him to fly to Aretas, King of Arabia Petræa, who, on condition of receiving large grants of territory, undertook to reinstate Hyrcanus. Aristobulus II was first defeated by Aretas and the partisans of Hyrcanus, and next besieged in the Temple-fortress of Jerusalem.

Meanwhile, the great Pompey had been pursuing his conquests in Asia, and had just detached his lieutenant Scaurus with instructions to submit Syria. Soon after his arrival at Damascus, Scaurus hastened to Judæa, on the borders of which messengers from both Hyrcanus and Aristobulus offered him sums of money in return for his assistance. The offers of Aristobulus were accepted because he was in possession of the Temple treasury, and Aretas received orders to break up the siege of the Temple-fortress.

Before long, however, Pompey arrived in person at Damascus, where he was met by three ambassies from Judæa, namely, those of the two brothers, and one sent by the Jewish nation. Hyrcanus appealed to his birthright; Aristobulus urged the incompetency of Hyrcanus, and the deputies of the Jewish nation expressed the wish to get rid of the monarchical form of government altogether, and to have their ancient priestly constitution restored. The request of the Jewish deputies found no response, and the examination of the rival claims of the Asmonean princes was postponed by the wary *imperator* till after he had submitted Aretas and his country to Rome, although he had practically settled the question in his mind in favor of the weak Hyrcanus, who would present fewer obstacles to the prospective annexion of

Judæa to the Roman empire (JOSEPHUS, Antiquities of the Jews, book xiv, chaps. i–iii, § 3).

2. **Action of Pompey in Jerusalem.** Apprehensive of the fate that threatened him, Aristobulus did not wait quietly for Pompey's decision; whereupon the latter marched at once against him, and laid siege to Jerusalem. Then it was that Aristobulus's courage failed him altogether, and that having gone to the Roman camp, he agreed to surrender the Jewish capital. The gates of the city were indeed thrown open to the Roman legions, but the Temple-fortress withstood three months the efforts of the troops of Pompey. At length, on a Sabbath-day, the sacred precincts were taken by storm, and a fearful carnage followed. The great conqueror penetrated into every part of the Temple of Jehovah, but through policy, he left untouched the treasures it contained, and even gave orders for the resumption of the Temple services.

With this finished the short era of independence which the Machabees had secured to their country (B. C. 63). Hyrcanus II was appointed *high priest* and *ethnarch*, that is ruler of the country; he was not allowed to wear the royal diadem, and his jurisdiction was limited to Judæa, which became tributary to Rome, as a part of the government of Syria. All the surrounding Hellenistic cities and Samaria were withdrawn from Jewish allegiance and the walls of Jerusalem were demolished; after which Pompey proceeded homewards, taking with him to grace his triumphal entry Aristobulus, and his two sons and two daughters, together with numerous Jewish captives. The captives then brought to Rome increased considerably, if indeed they did not begin, the Jewish community in the capital of the Roman empire (JOSEPHUS, Antiquities of the Jews, book xiv, chap. iii, § 4; chap. iv).

§ 3. *Herod the Great.*

1. **Origin and Rapid Fortune of the Herodian Family.** The Herodian family took its rise in Idumæa, a district, the conquest and conversion of which by John Hyrcanus has already been noticed. The founder of this family was Antipas, who was made governor of Idumæa by Alexander Jannæus, and who was succeeded in this office by his son Antipater, the father of Herod the Great. The ambitious Antipater successfully interfered in the unhappy strife between Hyrcanus II and Aristobulus II, and on the taking of Jerusalem by Pompey and the appointment of Hyrcanus as high priest and ethnarch of *Judæa proper*, he became the virtual ruler of the land with Hyrcanus as a mere puppet in his hands.

When Pompey was finally defeated by Julius Cæsar at Pharsalia (48 B. C.), the prospects of Antipater and Hyrcanus, who naturally enough had held out for the great conqueror of Jerusalem, seemed rather dark. But they quickly changed sides, and timely help in men and personal influence given to Cæsar in Egypt secured to Antipater the title of Procurator of Judæa, which was then restored to its former extent, and to Hyrcanus the permission of rebuilding the walls of the Holy City (B. C. 47, cfr. JOSEPHUS, Antiquities of the Jews, book xiv, chap. viii).

2. **Early Relations of Herod with the Romans and the Asmoneans.** To be better able to control the whole extent of territory now so immediately and openly intrusted to him by Rome, Antipater appointed his two sons governors: the elder, **Phasaelus**, of Jerusalem; the younger, Herod, only twenty-five years old, of Galilee. Herod was a man of keen intellect, strong will and ruthless ambition. He was noted as a fearless rider, and no one threw the spear so straight to the mark or shot his arrow so constantly into the

centre. It was most likely because of these strong features of Herod's character, in striking contrast with those of Hyrcanus, that the latter loved the new governor of Galilee " as his own son " (R. W. Moss, From Malachi to Matthew, p. 192).

In Galilee Herod soon displayed the energy which ever characterized him. He crushed a guerilla warfare, put to death its leader and nearly all his associates. This aroused the indignation of the patriots of Jerusalem, and Herod, as professing the Jewish religion, was summoned to appear before the great Sanhedrim, for having arrogated to himself the power of life and death. He appeared, but escaped condemnation through the interference of Hyrcanus, and took refuge near Sextus Cæsar, the president of Syria.

On the murder of Julius Cæsar (B. C. 44), and the possession of Syria by Cassius, Antipater and Herod again changed sides, and in return for substantial services Herod was recognized as governor of Cœle-Syria. When the battle of Philippi (B. C. 41) placed the Roman world in the hands of Antony and Octavius, the former obtained Asia. Once more Herod knew how to gain the new ruler, and he became **Tetrarch** of Judæa, with the promise of the crown, if all went well (Josephus, Antiquities of the Jews, book xiv, chaps. ix–xiii, 2).

3. **Herod becomes King of Judæa.** Forced, the following year (B. C. 40), by an irruption of the Parthians, who had espoused the cause of his rival, Antigonus (the son of Aristobulus II), to abandon Jerusalem, Herod first betook himself to Egypt, and then to Rome. There, owing chiefly to the influence of Antony, he was declared King of Judæa by the Roman Senate, and, preceded by the consuls and the magistrates, he walked in procession between Antony and Octavius to the Capitol, where the usual sacrifices were offered and the decree formally laid up in the archives.

After an absence of barely three months, Herod was again in Palestine, where at the head of an army he soon made himself master of Galilee. He next set himself at work to take the Holy City. But before investing it — which he did in the early spring of B. C. 37 — he repaired to Samaria to wed the unfortunate Machabean princess, Marianne, betrothed to him five years before. The uncle of that ill-fated queen was Antigonus, whom Herod now besieged in Jerusalem. After a siege of six months Jerusalem fell, and a fearful scene of carnage ensued. At length Herod, by rich presents, induced the Romans to leave Jerusalem, carrying Antigonus with them (June, 37 B. C. (cfr. JOSEPHUS, ibid., book xiv, chaps. xiv-xvi). Herod, the Idumean, now ascended the throne of Judæa, and thereby put an end to the last Jewish dynasty. As Our Lord was born "in the days of Herod, the King of Judæa" (Luke i, 5), the reign of this prince forms a real part of Our Lord's time: we will therefore reserve the narrative of its events for our study of the Life of Christ.

# SYNOPSIS OF CHAPTER XXX.

## THE JEWS OF THE DISPERSION.

---

**I. EASTERN OR ARAMAIC SECTION:**
1. *Its Origin and Principal Settlements.*
2. *Social Condition and Political Influence.*
3. *Religious and Patriotic Relations with Palestine.*

---

**II. WESTERN OR GREEK SECTION:**
1. *Its Origin and Rapid Spread through*
   - Northern Africa.
   - Syria and Asia Minor.
   - Greece and Italy.
2. *Principal Centre: Alexandria:*
   - Situation and description.
   - Commerce and civilization.
   - Position of Jews.
3. *Social Intercourse with Heathens:*
   - Mutual aversion.
   - Mutual influence.
4. *Religious Condition:*
   - Faithfulness to Jehovah and His law.
   - Close union with Palestine (Books of Wisdom and Ecclesiasticus).

---

**III. RESULTS OF THE DISPERSION:**
1. *Establishment of Synagogues Everywhere.*
2. *Change of Language.*
3. *Spread of Monotheistic Belief and Messianic Hopes.*

## CHAPTER XXX.

### THE JEWS OF THE DISPERSION.

To complete our rapid survey of Jewish history, there remains to speak of the countless Jews who, even before Our Lord's time, were scattered through pagan lands, and who, for this reason, were called the Jews of "**The Dispersion**" (cfr. II Mach. i, 27; Jas. i, 1; I Peter i, 1). They considered themselves as a portion of God's chosen people, looked upon Jerusalem as their metropolis, and carrying about with them the monotheistic belief, and the sacred Scriptures of their nation, they effectively concurred in preparing the world for the coming of the Messias and for the spread of His doctrine. They fall naturally under two great heads: (1) the Jews speaking Aramaic, like those of the mother country, and scattered through the East, formed the *Eastern* or *Aramaic* section of the Dispersion; (2) the Jews speaking Greek and settled in the West were the *Western* or *Greek* section, or "the Dispersion of the Greeks," as they are called in St. John vii, 35 (in the Greek).

§ *1. Eastern or Aramaic Section of the Dispersion.*

1. **Origin and Principal Settlements.** The Aramaic Dispersion owes its origin to the two great captivities which befell Israel and Juda in B. C. 721 and 588 respectively, and from which only small detachments of the Jews ever returned to the Holy Land. Its principal seats were the countries beyond the Euphrates, namely, Babylonia, Media, Assyria and Mesopotamia, in which the Jews, as Josephus says,

"were an immense multitude" (Antiq. of the Jews, book xi, chap. v, § 2). Important settlements existed also about the middle of the fourth century B. C. in Hyrcania on the Caspian Sea. On this side of the Euphrates there was a considerable "Jewish population in many places, notably in Palmyra, and in the province of Yemen in Arabia Felix" (SEIDEL, In the Time of Jesus, p. 164, cfr. also SCHURER, The Jewish People in the Time of Jesus Christ, division ii, vol. ii, p. 220, sq., English Translation).

2. **Social Condition and Political Influence.** Only scanty details concerning the history of the Eastern or Aramaic section of the Dispersion have come down to us, so that it is very difficult in the present day to draw anything like a faithful picture of the social condition and political influence of the Jews settled in the great countries of southwestern Asia. It may be said, however, that the insight allowed us by the books of Tobias, Esther, Daniel and Nehemias, and by the writings of Josephus, into the condition of the Aramaic-speaking Jews leads us to believe that they were both prosperous and influential. In the large Eastern cities they were very successful in the pursuit of trade and industry, whilst in the low countries of the Euphrates they carried on with no less success agriculture and cattle farming (cfr. JOSEPHUS, Antiq. of the Jews, book xviii, chap. ix). "In some of these countries they kept quite aloof from connection by marriage with the other inhabitants, but in other cases they were not so strict, and this gave rise to various epithets, intended to mark the degree of purity of the Jewish blood" (BLAIKIE, Manual of Bible History, p. 405). Under their political and social influence, many heathens became proselytes to the Jewish faith (Tobias i, 7), and there is hardly any doubt that their financial and social prosperity go a great length towards accounting for the fearful persecution which they underwent about the time of Our Lord, and in which upwards of 50,000

Jews were put to death in Mesopotamia, and for similar persecutions of which they often were the object in other districts of Asia.

3. **Religious and Patriotic Relations with Palestine.** Between the Jews dispersed in the East and those of Palestine a close and heartfelt union was ever maintained. This was due to a large extent to their community of language and probably also to the influence of the faithful priests who had remained in foreign lands. They had only synagogues as religious meeting-places, so that they naturally looked up to Jerusalem and its Temple as the centre of their national worship. It was to the Great Sanhedrim of Jerusalem, as to their supreme national and religious tribunal, that they looked for legal decisions, and every year sacred processions of Babylonian Jews, bearing their tribute and first-fruits to the Temple, regularly travelled by thousands to offer sacrifices in the Holy City and worship Jehovah in His Holy Place (cfr. Tobias i, 6).

Sincere patriots they ever were towards the mother country, and their position on "the eastern borders of the Roman Empire, till Trajan — as subjects of the Parthians and subsequently of those eastern provinces which could never be kept under subjection by the Romans — made their attitude always of political importance to the Empire. P. Petronius, legate of Syria, esteemed it dangerous in the year 40 B. C. to excite in them a hostile disposition towards Rome, and a little later, during the Vespasian war, the insurgents sought to incite their co-religionists beyond the Euphrates to hostilities against Rome" (SCHURER, loc. cit., p. 224).

§ *2. Western or Greek Section of the Dispersion.*

1. **Origin and Rapid Spread.** It is not improbable that long before the time of Alexander the Great there was

a fair sprinkling of Hebrew settlers among the mixed population of Lower Egypt. It is only, however, to this great conqueror of Persia and Egypt that the Western or Greek Dispersion may be said to owe its origin. He it was, as we saw in a preceding chapter, who attracted to the new Egyptian capital he had built to perpetuate his name a large number of Jews by granting to them equal civic rights with his Macedonian colonists. Thus did he set an example which his successors on the throne of the Pharaos, notably Ptolemy I, son of Lagus, and Ptolemy II, Philadelphus, were not slow to imitate. The Greek Dispersion thus powerfully started, spread rapidly westward along the coast of Africa to Cyrene and the towns of the Pentapolis, and inland southward to the territory of Ethiopia (cfr. II Mach. ii, 24; i, 1; Acts ii, 10; viii, 27; Matt. xxvii, 32, etc.).

Nor were the successors of Alexander in Western Asia less desirous than the Ptolemies of Egypt to establish Jewish colonies in their dominions. Seleucus I, who was fully aware of the aptitude of the Jews as colonists, invited them to come and dwell in the city of Antioch he had but recently founded, and his invitation was gladly responded to by many who on their settling there were governed by an ethnarch of their own and admitted to the same advantages as the Greeks. We also learn from Josephus that Antiochus the Great settled 2,000 Jewish families from Mesopotamia and Babylonia in Lydia and Phrygia, two important provinces of Asia Minor, granting to them at the same time the use of their own laws, extensive territorial possessions and exemption from all tribute for ten years (Antiquities of the Jews, book xii, chap. iii, § 4). As Antiochus had foreseen, this part of his dominions became very prosperous, and the Jews soon multiplied in all the commercial centres of Asia Minor, such as Ephesus, Pergamus, Miletus, Sardis, etc. From Asia Minor they also found their way into Greece and other parts of Europe, the Archipelago, where they settled in no small numbers, supplying them with a natural bridge between the Asiatic and European continents. The decree of the Roman consul Lucius, recorded in I Mach. xv, gives us a vivid impression of the extent to which they spread themselves in every direction not long after the death of Antiochus the Great, and the book of the Acts speaks of their important and old settlements in Philippi, Berea, Thessalonica, Athens and Corinth. The same book of the Acts makes also mention of a Jewish community in the capital of the Roman Empire. If the Jews appeared in Rome for the first time in the train of the captives of Pompey, their captivity was not of long duration, and under the protection of Julius Cæsar, who granted to them the same privileges as the Ptolemies and the Seleucidæ in Egypt and Syria, they rapidly multiplied in the capital and thence spread into several towns of Italy.

2. **Principal Centre of the Greek Dispersion.** Of the Greek Dispersion, Alexandria was unquestionably the metropolis because of the number, wealth and influence of its Jewish population. Founded by Alexander the Great, whence it derived its name, the city was situated on a narrow neck of land between the Mediterranean Sea and the Lake Mareotis. It was built in the form of the outspread cloak of a Macedonian warrior, and measured about four miles from east to west, and about one mile from north to south. Far different from the modern Egyptian Alexandria, it was laid out in straight, parallel streets cutting each other at right angles, and had four principal gates at the cardinal points. Its two principal streets, about 200 feet wide, were lined with magnificent houses, temples and public buildings, and at their intersection there was a spacious square from the centre of which vessels sailing either on the Mediterranean to the north, or on the lake to the south, could be seen coming in under full sail. The fleets of Asia and

Europe could easily meet in the commodious and safe harbor of Alexandria, and a magnificent light-house had been built for the guidance of sailors at the eastern point of the Island of Pharos about one mile off at sea. The climate of the city was healthy, and it was well supplied with fresh water by a subterranean aqueduct.

Alexandria had excellent commercial connections with Arabia and India, the tribes living in the deserts west and south, and the nations or cities along the coasts of the Mediterranean, and in consequence, it had become in the time of Strabo "the greatest emporium in the world." Apart from its architectural splendor and commercial prosperity, the Egyptian capital was celebrated for its stirring intellectual life. The famous Museum founded by Ptolemy I contained a magnificent royal library together with dwellings for scholars, poets and artists who came hither from all parts of the world to live in this great centre of Greek and Eastern literature and art, and to listen to the greatest masters of the time.

The three sections into which Alexandria was divided corresponded to the three great classes of its inhabitants: Greeks, Egyptians and Jews. From the very beginning of the city the Jewish element was considerable for its number and political privileges, and under the Ptolemies it grew so steadily that in the time of Philo it occupied more than two out of the five districts of Alexandria. The Jews formed a large independent municipal community within or co-ordinate with the rest of the city, and governed themselves under the presidency of an ethnarch. Their wealth was very considerable, and some among them occupied important positions in the Egyptian army. They had a magnificent synagogue, and their Sanhedrim was second only to that of Jerusalem.

3. **Social Intercourse with Heathen Nations.** Whilst the Jews of Palestine and especially those of Jeru-

salem could, under the powerful influence of the Pharisees, succeed pretty well in avoiding contact and exchange of ideas and customs with the pagans, those of the Greek Dispersion, whether in Alexandria, in Antioch or in the other cities and towns of the Greco-Roman world, could not help being brought in daily contact with Greek culture and civilization. This unavoidable intercourse between Jews and Gentiles soon presented a twofold aspect: the one of mutual aversion, and the other of mutual influence, which can easily be traced to the striking peculiarities of either party.

Nothing, for instance, appeared more ridiculous to the Gentiles than the practice of circumcision, the abstinence from swine's flesh and a strict Sabbatarianism. A religion, like that of the Jews, without images and pictures, was naturally regarded as barbarous or even treated as atheistic, whilst many of its rites were called absurd or contemptible. Again, in the name of their religion, the Jews claimed so many privileges in addition to those they already possessed as citizens of a particular city or as citizens of the empire, they sent so much money to their Temple in Palestine, and showed themselve so exclusive of the pagans on many public occasions, that they naturally excited a deep aversion on the part of the heathen statesmen and multitudes. Add to this the great self-esteem of the Jews which, in the eyes of Greeks and Romans, rested on nothing but glories which belonged to bygone centuries, an unconcealed antipathy of foreign races and religions, a commercial success not perhaps always due to the exclusive use of lawful means, and finally slanderous reports circulating freely about the Jewish race, and it will be easy to understand the terms of contempt and aversion constantly met with about the Jews in heathen writers, and the occasional outbreaks of violence on the part of pagan multitudes against the dispersed children of Israel (cfr. II Mach. i, 27; SCHURER, The Jewish People in the Time of Jesus Christ, division ii, vol. ii, p. 291, sq).

Thus then, the Gentiles found in the peculiarities of the Jewish race much which was calculated to foster their contempt and aversion towards the Jews of the Western Dispersion, and naturally enough this very contempt and aversion were keenly resented by the Jews, who considered themselves as the chosen people of God and the inheritors of the Divine blessings promised to their forefathers. The Gentiles appeared also contemptible and hateful to the Greek-speaking Jews because of their idols, of their superstitious and immoral practices, especially, as it oftentimes happened, when the pagan populations or authorities did everything in their power to compel them to apostatize from the pure and ennobling worship of the living God.

These and other such peculiarities of either Jew or Gentile explain their mutual aversion, which of course varied in intensity according to circumstances of time and place. But there were other features of Jewish as well as of Greek life which were calculated to counteract, to some extent, this mutual antipathy.

It is beyond doubt, for instance, that under the efforts of the Jews in apologetic works, in daily intercourse, etc., the superiority of monotheistic belief and of public and private morality as inculated in the sacred books of the Jewish nation appeared manifest to many men and women of the Gentile world, and effectively led many of them to embrace Judaism. Women, in particular, felt especially attracted by the mystery of the synagogue, by the superior condition assigned to their sex in the Jewish religion; hence they became proselytes of Judaism in large numbers, and naturally drew the attention of the domestic circle to the belief they had adopted. Further, the Jews of the Greek Dispersion were careful not to enforce too strictly upon those whom they saw inclined towards the pure worship of Jehovah the ritualistic features of their religion which were most objected to by pagans at large, and this, together with the brotherly love exhibited by the members of the Jewish communities towards one another, contributed powerfully to dispel the prejudices and even to win the admiration of the heathens.

Whilst the Jews exerted such deep and widespread influence upon the Greco-Roman world, they themselves underwent, to a considerable extent, the influence of Greek thought and culture. In the Dispersion, the cultured Jew was not simply a Jew, he was also a Greek in respect of language, of education and social manners and customs, by the sheer force of his surroundings, and in many points, particularly of a ritualistic nature, he gradually became more or less relaxed. Again, the close study of pagan authors and notably of Greek classics, even when pursued with a view to defend or propagate the Jewish creed, was not without some influence upon the manner in which this same Jewish creed was conceived of by the Jews, or presented by them to the acceptance of the pagans. Indeed, this Hellenistic influence, imperceptible at first, led ultimately to that form of Alexandrine religious thought which has been called *syncretism* (that is, the blending into one system of Jewish belief with Greek speculation), which we find fully developed in the writings of Philo, and which from Alexandria spread far and wide (cfr. FOUARD, St Peter, chap. iii).

4. **Religious Condition of the Greek-speaking Jews.** Of course, the influence just described of Greek thought, forms of expression and philosophical speculation upon the Greek-speaking Jews never extended much beyond a comparatively narrow circle of Jewish thinkers and apologists. The great bulk of the dispersed Jews in Egypt, as well as in the other countries of the Greco-Roman world, ever remained under the full power of the early training received at home and completed in the synagogues erected almost everywhere by the dispersed Jews, and this was distinctively Jewish in tendency, belief and practice. We must picture them to us

as perfectly regular in their attendance at the Divine worship in the synagogues such as it was conducted there, that is limited to prayer in common, public reading and exposition of the Sacred Books. They were also faithful in carrying out as much of the Mosaic observances as was compatible with their condition far from Jerusalem and its Temple. Like their brethren dispersed in the Eastern countries, they sent rich offerings to the Holy City, appealed to the Great Sanhedrim of Jerusalem for final legal decisions, and received with joy mingled with reverence the exhortations and instructions of those scribes who from time to time came to them from Jerusalem, the acknowledged metropolis of all the Jews. Finally, to go up to offer sacrifices in the Temple of Jerusalem annually on the great Paschal festival, or, if he lived too far off for that purpose, to make a pilgrimage there once or more in his lifetime, was held by every Jew to be an essential part of his religion.

This close union between the Jews of the Western Dispersion and Palestine as the centre of their religion is particularly remarkable in connection with the Jews of Egypt, who having a temple of their own at *Leontopolis*, a few miles northeast of Cairo, conducted there the worship of Jehovah on the same lines as in Jerusalem, since the middle of the second century before our era.

Two facts more deserve special notice in connection with the religious life of the Jews of Alexandria, (1) the composition of the inspired book of *Wisdom* in their language and in their midst, about the middle of the second century before Christ, (2) the translation into Greek, made in Egypt about 130 B. C., of the inspired book of *Ecclesiasticus*, which the Egyptian Jews had probably received from those of Jerusalem some time after its composition, and very large fragments of which in the original Hebrew have been recently discovered (cfr. Revue Biblique, October 1, 1897, p. 573, footnote 2).

### § 3. *Results of the Dispersion.*

**1. Establishment of Synagogues Everywhere.** When after this rapid survey of the Eastern and Western Dispersion we try to sum up its principal results, we find that the first is the establishment of Jewish synagogues through the various districts of the Roman Empire. These places of religious worship in which Moses and the Prophets were read, tended, of course, to diffuse the expectation of the Kingdom of Heaven, but more particularly they were places into which the Apostles and early preachers of Christianity were free to penetrate, and in which they were naturally invited as strangers to address an exhortation to the assembled brethren. This was a splendid opportunity for them to preach the Gospel, and they naturally availed themselves of it. Starting from the passages of Holy Writ which had just been read, they announced boldly the fulfilment of the Law and the Prophets in the Person and Mission of Our Lord and Savior Jesus Christ.

**2. Change of Language.** A second important result of the Dispersion is the change which took place among the Jews scattered in the Greco-Roman world. It can readily be seen that their adoption of the Greek language as their vernacular, and more particularly as the language of their literature and of their liturgy placed many religious truths within the reach of the heathen. It introduced also into the Greek language numerous words and modes of expression required by Hebrew thought, and gradually moulded it into that *Hellenistic* Greek, as it has been called, which the early preachers of the Gospel and inspired New Testament writers were to use as a language almost entirely fitted already to convey the great truths they had to announce.

3. **Spread of Monotheistic Belief and Messianic Hopes.** The third and most important result of the Dispersion, was such a spread of the monotheistic belief and Messianic hopes of Israel as to prepare effectively the Gentiles for Christianity. Had all the Jews of the Captivities returned to the Holy Land and re-established there Judaism in its strictest form, the heads of the Jewish commonwealth would never have realized the necessity of divesting their religion of what were, after all, only its transient features. They would never have felt compelled, for instance, to dispense the pagans who wished to become worshippers of the true God, from the hateful rite of circumcision and other such practices of the law however utterly incompatible with surroundings different from those of Palestine. As a necessary consequence, the belief and worship of the sole true God as we see it spread by the Dispersion, namely, unfettered by the complicated and burdensome system of legal enactments, would never have existed as a transition from Judaism to Christianity, as a preparation of the Gentile world for the universal religion in which "the Father must be adored in spirit and in truth" (John iv, 21-24).

In like manner, without the Dispersion, the expectation of the Messias would have been practically confined to the limits of the Holy Land; whereas the dispersed Jews carrying everywhere their prophetical books, spread far and wide the hope of a great Deliverer, and thus directed the eyes of all peoples towards the One who was soon to appear as the Teacher and Redeemer of all nations.

# INDEX.

AARON, spokesman of Moses, 61, 103; death of, 120.
Abdias, 280.
Abiathar, 194, 203, 207, 214.
Abimelech, 12, 153, 160.
Abner, 197.
Abraham, 1; ancestor of the Jews, 7; call of, 8; wanderings of, 8; relations with Chanaanites, 10; relations with Egypt, 10, 11; domestic life of, 13, sq.; burial-place of, 15; life of faith of, 23–26; blessings bestowed upon him, 24; character of, 24, 35; father of the faithful, 25; ancestor of the Christians, 25, 26.
Absalom, 207.
Achab, 245, sq.; idolatry under, 246, 259.
Achaz, 194, 253, 262; frightful idolatry of, 262.
Achimelech, 193.
Acre, 114; plain of, 115, 238.
Adonias, 207, 213, 214.
Agar, 13, 14.
Aggeus, 282, 315.
Akabah, Gulf of, 102, 105, 119.
Alcimus, 342, sq.
Alexander, Bales, 343; Jannæus, 348, 350, sq., 353; the Great, 324, 331, 364.
Alexandra, 348, 351, 354.

Alexandria, 326, 330, 336; foundation of, 325; description of, 365; commerce of, 366; Jews in, 366.
Altar of Holocausts, 84, 86, 97; of incense, 84.
Amalec, Amalecites, 104; their attacks on Israel, 72, 157, 159; attacks on Saul, 186, 194.
Ammon, Ammonites, 119, 122, 131, 132, sq., 157, 204.
Amorrhites, 9, 104, 122, sq., 175, 204.
Amos, 252, 279.
Amri, 244, sq.
Angel of Jehovah, 13; belief in angels developed, 308.
Animals, why offered to Jehovah, 92; clean and unclean, 94.
Anna, 172.
"Anointed of Jehovah," applied to kings, 179.
Antigonus, General of Alexander, 325, sq.; son of Aristobulus II, 358, 359.
Anti-Lebanon, 110.
Antioch, 332, 337.
Antiochus III, 330, 364; IV, 332, sq.; persecutes Jews, 336, sq.; VI, 345; VII, 349.
Antipater, 355, 357, sq.
Antony, 358.
Aod, 157.
Aphec, 173.

[373]

## INDEX.

Apis, bull, 76.
Apollonius, 331, 336, 341.
Arabah, the, 105, 119.
Arabia, 110, 216, 355.
Aretas, 355.
Aristobulus I, 348; II, 354, 356, sq.
Ark of the Covenant, description of, 84, sq.; like to Egyptian Naos, 85; preceding Israel, 101, 224; capture of, 168; on Mount Sion, 202.
Arnon, River, 110, 112, 120, sq.
Artaxerxes I, 316, 318, 320; II, 320.
Asa, 242, 256, 257.
Asaph, 203.
Asarhaddon, 266; II, 298.
Aser, 142.
Asiongaber, 217.
Asmonean, 353, 355.
Assideans, 340, 342, 351.
Assuerus, 316.
Assurbanipal, 266.
Assyria, 238, 250, 254, 263, 361.
Astarthe, 134, sq., 245, 265.
Athalia, 259, 260, 261.
Atonement, the day of, 88, 98.
Azarias, King, 261.

BAAL, 123, 134, sq., 159, 260.
Baasa, 256.
Babylon, 8, description of, 298; capture of, 300, 306.
Babylonia, 8, 238, 254, 297, 324; history of, 298, sq.
—— civilization of, 300, sq.
—— religion of, 303, sq.
—— captivity in, 304, sq.
Balaam, 124, 125.
Baltassar, 300.
Banias, 201, 220.
Barac, 158.
Baruch, 279.
Basan, 121.

Bedouin, 9, 108, 149.
Bel or Belus, 298, 303.
Benadad, 248, 257.
Benjamin, 34, 38, 43; tribe of, 141, 169, 321.
Bersabee, 10, 53, 176.
Bethel, 9, 34, 175.
Bethlehem, 34, 169, 190, 194.
Bethoron, 138, 139, 341, 342.
Bethsabee, 206, 208, 212, 213.
Birthright, 28, 30.
Borsippa, 297, 299.
Breastplate of high priest, 87.
Brick-making in Egypt, 56, 57, 62.
Burnt-offerings, 99.

CADES, 10, 102, 103, 106, 118, 134.
Cæsar, Julius, 357, 358, 365; Sextus, 358.
Caleb, 104, 142.
Calf, golden, at Sinai, 72; at Dan and Bethel, 243.
Candlestick, golden, 84, 86.
Captivity of Israel, 254; of Juda, 269; of Babylon, 297, sq., 304, sq.; end of, 311.
Cariathiarim, 174, 202.
Carmel, Mount, 113, 247.
Castes, how prevented in Israel, 99.
Cedron, 199.
Census, at Sinai, 101; under David, 207; of Zorobabel and Nehemias, 318.
Ceremonial law, 90, sq.
Chaldæa, 7, 267.
Chaldean, 8, 286, 297, 298; account of Genesis, 303.
Champollion, 48, 257.
Chanaan, land of, 8, 9, 25, 34; advance to, 118, sq.
—— inhabitants of, 131, sq.; partition of, 140, sq.

Chanaanites, relations of, with Abraham, 10; descendants of Cham, 131; civilization of, 133, sq.; religion of, 134, sq.; remains of, in Palestine, 150.
Character, of Abraham, 24, 35; of Isaac, 35; of Jacob, 35, sq.; of Esau, 36; human character of Mosaic law, 81; of Moses, 128, sq.; of David, 208, sq.
Cherubim, 85, 224.
Chronology of royal period, 271.
Circumcision, 14, 25, 26.
Cison River, 116.
Cities of refuge, 143.
City, Holy (see Jerusalem).
Civilization, 1; of Egypt, 49, sq.; of Chanaan, 133, 134; of Babylonia, 300, sq.; Greek, 328.
Clean and unclean, animals, things, conditions, 94, sq.; in Babylonia, 304.
Contract tablets, 301, sq.
Courses of priests, 203.
Courts of Tabernacle, 97; of Temple, 224, sq., 316.
Covenant, 1, 25, 77; renewal of, 319; angel of the, 283.
Cuneiform, 11, 302.
Cyrus, 300; liberator of Jews, 311; decree of, 311, 315.

DAMASCUS, 9, 141, 251, 312, 355.
Dan, tribe of, 141, 168.
Daniel, 281, sq., 324, 299, 305, 362.
Darius, 315.
David, 170, 188; origin and early life, 189, sq.; first introduction to Saul, 191; relations with Saul, 192, sq.; wanderings of, 193, sq.; king in Hebron, 197; king over all Israel, 198, sq.; capital and court of, 199; city of, 199; political administration of, 200, sq.; ecclesiastical arrangements, 202; a prophet, 202; outward relations, 203; barbarity of his wars, 204, sq.; extension and prosperity of his empire, 205; fall and punishment, 206; death of, 208; Psalms of, 209; a type of Christ, 209.
Dead Sea, 15, footnote 1; 110.
Debbora, 152, sq., 157, sq.
Dedication of Solomon's Temple, 225; of Zorobabel's Temple, 315.
Delta, the, 47.
Demand for a king, 177.
Demetrius II, 343, sq.
Departure from Egypt, 64, sq.; from Sinai, 101; from Babylonia, first, 311, sq.; second, 320.
Deuteronomy, 126, sq., 267.
Dispersion, the, 361; Eastern, 361, sq.; Western, 363, sq.; intercourse with pagans, 366, sq.
Disruption of Solomon's kingdom, causes, consequences of, 235, sq.
Divination, heathen, contrasted with prophetical inspiration, 275.
Dothain, 39, 159.
Dreams of Joseph, 38; of Joseph's co-prisoners, 42; of Pharao, 42.
Drink-offerings, 92.
Dynasties, principal Egyptian, 49.

EBAL, Mount, 84, 115.
Ecclesiasticus, 326, 370.
Edom, 119, 121.
Edomites, 26, 313.
Egypt, 9, 270; physical description of, 47; history of, 48, sq.; civilization of, 49, sq.; length of stay in, 66.
Elders, 61, 103, 198, 353.

Eleazar, 14; son of Aaron, 87, 154.
Eleazar II, 326.
Elias, 246; slays priests of Baal, 247; miracles of, 247, sq.
Eliasib, 319, 320.
Elim (Wady Gharandel), 71.
Eliseus, 249.
Endor, witch of, 189.
Enoch, book of, 350.
Ephod, 87.
Ephraim, son of Joseph, 55; tribe of, 141, 142, 235; rivalry with tribe of Juda, 235.
Esau, 28, sq.; character of, 36.
Esdrælon, plain of, 114, 115, 142, 189.
Esdras, 320; works ascribed to him, 312, 317, sq., 321, sq.
Essenes, 353.
Esther, book of, 317, 362.
Ethnarch, 356, sq.
Et Tih, 104, sq.
Euphrates, 8, 9, 33, 297, 320.
Exile of Babylon, 304, sq.; return from, 311, sq.
Exodus from Egypt, 59, sq.; the new, 312.
Expiatory sacrifices, 91.
Ezechias, 263.
Ezechiel, 281, sq., 304.

Famine in Chanaan, 9; in Egypt, 43, 48.
Fellahin, 57.
Festivals, Mosaic, 95, sq.
First-born of Egyptians smitten, 64.
First-fruits, 92, 363; why offered to Jehovah, 93.
Forty years' wandering, why imposed, 106.
Future life, Egyptian belief in, 52; not mentioned in Pentateuch, 83; Babylonian belief in, 304.

Gad, 141, 203.
Gabaa, 169, 203, 215.
Gabaon, 138, 215.
Galaad, 33, 113, 161.
Galgal, 138, 139, 175, 178, 181.
Galilee, 114, 358, 359.
Garizim, Mount, 138, 320, 349.
Garments of priests, 86; of high priests, 87.
Gedeon, 152, 159, sq.
Gelboe, 188, sq., 194, 197.
Genesareth, 115; Lake of, 116.
Gergesites, 133.
Gessen, land of, 54.
Geth, David in, 194.
Gifts obtained from Egyptians by Israelites, 66.
Godolias, 270.
Golan, 112.
Goliath, 191.
Greek language adopted by Western Dispersion, 369, sq.

Habacuc, 280.
Haran, 8, 30, sq., 297, 312.
Hauran, 112.
Hazeroth, 103.
Hebrew, Abraham, the, 15.
Hebron, 9, 16, 34; a place of worship, 94, 114, 139, 197, 313.
Heli, 152; of the line of Ithamar, 154; his judgeship, 167, sq.; death of, 173.
Heliodorus, 332.
Heliopolis, 43.
Hellenism, meaning of, 328; rise of, 328; growth of, 333, 336, sq., 343.
Hermon, Mount, 121, 140; Little, 114, 188.

Herod the Great, 348, 355, 357.
Hethites (Hittites), 131, 133, 215, 312.
Hieroglyphics deciphered, 48, 49, 134.
High Priest, sacred character of, 87; special garments of, 87; privileges of, 87, 88; rule of high priests, 324, sq.
Hiram, 199, sq., 216.
History, Jewish, introduction to, 1–5; of Egypt, 48, sq.; of Babylonia, 298, sq.
Hittites (see Hethites).
Holidays, Mosaic, 95, sq.
Holiness of Jewish people, 79; how promoted by sacrifices, 90, sq.
Holocausts, 91; special meaning of, 93.
Holy Place, 84, 86; Holy of Holies, 84, 88, 99, 224; Most Holy Place, 330.
Hor, Mount, 119, sq.
Horeb, Mount, 61; probably Mount Serbal, 72.
Hospitality, Eastern, 21, 22.
Human sacrifices, were they offered to Jehovah? 163.
Hyksos, 53, 56.
Hyrcanus, John, 348, 349, sq., 351; I, 353; II, 354, sq., 357.

IDOLATRY, why punished by Mosaic law, 81; why a great danger to Israel, 135, sq.; under Judges, 154, sq.; under Solomon, 231, sq.; in kingdom of Juda, 257, sq.; of Manasses, 265, sq.; etc.
Idumæa, 357.
Idumean, 349, 359.
Incense, altar of, 84; why offered, 93.

Inspiration of prophets contrasted with divination, 275.
Ipsus, battle of, 326.
Isaac, 14; of secondary importance in Jewish history, 28; burial of, 34; character of, 35, 36.
Isaias, 262, 264, 280.
Isboseth, 197, 235.
Ismael, Ismaelites, 13, 39, etc.
Israel, Jacob, so named, 33; kingdom of, 237; political and religious organization, 242, sq.; Israel and Juda, kingdoms of, compared, 238, sq.; destruction of kingdom of, 253.
Israelites, prosperity in Egypt, 55, sq.; persecution in Egypt, 56, 60; life of, in the Wilderness, 107, 108.
Issachar, tribe of, 142.
Ithamar, 154.

JABES Galaad, 180.
Jabin, 140, 158.
Jaboc 33, 112, 121, sq.
Jacob, importance in Jewish history, 28; secures last blessing, 30; at Bethel, 31; in Haran, 31, sq.; vows exclusive worship to Jehovah, 31; character of, 35, sq.; grief of, 40; in Egypt, 53, sq.; blesses Juda, 54; burial of, 54, sq.
Jaddus, 324.
Jahel, 158.
Jasa (Jahaz), battle of, 122.
Jason, 332, sq.; of Cyrene, 350.
Jebel Musa, 74, sq.
Jebusites, 131, 133, 199.
Jechonias, 282.
Jehu, 249, sq.
Jephte, 162; questions connected with his vow, 162, sq.

Jeremias, 267, 268, 270, 280, 304.
Jericho, 123, 245, 346; captured by Josue, 137, 138.
Jeroboam, 233, 236; aim, on the throne, 241; connects religious innovations with history of the past, 242, sq.
Jeroboam II, 251, sq.
Jerusalem (Uru' Salim), 12; in time of David, 199; destroyed by Nabuchodonosor, 269, sq.
Jethro, 60, sq.
Jezabel, 245.
Jezrael, 159, 245, 250.
Joab, 199, 201, 207, 214.
Joachaz, 251, 268.
Joakim, 268.
Joas, 251, 260.
Joatham, 261.
Job, 219.
Joel, 280.
Joiada, 220, 260, 261, 320.
Jonas, 251, 279.
Jonathan, son of Saul, 185, 188, 198; son of Mathathias, 339; Machabeus, 343, sq.; renews treaty with Rome, 344.
Joppe, 238, 345.
Joram, of Israel, 250; of Juda, 259.
Jordan, valley, 115; river, 115, 116; fords of, 159; miraculous crossing of, 137.
Josaphat, 248, 258.
Joseph, 34; life in Chanaan, illustrated, 38, 39; in Putiphar's house, 40, 41; in prison, 41, 42; interprets dreams, 42; elevation of, 43; kindness to his brothers, 44; character of, 44; type of Christ, 45; death of, 55.
Josephus, 325, 327, 348, 361, 364.
Josias, 267.

Josue, successor of Moses, 136; conquers Palestine, 137, sq.; stopping of the sun by, 139; special territory of, 142; death and burial-place of, 143, 144.
Jubilee, 96.
Juda, Jacob's son, 39, 53; blessed by Jacob, 54; tribe of, 141, 235, 321; kingdom of, 237, 256, sq.; destruction of kingdom of, 269, sq.
Juda and Israel, kingdoms of, compared, 238, sq.
Judæa, 114; tributary to Persia, 311, sq.; to Macedonia, 324; to Egypt, 326, 329; to Syria, 329, sq.; a part of Syria, 356; to Rome, 365.
Judas Machabeus, 339, 340; makes alliance with Rome, 342.
Judges, 1; qualities required in, by Mosaic law, 82; time of the, 146, sq.; meaning of title of, 148, 151; social condition during time of, 148, sq.; domestic life under, 149; limited power of the, 152; how appointed, 151, sq.; religious organization under the, 153, sq.
Judith, book of, 266.

KARNAK, 134, 257.
King, popular demand for a, 176.

LABAN, 31, sq.
Lachis, 139, 264.
Lamb, paschal, 97.
Land, Mosaic laws regarding, 96; of Chanaan, of Promise (see Chanaan, Palestine).
Language, change of, in Western Dispersion, 371.
Laomedon, 325.
Laver (or "sea") of brass, 225.
Law, book of the, discovered, 267.

# INDEX.

Law Mosaic, main purposes of, 79; general features of, 80; public reading of, 98, 170, 258, 319; "a prophecy," 278, 321, 352.
—— civil, 80, 81; constitutional, 80; criminal, 81.
Lebanon, 110.
Length of stay in Egypt, 66; in Babylon, 307, etc.
Leprosy, 94.
Levi, tribe of, 85, 143.
Levites, 85; cities of, 143; under the Judges, 154, 201, 203.
Life of the Israelites in the Wilderness, 107, sq.
—— Jews in Babylonia, 304, sq.
Loaves of proposition, 84, 86.
Lot, 9, 15.
Lysias, regent of Syria, 341.

MAACHA, 258.
Machabee (Machabeus) name of, 340, 343; books of Machabees, 350.
Machabean, 359, etc.
Machpelah, cave of, 15, 55.
Madian, 60, 73, 122, sq., 160.
Mageddo, 158, 226, 250, 268.
Mahanain, 33, 197.
Malachias, 282.
Mambre, 9, 34.
Manasses, son of Joseph, 55; half-tribe, east of Jordan, 125, sq., 141; west of Jordan, 142, 159; king, 265, sq.; the high priest, 329.
Manna, not a mere natural product, 73, 108.
Mara, 71.
Marriage, Eastern customs, 31, 301.
Mary, sister of Moses, 59, 103, 118.
Masphath, 174, 175, 179.

Mathan, 261.
Mathathias, 339, 353.
Medes (Media), 324.
Melchisedech, 11, 12.
Menelaus, 333, sq.
Meneptah I, 60, 65.
Menes, 49.
Mercy-seat, 84, 99.
Merom, lake of, 116, 140.
Merodach Baladan, 265.
Mesa, King, 248.
Mesopotamia, 33, 157, 312, etc.
Messias, 202, 283, 372; predicted by prophets, 288; belief in, developed in Babylon, 307, sq.; belief in, kept up by Pharisees, 352.
Michas and the Danites, 154, 168.
Micheas, 280.
Mighty men of David, 201.
Miphiboseth, 198.
Miracles in Egypt, 61, sq.; of Elias, 247, sq.
Moab, 119, 122, sq., 259.
Moabite stone, 248.
Modin, 339.
Monarchy, beginning of the, 172, sq.; first opponents of, 179, 181, 200; restoration of, after exile, 314.
Monotheism, absolute, in Mosaic law, 82, 83.
—— Jewish monarchy, a danger to, 278.
—— not the religion of Cyrus, 311.
Moon (new), 95.
Moria, 199, 223.
Moses, birth, early life, 59, 60; flight to Madian, 60; sent to Pharao, 61, sq.; last discourses of, 126, sq.; successor of, 126; death of, 127; character of, 128, sq.
Mugheir (Ur), 7.

NABONAHID, 300.
Nabopolassar, 269, 298.
Naboth, 248.
Nabuchodonosor, invasions of, 268, sq., 297, 304; gigantic works of, 299; Lycanthropy of, 300, 302, 312.
Nachor, 8.
Nahum, 280.
Nathan, 202, 208, 213.
Nazarite, 165, 172.
Nebo, Mount, 127.
Nechao, 268.
Negeb, 9, 105.
Nehemias, 317, 320, 322; first mission of, 318, 362.
Nephtali, tribe of, 142, 246.
New moon, festival of, 95.
Nile, river, 47; its water, 48; plague of, 62, sq.
Nineveh (Ninive), 251, 264, 298, 300, 307, 312.
Nisan, month, 97.
Nomad life, in general, 18; particulars of, 19-23.

OBED, 169.
Ochozias, 248, sq., 250.
Octavius, 358.
Odollam, cave of, 194.
Offerings, meat and drink, 92; for sin, 99; burnt, 99.
Og, King, 122, 125.
Olives, Mount of, 231.
Onias I, 325; II, 329; III, 331.
Ophir, 217, 218.
Osee, 252; King of Israel, 253; prophet, 279.
Othoniel, 157.
Oza, 202.

PACIFIC sacrifices, 91.

Palestine, names of, 110; geography of, 110, sq.
—— Eastern, described, 111, 113; political divisions of, 121, sq.; conquest of, 122-125.
—— Western, described, 111, sq.; conquered, 125, 130, sq., 136, 140; inhabitants of, 131, sq.
Palmyra (Tadmor), 226.
Panium, Mount, battle of, 330.
Parthians, 358.
Paschal, festival, 96, sq.; an agricultural feast, 97.
—— lamb, 97.
Passage of Red Sea, 67; miraculous character of, 68; traditions about, 69.
Passover, 64, sq., 97; at Sinai, 101, 316.
Patriarchal age, 5, 7, etc.
Pentecost, 97.
Phacee, 253.
Phaceia, 253.
Phanuel, 33, 241.
Pharao, 9; power in Egypt, 50; opposes Moses, 60, sq.; father-in-law to Solomon, 214.
Pharan, 102, 105.
Pharisees, 351, sq.; tenets of, 351, sq.
Phenicia, 110, 114, etc.
Pherezites, 131, 133, etc.
Phihahiroth, 67.
Philistia, 115.
Philistines, 119, 174, 176, 185, etc.; and Samson, 165, sq.
Phinees, 124, sq.
Phithom, 56.
Phul (Teglathphalasar), 253.
Plagues of Egypt, 62; analogous with, yet different from natural scourges, 63; derisive of Egyptian gods, 64.

Plains in Palestine, 114, sq.
Polygamy, 22, 32, 51, 172, 199, sq., 230, 245, 301.
Pompey, 348, 355, sq., 365.
Predictions (see Prophets).
Priests, Egyptian, 50, sq.; not a caste in Israel, 80; high, 84, sq.; simple, 84, sq.; function of high, on day of atonement, 98, sq.
—— of Baal and Astarthe, 246.
—— in Babylonia, 303, sq.
Prophecy, meaning of word, 273; the Law "a Prophecy," 278.
Prophetical order, 273, sq.; history of, 277, sq.; general results of, 294, sq.
Prophets, schools of, 175, 276; prophets, 200; meaning of name, 273; mission of, 273, sq.; inspiration of, 274; sons of the prophets, 276; Moses a prophet, 277; before captivity, 279, sq.; writings of, 279; after the exile, 281, sq.; opposition of, to calf worship, 281; to Jewish law and priesthood, 281; to idolatry, 281, 295; predictions of, supernatural character of, 285, sq.; objects of predictions, 287, sq.; characteristics of predictions, 289; influence of prophets, 291, sq.; obstacles to, 291, sq.; means of success of, 293, sq.
Proselytes, 362.
Proverbs, 219.
Psalms, 209, 350.
Ptolemais, 344.
Ptolemy I, 325, 364; Soter, 326; II, Philadelphus, 326, 364; III, 329; IV, 330; V, 330.
Punishments in Mosaic law, 81, 82.
Purim, festival of, 317.
Purity, laws about legal, 94.

Putiphar, meaning of, 40.
Pyramids, 49.

QUAILS sent to Israel, 73, 103.

RACHEL, 31, sq., 38.
Rama, 242, 256.
Ramesses, city of, 56; Ramesses II, 56, 57.
Ramoth Galaad, 249.
Raphidim (Wady Feiran), 72.
Ras Sufsafeh, 74, 75.
Rebecca, 15, 29.
Red Sea, passage of, 67, 102.
Refuge, cities of, 143.
Religion, 1; of Egypt, 51, 52; of Chanaan, 134, sq.; of Babylonia, 303, sq.; of Jews in Babylonia, 306, sq.
Resurrection of dead, 307.
Revolt of ten tribes, 236, sq.
River of Egypt, 104, 110.
Roboam, 236, 256, sq.
Rome, 342, 349. 356, 365.
Romans, 342, 356, sq., 359.
Ruben, tribe of, 140, sq.
Ruth, 169, sq.

SABBATH, 95, etc.; festivals connected with, 95; Sabbatic year, 96, 98.
Sacrifice, of Isaac, 14; expression of religious worship, 90; bloody and unbloody, 90, sq.; chief objects of, 91, sq.; common features to all bloody, 91; place of, 93; human, in honor of Jehovah? 163.
Sadducees, 351, sq., 354.
Sadoc, 203.
Salem, 252.
Salmanasar II, black obelisk of, 251.
—— IV, 253.

Samaria, kingdom of, 238, sq., 349, 369; city of, 239, 250; foundation of city of, 244; destruction of, 254, 313.
Samaritans, 320; hatred of Jews, 315, sq.; temple of Mount Garizim, 320.
Samgar, 157.
Samson, 152; how a judge, 164; strength of, 165; historical character of exploits, 166.
Samuel, 152, 278; early life and judgeship of, 172, sq.; offers sacrifice to Jehovah, 175, footnote 1; resents demand for a king, 177; withdraws, 181; anoints David, 190; founder of schools of prophets, 276.
Sanaballat, 318, 320.
Sanhedrim, 103; origin and powers of, 353, sq., 358, 363.
Sarai (Sara), 11, 12; character of, 14.
Saron, 115.
Sasabassar, 312.
Saul, election of, 177; meeting with Samuel, 178; anointing of, as king, 178; victory over Ammonites, 179, sq.; military achievements of, 184; rejected by God, 185, sq.; character of, 186, sq.; death of, 189.
Schools of the prophets, 175, 276.
Scribes, 289, 321, 338.
Scripture, Holy, and Esdras, 321, sq.
Sea, Red, 14; Great or Mediterranean, 110, sq.; coast, 113, sq.
Seba, 207.
Sects, Jewish, 351, sq.
Sedecias, 209.
Sehon, 122.
Seir, Mount, 34, 102.

Seleucus I, 326, 331, 364; IV, 331.
Sennacherib, 264; army of, destroyed, 265.
Septuagint, translation of Old Testament, 66, 191.
—— origin of, 326, sq.
Serbal, Mount, 72.
Serpent, brazen, 121, 264.
Sesac, 257.
Shepherd, life of, 32, 190.
Shibboleth, 164.
Sichem, 9, 34, 160, 239, 241, 349.
Sicle (Shekel), 194, 319.
Sidon, 245.
Silo, 153, 168.
Simeon, tribe of, 141.
Simon I, the Just, 326, 329; II, 330; Simon Machabeus, 339, 340, 344, sq., 348, 353.
Sinai, journey to, 71; description of, 74; fitness for giving of the law, 74; from Sinai to Cades, 101, sq.
Sion, 125, 199.
Sisara, 158, sq.
Slaves, 39; among nomads, 22; in Mosaic law, 81, etc.
Socoth, 34.
Sodom, destruction of, 15, footnote 1.
Solomon, 208, 251; how brought up, 212, 213; inaugurated king, 213; first acts of, 213, sq.; commerce by land, with Egypt, 215; with Arabia, 216; with Phenicia, 216; commerce by sea, 216, sq.; temple of, 216, 222, sq.; intellectual life of, 218, sq.; wisdom of, 218; proverbs of, 219; military and political organization, 220; extension and peace of his States, 221; public works in Jerusalem and provinces, 222–227; palace of, 226; decline and disruption of kingdom

of, 229, sq.; despotism, 230; polygamy of, 230; idolatry of, 231, 232; end of, 234.
Sophonias, 280.
Spices, 39.
Spies, sending of the twelve, 104.
Stations in the wilderness, 106, sq.
Suez, 105; extent of gulf of in Moses' time, 67.
Sur, wilderness of, 13.
Susa, 297, 317.
Suzanna, 306.
Synagogue, the Great, 321, 326.
Synagogues, local, origin of, 308, 322, 369.
Syria, 250, 299, 325.
—— Cœle-Syria, 322, 325, 358.

TABERNACLE, description of the, 84; ministers of, 85, sq.; how far sole place of sacrifice, 93, 94, 97; construction of, 101, 215.
Tabernacles, Feast of, 98, 243, 314, 319.
Tabor, Mount, 114, 142.
Tanis, 54.
Teglathphalasar, 253, 263.
Tel el-Amarna, tablets, 11.
Temple, construction of, projected by David, 202; of Solomon, 216, 222, sq.; of Zorobabel, 314, 316.
—— Chaldean, 8; on Garizim, 320, 349; rededicated by Judas, 341, 356.
Tents, 19; arrangement of, 20.
Thare, 8.
Tharsis, 216.
Theocracy, 2, 77, 80, 308, 326, 328.
Thersa, 239, 244, 252.
Tigris, 7, 297, 312.
Tithes, assigned to priests and Levites, 86, 319.

Tobias, book of, 246, 308, 362; son of Tobias, 329.
Traditions, Jewish, 321.
Treasury, temple, 320, 355.
Triads in Egyptian religion, 52, 83, footnote 1.
—— in Babylonian religion, 303.
Tribes, jealousy among, 235.
Trumpets, Feast of, 96.
Tryphon, 344, sq.
Twelve, tribes, 101, 313; divisions of land under Solomon, 220.
Two brothers, Egyptian tale of the, 11, 41.
Tyre, 216, 245, 324, 333.
Tyropœon valley, 199.

UNCLEANNESS, laws regarding, 94, sq.
Unity of Sanctuary, 93, 94; under the Judges, 153.
Unleavened bread, 97.
Ur of the Chaldees, 7.
Urim and Thummim, 87, 316.

VICTIMS for sacrifice, 91, 92.
Visions of Abraham, 9, 24; of Jacob, 30, 33; of Samuel, 173; of prophets 275.
Volcanoes, extinct, east of Jordan, 112.
Vow of Jephte, 162, sq.

WADY, el Arabah, 119; Feiran (Raphidim) 72; Gharandel (Elim), 71.
Wandering, life, 19, sq.; forty years', 106, sq.
Wells in the East, 13.
Wilderness, of Sin, 72, 105; of the Wandering 104, 121; of Pharan, 14, 102, 105; of Judæa, 114.

Wisdom, Book of, 370.
Women, condition of, in Egypt, 41; in Babylonia, 301; among nomads, 22.

XERXES I, 316, sq.

YARMUK, river, 112.

Year, Sabbatical, 96, 98; of Jubilee, 96.

ZABULON, tribe of, 142.
Zacharias, King, 252; son of Joiada, 261; the prophet, 282, 315.
Zerka, river, 116.
Zorobabel, 312, 314, 322.

www.ingramcontent.com/pod-product-compliance
Lightning Source LLC
Chambersburg PA
CBHW032023220426
43664CB00006B/342